THE ETHICS OF POLICING

The Ethics of Policing

New Perspectives on Law Enforcement

Edited by
Ben Jones *and* Eduardo Mendieta

NEW YORK UNIVERSITY PRESS
New York

NEW YORK UNIVERSITY PRESS
New York
www.nyupress.org

© 2021 by New York University
All rights reserved

References to Internet websites (URLs) were accurate at the time of writing. Neither the author nor New York University Press is responsible for URLs that may have expired or changed since the manuscript was prepared.

Library of Congress Cataloging-in-Publication Data
Names: Jones, Ben, 1985– editor. | Mendieta, Eduardo, editor.
Title: The ethics of policing : new perspectives on law enforcement /
  edited by Ben Jones and Eduardo Mendieta.
Description: New York : New York University Press, [2021] |
  Includes bibliographical references and index.
Identifiers: LCCN 2020047254 | ISBN 9781479803729 (hardback) |
  ISBN 9781479803736 (paperback) | ISBN 9781479803743 (ebook) |
  ISBN 9781479803750 (ebook)
Subjects: LCSH: Police ethics. | Law enforcement—Moral and ethical aspects.
Classification: LCC HV7924 .E868 2021 | DDC 174/.93632—dc23
LC record available at https://lccn.loc.gov/2020047254

New York University Press books are printed on acid-free paper, and their binding materials are chosen for strength and durability. We strive to use environmentally responsible suppliers and materials to the greatest extent possible in publishing our books.

Manufactured in the United States of America

10 9 8 7 6 5 4 3 2 1

Also available as an ebook

CONTENTS

Introduction: Police Ethics after Ferguson   1
Ben Jones and Eduardo Mendieta

PART I. THE ROLE OF POLICE

1. Clashing Narratives of Policing? The Quest for Lawful versus Effective Policing and the Possibility of Abolition as a Solution   25
Tracey L. Meares

2. Legitimate Policing and Professional Norms   39
Jake Monaghan

3. Reward and "Real" Police Work   66
Michael Sierra-Arévalo

PART II. USE OF FORCE

4. Soldiers and Police   93
Michael Walzer

5. When Police Do Not Need to Kill   107
Franklin Zimring

6. Prioritization of Life as a Guiding Principle for Police Use of Deadly Force   120
David Klinger

PART III. RACE, BIAS, AND RESISTANCE

7. Policing Narratives in the Black Counterpublic   149
Vesla Weaver

8. Police Ethics through Presidential Politics and Abolitionist Struggle: Angela Y. Davis and Erica Garner   179
Joy James

PART IV. POLICING'S PAST AND FUTURE

9. Police and Slave Patrols: A History of State-Sponsored White-on-Black Violence 205
   Sally Hadden

10. From Protection to Predation: Policing as the Pursuit of War by Other Means in the Third Reich 222
    Nicolas de Warren

11. Police, Drones, and the Politics of Perception 248
    Lisa Guenther

12. Predictive Policing and the Ethics of Preemption 268
    Daniel Susser

Acknowledgments 293

About the Editors 295

About the Contributors 297

Index 301

Introduction

Police Ethics after Ferguson

BEN JONES AND EDUARDO MENDIETA

Killings by police in recent years have sparked mass protests and put policing at the center of national debate. An initial turning point came in 2014. Questionable police force was to blame for the deaths of Eric Garner in New York City, Michael Brown in Ferguson, and Tamir Rice in Cleveland. Quickly, their deaths became national and even international stories. In the years that followed, many more—Walter Scott, Freddie Gray, Samuel DuBose, Alton Sterling, Philando Castile, Terence Crutcher, Breonna Taylor, George Floyd, and others—would become known to the public in their deaths, added to the long list of Black lives ended by police.

This sudden interest in police practices marked a dramatic shift in the status quo. For decades, high rates of killings by police had made the United States an outlier but had failed to generate much national concern. When high-profile killings by US police in 2014 prompted public interest in the scope of this problem, reporters and researchers found themselves in an embarrassing position: they could not even say how many of these killings occur annually. At the time, no entity maintained accurate US data on them (Zimring 2017, 23–40, 74–90). Media outlets began tracking killings by police (*Washington Post* 2015; *Guardian* n.d.), scholars called for more research (Soss and Weaver 2017), a presidential commission was formed and investigations were launched by the Department of Justice (President's Task Force on 21st Century Policing 2015; United States Department of Justice 2015, 2017), and lawmakers and reformers championed proposals to limit the use of force by police (Police Executive Research Forum 2016; California State Legislature 2018; Campaign Zero 2018).

Despite all this attention being paid to policing, many departments and local governments resisted meaningful reform. The number of individuals killed by police each year in the US remained steady, at over a thousand a year (Mapping Police Violence 2020). With disturbing regularity, videos of questionable killings and police brutality kept coming out, and little seemed to change. Things reached a breaking point in 2020 when video surfaced of a Minneapolis police officer putting his knee to George Floyd's neck for nearly nine minutes until he suffocated to death (Hill et al. 2020). Massive protests broke out across the US and the world, as frustration over the lack of change boiled over. In a development reminiscent of the civil rights movement, momentum for reform gained strength as video captured police arresting reporters and brutally attacking peaceful protesters (Hubler and Bosman 2020). These developments reiterated the impression that policing in the US was deeply broken and transformative change urgently needed.

Floyd's death and the ensuing protests also reshaped the debate over policing. Bills to ban chokeholds and increase transparency of officer misconduct, which had languished for years, quickly passed in state legislatures in response to the protests (Li and Lodhi 2020). Both Republicans and Democrats in Congress rushed to introduce federal legislation to reform police practices (Cochrane and Broadwater 2020). And ideas once dismissed as politically impossible, such as reallocating funds from law enforcement to social services, gained traction in a number of local governments (Stockman and Eligon 2020). This combination of legislative action and grassroots protests came at a time of national reckoning with policing's role in systemic racism throughout US history, from slave patrols to the present.

This history has resulted in deep distrust of law enforcement, no more so than in communities of color. Beyond just decrying those actions by police that killed Garner, Brown, Rice, and Floyd, protesters have made clear that the sources of discontent run much deeper. Killings by police are symptoms of entrenched patterns of discrimination. This discriminatory violence at the hands of the state hits Black men hardest, but as Angela J. Davis (2017, xiv) points out, others suffer too: "Black women, Latino/a men and women, Native Americans, and other people of color also experience violence at the hands of the state and discriminatory treatment in the criminal justice system as do people who are gay, lesbian, and/or transgender."

There is no shortage of investigations confirming discriminatory police practices. After police killed Michael Brown, the US Department of Justice's Civil Rights Division investigated the Ferguson Police Department. It found a department focused on generating revenue that targeted poor Black neighborhoods. As the report details, "many officers appear to see some residents, especially those who live in Ferguson's predominantly African-American neighborhoods, less as constituents to be protected than as potential offenders and sources of revenue" (United States Department of Justice 2015, 2). Furthermore, this mindset fostered a climate where officers used excessive force largely with impunity. Other Department of Justice investigations found similar patterns of racial disparities and excessive force in the Baltimore, Chicago, and Cleveland police departments (United States Department of Justice 2017).

As these recent investigations illustrate, high-profile killings put a spotlight on a host of issues that threaten the legitimacy of the police. In a democratic state, there is the expectation that police enforce the law fairly and protect basic rights. When officers fail to, there must be mechanisms to ensure meaningful accountability and prevent future abuses. Questionable killings by police and lack of accountability cast doubt on the legitimacy of current practices.

Such incidents point to the need to reevaluate the role of police, including the ethical and legal principles that should guide their work. Most obviously, recent killings raise questions about police use of force and what rules should govern it (see Jones forthcoming). There is a strong case for reforms to prohibit tactics and force that threaten life unnecessarily. But such reforms alone cannot address the ethical concerns that loom over policing today. Even when police do not use lethal force, they still enforce the law in unfair and discriminatory ways that erode public trust. That is especially true when officers operate under the shadow of historic injustices that create suspicions about their role. Past wrongs influence perceptions of policing today, and any analysis of police ethics must be sensitive to that history. The future of policing also deserves close analysis. As new technologies are created, they have the potential to make police more effective, but also to augment their power in ways that exacerbate, and further entrench, existing injustices.

Making progress on these challenges requires perspectives from a wide range of fields—Black studies, criminology, history, law, philosophy, political science, sociology, and others—in conversation with one another. This volume provides such interdisciplinary perspectives on the ethical challenges that face policing today. Events in Ferguson, Cleveland, Baltimore, New York City, Louisville, Minneapolis, and elsewhere make clear that policing too often falls short of our normative expectations for it. The contributions here aim to clarify what ethical principles should guide police, where current practices fall short, and what strategies hold the most promise for addressing these failures.

The Philosophy and Role of Policing

The ethics of policing is a theme at the very foundation of political philosophy. The word *police* has its etymology in the Greek term *politeia* (Knemeyer 1980), the Greek title of Plato's book known today as *The Republic*. A more appropriate translation of *politeia* would be "constitution" (see Menn 2006; Moore 1975). The dialogue of the *Politeia* features Plato's teacher Socrates, who sets out to describe a completely just, beautiful, wise, and well-ordered city (Plato 2004, 427e). Notably, a key feature of this ideal city is the education and training of what some translators call "soldier-police" (Reeve 2004, xxx), who are tasked with securing the peace of the city and fending off external aggressors. These soldier-police are the city's guardians, which Plato (2004, 375d–375e) compares to "noble hounds" due to their ability to discriminate between friend and foe. The guardians possess various virtues that help them excel in protecting the city: speed, strength, energy, courage, wisdom, and eagerness to learn. Interestingly, the philosopher-kings later described in the *Politeia*—the wisest members of Plato's ideal city—are a subset of these guardians. By embodying a range of virtues, the guardians stand out as moral exemplars in their role of seeing after the city's peace and security. So already in Plato's foundational text, the role of guardian, the police-soldier, is entangled with ethical expectations and normative assumptions.

Further insight into the concept of policing comes from Franz-Ludwig Knemeyer, who traces the genealogy of the German word *Polizei*. Noteworthy in this genealogy is that, from the fifteenth through the eighteenth century, the meaning of *Polizei* remained fairly stable, referring to the condition in which subjects "conducted themselves in an orderly, modest, courteous, and respectable fashion wherever human life was organized communally" (Knemeyer 1980, 174). The term *Polizei* referred to a state or condition of society, while also referring to the means for securing, preserving, and augmenting that well-ordered state. In the former sense, it referred to what we call the social order or the set of conventions that regulate interactions among citizens.

At times in the history of political and social thought, some have proposed less rich understandings of policing. As policing became the object of legal regulation, there was an attempt to downplay its moral role. This transformation makes the police an administrative arm of the state that ensures the "domination of Law" (Knemeyer 1980, 188). In many classical theories of the state, the state's coercive power has this impersonal and terrifying aspect. Perhaps no thinker better illustrates this point than Thomas Hobbes (2012), who portrays the civil sovereign as a Leviathan—a biblical monster that strikes fear into whoever encounters it. This understanding of state power, though compelling in certain aspects, runs the risk of simplifying the complexities and nuances involved in interacting with actual agents of the state. The coercive face of the state remains in many contexts a *human* face, with the potential to exhibit the best or worst of human nature.

Didier Fassin, in particular, draws attention to the intimate ways we experience the state. He tellingly writes:

> The proximity with the agents [of the state] reveals the warmer side of the state, so to speak. It is more than a bureaucracy with rules and procedures. Officers, magistrates, guards, social workers, mental health specialists also act on the basis of values and affects. Justice and fairness, concern or indifference, empathy or indignation, admiration or distrust are part of their experience in their relations, not only with their public but also with their colleagues, their superiors, and their institutions. They inform their daily decisions and actions but are also informed by the ethos of their profession and the ethical climate of the public sphere. (Fassin 2015, x)

The social and political institutions that make up the state, through which its force and administrative power are enacted, inevitably have a moral dimension. They comprise what Fassin (2015) calls the "moral world of institutions." The police, perhaps unlike any other manifestation of state power, must articulate, present, and enact that moral world. They express the moral ideals not only of their profession, but also of the broader community.

Any analysis of police ethics thus must pay close attention to the moral world in which they exist. To quote Fassin again: "The work of law enforcement agents is inscribed within a moral economy, rests on moral arguments, constructs moral communities, engages moral subjectivities, and provokes moral conflicts—all elements that are indispensable when considering how to make sense not only of what is standard practice in their interactions with their public, but also the forms of deviance like brutality and cruelty, racism and discrimination" (Fassin 2015, 94). The police are part of our moral world and, as such, should be more than simply the cold and violent face of the state. At their best, they are its beneficent and moral manifestation.

When speaking about the moral dimension of policing, we must remember the bidirectional nature of ethical obligations, expectations, and accountability. The moral climate of a society is gauged not simply by how police interact with members of the community, but also in how the police are treated by that community. We find this idea, too, in Plato's *Politeia*, which envisions the state providing its guardians with the education, training, and support necessary to become moral exemplars and carry out the difficult role bestowed on them. In other words, police help their community achieve its ideals and vice-versa. But that is only possible if both sides fulfill their obligations to each other.

Police Ethics and Democratic Legitimacy

When police fail to be moral exemplars, are negligent in their duties, and abuse their powers, their action most obviously undermines the legitimacy of law enforcement institutions. There is extensive research showing that police lose legitimacy in people's eyes if they act in ways that violate basic norms of fairness and procedural justice (see Tyler 2004; Meares 2013). But it is important to recognize that such failures by police pose even broader threats: they put in jeopardy the legitimacy of the state as a whole. For one way people encounter and experience the state is through their interactions with police. When police are corrupt, threaten fundamental rights, and act as forces of predation rather than protection, that inevitably influences how people understand the state's role and their relation to it. Unjust policing can transform the state in people's minds from a source of support and protection into a danger to be on guard against.

Police work presents no shortage of threats to government legitimacy. Notably, police exercise a great deal of discretion in their jobs that they can abuse. Discretion can transform the permission to use coercion in enforcing the law into a license for excessive force and police brutality. It also can lead to discriminatory enforcement of the law, in which police reserve harsh enforcement practices for certain groups and allow others to break the law with impunity. Such abuses of discretion often require democratic institutions overseeing law enforcement to step in and specify more precisely the boundary between discretionary powers and illegality, while holding officers who cross these boundaries accountable. But even after these interventions, police discretion will still persist. Officers confront such a wide array of circumstances and challenges that it is impossible to completely specify in advance how they should act. Policing, in fact, is one of the few professions where discretion tends to increase the lower one's position in the organizational hierarchy, with cops working on the street exercising broad discretion (Wilson 1978, 7–8). That aspect of policing makes cultivating ethical judgment in officers all the more critical.

Because discretion is inextricably tied to police work, it is difficult to fully eliminate the risk that some officers will abuse their power. But when widespread discontent over policing surfaces, it usually stems from deeper, more systemic ills than just a few rogue officers behaving badly. Police reflect the society in which they operate, and this can put officers in situations where they have a chance to succeed or, conversely, in situations where success is impossible. For instance, if society allocates grossly insufficient resources to care for those with intellectual disability or mental illness, it should come as no surprise when problems arise in police interactions with these populations. Underlying systemic injustices do not mean that individual officers are morally off the hook for violating their legal and ethical obligations. Stressful background conditions and a lack of resources can help explain such violations without excusing them. At the same time, if we see unjust police practices, it is important to keep in mind how they often reflect and exacerbate more widespread injustices within society.

That raises a question: how should we understand and develop ethical and legal principles for police who operate in a world far from ideal? The field of police ethics must engage in what political philosophers call nonideal theory. Whereas ideal theory outlines what normative principles should guide action under conditions of perfect justice, nonideal theory investigates how normative principles may look different under conditions of injustice (see Valentini 2012).

An example of the type of question nonideal theory takes up is how police should enforce unjust yet democratically approved laws. One can make the case that certain harsh drug and immigration laws fall into this category. Intuitions pull in different directions as to how police should enforce such laws. On the one hand, the police are ultimately answerable to the people and have some obligation to carry out laws enacted by democratic institutions. On the other hand, unjust laws cause real harms—depriving people of liberty and tearing families apart. Officers often have the power to avoid or mitigate these harms, depending on how they enforce the law. The discretion enjoyed by officers makes this ethical question particularly pressing. Since the many laws in place render it impossible to fully enforce all of them, police cannot avoid prioritizing the enforcement of some laws over others. This fact complicates the relationship between the police and the law. Even in a democratic society with legitimate political institutions, the idea that police should simply enforce the law proves insufficient as an overarching principle to guide their work. Police work, it seems, also comes with the ethical responsibility of evaluating the law and which aspects of it to prioritize (for more on this point, see Monaghan 2018).

Though nonideal theory is necessary for police ethics, it would be a mistake to treat all current injustices in society as fixed and restrict our normative ambitions for policing to those confines. The legitimacy of the police is intricately bound up with the legitimacy of other institutions within society. Police ethics requires thinking through what other aspects of society must change to create an environment where officers can fulfill the loftier goals associated with their role. To put officers in a position where they truly have a chance to succeed, it often will be necessary to pursue reforms beyond just those narrowly focused on law enforcement (e.g., more robust services for those with intellectual disability or mental illness). The field of police ethics has to allow space for envisioning policing under more ideal conditions and the societal transformations needed to move toward that goal.

For those engaged in the difficult work of reforming police and other institutions to remedy injustice and bolster their legitimacy, both the shadow of the past and specter of the future loom over these efforts. Historical injustice and rapidly changing technologies complicate the ethical challenges that face police and the institutions overseeing them. The next two sections consider each of these factors in turn.

Policing's Past and Its Legacy Today

In public opinion surveys, most White Americans express having "a great deal" or "quite a lot" of confidence in the police. The police consistently rank as one of the institutions Americans trust the most, far surpassing the media, schools, and Congress (Jones 2020). Such findings give the impression that concerns about lack of public trust in the police are overblown. A closer look at the poll numbers, though, reveals sharp divisions in society. Black Americans have more negative views of the police than White Americans. According to a 2020 Gallup poll, less than a fifth of Black Americans have much confidence in the police (Jones 2020). This gap in attitudes is not a recent phenomenon but rather a longstanding one (Weitzer and Tuch 2006). So though the police enjoy trust in some segments of society, in others they clearly lack it.

This trust gap stems in part from disparities in how police enforce the law. Empirical research finds that police in the US use more aggressive enforcement strategies against people of color, a discrepancy that cannot be explained by different levels of criminality between racial groups. African Americans are more likely to experience investigatory stops—where police pull over a driver or frisk a pedestrian in search of guns, drugs, or other contraband—and are less likely to be found with contraband during such stops (Gelman, Kiss, and Fagan 2007; Baumgartner, Epp, and Shoub 2018; Epp, Maynard-Moody, and Haider-Markel 2014). The use of SWAT teams and militarized policing is also more common in Black communities, even after controlling for crime rates (Mummolo 2018).

How aggressive policing strategies came to be implemented is a complex story. Sometimes blatant racism has had a role in motivating policy, as one official in the Nixon administration admitted was the case with the war on drugs (Baum 2016). But a variety of other factors also contributed to the implementation of aggressive law enforcement measures. As James Forman Jr. (2017) documents in *Locking Up Our Own*, a number of African American leaders championed tough-on-crime measures because they saw them as remedies to high-crime rates in their communities. Though different motivations contributed to the development of aggressive policing practices, once implemented they resulted in racially disparate outcomes. People of color come into contact with the police and criminal justice system at higher rates. Such interactions, often perceived as unjustified and as harassment, have the effect of eroding confidence in police and government institutions generally (Weaver and Lerman 2010; Lerman and Weaver 2014; Tyler, Fagan, and Geller 2014).

Importantly, racial disparities in law enforcement do not occur in a historical vacuum. They take place against a historical backdrop in which police played a central role in protecting institutions that deprived minority groups of basic rights. This past can have profound effects on the meaning of police interactions today. Police ethics has to take into account the historical context in which officers do their work—otherwise it risks being grossly deficient.

In US history, several notorious features about policing stand out. Slave patrols emerged during the colonial period and represented an innovation in law enforcement. These patrols played a significant role in the development of the police, especially in the South. As Sally Hadden explains,

> patrols . . . function[ed] in many ways like police groups: breaking up nighttime gatherings, hauling in suspicious characters, trying to prevent mischief before it happened, or capturing the lawbreakers after the fact. The big difference was that in the South, the "most dangerous people" who were thought to need watching were slaves—they were the prime targets of patrol observation and capture. The history of police work in the South grows out of this early fascination, by white patrollers, with what African American slaves were doing. Most law enforcement was, by definition, white patrolmen watching, catching, or beating black slaves. (Hadden 2001, 4)

Slave patrols ended after the Civil War, but continued to influence policing. Southerners understood law enforcement as the responsibility of Whites, and police forces were often entirely White, like the slave patrols that preceded them. Imitating these patrols, some law enforcement officials after the Civil War engaged in brutal tactics to terrorize Blacks and maintain White supremacy. It comes as little surprise, then, that freedmen often saw little difference between slave patrollers and the police: both brutalized Black Americans with impunity (Hadden 2001, 218–20).

During the Jim Crow era, lynching developed as a tool for maintaining White supremacy partly due to law enforcement's complicity. Lynchings lacked legal sanction and, in this sense, represented a challenge to formal institutions of law and punishment. Some in law enforcement decried lynchings, and there are examples of officials going to heroic lengths to prevent them. Sheriff Sherman Ely of Lima, Ohio, almost ended up lynched himself in 1916 when a mob demanded a Black prisoner in his custody, but he managed to save the prisoner and barely escape with his own life. The NAACP later recognized him for his courage (Dray 2003, 222–23). Yet, in other cases, law enforcement turned a blind eye to mob violence and allowed lynchings, making no attempt to stop them (see, e.g., *United States* v. *Shipp* 1906; Downey and Houser 1991). Most egregiously, some law enforcement officers played an active role in these acts of terror by seizing victims and delivering them to lynch mobs. As late as 1964, law enforcement cooperated with Klansmen to lynch three civil rights workers in Mississippi (Dray 2003, 446–56).

Police also employed other forms of violence beyond lynching to defend Jim Crow. Some of the most indelible images from the civil rights movement include police using dogs to terrorize, intimidate, and attack peaceful protesters. When called upon by local officials to defend discriminatory laws with force, police rarely hesitated. In fact, as infamous figures like Birmingham police commissioner Bull Connor remind us, they often did so with enthusiasm.

This history inevitably impacts how policing is perceived today. When racial bias infects current police practices, it is not a mere aberration or an isolated injustice. Instead, it is part of a much longer chain of harms that have fallen disproportionately on Black people. This link between past and current wrongs can severely undermine trust in the police, who come to be viewed as a force that perpetuates injustice and lacks legitimacy.

Beyond just influencing others' perceptions of police, history can influence how police perceive those they encounter. Bryan Stevenson (2017, 4) calls attention to the "presumption of guilt and dangerousness" that burdens people of color—in particular young Black men—in their interactions with police (see also Butler 2017). We see this presumption at work when police in White neighborhoods aggressively stop and threaten Black men with lethal force simply for being there—something Stevenson himself and countless others have experienced firsthand.

Stevenson makes a compelling case that, to understand policing challenges today, we must understand the history of racial injustice that led up to them. He urges an honest reckoning with this history and its legacy: "The issue of racially motivated police violence or racial disparities in sentencing can't be viewed simply as a consequence of bad police officers or racially biased judges. There are deep historical forces that have created the problems so clearly seen in America's criminal justice system" (Stevenson 2017, 4–5). Past injustices reverberate today. We make a grave error ignoring this past, for such neglect renders any ethical prescriptions for policing incomplete.

A historically informed approach to police ethics places a high priority on officers' being sensitive to how past injustices shape their and others' perceptions. History creates certain ethical obligations for officers, which include recognizing the real harms suffered by communities of color and how they undermine trust in the police. Dismissing these concerns only entrenches already substantial barriers between the police and those they serve.

There are many concrete steps police can take to recognize historic injustices and participate in the difficult work of addressing them. The Equal Justice Initiative, for instance, is engaged in the project of setting up markers to remember victims of lynching. Stevenson (2017, 25) calls on law enforcement leaders to be present at these dedications and to apologize for the failure of police to protect people of color threatened by racial terror. In recent years, some law enforcement officials have come forward to apologize for the role police have played in historic injustices. Wellesley Police Chief at the time, Terrence Cunningham, gave a statement in 2016 on behalf of the International Association of Chiefs of Police (IACP) acknowledging that there have been times when police were "the face of oppression." The statement went on to apologize for "the role that our profession has played in society's historical mistreatment of communities of color" (Jackman 2016). In addition to such statements, some law enforcement agencies now support training programs focused on teaching officers about historic injustices. One program through the United States Holocaust Memorial Museum (n.d.) covers some of the most egregious police practices—those of Nazi Germany—with the goal of providing officers new perspectives on their role and the ethical lines they should never cross.

But though police have taken some steps in recognizing, apologizing for, and learning from historic injustices, much work remains. Some in law enforcement are hostile to the idea of addressing past injustices. When Cunningham delivered IACP's statement apologizing for the police's role in historic injustices, he received a standing ovation from IACP's membership, but officials from other organizations—like the Fraternal Order of Police—quickly dismissed it (Jackman 2016). This reaction highlights the resistance that efforts to address historic injustices face from some segments of law enforcement.

The Promise and Peril of New Technology

Beyond looking at the past, a compelling account of police ethics must also consider how innovations will shape the future of law enforcement and their normative implications. New technology is having profound effects on what policing looks like, a trend that shows no sign of slowing down. In the wake of concerns sparked by Ferguson and other high-profile incidents, some see technology as a remedy to many of the problems that plague policing.

Without question, new technology provides law enforcement with tools they previously lacked. It is now feasible to equip police officers with body cameras to record their interactions. The hope is that this technology will discourage excessive force, increase accountability, and build trust with communities by showing a commitment to transparency (Stoughton 2018). Other technology, like Tasers, gives police a tool to incapacitate uncooperative and dangerous suspects without having to use a firearm. More police agencies now also rely on predictive analytics to inform how they dedicate resources to fight crime (Joh 2014).

Not surprisingly, those designing and selling these new technologies often view them with great optimism. Rick Smith, CEO of Axon—which supplies Tasers and body cameras to law enforcement agencies—describes his company's vision: "firing hot projectiles of lead shrapnel at people—we want to make that a ridiculous concept, because it's a brutal, outdated, terrible thing to do" (Goodyear 2018). Companies like Axon have found increased demand for their products in the wake of Ferguson—body cameras, in particular. When Michael Brown was shot and killed by Officer Darren Wilson in Ferguson, witness accounts of the incident varied widely, without video to verify what actually happened. Afterward, the Department of Justice began issuing grants to enable law enforcement agencies to adopt body cameras. Though only a handful of departments used body cameras before 2014, by 2018 over half of them had adopted the practice (Goodyear 2018).

Technologies like body cameras deserve consideration in the wake of Ferguson and the concerns it raised, and evidence suggests they have some effectiveness in reducing officer use of force (Maskaly et al. 2017). But it is a mistake to expect technology to offer quick fixes—such expectations are rarely met. High-profile killings by police and the investigations they prompted brought to light systemic failures that point to the need to transform the culture of many police agencies. Introducing new technology into institutions that otherwise remain the same is a recipe for failure. Consider the problem of excessive force. Equipping officers with Tasers by itself fails to fix the problem, and in fact introduces another weapon with the potential for abuse. The adoption of less lethal weapons like Tasers only succeeds if it is part of a more robust framework of training, guidelines, and systems of accountability that prioritize protecting life and avoiding unnecessary force (Alpert and Dunham 2010).

In addition, technology often raises new ethical concerns. If these concerns are overlooked or dismissed, the adoption of new technology can backfire by undermining police legitimacy rather than improving it. Equipping officers with body cameras has been a popular reform to strengthen accountability, but it also raises worries about more intensive surveillance and policing, especially in marginalized communities. Similar concerns also apply to the growing use of predictive analytics by police agencies. It is essential to consider the potential harms of new technology and to take steps to mitigate them, while also leaving open the option of avoiding certain kinds of technology if appropriate safeguards cannot be put in place.

In short, the field of police ethics must pay close attention to new technology and whether it advances normatively worthwhile goals. Other fields, like just war theory, have had to develop with the emergence of new technology, as philosophers, ethicists, and legal scholars have grappled with what role (if any) the technology should have in war. A similar task faces those studying police ethics, especially now as technology reshapes law enforcement in dramatic ways.

Overview of What's to Come

The chapters that follow explore in depth the ethical challenges that loom over policing in the aftermath of Ferguson. The volume tackles these issues in four parts: I. The Role of Police, II. Use of Force, III. Race, Bias, and Resistance, and IV. Policing's Past and Future.

Part I examines the proper role of police in a democratic society, and how certain practices and developments today can distort understandings of police work. Law professor Tracey L. Meares, a member of President Barack Obama's Task Force on 21st Century Policing, opens this section with her chapter "Clashing Narratives of Policing? The Quest for Lawful versus Effective Policing and the Possibility of Abolition as a Solution." In response to persistent racial disparities in policing and excessive force, especially in marginalized communities, calls to abolish or defund the police have become a rallying cry for many progressives. Meares explains that police abolitionism is more nuanced and compelling than how it is often portrayed. The legacy of racial violence and oppression influences policing and other criminal justice institutions today. Many aspects of these institutions *need* to be uprooted and abolished. But abolition—whether of slavery at an earlier period or policing today—also requires building new structures to address community needs that will persist even after the old structures are dismantled. As Meares understands police abolition, it involves the transformation of the police into an institution that cooperates with communities to ensure their safety and that is truly a public good.

The next chapter of Part I, "Legitimate Policing and Professional Norms" by philosopher Jake Monaghan, focuses on cultivating epistemic and "improvement" norms in law enforcement. Monaghan attributes some failures in policing today to inadequate attention to reforming practices in light of new evidence. Using the medical profession as a comparison, Monaghan argues that law enforcement agencies have ethical obligations to evaluate themselves in light of the latest research, as well as to support ongoing research on best practices. Though some groups and agencies have taken steps in this direction, much work remains to be done if policing is to become a profession that is truly self-critical and committed to self-improvement.

Sociologist Michael Sierra-Arévalo closes Part I with his chapter "Reward and 'Real' Police Work." In it he presents and analyzes new data that offer insights into the activities police agencies value most. Consistent with popular narratives of what real police work entails, Sierra-Arévalo finds that departmental awards place an emphasis on recognizing dangerous, stereotypically masculine actions related to fighting crime and making arrests. Such findings raise questions about current incentives within police departments and how they influence officers' understandings of their roles. If we hope to promote a guardian mentality rather than a warrior mentality in policing, one that prioritizes compassion and respect in community interactions, Sierra-Arévalo suggests that incentive structures in departments need to change.

Part II turns to an issue at the center of many recent debates over policing—use of lethal force. In "Soldiers and Police," political theorist Michael Walzer draws on his extensive work on just war theory to highlight key distinctions between the military and law enforcement. Walzer expresses grave concerns over the militarization of the police and how it transforms their relationship with society. Though police investigate and sometimes witness brutal crimes, Walzer cautions against officers viewing suspects and criminals as enemies they are at war against. In his view, officers take a dangerous step when they see themselves as part of a war, for that mindset opens the door to abusing the very rights liberal democracies aim to protect.

Then, in "When Police Do Not Need to Kill," criminologist Franklin Zimring makes the case that hundreds of killings by police each year in the US are avoidable. In almost half of these incidents, suspects have no firearm and involve circumstances where officers rarely need to use lethal force. Zimring also presents evidence showing that mortality rates increase dramatically the more times a suspect is shot. In light of this evidence, Zimring calls on police administrators to implement more stringent "don't shoot" and "stop shooting" rules, which could significantly reduce the number of killings by police without putting officers at greater risk.

The last chapter of Part II, "Prioritization of Life as a Guiding Principle for Police Use of Deadly Force," by criminologist and former police officer David Klinger, situates the role of lethal force within an ethical framework of protecting life. Klinger finds that efforts to completely eliminate killings by police are dangerous, since they fail to recognize that lethal force is sometimes necessary to protect innocent life against unjust threats. To illustrate, he examines several recent incidents involving police use of force and how reluctance to use lethal force can result in avoidable officer and civilian casualties. For Klinger, police cannot always avoid lethal force, but they need clear ethical principles to guide them when they are deciding whether to use it. In particular, he recommends wider adoption of the prioritization-of-life framework used by SWAT teams—which prioritizes the lives of (1) innocent citizens, then (2) police officers, and finally (3) suspects—in programs that train officers on use of force.

Part III takes up the ethical challenge of how to confront the problem of racial bias in policing. Political scientist Vesla Weaver opens the section with "Policing Narratives in the Black Counterpublic," which explores what she terms "race–class subjugated communities" and how they experience police. Standard survey methods often fail to capture the views of marginalized communities, those most impacted by aggressive police tactics. Weaver reports on the findings of an innovative methodology designed to overcome this obstacle: the use of Portals, which allow people in race–class subjected communities to communicate with each other about their experiences with police. Drawing on these and other data, Weaver argues that police fail poor communities of color by both *over*-policing and *under*-policing them. Police aggressively enforce minor violations in these communities—often to generate revenue—while seeming absent when they are needed to protect lives and solve serious crimes.

The other chapter of Part III features a contribution by critical race theorist Joy James. In "Police Ethics through Presidential Politics and Abolitionist Struggle: Angela Y. Davis and Erica Garner," James looks at advocacy against police violence in communities of color in the wake of deep personal loss. The chapter focuses on the advocacy of Erica Garner after her father was killed by a police chokehold in 2014. Garner refused to be coopted by politicians and others whose cozy relationships with police, in her view, prevented them from calling out their abuses. As a result, Garner often received little institutional support for her advocacy. James contrasts Garner with more established figures like Angela Y. Davis, and raises concerns about diluting radical messages in the hope of gaining broader acceptance. Such an approach, James worries, risks rendering advocacy impotent in the face of unjust police practices that destroy communities of color.

Part IV concludes the volume by considering the ethical challenges posed by both the past and future of policing. In "Police and Slave Patrols: A History of State-Sponsored White-on-Black Violence," historian Sally Hadden traces the emergence of slave patrols and their impact on policing's development in the American South. After slavery, the Ku Klux Klan drew on slave patrol practices to terrorize Black Americans, often with the cooperation of local law enforcement. Hadden closes the chapter by calling on officers to study more closely the role of the police in exacerbating racial oppression in the US, so as to better understand how this history contributes to distrust of police today.

Philosopher Nicolas de Warren examines another episode from policing's past in "From Protection to Predation: Policing as the Pursuit of War by Other Means in the Third Reich." De Warren uses Nazi Germany as a case study in how policing can become utterly corrupted. Echoing themes from Walzer's opening chapter, de Warren explains the transformation of the Nazi police into a tool of war against enemies of the state. Germany's police forces ceased to serve a protective function, becoming instead forces of predation in the service of a totalitarian regime. De Warren's case study stands as an instructive warning of the dangers that come with removing legal and ethical restraints on police as part of efforts to advance political ends.

The following chapter by philosopher Lisa Guenther, "Police, Drones, and the Politics of Perception," also raises concerns about the predatory mindset in policing but with an eye toward the future. Specifically, Guenther explores the ethical implications of police use of drones and other surveillance technology. Though framed as a less invasive tool, such technology represents for Guenther a dangerous expansion of state power, especially in marginalized communities most harmed by aggressive policing. Constant surveillance intensifies policing, which should prompt concern given that over-policing and predatory practices to generate revenue were *already* problems before these new technologies became widely available.

In the final chapter, "Predictive Policing and the Ethics of Preemption," data ethicist Daniel Susser examines the increasing use of machine learning technology by police. Such technology analyzes data to identify patterns in an effort to make predictions about future crime and how to limit it. Champions of this technology see it as a valuable tool that can help police prevent crime before it occurs. Susser, however, raises ethical concerns about using this technology for preemptive policing. Since the technology relies on historical data often infected by racial bias, it can reproduce this bias in its predictions and recommendations. An even more basic worry with preemptive policing, argues Susser, is that it makes harmful assumptions about individuals and fails to recognize them as ethical agents. Preemptive policing aims to reduce overall crime, but does so by treating suspects and at-risk individuals in an instrumental fashion. For Susser, predictive analytics belong in the hands of those with more direct obligations to at-risk individuals, who can use such tools to further their development (e.g., social workers).

As these contributions highlight, policing faces no shortage of challenges in the aftermath of Ferguson. High-profile killings by police, investigations of departments, and community protests have brought to light deep concerns about the legitimacy of many current police practices. Ignoring these concerns risks further undermining community trust in the police and, in turn, making officers' jobs more difficult. Now is a critical time to reexamine what ethical principles should guide policing, identify where current practices fall short, and pursue remedies. Our hope is that the chapters that follow contribute to these urgent tasks.

BIBLIOGRAPHY

Alpert, Geoffrey, and Roger Dunham. 2010. "Policy and Training Recommendations Related to Police Use of CEDs: Overview of Findings from a Comprehensive National Study." *Police Quarterly* 13 (3): 235–59.

Baum, Dan. 2016. "Legalize It All." *Harpers*, April 2016. https://harpers.org.

Baumgartner, Frank, Derek Epp, and Kelsey Shoub. 2018. *Suspect Citizens: What 20 Million Stops Tell Us about Policing and Race.* New York: Cambridge University Press.

Butler, Paul. 2017. *Chokehold: Policing Black Men.* New York: New Press, 2017.

California State Legislature. 2018. AB-931 Criminal Procedure: Use of Force by Peace Officers. California Legislative Information, 2017–2018 Regular Session. http://leginfo.legislature.ca.gov.

Campaign Zero. 2018. "Limit Use of Force." www.joincampaignzero.org.

Cochrane, Emily, and Luke Broadwater. 2020. "Here Are the Differences between the Senate and House Bills to Overhaul Policing." *New York Times*, June 17, 2020. www.nytimes.com.

Davis, Angela J. 2017. "Introduction." In *Policing the Black Man: Arrest, Prosecution, and Imprisonment*, edited by Angela J. Davis, xi–xxiv. New York: Pantheon Books.

Downey, Dennis, and Raymond Hyser. 1991. *No Crooked Death: Coatesville, Pennsylvania, and the Lynching of Zachariah Walker.* Urbana, IL: University of Illinois Press.

Dray, Philip. 2003. *At the Hands of Persons Unknown: The Lynching of Black America.* New York: The Modern Library.

Epp, Charles, Steven Maynard-Moody, and Donald Haider-Markel. 2014. *Pulled Over: How Police Stops Define Race and Citizenship.* Chicago: Chicago University Press.

Fassin, Didier, ed. 2015. *At the Heart of the State: The Moral World of Institutions.* London: Pluto Press.

Forman, James, Jr. 2017. *Locking Up Our Own: Crime and Punishment in Black America.* New York: Farrar, Straus and Giroux.

Gelman, Andrew, Alex Kiss, and Jeffrey Fagan. 2007. "An Analysis of the New York City Police Department's 'Stop-and-Frisk' Policy in the Context of Claims of Racial Bias." *Journal of the American Statistical Association* 102 (479): 813–23.

Goodyear, Dana. 2018. "Can the Manufacturer of Tasers Provide the Answer to Police Abuse?" *New Yorker*, August 20, 2018. www.newyorker.com.

Guardian. n.d. "The Counted: People Killed by Police in the US [2016]." Accessed October 23, 2020. www.theguardian.com.

Hadden, Sally. 2001. *Slave Patrols: Law and Violence in Virginia and the Carolinas.* Cambridge, MA: Harvard University Press.

Hill, Evan, Ainara Tiefenthäler, Christiaan Triebert, Drew Jordan, Haley Willis, and Robin Stein. 2020. "How George Floyd Was Killed in Police Custody." *New York Times*, May 31, 2020. www.nytimes.com.

Hobbes, Thomas. 2012. *Leviathan.* Edited by Noel Malcolm. New York: Oxford University Press.

Hubler, Shawn, and Julie Bosman. 2020. "A Crisis that Began with an Image of Police Violence Keeps Providing More." *New York Times*, June 5, 2020. www.nytimes.com.

Jackman, Tom. 2016. "U.S. Police Chiefs Group Apologize for 'Historical Mistreatment' of Minorities." *Washington Post*, October 17, 2016. www.washingtonpost.com.

Joh, Elizabeth. 2014. "Policing by the Numbers: Big Data and the Fourth Amendment." *Washington Law Review* 89 (1): 35–68.

Jones, Ben. Forthcoming. "Police-Generated Killings: The Gap between Ethics and Law." *Political Research Quarterly*.

Jones, Jeffrey. 2020. "Black, White Adults' Confidence Diverges Most on Police." Gallup, August 12, 2020. https://news.gallup.com.

Knemeyer, Franz-Ludwig. 1980. "Polizei." *Economy and Society* 9 (2): 172–96.

Lerman, Amy, and Vesla Weaver. 2014. *Arresting Citizenship: The Democratic Consequences of American Crime Control*. Chicago: Chicago University Press.

Li, Weihua, and Humera Lodhi. 2020. "The States Taking on Police Reform after the Death of George Floyd." FiveThirtyEight, June 18, 2020. https://fivethirtyeight.com.

Mapping Police Violence. 2020. "National Trends." https://mappingpoliceviolence.org.

Maskaly, Jon, Christopher Donner, Wesley Jennings, Barak Ariel, and Alex Sutherland. 2017. "Effects of Body-Worn Cameras (BWCs) on Police and Citizen Outcomes: A State-of-the-Art Review." *Policing: An International Journal* 40 (4): 672–88.

Meares, Tracey. 2013. "The Good Cop: Knowing the Difference between Lawful or Effective Policing and Rightful Policing—and Why It Matters." *William & Mary Law Review* 54 (6): 1865–86.

Menn, Stephen. 2006. "On Plato's Πολιτεία." *Proceedings of the Boston Area Colloquium in Ancient Philosophy* 21 (1): 1–55.

Monaghan, Jake. 2018. "On Enforcing Unjust Laws in a Just Society." *Philosophical Quarterly* 68 (273): 758–78.

Moore, J. M. 1975. "Introduction to *The Constitution of Athens*." In *Aristotle and Xenophon on Democracy and Oligarchy*, translated by J. M. Moore, 143–46. Berkeley, CA: University of California Press.

Mummolo, Jonathan. 2018. "Militarization Fails to Enhance Police Safety or Reduce Crime but May Harm Police Reputation." *Proceedings of the National Academy of Sciences* 115 (37): 9181–86.

Plato. 2004. *The Republic*, 3rd ed. Translated by C. D. C. Reeve. Indianapolis, IN: Hackett Publishing Company.

Police Executive Research Forum. 2016. *Guiding Principles on Use of Force*. Washington, DC. www.policeforum.org.

President's Task Force on 21st Century Policing. 2015. *Final Report*. Washington, DC: United States Department of Justice.

Reeve, C. D. C. 2004. "Synopsis." In Plato, *Republic*, 3rd ed., translated by C. D. C. Reeve, xxx–xxxiii. 3rd ed. Indianapolis, IN: Hackett Publishing Company.

Soss, Joe, and Vesla Weaver. 2017. "Police Are our Government: Politics, Political Science, and the Policing of Race-Class Subjugated Communities." *Annual Review of Political Science* 20: 565–91.

Stevenson, Bryan. 2017. "A Presumption of Guilt: The Legacy of America's History of Racial Injustice." In *Policing the Black Man: Arrest, Prosecution, and Imprisonment*, edited by Angela J. Davis, 3–30. New York: Pantheon Books.

Stockman, Farah, and John Eligon. 2020. "Cities Ask If It's Time to Defund Police and 'Reimagine' Public Safety." *New York Times*, June 5, 2020. www.nytimes.com.

Stoughton, Seth. 2018. "Police Body-Worn Cameras." *North Carolina Law Review* 96 (5): 1363–1423.

Tyler, Tom. 2004. "Enhancing Police Legitimacy." *Annals of the American Academy of Political and Social Science* 593: 84–99.

Tyler, Tom, Jeffrey Fagan, and Amanda Geller. 2014. "Street Stops and Police Legitimacy: Teachable Moments in Young Urban Men's Legal Socialization." *Journal of Empirical Legal Studies* 11 (4): 751–85.

United States Holocaust Memorial Museum. n.d. "Law Enforcement and Society: Lessons of the Holocaust." www.ushmm.org.

United States Department of Justice. 2015. *Investigation of the Ferguson Police Department*. March 4, 2015. www.justice.gov.

United States Department of Justice. 2017. *Federal Reports on Police Killing*. Brooklyn, NY: Melville House Publishing.

United States v. Shipp. 1906. 203 US 563.

Valentini, Laura. 2012. "Ideal vs. Non-ideal Theory: A Conceptual Map." *Philosophy Compass* 7 (9): 654–64.

Washington Post. n.d. "994 People Shot Dead by Police in 2015." www.washingtonpost.com.

Weaver, Vesla, and Amy Lerman. 2010. "Political Consequences of the Carceral State." *American Political Science Review* 104 (4): 817–33.

Weitzer, Ronald, and Steven Tuch. 2006. *Race and Policing in America: Conflict and Reform*. New York: Cambridge University Press.

Wilson, James. 1978. *Varieties of Police Behavior: The Management of Law and Order in Eight Communities*. Cambridge, MA: Harvard University Press.

Zimring, Franklin. 2017. *When Police Kill*. Cambridge, MA: Harvard University Press.

PART I

The Role of Police

1

Clashing Narratives of Policing?

The Quest for Lawful versus Effective Policing and the Possibility of Abolition as a Solution

TRACEY L. MEARES

There is a debate within both scholarly and popular writing focused on the appropriate role for police. Among the various strands of this debate is a clash between two modes of policing: policing that is considered effective, on the one hand, and policing that is lawful, on the other. By *effective*, I mean something very specific: the idea that police can and should engage in strategies and tactics designed to reduce and suppress crime. When I refer to *lawful policing*, I mean the idea that compliance with the law as police officers carry out their tasks should be policing's highest priority. Whatever else police do, this view holds, they must always be attentive to legal constraints on their activities and especially constraints provided by constitutional law. It should be obvious that these two notions hardly need to be conceptualized as "clashing." Indeed, I hope many readers are thinking that it is problematic to discuss them as competing visions. As I will explain below, however, when one looks to the scholarly literature on these two topics—especially the criminological and legal literatures—it is easy to see that they *have* been in competition. The rest of this essay will describe these two ideas of policing and then explain how the contemporary moment of police reform provides an opportunity for reconciliation of them. In a third section, the essay will turn to the nascent idea of police abolition as a new challenge to current work on reform. That section will offer some ideas about how an abolition framework might helpfully advance thinking both on the seeming clash between effective and lawful policing as well as more generally, the ethics of policing.

Effective Policing

Policing as effectiveness is congruent with how many police agents think of themselves. If you ask a police officer what policing is for, she is likely to say, "The job of the police is to keep the public safe." Many, including the police themselves, take that statement to mean that police ought to be effective "crime fighters" (Steden, Wal, and Lasthuizen 2015). And, crime fighting, in turn, is often construed in terms of police enforcing the law against so-called "bad guys." In a world in which crime, especially violent crime, is high, it makes sense for state and municipal government to set as a task for themselves addressing such problems.

The importance of crime reduction as a top agenda item for state and local governments is a relatively recent phenomenon, however, as the idea that police could do anything to address and reduce crime in a substantial way has become salient only during the last thirty years or so. From roughly the late 1960s, coinciding with the publication of the ground-breaking report *The Challenge of Crime in a Free Society* by the President's Commission on Law Enforcement and Administration of Justice (1967), which detailed the relationship between so-called root causes, until the mid-1990s, coinciding with the passage of the Violence Crime Control and Law Enforcement Act of 1994 (popularly known as the Clinton administration's Crime Bill), it was generally thought that police could not do much about crime. David Bayley, in his 1994 book *Police for the Future*, sums up this view: "The police do not prevent crime. That is one of the best kept secrets of modern life. Experts know it. The police know it, but the public does not know it. Yet, the police pretend that they are society's best defense against crime and continually argue that if they are given more resources, especially personnel, they will be able to protect communities against crime. This is myth" (Bayley 1994, 3). Thought leaders at the vanguard of the professionalism era in policing during the 1970s thought that police should focus on tasks such as bringing offenders to justice regardless of whether such work affected the crime rate, or peacekeeping tasks such as intervening in domestic disputes, or providing help and assistance to those in need, or even traffic control. Although some practitioners writing about the then-nascent "police science" in the late 1950s and early 1960s tried to encourage excitement among police executives about the idea of addressing crime by focusing on "troubled youth," this work did not emphasize the idea that the core role of the police was their ability to reduce crime (e.g., Winters 1957, Lunden 1961).

Today, there is a federal Community-Oriented Policing Services (COPS) Office located in the Department of Justice (it was established in 1994, during the Clinton Administration). Today, police executives' careers live or die on the basis of a city's crime rates. Today, innovations in both policing strategies, such as COMPSTAT, and innovations in econometric methods of assessing whether policing strategies or tactics are causally related to declines in crime have changed the conversation regarding whether or not police are effective at reducing crime. The question posed instead (Zimring 2012) is: how much of a difference do police make, with respect to crime?

Lawfulness

Lawfulness is another way of articulating the good in policing. Policing is fundamentally about law, and law permeates policing. The difference between *policing*, as most understand the term, and *vigilantism* is the rule of law. Evaluating policing in terms of its lawfulness is accordingly one of the most important aspects of democratic society (for more, see Meares 2008, 1867). Many varied types of law are relevant to policing. They include municipal ordinances, state constitutional law as well as state statutes, federal statutes, international treaties, and, of course, the United States Constitution (Harmon 2011). Additionally, the internal regulations of policing agencies themselves are another source of law, as they are essentially administrative agency rules. There is very little scholarship regarding most of these forms of lawful policing because proponents of lawful policing tend to focus on only one source of law, federal constitutional law.

Of course, given that even before the focus on effectiveness, as I have described it above, police were tasked with playing some role in ensuring that members of the public obey laws that the polity has adopted for its governance, policing as upholding the law could be considered just an aspect of the police-effectiveness vision of policing. Typically, however, those who demand police lawfulness are not talking about police enforcing the criminal laws that a polity has adopted. Rather, they are talking about police commitments to lawfulness when carrying out the tasks of enforcing criminal laws. These commitments include adherence to constitutional law, and specifically constitutional criminal procedure, which specifies the jurisprudence of when police can interact with suspects on the street; what procedures they must engage in before searching or seizing someone; how interrogations must be conducted; and what kind of authority they have to maintain public order. These commitments refer to what Rachel Harmon calls the "conventional paradigm" of police regulation (Harmon 2011, 765).

This conventional paradigm casts policing as a necessary evil in that the conception of policing imagines the enterprise as a trade-off between the risk of arbitrary or oppressive enforcement and individual rights, which always results in less liberty for individuals. In this world, the ideal is less policing, full stop. This view lends itself to a description of problematic policing in purely legal terms. Stop, question, and frisk (SQF) practices are called into question because they are said to not comport with the Fourth Amendment. And, if the problem is constitutional transgression, then the answer is, in turn, more constitutional compliance (see, e.g., Maclin 1998).

Dueling Narratives

The criminological research supporting police effectiveness as crime reduction, with its focus on the econometrics of tactics and strategies to reduce crime, has largely ignored the lawfulness or unlawfulness of the police action taken to achieve it. On occasion, the rare social scientist might point to police lawbreaking as a potential "cost" to balance against the benefit of policing that effectively reduces crime (e.g., Taylor and Lawton 2012), but for the most part, social scientists seem to presume that policing takes place lawfully. This is extremely problematic in a world in which the public is bombarded daily with police excess in the name of effective policing and when it has increasingly become obvious—though scholars have known it for years—that police operate in the street with great discretion, largely alone, and without direct supervision (Davis 1969).

The effective policing camp's blind spot in this area has allowed scholars concerned with the lawfulness of police action to write as if police effectiveness was largely irrelevant to their own work.[1] For example, consider the words of Judge Shira Scheindlin. In her opinion in *Floyd v. New York City* (2013), Scheindlin cabined off the relevance of law enforcement effectiveness from her assessment of the constitutional violations in question. When the defendants attempted to present evidence on the effectiveness of SQF in reducing crime in the City of New York, the judge refused to allow it, stating that "this case is not about the effectiveness of stop and frisk in deterring or combating crime. This Court's mandate is solely to judge the constitutionality of police behavior, not its effectiveness as a law. . . . 'The enshrinement of constitutional rights necessarily takes certain policy choices off the table.'" Scheindlin's statement encapsulates the view that police adherence to strict dictates that constrain discretion always results in more liberty for individuals, and the higher levels of crime that we might experience as a result of less policing is simply a price we pay for more freedom in society. But this view is somewhat odd if it is reasonable to believe that the state should be responsible in some way for public safety while simultaneously observing legal constraints, and to believe that a world with lower levels of violence would also increase individual freedom (Sharkey 2018).

Elsewhere in both legal and social science literatures, I have described a vision of policing that is attentive to both lawfulness and effectiveness but also captures important dimensions beyond police activities designed to reduce crime and those relevant to compliance with legal dictates (see, e.g., Meares 2013 and Meares, Tyler, and Gardener 2015). Grounded in the social psychological concept of legitimacy, this approach to policing emphasizes what psychologists call the procedural justice of police action. Note that in defining legitimacy in this way I am not offering a philosophical justification for when people ought to defer to authorities. My claim is descriptive in that I will explore the extent to which people do defer (or at least say that they do) (Tyler 2006). Attention to the procedural justice of policing problematizes the ease with which policing organizations point to public safety as the primary justification for their existence and as the obvious explanation for what they do.

According to scholarship on procedural justice, people systematically focus on a few dimensions when evaluating police and other legal authorities (Tyler 2004; Tyler and Wakslak 2004). First, participation is an important element. People report higher levels of satisfaction in encounters with authorities when they have an opportunity to explain their situation and perspective on it. Second, people care a great deal about the fairness of decision-making by authorities. That is, they look to indicia of the decision maker's neutrality, objectivity, factuality, consistency, and transparency. Third, people care a great deal about how they are treated by organization leaders. Specifically, people desire to be treated with dignity, with respect for their rights, and with politeness. Fourth, in their interactions with authorities, people want to believe that authorities are acting out of a sense of benevolence toward them. That is, people attempt to discern why authorities are acting the way they do by assessing how they are acting. They want to trust that the motivations of the authorities are sincere, benevolent, and well intentioned. Together these indicia comprise a model of procedural justice that is the basis of legitimacy (Blader and Tyler 2003). A robust body of social science evidence from around the world shows that people are more likely to voluntarily obey the law when they believe that authorities have the right to tell them what to do (Tyler 2007).

The dynamic of the legitimacy account is social rather than instrumental, which means that the account is not concerned with how people think about maximizing their utility in terms of the particular outcomes of any situation, but instead is concerned with how people understand their relationship to one another, their position in a group to which they belong, and the relationship of their group to other groups. People tend to seek a favorable social identity within the groups to which they belong. People also seek a favorable social status for their group vis-à-vis other groups. Psychologists Allan Lind and Tom Tyler (1988) explain that people care about procedural justice because it provides them with important informational signals that they view as relevant to their identities. How a police officer, as a representative of the state, treats an individual, provides that person with crucial information about how the state views that person and the group to which she belongs. Thus, the ubiquity of videos documenting negative treatment especially of people of color by police, no matter their race, fuels the perception that some groups have lower status than others. Indeed, the treatment doesn't even have to be overtly negative; rather, the knowledge that there is differential treatment by state authorities of different groups will fuel a negative perception (Epp, Maynard-Moody, and Haider-Markel 2014; Voigt et al. 2017).[2]

Research suggests, importantly, that procedural justice leads to perceptions of legitimacy and that legitimacy is in turn associated with compliance with the law and with cooperation with legal authorities (Meares 2008). This conclusion further leads to important criticisms of both the effective policing and lawful policing views. With respect to effectiveness as a goal for policing, research on procedural justice and legitimacy means that the oft-cited chestnut proffered by many criminal justice policy-makers, that deterrence-based "get-tough-on-crime" approaches are the only way to address and reduce crime, is likely incorrect (National Academies of Sciences, Engineering, and Medicine 2018, 211–49). With respect to focusing solely on lawfulness in policing, research on procedural justice underscores the idea that the conventional view of police regulation through lawfulness can miss important factors the public cares about when evaluating police. More specifically, constitutional law, the primary code of police regulation, does not emphasize factors such as the importance of the quality of police treatment and does not discuss the impact of police work on individual dignity, identity, or status, which all are key aspects of procedural justice and key components of the public's conclusions regarding legitimate police authority. Of course, while constitutional law could focus on these things, importantly, it does not now do so (Meares, Tyler, and Gardener 2015).

Police Abolition

Police abolition has become a prominent demand in what I call the "reform space"—although it is probably better described as the "*transform* space." I have suggested that policing must be abolished before it can be transformed and that critics of police abolition caricature the abolitionists' view when they assume that police abolition simply means no more police (for more on this point, see Meares 2017). The attack on abolitionists is unsurprising given that it comes from those who are committed to the notion that crime reduction by police is self-justifying—an approach that too many proponents of effectiveness take. This argument is a straw man. Obviously, residents of cities such as Chicago, Baltimore, or Milwaukee are struggling with unacceptably high levels of violence and are concerned with reducing it. In Chicago, for example, protests against police violence shut down Lake Shore drive after the police killing of Laquan MacDonald became public (NBC Chicago 2015), and protests against the failure of city government to address high levels of violence in some neighborhoods shut down the Dan Ryan Expressway, the main highway through the city's South Side (Wang 2018).

Mariame Kaba, a prominent abolitionist, has argued that "prison abolition is two things: It's the complete and utter dismantling of prison and policing and surveillance as they currently exist within our culture. And it's also the building up of new ways of intersecting and new ways of relating with each other" (Dukmasova 2016). Of course, residents of the cities I just named and many more care about being safe—from each other and from police excesses.[3] Now, however, I want to shift slightly to point out a few issues in the argument of the abolitionists. I consider what I am doing here a very friendly amendment to their work.

The issue can be easily seen by going back to Kaba. She makes two points: (1) one about dismantling and (2) one about building up.

Much of the energy that fuels the abolition movement in criminal justice is understandably focused on dismantling the excesses that have built up over time, whether we focus on the millions of people who have been incarcerated or otherwise processed by criminal justice corrections, or whether we are focused on my subject of interest—policing. With respect to policing, excess is a watchword. The police do too much stopping, frisking, and engagement with civilians to enforce low-level ordinances that have little connection to the real problems people face (see Weaver's contribution in this volume). There is also too much police violence. While we do not—shockingly—have good and accurate counts of the number of individuals killed by police every year, in the last few years our best estimate of that count has not dipped below one thousand (Bialik 2016).

It is also the case that violence in neighborhoods remains a problem for too many residents of primarily urban spaces. Violence remains a problem despite the critical benefit of the decline in homicide over the last three decades. To get a sense of the magnitude of that decline, consider sociologist Patrick Sharkey's stunning statistical observation: the decline in homicide rates among African American men in the United States has been so substantial that the resulting increase in life expectancy we now observe for members of that group is what we would expect to see if African American men no longer suffered from obesity (Sharkey 2018). Given that violence remains a problem for so many people, we should be concerned that a focus on dismantling without a theory of the goal of building up puts us at risk of just reducing the bad. This is notable, but it is inadequate. Reduction of the bad is certainly more humane, but it's not a citizenship project.

The history of abolition has something to teach us on this point. Paul Butler, my friend and colleague, is working on a new project on abolition, a project that involves applying criminal law concepts to understandings of abolition. His new work is attentive to W. E. B. Du Bois's ([1935] 2014) magisterial work *Black Reconstruction*, which teaches us that the abolition of slavery was never just about eradicating the legal category of enslaved people; it was also—critically—about the project of establishing *citizenship* for the formerly enslaved. Note the relationship between this idea and Kaba's conception of abolition. Both are about dismantling, but both are also about building up.

My argument is that policing is a project of citizenship because it ought to be conceptualized—and then carried out—as a public good. Public goods are, canonically, goods that are non-rivalrous and nonexcludable: anyone can enjoy them without diminishing their supply, and no one in the relevant group (e.g., a given city or nation) can be excluded even if they cannot afford to pay. We typically rely on the state to fund public goods through taxes because the state has a vested interest in making these goods available to its citizens and cannot rely on the market to provide them as they are not necessarily—or even ideally—profitable. An interesting discussion on the nature and scope of public goods has been unfolding lately in the political theory literature, and much of this discussion has focused on a private/public distinction that is interestingly and, maybe to some, surprisingly, relevant to police abolition.

So, for example, Neil Walker and Ian Loader (2007) in their recent book, *Civilizing Security*, worry about a decoupling of policing from the state, which could allow the potential provision of private, rather than public, policing. Bonnie Honig (2015) similarly writes about the encroachment of the neoliberal order on the provision of public goods.

These scholars' concerns reflect my own, which is that centering the state in the provision of public goods demands a special and communal focus on their provision. Thus, I have argued that when the public at large experiences the "good" of policing only by concentrating the costs of producing that good on a small group—such as Black people, and particularly Black men—it is hard to say that the good is "good" or even truly public. We need to create a kind of policing that we all can enjoy (Meares 2017).

Police transformation requires deep thinking about what it means to say that a public good is both public and good. When one considers the racialized origins of policing in America—from its roots in slave patrols (see Hadden's contribution in this volume) to its build-up during the early twentieth century as an immigrant-control brigade—it is clear that a necessary first step to redeeming this public good is to find a new symbolic language for thinking about its role in society. Walker and Loader (2007) argue similarly that there is a limitation with conceiving of police as a public good solely in utilitarian terms. Specifically, it risks a conception of that good as one enjoyed communally only by aggregating the benefits that individuals receive, which in turn leads to an assessment of the benefits and costs of the provision of that good in terms of efficiencies experienced at the individual level that are in turn aggregated up. This process leads more easily to imagining the provision of that good by some entity other than the state and, thus, to the possibility of the good not being provided at all. Instead, we need a way of conceiving of the good that demands its enjoyment by all people in common.

This is particularly crucial with regard to the role that police play in generating our understanding of ourselves as citizens (Loader 2006), so I want to argue that the project of coming up with this symbolic language is a task we all must engage in together. It is a necessary part of the building up, and we must do it while we are engaged in the task of dismantling what we do now. To put the argument slightly differently, dismantling without a theory of building up puts us at the same risk that Loader and Walker (2007) describe with regard to a purely utilitarian conception of the public good.

To make the argument more concrete, I want to borrow from political theorist Bonnie Honig (2015), who has recently made an argument about the importance of pursuing, in common, objects of common desires when theorizing democracy. Honig cautions against theorizing only about the *demos* (constitutions, proper procedures, commitments to formal equality, boundaries), and she urges us to think about the objects of democracy as well. She calls these objects "public things," pointing to parks, public transportation, schools, sewage systems, and prisons as examples. The idea of a public thing prefigures a public good. We have to commit to the public thing before we can do the work of the symbolic language that creates the good. As Honig says, "Being shared or public means that they are sites of confrontation and encounter, enjoyment and conflict, and they are accessible to all" (Honig 2015, 624).

As I close, let me turn back to the historical account of the abolition of slavery in the US. The passage of the Thirteenth Amendment to the US Constitution did not magically create a world in which formerly enslaved African Americans suddenly enjoyed the benefits of citizenship that had been denied for over 150 years. The tragically short twelve-year Reconstruction following the passage of the Thirteenth Amendment was designed to do some of that work. While progress was undeniably made—a fact that was strenuously denied for decades, even after the publication of Du Bois's ([1935] 2014) careful documentation of efforts of the formerly enslaved to create space for themselves as citizens in the new social order against all odds in *Black Reconstruction*—there was much work left to be done at the turn of the twentieth century.

The Civil Rights Movement of the 1960s is sometimes referred to as the Second Reconstruction, but even today many argue that a Third Reconstruction is needed, especially with respect to criminal justice matters.[4] My argument is simple. We must build up a conception of policing as a public good in order to fulfill the original promise of Reconstruction. In this way, we will not simply imagine a policing construct that "occupies the same footprint" as the space policing currently does (Davis 2003). Reconstructing the relationship that people of color, especially "race–class subjugated" people (Soss and Weaver 2017), have to criminal justice systems simply is necessary to make citizens out of all of us.

NOTES
1 The next section of this piece is based on a previously published article. See Meares (2013).
2 This theory implies that status enhancement can occur even in the face of punishment. Tyler and Fagan (2008) demonstrate that the police can give a person a

ticket or even arrest them while simultaneously enhancing police legitimacy if they are respectful and fair to the person they are dealing with.
3 Readers might find helpful a discussion of abolition between myself and Professor Vesla Weaver in a Boston Review podcast. See Meares and Weaver (2017).
4 For a short argument to this effect, see Meares (2015).

BIBLIOGRAPHY

Bayley, David H. 1994. *Police for the Future*. Studies in Crime and Public Policy. New York: Oxford University Press.

Bialik, Carl. 2016. "The Government Finally Has a Realistic Estimate of Killings by Police." FiveThirtyEight, December 15, 2016. https://fivethirtyeight.com.

Blader, Steven L., and Tom R. Tyler. 2003. "A Four-Component Model of Procedural Justice: Defining the Meaning of a 'Fair' Process." *Personality and Social Psychology Bulletin* 29 (6): 747–58.

Davis, Angela Y. 2003. *Are Prisons Obsolete?* New York: Seven Stories Press.

Davis, Kenneth Culp. 1969. *Discretionary Justice: A Preliminary Inquiry*. Baton Rouge, LA: Louisiana State University Press.

Du Bois, W. E. B. (1935) 2014. *Black Reconstruction: An Essay toward a History of the Part Which Black Folk Played in the Attempt to Reconstruct Democracy in America, 1860–1880*. New York: Oxford University Press.

Dukmasova, Maya. 2016. "Abolish the Police? Organizers Say It's Less Crazy than It Sounds." *Chicago Reader*, August 25, 2016. www.chicagoreader.com.

Epp, Charles R., Steven Maynard-Moody, and Donald P. Haider-Markel. 2014. *Pulled over: How Police Stops Define Race and Citizenship*. Chicago: University of Chicago Press.

Floyd v. New York City. 2013. 959 F. Supp. 2d 540.

Harmon, Rachel A. 2011. "The Problem of Policing." *Michigan Law Review* 110 (5): 761–817.

Honig, Bonnie. 2015. "Public Things: Jonathan Lear's Radical Hope, Lars von Trier's Melancholia, and the Democratic Need." *Political Research Quarterly* 68 (3): 623–36.

Lind, E. Allan, and Tom R. Tyler. 1988. *The Social Psychology of Procedural Justice*. New York: Springer.

Loader, Ian, and Neil Walker. 2007. *Civilizing Security*. New York: Cambridge University Press.

Loader, Ian. 2006. "Policing, Recognition, and Belonging." *ANNALS of the American Academy of Political and Social Science* 605 (1): 201–21.

Lunden, Walter A. 1961. "The Theory of Crime Prevention." *British Journal of Criminology* 2 (3): 213–28.

Maclin, Tracey. 1998. "*Terry v. Ohio*'s Fourth Amendment Legacy: Black Men and Police Discretion." *St. John's Law Review* 72 (3–4): 1271–1322.

Meares, Tracey L., Tom R. Tyler, and Jacob Gardener. 2015. "Lawful or Fair? How Cops and Laypeople Perceive Good Policing." *Journal of Criminal Law and Criminology* 105 (2): 297–344.

Meares, Tracey, and Vesla Weaver. 2017. "Abolish the Police? Is Policing a Public Good Gone Bad?" *Boston Review*, August 1, 2017. http://bostonreview.net.

Meares, Tracey. 2008. "The Legitimacy of Police among Young African-American Men." *Marquette Law Review* 92 (4): 651–66.

Meares, Tracey. 2013. "The Good Cop: Knowing the Difference between Lawful or Effective Policing and Rightful Policing—and Why It Matters." *William & Mary Law Review* 54 (6): 1865–86.

Meares, Tracey. 2015. "A Third Reconstruction?" Balkanization, August 14, 2015. https://balkin.blogspot.com.

Meares, Tracey. 2017. "Policing: A Public Good Gone Bad." *Boston Review*, August 1, 2017. https://bostonreview.net.

National Academies of Sciences, Engineering, and Medicine. 2018. *Proactive Policing: Effects on Crime and Communities*. Washington, DC: The National Academies Press.

NBC Chicago. 2015. "Protesters Call for Mayor Emanuel's Resignation in Citywide Walkout." December 9, 2015. www.nbcchicago.com.

President's Commission on Law Enforcement and Administration of Justice. 1967. *Challenge of Crime in a Free Society*. Washington, DC: United States Government Printing Office.

Sharkey, Patrick. 2018. *Uneasy Peace: The Great Crime Decline, the Renewal of City Life, and the Next War on Violence*. New York: Norton.

Soss, Joe, and Vesla Weaver. 2017. "Police Are Our Government: Politics, Political Science, and the Policing of Race-Class Subjugated Communities." *Annual Review of Political Science* 20 (1): 565–91.

Steden, Ronald van, Zeger van der Wal, and Karin Lasthuizen. 2015. "Overlapping Values, Mutual Prejudices: Empirical Research into the Ethos of Police Officers and Private Security Guards." *Administration & Society* 47 (3): 220–43.

Taylor, Ralph B., and Brian A. Lawton. 2012. "An Integrated Contextual Model of Confidence in Local Police." *Police Quarterly* 15 (4): 414–45.

Tyler, Tom R. 2004. "Enhancing Police Legitimacy." *Annals of the American Academy of Political and Social Science* 593: 84–99.

Tyler, Tom R. 2006. *Why People Obey the Law*. Princeton, NJ: Princeton University Press.

Tyler, Tom R., ed. 2007. *Legitimacy and Criminal Justice: International Perspectives*. New York: Russell Sage Foundation.

Tyler, Tom R., and Jeffrey Fagan. 2008. "Legitimacy and Cooperation: Why Do People Help the Police Fight Crime in their Communities?" *Ohio State Journal of Criminal Law* 6 (1): 231–275.

Tyler, Tom R., and Cheryl J. Wakslak. 2004. "Profiling and Police Legitimacy: Procedural Justice, Attributions of Motive, and Acceptance of Police Authority." *Criminology* 42 (2): 253–82.

Voigt, Rob, Nicholas P. Camp, Vinodkumar Prabhakaran, William L. Hamilton, Rebecca C. Hetey, Camilla M. Griffiths, David Jurgens, Dan Jurafsky, and Jennifer

L. Eberhardt. 2017. "Language from Police Body Camera Footage Shows Racial Disparities in Officer Respect." *Proceedings of the National Academy of Sciences* 114 (25): 6521–25.

Wang, Amy. 2018. "Anti-gun Violence Protestors Take over Chicago Highway." *Washington Post*, July 7, 2018. www.washingtonpost.com.

Winters, John E. 1957. "The Role of the Police in the Prevention and Control of Delinquency." *Federal Probation* 21: 3–8.

Zimring, Franklin. 2012. *The City that Became Safe: New York's Lessons from Urban Crime and Its Control*. New York: Oxford University Press.

2

Legitimate Policing and Professional Norms

JAKE MONAGHAN

On July 26, 2017, nurse Alex Wubbels was assaulted by Detective Jeff Payne. Detective Payne was ordered to collect a blood sample from an unconscious patient who had been in an automobile accident, though he was not suspected of being under the influence of drugs or alcohol. Wubbels explained that Payne could collect a blood sample only with a warrant, with the patient's formal consent, or if the patient were under arrest. When Wubbels refused to let Payne collect a blood sample because none of these criteria were met, Payne, under an order from Lieutenant James Tracy, charged toward Wubbels and dragged her outside. He placed her under arrest, cuffed her, and put her in a police vehicle.

Prior to the arrest, Wubbels was communicating with her supervisor, who also informed Payne that he did not have the authority to collect a sample. Another officer on the scene suggested to Payne that they get a search warrant. But Payne himself recognized that they lacked the probable cause for a search warrant. He later claimed that he had authority from Utah's "implied consent" law. Not only was this law changed ten years prior to the incident, the US Supreme Court had earlier ruled that blood tests require a warrant. Payne, apparently ignorant of the relevant laws and policies, and despite the protests of Wubbels, her supervisor, and security for the hospital, *and* despite the apparent hesitance of his fellow officer, arrested Wubbels (Hawkins 2017).

In the end, Wubbels was not charged, and she reached a settlement with Salt Lake City. After a period of paid administrative leave, Detective Payne was fired. Lieutenant Tracy was demoted (Wamsley 2017).

The Clash of Professional Norms

This case is noteworthy for a variety of reasons. Unlike many cases of police brutality, the officer's misbehavior occurred against a backdrop of his own safety and without any need for urgent action. It occurred despite the warnings of hospital staff that Payne was making a mistake, and despite another police officer voicing concern. Unfortunately, none of Payne's fellow officers intervened or objected more forcefully. The case is also noteworthy because Payne was fired. It is most noteworthy, for my purposes, because it throws into sharp relief the divergent informal norms of two service professions: medicine and law enforcement.

Public discourse around policing is often critical and calls for institutional change. Our formal institutions, however, are only as effective as the informal norms they operate on top of.[1] In light of that, this chapter examines some of the informal norms that govern policing with the aim of identifying possibilities for improvement. In particular, I'll focus on policing strategies and policies rather than individual police-citizen interactions. The professional norms in policing are partly responsible for the manner in which the law is enforced, and they need attention.

I begin with some remarks on the relationship between law enforcement and political legitimacy. This provides a useful set of tools for thinking about the ethics of law enforcement. I shall then use legitimacy requirements to evaluate the informal norms of policing. There are two kinds of norms that I shall focus on: epistemic and "improvement" norms. The state of these informal norms in policing indicates a deficiency in professionalism, broadly construed, within law enforcement. I should emphasize that my claim is not that these norms don't exist within law enforcement; it is rather that they are not robust enough. They aren't endorsed widely enough, aren't weighed strongly enough, or they fail to take priority over other norms. Further, there are institutional impediments to norm improvement. Understanding which informal, professional norms are desirable can help to recommend institutional reforms. The norms I shall discuss are relevant to the case described above, though they apply broadly. Achieving clarity about professional norms in policing is an important part of the project of professionalizing police work, a project begun about a century ago by August Vollmer.[2]

Law Enforcement Strategies and Political Legitimacy

Police ethics must concern itself with questions about individuals as well as institutions. When are individual officers permitted to engage citizens, and when are they permitted to enforce particular laws?[3] There are also questions about strategy and policy. How will officers in a department remove illegal guns from the streets, deter burglaries, deal with officer misconduct, or wage the day's battle in the war on drugs? What policies and strategies govern patrol officers, detectives, and others, given their tremendous amount of discretion?

Because police officers and other members of law enforcement are the ones who enforce many of the decisions of the state, law enforcement strategy is justified in large part by considerations of *normative* political legitimacy. By legitimacy I mean the property of being *morally permitted* to exercise political power.[4] This sense of "legitimacy" is normative, unlike the descriptive sense used in other work (Tyler 2004). Normative legitimacy is not determined solely by whether citizens believe a police officer or agency to be legitimate. Policing is a profession, but it is a political profession; the normativity here is partially political, so the justifications must be as well.

Suppose that political legitimacy is in fact a foundational component of the professional ethics of law enforcement. Does this make police ethics redundant on the grounds that it is explained entirely by whatever theory of legitimacy we have? Perhaps if the True Theory of Legitimacy says that a particular government and law are legitimate, agents of that government may enforce it, and if the True Theory of Legitimacy says that a particular government or law is illegitimate, agents of that government may not enforce it. On this view, how members of law enforcement should behave—their professional ethics—is determined entirely by whatever normative theory tells us about which governments and laws are legitimate.

This line of reasoning is mistaken. It glosses over an important issue, namely that legitimate governments and laws can be made illegitimate by bad law enforcement. Theories of political legitimacy are therefore incomplete without police ethics. Most readers will think that the government of New York City and most of its laws are legitimate. Even if officers in the New York City Police Department (NYPD) are permitted to stop cab drivers using fraudulent medallions, they are not permitted to shoot drivers using fraudulent medallions. Nor are they permitted to enforce the law selectively while giving their friends a pass. Either of these modes of enforcement would be illegitimate; police lack the permission to exercise these kinds of power. Any law can be illegitimately enforced. With enough illegitimate enforcement, an entire agency can become illegitimate. The Acapulco police department, for example, was so compromised by criminal organizations that the Mexican military disarmed it (Agerholm 2018). At some point, an organization goes from a bad law enforcement agency to a criminal gang or occupying force.

Finally, note that much of what law enforcement organizations do is not given to them directly by legislatures or the courts. This fact is often overlooked. Locke, for example, in discussing the importance of separating executive and legislative powers, claimed that the legislature has (he seems to mean sole) authority over "how the force for the commonwealth shall be employed" (Locke [1689] 1968, chapter 12, section 143). But this is, strictly speaking, false; it ignores the reality of how bureaucracies function. To put the point differently, it is insensitive to the fact that the decisions of electorates and legislative bodies will always under-determine modes of enforcement.

Discretion in law enforcement—about whether to engage a suspect in conversation or in pursuit, to write a motorist a ticket, to focus on small "broken windows" infractions or to focus on crime "hot spots," to prosecute an accused criminal on this charge or that, or to stack those charges—is largely unavoidable. Law enforcement strategy and policy occupies an intermediate zone between laws and particular instances of political power. For this reason we can't have a complete account of police or law enforcement ethics more generally by relying only on the True Theory of Legitimacy. In the following section, I use the NYPD's practice of stop, question, and frisk (SQF) as a way to emphasize this point.

Although police ethics requires input from a theory of legitimacy, I do not want to rely on a particular theory of legitimacy here. I shall remain agnostic on how to fully specify a theory of legitimacy and instead rely on a few legitimacy requirements that are rather widely endorsed. Enforcement is plausibly illegitimate when the enforcement strategy is *disproportionate*, *unequal*, or when it is *harsh* rather than lenient.

Let's take the proportionality requirement first. Suppose legislatures are permitted to regulate the supply of taxis in their jurisdiction. They are nevertheless not permitted to set the death penalty or a $10 million fine as the punishment for operating an unauthorized taxi. What makes this the case also applies to other aspects of law enforcement. Even if officers in New York City are permitted to arrest individuals operating a taxi without a medallion, they are not permitted to use lethal force to prevent a driver from picking up a passenger. They may only impound the driver's car, issue a ticket, refer the case to a prosecutor, or something along these lines. Lethal force would be disproportionate in a case like this. This means that police commanders may not adopt a taxi law enforcement strategy in their department that permits officers to use lethal force. If the cost of this is less than full compliance with that particular law, that is simply a cost of legitimate policing.

As William Blackstone famously put it, "the law holds it better that ten guilty persons escape, than that one innocent party suffer" (Blackstone 1765, book 4, chap. 27). We might disagree with Blackstone about whether such leniency is actually widely respected in law creation or enforcement, but we are unlikely to disagree that leniency in an imperfect political procedure is a necessary part of that procedure's legitimacy. When it comes to punishment, Blackstone's view that false positives are worse than false negatives not only seems clearly correct, it seems to apply naturally to other aspects of law enforcement. The Fourth Amendment's prohibition on unreasonable search and seizure is a manifestation of this: we have a somewhat (some would argue insufficiently) demanding justificatory requirement for a member of law enforcement to search or seize property. Even when contact with the criminal justice system doesn't result in legal punishment, it can still be seriously costly. Therefore, if the result of an enforcement strategy is a high false-positive rate or, in other words, is harsh rather than lenient, it is likely illegitimate.

Finally, consider the equality requirement. Legislatures are not permitted to create a system of laws that intentionally benefits some members of society at the expense of others. Some kind of political equality is necessary for political legitimacy. Here, too, it is clear that this requirement applies to law enforcement more generally. A police department that enforces drug laws against one criminal organization and not another is illegitimate, and not only because drug prohibition is not a legitimate use of political power. A police department that tends to enforce laws against one race or ethnicity and not another is likely illegitimate; at that point the department stops looking like a police force.

Police ethics is a matter of political philosophy. It is also a matter of professional ethics. It is especially interesting for the political philosopher because, as an interface between law and citizen, occupying a space between legislated policy and particular instances of political power, modes of law enforcement can be the difference between legitimate and illegitimate political power. It is especially interesting for the professional ethicist because the relationship between officer and citizen is regularly adversarial. In what follows, I shall draw together these two points to further develop a professional police ethics that is sensitive to the demands of political legitimacy.

Epistemic Norms and Professionalism

Good professions obey a variety of closely related epistemic norms. Before practicing medicine, medical professionals undergo years of rigorous training. Additionally, medical professionals change their professional behavior in response to research because they aim to provide patients with the best care possible. Many healthcare professionals enroll in "continuing education" programs in order to keep up with research developments, and many also make some effort to read medical journals. Other professionals, including lawyers, educators, and engineers, also participate in continuing education programs; it is often required by licensing bodies. Of course, not all healthcare professionals do this, but there is some normative expectation that they will.[5]

Note also that healthcare professionals are often the ones conducting the peer-reviewed research. Clinical trials that study the efficacy, risks, and best practices for new treatments are typically conducted by physicians and other healthcare professionals. Not only do members of the healthcare profession typically recognize an obligation to stay informed, there is also an expectation, a professional norm, that new medical knowledge will be discovered by members of the field.

So there are two distinct but related epistemic norms in healthcare: one of knowledge acquisition, and one of knowledge production. The normative expectation that healthcare as an institution will aim at the best outcomes possible, understood in terms of patient beneficence and autonomy, generates both of these epistemic norms.

It is a moral and professional failing to disregard these epistemic norms. Deficiencies in epistemic norms contribute to deficiencies with respect to legitimacy. Let us consider a controversial case study: SQF "Terry stops" in New York City. The US Supreme Court's decision in *Terry v. Ohio* allows police officers to detain individuals suspected of being engaged in criminal activity for a short period of time and to "pat down" individuals who are detained without violating the Fourth Amendment's prohibition on unreasonable searches and seizures. This decision laid the ground for New York City's controversial SQF policy. The adoption and continued defense of this strategy is but one example of a failure to satisfy epistemic norms within law enforcement.

Proponents of SQF claim it deters crime, with some attributing the historic drop in New York City crime to the policy. Members of the NYPD and the Michael Bloomberg administration are among these proponents.[6] The enforcement strategy has become intensely controversial, and many of its vocal proponents are members of law enforcement. Are they correct? Is SQF a legitimate enforcement strategy?

The SQF enforcement strategy is controversial not only in part because it is unclear whether the practice deters crime. It is controversial because it might result in violations of the rights of innocent citizens and because it is possibly carried out in a racist manner; at the very least, minorities clearly bear the majority of the burdens associated with SQF. Although Blacks and Hispanics are minorities in New York City, the vast majority of New Yorkers stopped, questioned, and frisked have been Black or Hispanic. The police practice might license the racist harassment of innocent citizens.

Bloomberg responded to this claim as mayor, claiming that the decision to engage a suspect is entirely about behavior, not race or ethnicity (Bloomberg 2013). Further, those who find the charges of racism directed at stop and frisk nothing more than political correctness run amok are keen to point out that minorities are stopped at rates that closely match the minority-against-minority crime rate.[7] This, however, is probably not true. In 2007, years before Bloomberg and others made this argument, Andrew Gelman and co-authors showed that "members of minority groups were stopped more often than whites, both in comparison to their overall population and to the estimated rates of crime that they have committed" (Gelman, Fagan, and Kiss 2007, 813–14).

There is the additional problem that the NYPD, in this context, might not be very good at identifying behavior that is actually indicative of criminality: from 2003 to 2013, the NYPD performed 1,241 stops per day on average, arresting only seventy-three people per day, again on average. That's a "success" rate of only six percent. Further, the practice, aimed largely at removing weapons from the streets, yielded only two arrests per day on average for illegal possession of a gun (Apel 2016, 62). The low number of arrests generated by these Terry stops suggests that physical appearance, rather than behavioral cues, could be the cause.

If SQF is in fact an instance of unequal policing, then its legitimacy as an enforcement strategy is partially undermined. The success rate calls into question both the proportionality and leniency of SQF.

Consider first the costs of SQF. Interactions with police, even when they don't lead to incarceration, can be harmful. They likely decrease the mental health or well-being of those stopped (Geller et al. 2014). Interaction with law enforcement has also been found to decrease political participation, which in turn can decrease the quality of democratic decision-making (Weaver and Lerman, 2010). Simply put, we need a rather strong justification for stopping someone, demanding a justification that they are not doing anything illegal, and physically touching and searching them if we are unsatisfied with their explanation. This is widely agreed upon by serious moral theories, and it is reflected in many legal jurisdictions.

What are the benefits of SQF? The main benefit touted by proponents is crime deterrence.[8] Crime rates did drop when the NYPD was practicing SQF. Crime rates in New York City began falling in the early 1990s *before* the adoption of SQF, however, probably in large part because of a sharp increase in the number of police officers employed by the city (Fagan et al. 2010, 309). At the very least, it is difficult to separate the deterrent effects of a larger police presence from the deterrent effects of controversial Terry stops.[9] Some empirical work has found that SQF has *no* effect on robbery and burglary rates (Rosenfeld and Fornango 2014). Yet, despite historically low crime rates, the rate of Terry stops in the city increased drastically from 2003 to 2008 under Bloomberg. And because citizens who have negative interactions with the police are less likely to communicate with them, part of the crime drop attributed to the policy could be simply a drop in crime *reports* (Apel 2016, 63). In addition to an increase in the size of the police force and possible reductions in crime report rates, there has also been a steady increase in the number of surveillance cameras in the city that could deter crime (Apel 2016, 61). In light of this, it is difficult to confidently attribute the crime drop to SQF.

Might the low arrest rate described above actually be evidence of the policy's success? Bloomberg relied on this very argument, claiming that stops that do not result in an arrest can still be legitimate. They can stop an assault or mugging before it begins, for example. While this is in principle true, we now know that this is unlikely to be the case, because crime rates did not rise when SQF was abandoned.[10]

SQF needs to have a deterrent effect in order for the force required by the enforcement strategy to be proportionate. If an enforcement strategy does not succeed in protecting or serving the community, then we have some evidence that the force does not meet the proportionality requirement, because we have force without anything to justify it. Consider an analogy with the proportionality requirement for permissible self-defense: if a method of self-defense harms innocent bystanders without having any tendency to neutralize the threat, that method is not justified on self-defense grounds.

If SQF does in fact turn out to have a deterrent effect, and its particular manifestation is not unequal, it still faces the following problem. Whereas we want our criminal justice procedures to be *lenient*, SQF is far from it. Crime rates fell during SQF and Terry stops continued to rise while crime rates fell. This means that SQF targeted more innocent citizens as time went on, and that the practice became increasingly harsh rather than maintaining an appropriate level of leniency.[11]

Normative evaluations of political power, whether domestic law enforcement or otherwise, must often be comparative. How does this method of enforcement compare to other *feasible* alternatives? Perhaps the SQF strategy is simply the best option available to us. Perhaps it does indeed have a deterrent effect. Without SQF, New York City may have descended into a Hobbesian war of all against all. If SQF were the only feasible strategy for avoiding such misery, it may well have been legitimate. Our law enforcement institutions would need some justification for that claim as part of the case for why SQF was legitimate. As far as I can tell, this justification does not exist. That crime rates fell in New York City prior to SQF suggests that other enforcement strategies that were more proportionate and appropriately lenient were available. As noted above, some empirical examination suggests that increased police presence, *but not the increased stops themselves*, reduces crime (MacDonald, Fagan, and Geller 2016).

A proper analysis of SQF in light of legitimacy requirements would have made it clear that the strategy should have been abandoned. The upshot is twofold: there are good reasons to think that SQF was an illegitimate enforcement strategy, and more robust epistemic norms in policing could have prevented the adoption, or shortened the duration, of the enforcement strategy experiment. The practice was abandoned in New York City, but not because the department concluded that it was ineffective or illegitimate. It was deemed unconstitutional.

The effects of insufficient epistemic norms in policing are far-reaching. Detective Payne, in the case discussed at the outset, clearly violates the epistemic norm of policing, the knowledge acquisition norm in particular. But he is not alone. In 2018, Sergeant Josh Rosenblatt, a legal instructor in the Baltimore Police Department, claimed that the police academy in Baltimore is passing officers who lack adequate knowledge of the Constitution and when it is legal to arrest or search citizens (Rector and Fenton 2018). The problem isn't isolated to the rank-and-file.

The epistemic norm deficiencies can be a cause for concern even when the policing seems not to suffer as a result. The Buffalo Police Department (BPD) is unusually good at not shooting suspects: they shot no one for a five-year period between 2012 and 2017. Whatever rules of engagement or use-of-force training strategies are being used in the department are thus more likely to be legitimate. But, worryingly, BPD officers do not seem to know what it is that they are doing right. In a story on the subject, the police union president told CNN that it may just be luck. The other five officers CNN spoke with were unable to offer an explanation for their exemplary performance. This state of affairs is clearly better than in many mid-sized American cities, but it is a cause for concern nevertheless (Lake 2017).

Law enforcement is as difficult and complicated as medicine, and it needs epistemic norms to match. Professional epistemic norms are important for ensuring that professional activity is competent. But that is not all. Epistemic norms are related to, or possibly partly constitutive of, "improvement" norms. Professional activity needs to be competent, but it is highly desirable that professionals recognize an obligation to raise the bar of competence. Epistemic norms play a crucial role in the improvement norms that govern medicine and other professions.

Keeping the Bad Apples from Spoiling the Bunch

Acquiring the knowledge necessary for competent professional activity makes it clear that there is much we don't know about the subject. When this is the case, the knowledge acquisition norm generates the knowledge production norm. This norm is not only an epistemic norm, it can also be described as an *improvement* norm. The improvement norm, however, extends beyond epistemic norms.

In medicine, the improvement norm is most clearly manifested in the research component of the profession. But it is also manifested in dexterity practice for surgeons. Soldiers and police alike demonstrate a recognition of this norm when it comes to physical fitness, marksmanship, and other "combat" skills that require practice. Likewise for other professions.[12] In the context of policing, the norm obviously requires more than exercise and target practice. It requires, among other things, having a more general concern with officer performance. Good policing cannot happen individually. The collective nature of policing implies that law enforcement professionals ought to be particularly concerned with the performance of their fellow officers in addition to their own. Let me unpack this claim.

Members of law enforcement, whether they're officers working a beat, detectives, or officers in managerial positions, are providing for the *general* security.[13] The force that police officers wield is not justified by appeal to considerations about the particular citizens an officer will interact with, but rather by appeal to considerations about the citizenry in general. In this way, the *adversarial* nature of policing is constitutive of its *collective* nature.

Practically speaking, when members of a community come to distrust some police, it undermines the efficacy of the police department. One officer's unprofessional, unethical conduct will mean that other officers (including officers from other agencies) are less effective at their jobs

(Tyler 2004). For example, municipalities that rely heavily on police departments for revenue (e.g., through fines) also have higher rates of unsolved property and violent crime (Goldstein, Sances, and You 2020). Moreover, when police brutality cases are publicized, citizens are less likely to call the police to report ongoing crime (Desmond, Papachristos, and Kirk 2016). Cynicism about law enforcement tends to decrease cooperation with the police and cynicism about one law enforcement agency tends to transfer to other agencies (Kirk et al. 2012).

So, an unprofessional, unethical police officer in one agency can undermine not only the effectiveness of his or her own agency, but also of other agencies as well. Good police officers then must be concerned with eliminating the so-called "bad apples" who are either badly motivated or badly performing. Not only do they undermine the goals of law enforcement, they risk delegitimizing the law enforcement organization itself. Thus, from the obligation to competently perform one's professional activity, and from the improvement norm, it follows that there must also be a strong *accountability* norm in law enforcement.[14]

There are useful similarities with medicine here as well. Some of the professional obligations commonly recognized in medicine are agent- and patient-relative, meaning that *this* provider has an obligation to *that* patient. Others, we might say, are agent- and patient-neutral, meaning they apply to all providers and are enjoyed by all patients (or perhaps even more broadly). Deceiving a patient into accepting a particular treatment violates both kinds of obligation. There is an obligation the provider has to the patient that is violated. There is also, plausibly, an obligation not to do things that damage the trust patients have in the healthcare system that is crucial to effective and permissible medical care.[15]

Police ethics includes both kinds of obligation. Members of law enforcement have obligations of the agent- and patient-relative variety. They also have neutral obligations. Indeed, this follows from the adversarial nature of policing: the foundational obligation to protect and serve exists toward the community in general, and satisfying that obligation typically brings police into contact with others who must be constrained in some way.

There are at least two components of the general accountability norm: an obligation to not interfere with the removal or punishment of a fellow professional for unethical conduct, and an obligation to bring unethical conduct to light. Let us call these the *non-interference* and *whistleblowing* norms.

The law enforcement profession has not fully recognized these norms. Take the NYPD's retaliation against Adrian Schoolcraft as an example. In that case, officers harassed the rare whistleblower in law enforcement as punishment for whistleblowing, and further attempted to interfere with the investigation of corruption within New York City's 81st Precinct station (Goodman 2013). The NYPD, more generally, rarely acts to punish police officers who lie under oath. Between 2010 and 2018, the Civilian Complaint Review Board received eighty-one complaints about officers lying; in only two of them did the NYPD's Internal Affairs Bureau uphold the Board's complaint (Goldstein 2018).

This is a familiar phenomenon. The so-called "blue wall of silence" means that officers are unlikely to report or testify about misconduct (Koepke 2000). When misconduct is brought to light, internal affairs investigations are often not objective, plausibly because they are not sufficiently institutionally independent. Police unions complain when misconduct is made public knowledge, and often advocate against police oversight.[16] The close relationship between prosecutors and police officers is another institutional impediment to accountability norms.

I should emphasize that my point is not that there is *no* accountability norm in policing. Rather, the claim is just that the norm seems to be rather weak and it is undermined by various institutional design problems. Further, as evidenced by the "blue wall of silence" mentality manifest in counterproductive police unions, there seems to be a rather strong competing anti-accountability norm.

In addition to negligent police unions and incentive problems for internal investigators and prosecutors, the size of policing agencies is another institutional impediment related to accountability. When, despite the prevailing tendencies, an officer is removed from the job because of misconduct, this is often short-lived. Incompetent officers can bounce from agency to agency until they eventually use lethal force without justification.[17] Officers can sometimes find employment after using lethal force without justification: four years after fatally shooting Tamir Rice, and one year after being fired by the Cleveland Police Department,

Timothy Loehmann was hired by the Bellaire, Ohio, police department (Haag 2018). The decentralized nature of policing is partly responsible for these problems.

The common complaint about "Monday-morning quarterbacking" further illustrates the state of accountability norms in policing. It does no good to criticize the quarterback the morning after the game when we've had the benefit of hindsight and experienced none of the pressures of the job. There is something to this complaint, but this way of thinking about access to knowledge can be taken too far. It is easy to be too deferential to the perspective of individual officers. In discussing the BPD's low rate of killing citizens, mentioned earlier, one officer had this to say: "I've lost—not close friends, but friends, because of the comments they've made about, you know, 'This cop was wrong.' Were you there? . . . I mean, you weren't there. That's why I wouldn't critique anybody—I would never critique another cop" (Lake 2017). Surely this officer is not an outlier in the profession in holding that the judgment of an officer in the line of duty is basically beyond reproach. We don't even have to take this officer literally for this to be objectionable. It would be absurd to think one is *never* entitled to critique an officer's performance; it is not much less absurd to think that one is *usually* not entitled to critique an officer's performance. Though the Monday morning quarterback complaint is right that we should take into account the way that the circumstances of the job can lead to blameless mistakes, it does not follow that any professional's conduct is beyond criticism. Members of law enforcement are exactly the people who need to be critical of unprofessional policing.

Before moving on, let me explicitly connect the improvement norms I've discussed in this section with the legitimacy requirements set out at the beginning. Recall that legitimate policing requires equal, lenient, and proportionate enforcement. When law enforcement professionals violate the accountability norm by failing to whistle-blow, by failing to cross the blue wall of silence, or by otherwise interfering an investigation, they are engaging in unequal policing. Officers are permitted to use discretion, but ignoring professional misconduct is very different from ignoring a speeder or a beer in a paper bag on the street. Unequal policing doesn't merely make particular instances of enforcement illegitimate, it risks rendering the entire agency illegitimate.

There is a final sense of accountability worth discussing in this section. Not only does the law enforcement profession need a more widespread recognition of the obligation to hold others accountable for their unethical conduct, the profession also needs more accountability for enforcement strategies more broadly. Currently, for the most part, law enforcement agencies do not commit themselves upfront to abandoning strategies that prove ineffective because they do not spell out what it would mean for an enforcement strategy to be ineffective. This means that we have no way of easily falsifying the empirical claims used to justify new or experimental enforcement strategies.

Being clear from the beginning what the failure conditions for a proposed enforcement strategy are opens law enforcement up to accountability. NYPD Chief Ray Kelly went on the record to say that if SQF were ended, violent crime would go up (Cushing 2013). We now know that it did not. Kelly responded not by admitting that he was wrong, but by criticizing the crime statistics (Boniello 2016). Perhaps Kelly is right that clean statistics would vindicate him, though that seems unlikely. A more robust ability to hold agencies accountable for their enforcement strategies would hopefully result in the abandonment of this strategy. This requires law enforcement to make falsifiable claims in support of enforcement strategies.

In Detective Payne's case, despite determinations from an internal affairs review and a Police Civilian Review Board that Payne acted wrongfully, Payne's police union complained that the investigation was "corrupted" by "premature" release of body camera footage. In response to an obviously illegitimate use of police force, citizens complained and the city acknowledged that wrongdoing occurred. Incredibly, these statements were considered "inflammatory" by the police union (Hunt and Ramseth 2017).

Conceptual Improvements in Policing

After World War II, medical ethics underwent a revolution. Before the Nuremberg Code, the Declaration of Geneva, the Declaration of Helsinki, and a series of precedent-setting court cases in the 1950s, medical ethics was dominated by considerations of welfare as conceived of by physicians. Medical paternalism was the norm. A variety of conceptual changes played a role in the change to autonomy-based medical ethics, clearly spurred in part by the horrors of involuntary medical experimentation. In particular, recognizing that (1) welfare is partly determined by autonomous preferences, and that (2) mere acquiescence isn't evidence of valid consent, made it clear that the principle of respect for autonomy was far weightier and demanding than had been recognized.

The stark contrast between medical ethics before and after the Second World War is another reason why this comparison is useful. It is easy for an optimist to look at the Black Lives Matter movement, law enforcement's unequivocal defeat in the war on drugs, and the changes demanded by the ongoing opioid epidemic, and see ourselves as being on the cusp of a similar drastic transition in policing. We must ask, then, what went into medicine's transition? How can we instigate a similar transition in policing?

We might say that the goals of medical care were "thicker" after the Second World War. The goals of medical care went from mere health to a holistic integration of the values of autonomy and wellbeing. In turn, this allowed us to change the way that we think about the goals or nature of medicine: acting only with the patient's informed consent became far more important than merely returning the patient to health. This had huge ramifications. Hospitals had to institute and refine consent forms and procedures. Advance directives and goals of care were created and made more nuanced. Hospitals instituted procedures to make patients aware of the importance of advance directives and having trustworthy, official proxy decision makers. This transition is still underway, of course, as evidenced by the American Medical Association's (n.d., Opinion 5.8) reluctance to recognize that active euthanasia is a legitimate tool in the physician's toolkit; there are remnants of the beneficence-before-autonomy medical ethic.

A similar distinction can be drawn in policing. The "thin" goals of policing are simply the successful apprehension and prosecution of criminals. Of course, no one thinks that this exhausts the goals of policing. The description given by the International Association of Chiefs of Police of the duties of police is a plausible description of the "thick" goals of policing: "The fundamental duties of a police officer include serving the community; safeguarding lives and property; protecting the innocent; keeping the peace; and ensuring the rights of all to liberty, equality and justice" (International Association of Chiefs of Police 1989). Satisfying the thin goals of policing does not guarantee that any of the thick goals will be satisfied. Just as good medicine requires medical professionals to recognize that health is not the final end of medicine, good policing similarly requires law enforcement professionals to recognize that successful arrests and prosecutions are not the final end of policing. A singular focus on crime deterrence and punishment in law enforcement would be like a singular focus on disease prevention and treatment in medicine. In other words, *moral clarity* about the goals of policing, and their lexical priority, is necessary for good policing.

Clarifying the goals and values of medicine allowed us to add tools to the toolkit. A medical profession aimed solely at the treatment of pathology has no room for palliative care. Palliative care, a multidisciplinary approach to managing harmful symptoms that came into existence roughly alongside the doctrine of informed consent, can occur alongside curative care, though it is often the sole component of end-of-life care.

A "pathocentric" conception of medicine has a hard time permitting organ transplants from healthy donors to patients on the grounds that, in performing this procedure, the surgeon is turning a healthy *person* into a *patient*. Joseph Murray, the first to transplant a human kidney, considered the transplant an ethical "compromise" on these grounds (Davis and Crowe 2009, 589). Fortunately, organ transplants are now core rather than peripheral medical procedures. There is now widespread agreement that medicine is not purely pathocentric.

Palliative care and organ transplants are reactions to the fact that the goals and values of medicine can conflict. Paying attention to value conflict can uncover possible professional improvements in policing as it has in medicine.

Recognizing the value conflict in emergency situations when resources are scare, medical professionals triage patients to treat the most serious problems first. Some police departments seemingly do not take seriously enough the need to prioritize among conflicting values. In 2015, for example, the Flint Police Department was gifted a new drug-sniffing dog.[18] Though under serious resource constraints and facing high levels of violent crime, the department deemed drug prohibition to be important enough to spend its limited time seeking out those who illegally possessed drugs. Perhaps the department thought that by enforcing drug laws police would be able to indirectly target violent crime. But this itself embodies a failure to recognize that the goals of law enforcement can conflict. Enforcing prohibition laws that generate a black market is often a major *cause* of violence. The goals of eliminating crime and protecting citizens are thus in tension. If, however, law enforcement looked beyond traditional law enforcement *methods* of achieving their goals, they could reduce this tension.

I have in mind the perhaps counterintuitive harm-reduction approach to treating the ills of drug abuse. Sometimes the solution to a problem is counterintuitive. For example, it is common for kidney transplant recipients to have *three* kidneys, because if their original kidneys are not necrotic, it is a net benefit to the patient to leave them in their body. Similarly, treating the individual and social problems of drug abuse by giving drug users a supervised injection site and a needle exchange may seem as counterintuitive as leaving pathological kidneys in a transplant patient. Yet we have compelling evidence that housing support, therapy, needle exchange centers, and so on are better at treating the problems of drug abuse than incarceration. Harm reduction characterizes the medical response to drug use. Law enforcement, on the other hand, is by and large skeptical of harm-reduction approaches. This is evidenced by how long they have taken to spill over into the law enforcement arsenal. One Ohio sheriff, for example, refuses to have officers carry naloxone despite the obvious fact that it is a successful way to reduce the death toll of the opioid epidemic (Siemaszko 2017).

Finally, sometimes professionals simply need better training regarding the moral obligations that follow from uncontroversial professional goals and norms. In some cases, it is very difficult to figure out what morality requires in a complex situation. But in many cases, what morality requires is quite clear. For example, the cost of interacting with police entails that police need to have a justification for engaging with citizens (where engaging means stopping citizens or otherwise using force). They may not engage with citizens randomly.

Lack of awareness of this concern on the part of police can have unfortunate consequences. In a bid to improve police-community relations, police in Halifax, Virginia, in 2016 thought it would be a good idea to have "random ice cream stops" where motorists would be pulled over and given ice cream. The officers reported that the motorists genuinely enjoyed the interaction, though there are clear incentives not to communicate one's displeasure in a situation like this (Criss 2016). If we put aside the challenge of eating ice cream while driving and simply grant that many motorists like the interaction, this is still a bad idea. It would be analogous to medical professionals performing random, benign medical procedures. Just because a random flu vaccination can be in some ways benign does not mean that it is justified. A medical professional who performed random benign medical procedures would be guilty of, among other things, ignorance of what their professional obligations require of them. The same analysis applies to officers conducting random ice cream stops.

The recent behavior of St. Louis police officers serves as a less benign example of this problem. After breaking up protests, an unfortunately large number of police officers were heard chanting "Whose street? Our street!" (Lartey 2017). These officers seem not to respect the constraints on the adversarial nature of policing; policing should never be "us" versus "them." When it is, legitimacy is likely lost.

Conclusion

I have argued that the proportionality, leniency, and equality requirements for political legitimacy apply directly to law enforcement strategies and rules of engagement. Those requirements can be fully met only when law enforcement, as a profession, recognizes more robust (and partially overlapping) epistemic and improvement norms. The epistemic norms include a knowledge acquisition norm and a knowledge production norm. The improvement norms, in addition to requiring the profession to engage in knowledge production, also include the accountability norms of non-interference, whistleblowing, and falsifiability. Finally, I argued that increased moral clarity, itself a professional improvement, paves the way for enforcement strategies that are more likely to be legitimate.

This analysis explains a variety of moral problems in policing and is motivated in part by the view that simply spending more money on training and punishing unprofessional, unethical, and criminal law enforcement agents will not fix our problems. Force is rarely the best method for changing bad behavior and bad outcomes. Instead, we want professions to be, as far as possible, self-regulating.

There are many plausible suggestions for reform. Police decertification could be pursued more aggressively, along with other reforms, at the state level (Puro, Goldman, and Smith 1997; Goldman 2016). Explaining the blue wall of silence to jurors could increase police accountability (Koepke 2000). Perhaps requiring officers to carry their own "malpractice" insurance would make some unprofessional officers unemployable (Ramirez et al. 2018). All of these face the well-known problem that policing in the United States is radically decentralized, making widespread reform difficult to achieve. To conclude, I would like to discuss just one possibility for rectifying the deficiencies in professional norms and legitimacy in policing: making law enforcement more multidisciplinary. Making law enforcement more multidisciplinary is likely to increase moral clarity and strengthen epistemic and improvement norms.

The successful transition from paternalism-dominated to autonomy-dominated medicine required further specialization. Hospitals tend now to employ clinical ethicists to take part in decisions about medical care. Having an "outsider" in the room helps to increase the salience of considerations apart from medical wellbeing. The ongoing transition to more fully respect autonomy at the end of life was facilitated by the creation of a new specialization, palliative care. Medical professionals are as susceptible to bad incentives as anyone, and adding the clinical-ethicist and palliative-care positions to the hospital hierarchy serves as a check against these risks. These new roles, though slightly antagonistic to the existing conceptual frameworks, have been thoroughly integrated into the medical profession. Mild antagonism can itself be responsible for rectifying the norm deficiencies identified here.

Adding more police ethics to the law enforcement curriculum is a way of making policing more interdisciplinary. One of the benefits of making medical ethics a required part of the typical medical education is that professionals have a shared language to think about competing values in the morally charged situations that inevitably arise. More fundamentally, it introduces new metrics on which to evaluate possible courses of action. The evaluation should not stop at "is it legal?" and "will it deter crime?" Work on (descriptive) police legitimacy has already had an influence on the profession, but a larger influence would be welcome.

In order to further take advantage of some of the useful, mild antagonism found in the medical profession, the administrative ranks of law enforcement agencies might also be diversified. If no one in administrative positions is concerned with legitimacy requirements, no one has to convince others that a given enforcement strategy is legitimate. These kinds of institutional antagonisms require people to take seriously the perspective of others, even if only one party gets their way. This could have the further effect of decoupling the *goals* of law enforcement from the *methods* of law enforcement.

One way to begin changing the norms is to change the selection effects involved in the hiring and staffing process. At the political level, we can encourage law enforcement agencies to work with criminologists and other social scientists, possibly by increasing the grant money for that kind of research. Even better, we should encourage law enforcement agencies to have members who engage in criminology research. Pairing researchers with police administrators trying out new enforcement strategies allows for more robust epistemic norms, more accountability, and a better division of labor. Bringing criminologists and other social scientists into law enforcement agencies would change an agency's culture. This happens to an extent now, of course, but the transition can be strengthened and accelerated.

Perspectives from moral philosophy, medicine, and social science would improve the informal, professional norms within policing. Corporations have specialization at the executive level; the makeup of the executive and the board of directors matters for how the firm behaves. We can induce change within policing by remaking police departments.

The Police Executive Research Forum has made a number of recommendations along these lines. It recommends equipping officers with naloxone and working with public health and social service agencies (Police Executive Research Forum 2017, 14). Richard Biehl, police chief in Dayton, Ohio, has equipped officers with naloxone to great success (Goodnough 2018). The National Police Foundation acknowledges the empirical evidence concerning the costs of SQF and the risks associated with the strategy (Police Foundation 2017). I hope to have provided a normative framework that explains why we badly need to amplify these kinds of voices within the law enforcement profession. Again, my point is not that these norms are nonexistent; rather, it is that they need to be strengthened and extended, while competing norms and institutional impediments to improving the norms need to be eliminated.

One might object that the entire analysis I've offered is suspect on the grounds that medical malpractice claims more lives than police malpractice. Perhaps medicine is not the exemplar I've claimed that it is.[19] Perhaps medicine even has a thing or two to learn from policing. In response, I should clarify that the medical profession has deep moral problems of its own. The profession has, however, made a serious effort to rein in its abuses over the past several decades as patient autonomy has been pushed to the core of medical ethics and practice.

A natural worry about increased professionalization in law enforcement is that, rather than improving the quality of law enforcement, more professionalization would actually make it worse by undermining democratic oversight and the possibility of democratic authorization. If the police are experts, why would they take guidance from the voters? There is much more to be said about the relationship between democratic values and legitimate policing, and about how to make policing more legitimate. For now, I hope to have made it clear that achieving an appropriate relationship between the sense of professionalism in law enforcement and democratic authorization requires us to revise the way we think of law enforcement and to make changes in our law enforcement institutions. Law enforcement strategies aren't legitimate just because they are pursued by legitimate agents or agencies. Good policing is exceptionally difficult in no small part because legitimacy requirements are demanding.

NOTES

1 Douglass North (1991) famously defines institutions as *including* informal constraints. All that matters for present purposes is that the manifestation of formal rules is highly dependent on informal norms.
2 August Vollmer is widely considered the "father of modern policing." Sarah Seo (2019) chronicles the relationship between Vollmer's drive to professionalize policing and the adoption of the automobile.
3 I take up these questions in earlier work (Monaghan 2017, 2018).
4 Not everyone uses "legitimacy" in this way. My usage follows Buchanan (2002).
5 The American Medical Association's (AMA) code of ethics has the following to say on the matter: "Physicians should strive to further their medical education throughout their careers, to ensure that they serve patients to the best of their

abilities and live up to professional standards of excellence" (AMA n.d., Opinion 9.2.6).

6   NYPD spokesman Paul J. Brown and Marc LaVorgna, then-spokesman for then-mayor Michael Bloomberg, both make this claim (Taylor 2011). Bloomberg (2013) himself endorses this claim.

7   See Bloomberg (2013) and Mac Donald (2010).

8   The practice of stop and frisk has received some support from criminologists. Weisburd et al. (2016) provide some evidence for thinking that the practice does deter crime, though they point out that it is not clear whether there are other, better police practices for deterring crime. They also point out that one of the costs of the policy beyond police resources could be diminished police legitimacy. It should be rather obvious, though, that the comparative information we lack is precisely what we would want to know in order to evaluate the practice.

9   MacDonald, Fagan, and Geller (2016) claim that the above-cited Weisburd study does not make this separation, undermining the conclusion Weisburd et al. (2016) draw.

10 Of course, it is possible that the NYPD's strategy for *documenting* Terry stops changed, while its Terry stop strategy did not.

11 See again Fagan et al. (2010, 311) and recall from Geller et al. (2014) that there are real costs associated with Terry stops.

12 In the medical profession, for example, the AMA's principles of medical ethics explicitly recognize this duty: "A physician shall continue to study, apply, and advance scientific knowledge, maintain a commitment to medical education, make relevant information available to patients, colleagues, and the public, obtain consultation, and use the talents of other health professionals when indicated." Further, it even recognizes a political manifestation of this duty: "A physician shall respect the law and also recognize a responsibility to seek changes in those requirements which are contrary to the best interests of the patient" (AMA n.d., Principles III, V).

13 The United States Supreme Court has ruled that police are not obligated to provide services to particular citizens (*United States v. Armstrong* 1996; *Town of Castle Rock v. Gonzales* 2005).

14 An accountability norm also follows from a weaker "competence" norm. Here, too, the AMA recognizes a relevantly similar professional obligation: "A physician shall uphold the standards of professionalism, be honest in all professional interactions, and strive to report physicians deficient in character or competence, or engaging in fraud or deception, to appropriate entities" (AMA 2016, Principle II).

15 This sort of concern underlies the attempt to restrict the sphere of permissible medical action to exclude things like cosmetic enhancement surgeries. See, for one example, Miller, Brody, and Chung (2000). For a more general discussion of trust in medicine, see Clark (2002). These are but two of many possible examples.

16 The Nashville Fraternal Order of Police opposed the measure to establish a citizen review board and funded an ad campaign against it (Gonzalez 2018).

17 See, for example, the case of Michael Rosefield, who left a number of police departments before shooting a fleeing suspect two hours into his new job with the East Pittsburgh police department (Mock 2018).

18 Sonitrol, a private security firm, paid for the dog and purchased naming rights for the German Shepherd, which it named Sonitrol (Young 2015).

19 Thanks to David Klinger for bringing this objection to my attention.

BIBLIOGRAPHY

Agerholm, Harriet. 2018. "Mexican Military Disarm Entire Police Force in Resort City of Acapulco 'Corrupted by Drug Gangs.'" *Independent*, September 26, 2018. www.independent.co.uk.

AMA (American Medical Association). n.d. "Code of Medical Ethics Overview." www.ama-assn.org.

Apel, Robert. 2016. "On the Deterrent Effect of Stop, Question, and Frisk." *Criminology and Public Policy* 15 (1): 57–66.

Blackstone, William. 1765. *Commentaries on the Laws of England in Four Books*. Philadelphia: J. B. Lippincott Company.

Bloomberg, Michael. 2013. "Michael Bloomberg: 'Stop and Frisk' Keeps New York Safe." *Washington Post*, August 18, 2013. www.washingtonpost.com.

Boniello, Kathianne. 2016. "Ray Kelly Says City 'Doesn't Feel Safer' without Stop-and-Frisk." *New York Post*, January 3, 2016. https://nypost.com.

Buchanan, Allen. 2002. "Political Legitimacy and Democracy." *Ethics* 112 (4): 689–719.

Clark, Chalmers C. 2002. "Trust in Medicine." *Journal of Medicine and Philosophy* 27 (1): 11–29.

Criss, Doug. 2016. "Traffic Stop Yields Sweet Surprise for Unsuspecting Drivers." *CNN*, August 1, 2016. www.cnn.com.

Cushing, Tim. 2013. "NYPD Chief Says Ending Stop and Frisk Will 'Hurt Minorities,' Result in A Surge of Criminal Activity." Techdirt, August 20, 2013. www.techdirt.com.

Davis, Daniel F., and Samuel J. Crowe. 2009. "Organ Markets and the Ends of Medicine." *Journal of Medicine and Philosophy* 34 (6): 586–605.

Desmond, Matthew, Andrew V. Papachristos, and David S. Kirk. 2016. "Police Violence and Citizen Crime Reporting in the Black Community." *American Sociological Review* 81 (5): 857–76.

Fagan, Jeffery A., Amanda Geller, Garth Davies, and Valerie West. 2010. "Street Stops and Broken Windows Revisited: The Demography and Logic of Proactive Policing in a Safe and Changing City." In *Race, Ethnicity, and Policing: New and Essential Readings*, edited by Stephen K. Rice and Michael D. White, 309–48. New York: New York University Press.

Geller, Amanda, Jeffery Fagan, Tom Tyler, and Bruce G. Link. 2014. "Aggressive Policing and the Mental Health of Young Urban Men." *American Journal of Public Health* 104 (12): 2321–27.

Gelman, Andrew, Jeffrey Fagan, and Alex Kiss. 2007. "An Analysis of the New York City Police Department's 'Stop-and-Frisk' Policy in the Context of Claims of Racial Bias." *Journal of the American Statistical Association* 102 (479): 813–23.

Goldman, Roger. 2016. "Importance of State Law in Police Reform." *Saint Louis University Law Journal* 60 (3): 363–90.

Goldstein, Joseph. 2018. "Promotions, Not Punishments, for Officers Accused of Lying." *New York Times*, March 19, 2018. www.nytimes.com.

Goldstein, Rebecca, Michael W. Sances, and Hye Young You. 2020. "Exploitative Revenues, Law Enforcement, and the Quality of Government Service." *Urban Affairs Review* 56 (1): 5–31.

Gonzalez, Tony. 2018. "Nashville Votes to Create Citizen Board to Oversee Police Misconduct." *Nashville Public Radio*, November 7, 2018. www.nashvillepublicradio.org.

Goodman, David J. 2015. "Officer Who Disclosed Police Misconduct Settles Suit." *New York Times*. September 29, 2015. www.nytimes.com.

Goodnough, Abby. 2018. "This City's Overdose Deaths Have Plunged. Can Others Learn from It?" *New York Times*, November 25, 2018. www.nytimes.com.

Haag, Matthew. 2018. "Cleveland Officer who Killed Tamir Rice Is Hired by an Ohio Police Department." *New York Times*, October 8, 2018. www.nytimes.com.

Hawkins, Derek. 2017. "'This is Crazy,' Sobs Utah Hospital Nurse as Cop Roughs Her Up, Arrests Her for Doing Her Job." *Washington Post*, September 1, 2017. www.washingtonpost.com.

Hunt, Stephen, and Luke Ramseth. 2017. "Accident Victim at Center of University Hospital Blood-Draw Controversy Dies." *Salt Lake Tribune*, September 26, 2017. www.sltrib.com.

International Association of Chiefs of Police. 1989. "Law Enforcement Code of Ethics." http://ethicscodescollection.org.

Kirk, David S., Andrew V. Papachristos, Jeffrey Fagan, and Tom R. Tyler. 2012. "The Paradox of Law Enforcement in Immigrant Communities: Does Tough Immigration Enforcement Undermine Public Safety?" *Annals of the American Academy of Political and Social Science* 641 (1): 79–98.

Koepke, Jennifer. 2010. "The Failure to Breach the Blue Wall of Silence: The Circling of the Wagons to Protect Police Perjury." *Washburn Law Review* 39 (2): 211–42.

Lake, Thomas. 2017. "The Trigger and the Choice: Part 3." *CNN*, August 2017. www.cnn.com.

Lartey, Jamiles. 2017. "Police Officers in St. Louis Chant after Breaking Up Protests." *Guardian*, September 18, 2017. www.theguardian.com.

Locke, John. (1689) 1963. *Two Treatises of Government*. Edited by P. Laslett. Cambridge: Cambridge University Press.

Mac Donald, Heather. 2010. "Distorting the Truth about Crime and Race." *City Journal*, May 14, 2010. www.city-journal.org.

MacDonald, John, Jeffrey Fagan, and Amanda Geller. 2016. "The Effects of Local Police Surges on Crime and Arrests in New York City." *PLOS One* 11(6): e0157223.

Miller, Franklin G., Howard Brody, and Kevin C. Chung. 2000. "Cosmetic Surgery and the Internal Morality of Medicine." *Cambridge Quarterly of Healthcare Ethics* 9 (3): 353–64.

Mock, Brentin. 2018. "The Problem with Suburban Police." *City Lab*, June 22, 2018. www.citylab.com.

Monaghan, Jake. 2017. "The Special Moral Obligations of Law Enforcement." *Journal of Political Philosophy* 25 (2): 218–37.

Monaghan, Jake. 2018. "On Enforcing Unjust Laws in Just Societies." *Philosophical Quarterly* 68 (273): 758–78.

North, Douglass C. 1991. "Institutions." *Journal of Economic Perspectives* 5 (1): 97–112.

Police Executive Research Forum. 2017. "The Unprecedented Opioid Epidemic: As Overdoses Become a Leading Cause of Death, Police, Sheriffs, and Health Agencies Must Step Up Their Response." September 2017. Washington, DC. www.policeforum.org.

Police Foundation. 2017. "5 Things You Need to Know About Stop, Question, and Frisk." March 2017. www.policefoundation.org.

Puro, Steven, Roger Goldman, and William C. Smith. 1997. "Police Decertification: Changing Patterns Among the States, 1985–1995." *Policing: An International Journal of Police Strategies & Management* 20 (3): 481–96.

Ramirez, Deborah, Marcus Write, Lauren Kilmister, and Carly Perkins. 2018. "Policing the Police: Could Mandatory Professional Liability Insurance for Officers Provide a New Accountability Model?" *American Journal of Criminal Law* 45 (2): 407–59.

Rector, Kevin, and Justin Fenton. 2018. "Baltimore Police Recruits Set to Hit the Streets with Poor Understanding of Law, Academy's Legal Instructor Says." *Baltimore Sun*, February 2, 2018. www.baltimoresun.com.

Rosenfeld, Richard, and Robert Fornango. 2014. "The Impact of Police Stops on Precinct Robbery and Burglary Rates in New York City, 2003–2010." *Justice Quarterly* 31 (1): 96–122.

Seo, Sarah A. 2019. *Policing the Open Road*. Cambridge, MA: Harvard University Press.

Siemaszko, Corky. 2017. "Ohio Sheriff Says His Officers Won't Carry Narcan." *NBC News*, July 7, 2017. www.nbcnews.com.

Taylor, Kate. 2011. "Borough President Seeks Limits on Stop-and-Frisk." *New York Times*, September 23, 2011. www.nytimes.com.

Terry v. Ohio. 1968. 392 US 1.

Town of Castle Rock v. Gonzales. 2005. 545 US 748.

Tyler, Tom R. 2004. "Enhancing Police Legitimacy." *Annals of the American Academy of Political and Social Science* 593 (1): 84–99.

United States v. Armstrong. 1996. 517 US 456.

Wamsley, Laurel. 2017. "Utah Nurse Arrested for Doing Her Job Reaches $500,000 Settlement." *NPR*, November 1, 2017. www.npr.org.

Weaver, Vesla M., and Amy E. Lerman. 2010. "Political Consequences of the Carceral State." *American Political Science Review* 104 (4): 817–33.

Weisburd, David, Alese Wooditch, Sarit Weisburd, and Sue-Ming Yang. 2016. "Do Stop, Question, and Frisk Practices Deter Crime? Evidence at Microunits of Space and Time." *Criminology & Public Policy* 15 (1): 31–56.

Young, Molly. 2015. "Sonitrol the Drug Dog Joins Flint Police Department." *MLive*, December 4, 2015. www.mlive.com.

3

Reward and "Real" Police Work

MICHAEL SIERRA-ARÉVALO

Contemporary attention to the behavior of police officers in the United States has revitalized longstanding debates around the ethos—the style of action (Swidler 1986, 276)—that characterizes the culture and street-level practice of police. Of particular note are the criticisms of aggressive, enforcement-centric policing stemming from the so-called "warrior" mentality of present-day policing that harms the well-being of communities and damages the legitimacy of the police (Stoughton 2014a). Existing research looking to explain adherence to such enforcement-centric policing points to organizational pressures that mandate enforcement activity (Eterno and Silverman 2006; Jermier and Berkes 1979; Wilson 1968), perverse monetary incentives for making frequent arrests (Moskos 2009), formal and informal training (Sierra-Arévalo 2021; Stoughton 2014a; Van Maanen 1978), and an occupational culture that valorizes heroic crime fighting over "guardian" policing often perceived as soft or feminine (Bittner 1974; Rabe-Hemp 2008; Stoughton 2016).

Unfortunately, existing research on how the police organization rewards or incentivizes particular kinds of police work is limited by its focus on *informal* rewards and a reliance on measures of officers' *perceptions* or *expectations* of what is likely to be recognized and rewarded within the police department (Johnson 2010; Mastrofski, Ritti, and Snipes 1994; Van Maanen 1974). Though perception of what is likely to be rewarded by superiors is undoubtedly an important consideration in research on officer behavior, reliance on perceptual measures to the exclusion of empirical indicators of formal organizational reward prevents firm conclusions about what kind of police activity is rewarded in practice. Further, existing research on the organizational determinants of officer behavior does little to consider how organizational rewards perpetuate longstanding conceptions of "real" police work as the dangerous and masculine activity of crime fighting. This oversight ultimately limits understanding of the active role that the police organization plays in construction of "real" police work and the police culture that valorizes this particular policing ethos.

To address this gap in existing literature, I analyze a novel dataset composed of five years of award data from the Elmont Police Department.[1] This content analysis of award narratives provides a descriptive view of what officer activities receive formal recognition from the police department, how different types of awarded police activity are framed by the police organization, and if the proportion of awards framed in different ways differs according to the gender of recipient officers. First, I describe the frequency of various empirical police activities being mentioned in award narratives, such as arrests, proactive activity, gun recovery, and drug recovery. I then analyze subjective features of the same award narratives, coding for descriptions of officers' activity as showing courage, heroism, respect, compassion, etc., and then combine codes to create measures of "real/warrior" and "soft/guardian" policing. Overall, more than 60 percent of awards mention real/warrior policing as compared to just over 28 percent that mention soft/guardian policing. Analysis of the male-versus-female individual-award pairings—for which I use the term *individual-awards*—shows no statistical difference in the proportion of individual-awards mentioning real/warrior policing. In comparison, 45.14 percent of male individual-awards describe soft/guardian policing versus 64.71 percent of female individual-awards. Following presentation of the full analysis of award data from the Elmont Police Department, I consider future directions for research on police awards, implications of current approaches to recording and rewarding police behaviors, and potential avenues for fostering conceptions of police work that can aid in enhancing the well-being of the public and the legitimacy of the police.

"Real" Police Work

Though police officers are the most encountered and visible agents of the criminal legal system, their work is often hidden from those whose communities are not the site of frequent police-public contact.

For these individuals, evaluations of police officers and police work are often forged through consumption of mass media, including primetime TV and popular films such as *Training Day* or *End of Watch*, which portray police work as a whirlwind of car chases, gun fights, violence, and triumphs of the police over dangerous criminals (Christensen, Schmidt, and Henderson 1982; Pautz 2016; Scharrer 2001). Such dramatic accounts of police work are embraced and echoed by police, who are encouraged by the public's expectations (i.e., demands) to perform policing in "idealized terms . . . which grossly exaggerate the actual work done by police" (Manning 1978, 13).

These idealized depictions of police work, even if out of step with decades of research showing the rarity of crime fighting in day-to-day police activity (Cordner 1979; Cumming, Cumming, and Edell 1965; Famega, Frank, and Mazerolle 2005), continue to serve as both reflections of and contributions to "real" police work—the street-level activities that are the purview of officers with "skills and special abilities" acquired "by virtue of [their] unique experience and training" (Van Maanen 1978, 226). In particular, both public and police conceptions of the "real" or ideal nature of the police role emphasize three overlapping definitions of police work: (1) police work as crime fighting, (2) police work as dangerous, and (3) police work as masculine. Together, these intersecting assumptions of what constitutes "real" police work continue to shape the structure, operation, and culture of US police departments.

"Real" Police Work as Crime Fighting

As already alluded to, "real" police work is frequently—if not predominantly—equated with crime fighting: the detection, pursuit, and apprehension of lawbreakers who represent an existential threat to public safety and the moral order. In some of the earliest ethnographic work on police, Westley (1953, 35) notes, "The apprehension and conviction of the felons is, for the policeman, the essence of police work. It is the source of prestige within and outside police circles, it has career implications, and it is a major source of justification for the existence of the police before a critical and often hostile public." The emphasis on crook-catching arose over time from within and outside the police occupation. From within, policing-as-crime-fighting became more engrained as the police occupation grew increasingly professionalized between the 1930s and 1960s. This shift began, in part, as a response to widespread corruption, inefficiency, and a lack of consistency in police training and operations (Fogelson 1977). Spearheaded by reform-minded chiefs like O. W. Wilson, police administrators began to incorporate new technology, enhanced educational requirements, and better supervision of patrol officers to address disorganized and ineffectual police (Kelling and Moore 1988).

Alongside these welcome changes, prevailing political winds from outside the policing occupation also contributed to a deepening entanglement of the police role with the mission of crime control. Namely, public fear of crime and urban disorder escalated in the mid-twentieth century and throughout the Civil Rights Era, providing a powerful bedrock of moral panic on which to create policy infrastructure aligned with a vision of police as crime fighters. Financially, the Johnson-era Law Enforcement Assistance Act of 1965 supported and legitimated the crime control role of police and, for the first time, established federal influence on local-level police operation. The pressing need for a class of professional crime fighters was further affirmed and supported in 1967 by the President's Commission on Law Enforcement and Administration of Justice and the National Advisory Commission of Civil Disorders, both of which pointed to local police as a necessary bulwark against disorder and lawlessness (Hinton 2016).

This notion of police-as-crime-fighters continued throughout the twentieth century and is a common thread that links the war on crime, the war on drugs, and the subsequent rise of the era of mass incarceration (Forman 2017; Hinton 2016; Western 2006). As a part of this historical shift in law and criminal justice policy, new police management paradigms emerged within the police milieu. Chief among these was CompStat, popularized by the New York City Police Department and now used by departments around the world (Police Executive Research Forum 2013). As a part of this model, data on criminal incidents and calls for service are combined with data on police citations, stops, and arrests to measure police effectiveness and guide police operations (Moore and Braga 2003). By relying on these particular data, police performance became empirically indistinguishable from enforcement activity, further contributing to a police profession whose mission, structure, and management became increasingly aligned with a definition of police as professional crime fighters. This equivalence between "real" police work and crime fighting continued through a period marked by historically low levels of US crime (Zimring 2006), and it continues to be a prominent feature of police training, culture, and street-level practice (Sierra-Arévalo 2021).

"Real" Police Work as Dangerous

Given the centrality of crime fighting to the police role, it is unsurprising that danger is a sine qua non of "real" police work. Scholars have long noted the role of danger in structuring the daily activities and culture of police (Skolnick 1966); in the US context, in particular, the threat posed by the ubiquity of easily accessible firearms poignantly underscores the reality of this danger (Banton 1964). The centrality of danger to police training, operations, and culture remains a consistent feature of policing in the twentieth-first century (Loftus 2010; Sierra-Arévalo 2019, 2021), with the potential for violence and death in police work reflected in judicial rulings that center the danger of patrol to justify continued expansion of police powers (Stoughton 2014b).

Much like the historical robustness of the crime-fighter orientation of "real" police work, the emphasis on danger is out of step with the mundanity of life on patrol. As Manning writes (1978, 13): "Most police work resembles any other kind of work: it is boring, tiresome, sometimes dirty, sometimes technically demanding, but it is rarely dangerous. Yet the occasional chase, the occasional shoot-out, the occasional triumph of some extraordinary detective work have been seized upon by the police and played up to the public." The emphasis on danger vis-à-vis the heroic crime fighting of "real" police work persists despite long-term decreases in crime and in line-of-duty officer deaths. Indeed, though post-Ferguson rhetoric spurred by the rise of the Black Lives Matter movement claims the existence of a "war on cops" (Mac Donald 2016), empirical assessment of the danger facing police officers does not support the contention that policing is now more dangerous than ever

(Maguire, Nix, and Campbell 2017; White, Dario, and Shjarback 2019; Sierra-Arévalo and Nix 2020). Nonetheless, belief in existence of this so-called "war on cops" persists among police administrators at the top of departmental hierarchies (Nix, Wolfe, and Campbell 2018), suggesting the paradoxical but no less consequential continuation of danger as a "ubiquitous cultural theme" in policing (Crank 2004, 160; Cullen et al. 1983).

More than simple rhetoric or a mundane feature of an ill-defined "culture," the emphasis on danger in policing and "real" police work is linked to a host of tangible and decidedly negative consequences. Most fundamentally, the danger of patrol work contributes to strong in-group cohesion among police (Skolnick 1966, 2002). Though beneficial insofar as it can create strong interpersonal bonds between officers who depend on one another while on patrol, the "us versus them" mentality engendered by this insular cohesion is associated with persistent and dire issues like police corruption and brutality (Kappeler, Sluder, and Alpert 1998; Niederhoffer 1967; Paoline, Myers, and Worden 2000; Punch 2009). The distrustful and oftentimes antagonistic footing of police who view the public as inherently dangerous encourages aggressive, "warrior" policing (Stoughton 2014a), as well as the increased use of paramilitary police units (i.e., SWAT teams) to execute low-level search warrants in the name of order and officer safety (Balko 2013; Kraska 2007).

"Real" Police Work as Masculine

"Real" police work is also linked to the perception and reality of a policing occupation that has long "been male in spirit and gender" (Crank 2004, 229). Though female representation among sworn police officers increased from 6 percent in 1983 to just over 12 percent in 2013 (Reaves 2015), the occupational environment of the policing profession continues to be one that, as a result of structural and cultural factors, maintains a "cult of masculinity" that can lead to the ostracization and abuse of women in policing (Loftus 2008; Silvestri 2017). In her study of gender and policing, Martin (1980) describes how masculine policing is tied to broader understandings of what it means to be a man, including the valorization of aggression, status attainment, self-reliance, and the avoidance of anything that might be perceived as feminine. Thus, traditional masculinity shapes understanding of what kind of work police should do, how this work should be done, and who is considered an ideal officer (Heidensohn 1992).

The masculine framing of policing is intimately tied to the dangerous crime fighting that, as already described, is central to dominant conceptions of "real" police work. Writing nearly twenty years after the initial entry of women into policing in any significant numbers, Martin (1999, 115) explains the equivalence between "real" police work and "men's" work: "Aggressive crime fighting is viewed by both police and the public as real police work and is visible, valued, and rewarded. The association of catching criminals with danger and bravery is what marks police work as 'men's work.'" The flipside to the valorization of dangerous, masculine crime fighting is the avoidance and denigration of behaviors considered soft or feminine, such as showing compassion, caring for victims, or dealing with children (Bittner 1974; Martin 1999). Though some female officers resist occupational pressures to avoid empathy or softness associated with feminine gender roles, others double down on the aggression and physical force equated with "real," masculine policing (Herbert 2001; Rabe-Hemp 2009). This gendered dichotomy underlies the assumption of female officers' unsuitability to police work in ways that continue to perpetuate negative experiences among female officers and structural inequalities in the hiring, retention, and promotion of women in policing (Archbold and Schulz 2008; Cordner and Cordner 2011; Dowler 2005). More broadly, the gendered construction of policing partitions police work into high-status, masculine crime fighting and low status, feminine work in ways that support longstanding resistance against the "feminization" of policing represented by less enforcement-centric activities like community policing (Martin 1999; Skogan 2008).

Incentivizing "Real" Police Work

Constructions of "real" police work as dangerous, masculine crime fighting contribute to an occupational environment resistant to the tenets of what today is conceptualized as "guardian" policing. In the tradition of community-oriented policing and more recent moves toward procedural justice, this approach emphasizes cooperation and fair, respectful interactions with the public to simultaneously enhance public safety and the legitimacy of the police (Meares 2016; Tyler 2004). Unfortunately, such approaches are often criticized within policing as "coddling recruits . . . and diminishing officer safety" (Rahr and Rice 2015, 6). As a result, "soft" approaches that are out of step with the crime-fighting ethos of "real" police work are disparaged and avoided by officers (Innes 2005).

In contrast, this occupational environment is fertile ground for the proliferation of what is today conceptualized as a "warrior" approach or mentality. This policing ethos rests on the uncontroversial position that police work can place officers in harm's way and, when that happens, officers should be prepared to take the steps necessary to survive and to protect other officers and the public. However, this simple, foundational belief has metastasized into a hegemonic worldview that frames the public as potential assailants instead of citizens in need of protection or potential allies in the co-production of public safety (Stoughton 2014a). Combined with the longstanding emphasis on the pursuit and capture of criminals as the defining mandate of the police occupation, the adversarial, enforcement-centered focus of warrior policing aligns well with the "real" policing paradigm and is encouraged within the police department in several ways.

First, the shift toward data-driven policing over the past thirty years has created an infrastructure that demands the recording of specific officer behaviors—namely stops, citations, and arrests that operationalize police activity (Dabney 2010). These indicators of "productivity" become proxies for skill and work ethic that are then taken into account when promoting officers to desirable positions like specialized gang, narcotics, and investigatory units outside patrol (Chambliss 1994; Moskos 2009; Walsh 1986).[2] Second, triumph over dangerous suspects is informally rewarded among officers trading "war stories" (Van Maanen 1978; Waddington 1999), as well as by line-level administrators whose "style" and use of informal rewards like vacation days or more desirable assignments encourage particular officer behaviors, such as arrests and uses of force (Engel 2000; Van Maanen 1983). Finally, research on officers' perceptions of departmental support and rewards show that arrest activity is more likely if officers believe such activity is likely to be recognized and rewarded by peers, superiors, and the police organization (Johnson 2009, 2010; Mastrofski, Ritti, and Snipes 1994).

This valuable body of research on the incentives that structure police behavior is, of course, not without its limitations. First, past research attuned to informal rewards such as status, prestige, and officers' individual-level alignment with notions of "real" police work are unable to speak to organizational-level rewards that encourage or discourage particular kinds of officer activity. Second, work that attends to supervisory recognition, promotion, and recognition by the police department is limited by its reliance on officers' perceptions of these organizational rewards. That is, while this existing research confirms that street-level behavior is influenced by officers' perceptions of whether a given behavior is likely to be valued and rewarded, how such rewards manifest in practice remain unanswered questions.

Data and Method

In the hope of addressing these limitations of past research, this analysis draws on a novel dataset of departmental awards given within the Elmont Police Department (EPD), a large, urban police department operating in a city with a population of fewer than one hundred thirty-five thousand. Award records for the years 2011 to 2015 were compiled by an internal EPD workgroup of sworn officers, all of whom were ranked sergeant or above, in advance of a 2016 EPD award ceremony where officers were recognized in front of their peers, friends, and family. Award nominations were reviewed by this committee, which approves nominations that meet the criteria of the particular awards for which individuals were nominated. Any officer is eligible to nominate any other officer or non-sworn individual for an award, though EPD administrators familiar with the nomination process stipulated that nominations are overwhelmingly concentrated in the patrol division and originate from sergeants who directly supervise patrol officers. Importantly, a single award can be given to either an individual or a group such as the intelligence unit or firearms unit, a particular squad of officers, or partnered officers.

The original EPD award data came in plain text format and was provided for use in this analysis by a senior EPD administrator who was

Table 3.1. EPD Award Data

	Total	Analytic Sample
Unique Awards	70	60
Unique Individuals	92	75
Individual-Awards	167	144

Table 3.2. Sample Characteristics

	Department	Individual-Awards	Unique Individuals
% Male	85	88.19 (N=127)	84.00 (N=63)
% Female	15	11.81 (N=17)	16.00 (N=12)

part of the award committee. Each award record lists a unique award identification number, the names of each individual who is a recipient or co-recipient of the award, and an award narrative that corresponds to that unique award. The narrative is the original text submitted by an officer nominating one or more individuals for a particular award. This award narrative, produced by an officer and later reviewed by a committee of other sworn officers, is the raw material by which awards are approved and represents a portrayal of activities and circumstances *for* police *by* police. As such, the award narratives can provide useful insights into how officers frame police work of various kinds when looking to commend and recognize others.

Table 3.1 provides basic descriptive information about the EPD award dataset. The complete dataset contains seventy unique awards, ninety-two unique individuals, and 167 unique individual-award pairings.[3] From this master list of awards, individual-awards were excluded that did not list a sworn police officer or which did not list an award narrative. Following these exclusions, sixty unique awards, seventy-five unique officers, and 144 individual-awards comprise the analytic sample.

Though demographic information was not included in the original award data, officer gender was imputed based on officers' names and crosschecked with the gender pronouns used in award narratives and/or newspaper articles mentioning officers. Table 3.2 displays the gender breakdown of the EPD, as well as the proportion and frequency of

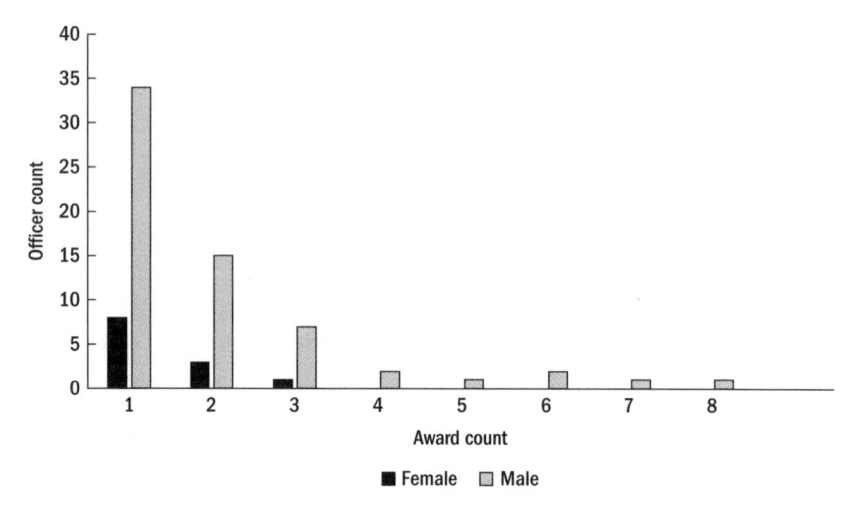

Figure 3.1. Awards per Officer by Gender.

individual-awards and unique individuals by gender. Compared to a department that is 85 percent male, 84 percent of the unique officers who received awards were male and nearly 89 percent of the individual-awards were given to male officers.

Figure 3.1, which displays the gender distribution of awards per officer, suggests that the elevated proportion of male individual-awards compared to the overall gender makeup of the EPD is driven by a greater number of male officers who received multiple awards. Overall, officers received an average of 1.95 awards per officer, male officers received an average of 2.02 awards per officer, and female officers received 1.33 awards per officer.

To investigate which police activities receive awards and how these activities are framed in police award narratives, each award narrative was coded in Microsoft Excel in two stages, the first stage focusing on objective content and the second on subjective content. Objective content included explicit mention of the following police activities: arrest, gun recovery, drug recovery, proactive or self-initiated activity (e.g., investigation, stops, searches), the arrest or pursuit of felons or those who committed felonies, foot chases, and vehicle pursuits. Awards were also coded for subjective content informed by mention of respect, compassion, restraint, professionalism, class, sensitivity, helping victims, humanistic or humanity, preventing crime, reducing crime, fighting crime, enhancing public safety, risking an officer's own safety, danger, high stress situations, bravery, courage, and heroism. After an initial round of coding, related concepts were combined into seven categories, which included: respect, compassion/care, restraint/de-escalation, professionalism/class, crime fighting, heroism/courage, and danger.

The first stage of analysis provides a descriptive overview of the frequency and percentage of unique awards that mention each objective and subjective characteristic. Additionally, this section of the analysis looks for differences in the proportion of awards that contain each objective and subjective characteristic across officer gender. In light of the small sample size, particularly when performing subgroup analysis by gender, Fisher's exact test is used to test for difference in the proportion of awards mentioning a particular characteristic by officer gender. The second stage of the analysis focuses in on the subjective characteristics in the award narratives and combines the seven categories into real/warrior policing—composed of crime fighting, heroism/courage, and danger categories—and soft/guardian policing—composed of respect, compassion/care, professionalism/class, and restraint/de-escalation. Using these new composite measures, I compare the proportion of unique awards and individual-awards that mention real/warrior and soft/guardian policing within each gender to see whether male and female individual-awards describe a particular type of policing more than the other.

Results

The first stage of this analysis begins with a descriptive overview of how often particular objective characteristics were mentioned in award narratives. As shown in Table 3.3, more than 86 percent of unique award narratives explicitly mention an arrest. Similarly, some 83.3 percent of award narratives mention contact with a felon or a felony arrest, specifically. This pattern is notable given that felony arrests are far less common than arrests for low-level offenses such as public intoxication, misdemeanor assault, or petty theft, and aligns well with prior research, which finds that felony arrests are prized among police officers and rewarded by police departments (Way and Patten 2013; Westley 1970). The next most common objective feature is the recovery of a firearm

TABLE 3.3. Objective Award-Level Descriptives

	Frequency	%
Arrest	52	86.67
Gun Recovered	39	65.00
Drugs Recovered	10	16.67
Proactive	28	46.67
Felon(ies)	50	83.33
Foot Chase	22	36.67
Car Chase	9	15.00

(65.00 percent), followed by proactive activity (46.67 percent), foot chases (36.67 percent), and drug recovery (16.67 percent). Table 3.4 displays the frequency and percentage of each subjective characteristic in the award narratives. The three most common subjective categories are danger (40.00 percent), heroism/courage (36.67 percent), and crime fighting (25.00 percent), with the least common being restraint/de-escalation (15.00 percent), compassion/care (11.67 percent), and respect (1.67 percent).

Because any award narrative can list more than one objective or subjective characteristic, it is not possible to statistically compare differences in the proportion of awards that mention a given characteristic. Still, that arrest, felon(ies), and gun recovery are mentioned in more than half of the unique award narratives suggests that these particular objective features are commonly focused on by officers who write the original award nominations and are common in awards given by the EPD. Similarly, descriptive results for subjective characteristics show that danger, heroism/courage, and crime fighting—concepts closely aligned with notions of dangerous, masculine crime fighting—are mentioned more often than respect, compassion/care, and restraint/de-escalation.

Table 3.5 compares the proportion of male and female individual-awards that mention each objective award characteristic. Proactive activity and gun recovery are mentioned in a significantly greater proportion of male individual-awards as compared to female: 43.75 percent versus 12.5 percent, and 59.39 percent versus 18.75 percent. The proportion of male individual-awards that include drug recovery or a

TABLE 3.4. Subjective Award-Level Descriptives

	Frequency	%
Respect	1	1.67
Compassion/Care	7	11.67
Restraint/De-escalation	9	15.00
Professionalism/Class	12	20.00
Crime Fighting	15	25.00
Heroism/Courage	22	36.67
Danger	24	40.00

TABLE 3.5. Objective Individual-Award Characteristics

	Total Sample		Male		Female		
	Frequency	%	Frequency	%	Frequency	%	Fisher Test
Arrest	113	78.47	102	79.69	11	68.75	0.338
Gun Recovered	79	54.86	76	59.38	3	18.75	0.003*
Drugs Recovered	25	17.36	25	19.53	0	0.00	0.075+
Proactive	58	40.28	56	43.75	2	12.50	0.016*
Felon(ies)	100	69.44	87	67.97	13	81.25	0.776
Foot Chase	48	33.33	46	35.94	2	12.50	0.09+
Car Chase	22	15.28	21	16.41	1	6.25	0.467

* $p < .05$
+ $p < .10$

foot chase does not differ significantly from the proportion of female individual-awards. More importantly, the small total sample size and even smaller subgroups makes a simple comparison of the difference between the proportions of male and female individual-awards on these objective characteristics useful; indeed, with 19.53 percent of male individual-awards mentioning proactive activity versus 0 percent of female individual-awards, and 35.94 percent of male individual-awards mentioning foot chases versus 12.50 percent of female individual-awards, there appear to be marked gender differences in individual-awards even if they are not statistically significant.

TABLE 3.6. Subjective Individual-Award Characteristics

	Total Sample		Male		Female		
	Frequency	%	Frequency	%	Frequency	%	Fisher Test
Respect	8	5.56	6	4.69	2	12.50	0.218
Compassion/Care	25	17.36	18	14.06	7	43.75	0.008*
Restraint/De-escalation	21	14.58	20	15.63	1	6.25	0.468
Professionalism/Class	29	20.14	23	17.97	6	37.50	0.094+
Crime Fighter	47	32.64	43	33.59	4	25.00	0.582
Heroism/Courage	55	38.19	50	39.06	5	31.25	0.598
Danger	48	33.33	47	36.72	1	6.25	0.021*

* $p < .05$
+ $p < .10$

Turning to subjective characteristics of individual-awards by gender (see Table 3.6), notable differences appear in the proportion of individual-awards that mention compassion/care and danger. A significantly greater proportion of female individual-awards (43.75 percent) mention compassion/care compared to male individual-awards (14.06 percent), while a greater proportion of male individual-awards (36.72 percent) mention danger compared to female individual-awards (6.25 percent). These results are in line with past research describing gendered definitions of police work that define compassion as a feminine quality and, conversely, the confrontation with danger as male work (Martin 1999). Finally, though the gender difference along the professionalism/class category is not significant at the 0.05 level, there is a sizeable difference between the proportion of female (37.50 percent) and male (17.97 percent) individual-awards that mention this subjective characteristic.

Finally, Table 3.7 shows the frequency of real/warrior and soft/guardian policing being mentioned in awards, while Table 3.8 compares the proportion of awards across genders falling into the real/warrior and soft/guardian composite categories formed from the subjective characteristics detailed in Table 3.4. Given that the real/warrior and soft/guardian policing are constructed from subjective characteristics that were differentially represented in award narratives, it is unsurprising

TABLE 3.7. Award-Level Real/Warrior versus Soft/Guardian Policing

	Frequency	%
Real/Warrior	37	61.67
Soft/Guardian	17	28.33

TABLE 3.8. Individual-Award Real/Warrior versus Soft/Guardian Policing

	Total Sample		Male		Female		Fisher Test
	Frequency	%	Frequency	%	Frequency	%	
Real/Warrior	80	55.56	73	57.48	7	41.18	0.425
Soft/Guardian	65	45.14	54	42.52	11	64.71	0.061+

+ p <.10

that disparities also appear across award narratives when comparing the composite real/warrior and soft/guardian categories: 61.67 percent of unique award narratives describe real/warrior policing, with only 28.33 percent describing soft/guardian policing.

Turning to Table 3.8, there is no statistically significant difference between the proportion of male and female individual-awards that describe real/warrior policing. In contrast, there is a marked difference in soft/guardian policing, with 45.14 percent of male individual-awards mentioning soft/guardian policing as compared to 64.71 percent of female individual-awards. Though this difference does not reach statistical significance at the 0.05 level, that it is statistically significant at the 0.1 level with such a small sample size is at the very least suggestive of a gender difference in the proportion of awards that mention soft/guardian policing.

Conclusion

Following a series of highly publicized police killings of unarmed, minority men, President Obama's Task Force on 21st Century Policing pointed to police culture as an important contributor to persistent inequalities in US policing. The Task Force suggested the need for cultural change among police as a necessary avenue for reform in the practice of police work, stating that, "Law enforcement culture should embrace a guardian—rather than a warrior—mindset" (President's Task Force on 21st Century Policing 2015, 1) to enhance public trust and police legitimacy. To aid in this cultural shift, they posited the need for new training, the cessation of for-profit enforcement policies, and the adoption of procedural justice principles that would move policing away from aggressive, often antagonistic enforcement toward an emphasis on compassion, cooperation, and respect (Rahr and Rice 2015; Stoughton 2016).

The analysis presented in this chapter suggests another mechanism for the (re)production and potential reform of police culture: departmental awards. Such awards are a formal mechanism for the recognition of particular types of police activity that reflect and reproduce longstanding understandings of what kind of work is valued within policing. Because the award narratives used in award nominations are produced by officers, analysis of these narratives provides a rich view into the kinds of work that police officers themselves see worthy of nominating and how such work is framed. Given the focus of award narratives on arrest, guns, heroism, and danger, it seems clear that police officers embedded in the occupational culture of policing continue to value work in step with stereotypical notions of "real" police work and the contemporary warrior mentality. When these nominations manifest in departmental awards, this particular ethic of policing is formally amplified by the police organization. Awards perpetuate the cultural significance of these comparatively rare activities while also obfuscating necessary and far more common non-enforcement tasks that comprise the bulk of police work.

Further, that the proportion of individual-awards that mention real/warrior policing does not differ between male and female officers but that there is some degree of disparity for soft/guardian awards points to the active construction of gendered police work and a broader, occupational-level policing culture. Though award data cannot definitively speak to whether or not female officers engage in soft/guardian work at higher rates than their male counterparts, that soft/guardian policing is mentioned more in female individual-awards indicates female officers are disproportionately recognized for such work relative to male officers. This provides evidence of a formal organizational mechanism that, as described in past research, constructs care, compassion, and emotional labor as the domain of female police officers (Garcia 2003; Martin 1999). By the same token, the lack of a gender disparity in award descriptions of real/warrior policing points to the co-construction of gender and "real" police work (Rabe-Hemp 2009). While female officers are rewarded for stereotypically feminine police work, their parity with male officers vis-à-vis real/warrior activities suggests that female officers perform and are rewarded for police work traditionally associated with the ethos of dangerous, masculine crime fighting.

Of course, caution is merited when interpreting and extrapolating from the results of this analysis given the limitations of the data employed. First, the award narratives that comprise the award dataset correspond to awards for which at least one officer was able to attend the award ceremony and only officers who attended the ceremony were named. Thus, this dataset is likely to underestimate the total number of awards and recipient officers and may be selecting on officers who were more likely—perhaps because of seniority, schedule, or other officer-level characteristics—to attend the award ceremony. Second, because these data are from a single department, it is impossible to say how pervasive the patterns observed in the EPD are within the police occupation writ large; whether such patterns hold in other departments that differ in terms of training, policies, state law, and myriad other structural characteristics remains unclear. Third, because the type of police work that is eligible to receive awards is constrained by what officers deem worthy of bringing to the attention of the police organization in the first place, it is also important to consider what work is *not* being nominated for awards and why. For example, though certain types of work are rewarded more often than others in the EPD, award data is unable to adjudicate whether male and female officers *engage* in some behavior more or are *recognized* for a given behavior at different rates. Similarly, it may be the case that certain officers or supervisors of different "styles" are more likely to nominate officers for awards, may focus on particular kinds of work to the exclusion of others, or are prone to recognize some officers but not others for the same kind of work (Van Maanen 1983).

Despite these limitations, there is ample room for future researchers to investigate police awards and the type of work they recognize in departments large and small, rural and suburban, and across regions of the US. Additionally, research on formal incentives within police departments should incorporate data on calls for service, detailed officer and supervisor characteristics (e.g., age, gender, race/ethnicity, years of service, specialized training, assignment), and incident-level records of stops, arrest, and uses of force. These data will help elucidate patterns in the type of work in which officers engage, which officers engage in that work, who is recognized for such work, and who recognizes (or ignores) particular work. This will ultimately provide a more complete delineation of how awards function as a mechanism for the perpetuation of occupational assumptions about what policing is and the police behaviors shaped by these assumptions.

It is also vital to recognize the practical implications of existing data within US police departments being heavily (if not exclusively) focused on enforcement-related activities. This is not to say that enforcement-related data should not be recorded; such data are necessary for increasing transparency, enhancing police accountability, and ensuring that the awesome powers with which police are entrusted are used legally and equitably. However, the emphasis on enforcement data is reflective of the fact that neither the EPD nor, to my knowledge, any other US police department systematically collects department-wide, officer-level data on positive, non-enforcement contact with citizens. This represents a clear structural shortfall that frustrates the incentivization of the respectful, compassionate, and cooperative behaviors of the guardian officer. Simply put, what a police department rewards is fundamentally constrained by what it records.

Of course, that departmental data does not focus on guardian behaviors does not doom departments to only reward warrior activities. Indeed, nearly 30 percent of Elmont Police Department awards between 2011 and 2015 mentioned guardian-style policing of some kind. Outside the EPD, the Philadelphia Police Department under the leadership of Commissioner Charles Ramsey instituted new awards for de-escalation, and the Los Angeles Police Department (LAPD) recently began to issue a Preservation of Life award. As encouraging as these developments are, they are also often met with resistance from within the police occupation. For example, the LAPD's new award was opposed by the union representing officers on the grounds that such an award increases the danger faced by officers on patrol (Gilbert 2017). This resistance to the expansion of what police work merits formal recognition is also a reflection of occupational understandings of policing as equivalent to dangerous, masculine crime fighting, and is part and parcel of broader resistance to change in policing (Cohen 2017; Stoughton 2016).

The challenges to realizing widespread change in policing notwithstanding, there are concrete steps that departments can take to build the infrastructure necessary to document and reward police behavior in line with a guardian mentality. In particular, departments must expand the range of documented officer behaviors beyond stops, searches, arrest, and uses of force. Though it might be viable to have officers self-report cooperative, non-enforcement activity, the onus of such street-level reporting need not necessarily fall exclusively on officers. Just as departments have incorporated procedures and technologies to track complaints against officers (Walker and Archbold 2013), departments should implement the means for citizens to report instances in which officers embody the fair and respectful actions of the guardian. Given the proliferation of body-worn cameras, supervisors could use random review of camera footage to, instead of only looking for violations, document positive, non-enforcement contact that has been causally linked to improved police legitimacy (Peyton, Sierra-Arévalo, and Rand 2019). Armed with records of these behaviors, police supervisors would be better able to concretely recognize and reward guardian policing. Beyond departmental rewards, officer- and citizen-generated reports of guardian activities should be incorporated into departmental promotions and other organizational processes that can incentivize respectful, cooperative policing and enhance police legitimacy.

NOTES
1 Per my IRB protocol, I use a pseudonym for the US police department that provided award data and anonymize officers mentioned in award narratives to ensure officers cannot be identified.
2 Further, Moskos (2009) notes that enforcement activity sometimes comes with direct monetary incentives: officers in places like Baltimore know that more arrests mean a higher likelihood of lucrative overtime hours to appear in court—a phenomenon referred to as "collars for dollars."

3 Note, the number of individual-awards is not the sum of unique awards and unique individuals because individuals can receive multiple awards. Individual-awards refer to each pairing of award and individual recipient, as opposed to unique awards which correspond to a particular award that can have one or more recipients.

BIBLIOGRAPHY

Archbold, Carol A., and Dorothy Moses Schulz. 2008. "Making Rank: The Lingering Effects of Tokenism on Female Police Officers' Promotion Aspirations." *Police Quarterly* 11 (1): 50–73.

Balko, Radley. 2013. *Rise of the Warrior Cop: The Militarization of America's Police Forces*. New York: PublicAffairs.

Banton, Michael. 1964. *The Policeman in the Community*. New York: Basic Books.

Bittner, Egon. 1974. "Florence Nightingale in Pursuit of Willie Sutton: A Theory of the Police." In *The Potential for Reform of Criminal Justice*, edited by Herbert Jacob, 11–44. Beverly Hills, CA: Sage Publications.

Chambliss, William J. 1994. "Policing the Ghetto Underclass: The Politics of Law and Law Enforcement." *Social Problems* 41 (2): 177–94.

Christensen, Jon, Janet Schmidt, and Joel Henderson. 1982. "The Selling of the Police: Media, Ideology, and Crime Control." *Contemporary Crises* 6 (3): 227–39.

Cohen, Ryan. 2017. "The Force and the Resistance: Why Changing the Police Force Is Neither Inevitable, Nor Impossible." *University of Pennsylvania Journal of Law and Social Change* 20 (2): 105–24.

Cordner, Gary. 1979. "Police Patrol Work Load Studies: A Review and Critique." *Police Studies: International Review of Police Development* 2 (2): 50–60.

Cordner, Gary, and AnnMarie Cordner. 2011. "Stuck on a Plateau?: Obstacles to Recruitment, Selection, and Retention of Women Police." *Police Quarterly* 14 (3): 207–26.

Crank, John P. 2004. *Understanding Police Culture*, 2nd ed. New York: Routledge.

Cullen, Francis T., Bruce G. Link, Lawrence F. Travis, and Terrence Lemming. 1983. "Paradox in Policing: A Note on Perceptions of Danger." *Journal of Police Science & Administration* 11 (4): 457–62.

Cumming, Elaine, Ian Cumming, and Laura Edell. 1965. "Policeman as Philosopher, Guide and Friend." *Social Problems* 12 (3): 276–86.

Dabney, Dean. 2010. "Observations Regarding Key Operational Realities in a Compstat Model of Policing." *Justice Quarterly* 27 (1): 28–51.

Dowler, Kenneth. 2005. "Job Satisfaction, Burnout, and Perception of Unfair Treatment: The Relationship Between Race and Police Work." *Police Quarterly* 8 (4): 476–89.

Engel, Robin Shepard. 2000. "The Effects of Supervisory Styles on Patrol Officer Behavior." *Police Quarterly* 3 (3): 262–93.

Eterno, John A., and Eli B. Silverman. 2006. "The New York City Police Department's Compstat: Dream or Nightmare?" *International Journal of Police Science & Management* 8 (3): 218–31.
Famega, Christine N., James Frank, and Lorraine Mazerolle. 2005. "Managing Police Patrol Time: The Role of Supervisor Directives." *Justice Quarterly* 22 (4): 540–59.
Fogelson, Robert M. 1977. *Big-City Police*. Cambridge, MA: Harvard University Press.
Forman, James, Jr. 2017. *Locking Up Our Own: Crime and Punishment in Black America*. New York: Farrar, Straus and Giroux.
Garcia, Venessa. 2003. "'Difference' in the Police Department: Women, Policing, and 'Doing Gender.'" *Journal of Contemporary Criminal Justice* 19 (3): 330–44.
Gilbert, Curtis. 2017. "Not Trained to Not Kill." *APM Reports*, May 5, 2017. www.apmreports.org.
Heidensohn, Frances. 1992. *Women in Control? The Role of Women in Law Enforcement*. New York: Oxford University Press.
Herbert, Steve. 2001. "'Hard Charger' or 'Station Queen'? Policing and the Masculinist State." *Gender, Place & Culture* 8 (1): 55–71.
Hinton, Elizabeth. 2016. *From the War on Poverty to the War on Crime: The Making of Mass Incarceration in America*. Cambridge, MA: Harvard University Press.
Innes, Martin. 2005. "Why 'Soft' Policing Is Hard: On the Curious Development of Reassurance Policing, How It Became Neighbourhood Policing and What This Signifies about the Politics of Police Reform." *Journal of Community & Applied Social Psychology* 15 (3): 156–69.
Jermier, John M., and Leslie J. Berkes. 1979. "Leader Behavior in a Police Command Bureaucracy: A Closer Look at the Quasi-Military Model." *Administrative Science Quarterly* 24 (1): 1–23.
Johnson, Richard R. 2009. "Explaining Patrol Officer Drug Arrest Activity through Expectancy Theory." *Policing: An International Journal of Police Strategies & Management* 32 (1): 6–20.
Johnson, Richard R. 2010. "Making Domestic Violence Arrests: A Test of Expectancy Theory." *Policing: An International Journal of Police Strategies & Management* 33 (3): 531–47.
Kappeler, Victor E., Richard D. Sluder, and Geoffrey P. Alpert. 1998. *Forces of Deviance: Understanding the Dark Side of Policing*, 2nd ed. Prospect Heights, IL: Waveland Press.
Kelling, George L., and Mark H. Moore. 1988. "The Evolving Strategy of Policing." *Perspectives on Policing* 4: 1–16.
Kraska, Peter B. 2007. "Militarization and Policing—Its Relevance to 21st Century Police." *Policing: A Journal of Policy and Practice* 1 (4): 501–13.
Loftus, B. 2008. "Dominant Culture Interrupted: Recognition, Resentment and the Politics of Change in an English Police Force." *British Journal of Criminology* 48 (6): 756–77.
Loftus, B. 2010. "Police Occupational Culture: Classic Themes, Altered Times." *Policing and Society* 20 (1): 1–20.

Mac Donald, Heather. 2016. *The War on Cops: How the New Attack on Law and Order Makes Everyone Less Safe*. New York: Encounter Books.

Maguire, Edward R., Justin Nix, and Bradley A. Campbell. 2017. "A War on Cops? The Effects of Ferguson on the Number of US Police Officers Murdered in the Line of Duty." *Justice Quarterly* 34 (5): 739–58.

Manning, Peter K. 1978. "The Police: Mandate, Strategies, and Appearances." In *Policing: A View from the Street*, edited by Peter K. Manning and John Van Maanen, 7–31. New York: Random House.

Martin, Susan Ehrlich. 1980. *Breaking and Entering: Policewomen on Patrol*. Berkeley, CA: University of California Press.

Martin, Susan Ehrlich. 1999. "Police Force or Police Service? Gender and Emotional Labor." *ANNALS of the American Academy of Political and Social Science* 561 (1): 111–26.

Mastrofski, Stephen D., R. Richard Ritti, and Jeffrey B. Snipes. 1994. "Expectancy Theory and Police Productivity in DUI Enforcement." *Law & Society Review* 28 (1): 113–48.

Meares, Tracey L. 2016. "Policing in the 21st Century: The Importance of Public Security." *University of Chicago Legal Forum* 2016: 1–12.

Moore, Mark H., and Anthony A. Braga. 2003. "Measuring and Improving Police Performance: The Lessons of Compstat and Its Progeny." *Policing: An International Journal of Police Strategies & Management* 26 (3): 439–53.

Moskos, Peter. 2009. *Cop in the Hood: My Year Policing Baltimore's Eastern District*. Princeton, NJ: Princeton University Press.

Niederhoffer, Arthur. 1967. *Behind the Shield: The Police in Urban Society*. Garden City, NY: Doubleday.

Nix, Justin, Scott E. Wolfe, and Bradley A. Campbell. 2018. "Command-Level Police Officers' Perceptions of the 'War on Cops' and De-Policing." *Justice Quarterly* 35 (1): 33–54.

Paoline, Eugene A., Stephanie M. Myers, and Robert E. Worden. 2000. "Police Culture, Individualism, and Community Policing: Evidence from Two Police Departments." *Justice Quarterly* 17 (3): 575–605.

Pautz, Michelle C. 2016. "Cops on Film: Hollywood's Depiction of Law Enforcement in Popular Films, 1984–2014." *PS: Political Science & Politics* 49 (2): 250–58.

Peyton, Kyle, Michael Sierra-Arévalo, and David G. Rand. 2019. "A Field Experiment on Community Policing and Police Legitimacy." *Proceedings of the National Academy of Sciences* 116 (40): 19894–98.

Police Executive Research Forum. 2013. *Compstat: Its Origins, Evolution, and Future in Law Enforcement Agencies*. Washington, DC: Police Executive Research Forum. www.bja.gov.

President's Task Force on 21st Century Policing. 2015. *Final Report*. Washington, DC: US Department of Justice.

Punch, Maurice. 2009. *Police Corruption: Deviance, Accountability and Reform in Policing*. New York: Routledge.

Rabe-Hemp, Cara E. 2008. "Female Officers and the Ethic of Care: Does Officer Gender Impact Police Behaviors?" *Journal of Criminal Justice* 36 (5): 426–34.

Rabe-Hemp, Cara E. 2009. "POLICEwomen or PoliceWOMEN?: Doing Gender and Police Work." *Feminist Criminology* 4 (2): 114–29.

Rahr, Sue, and Stephen K. Rice. 2015. "From Warriors to Guardians: Recommitting American Police Culture to Democratic Ideals." *New Perspectives in Policing* (April): 1–16.

Reaves, Brian A. 2015. "Local Police Departments, 2013: Personnel, Policies, and Practices." Washington, DC: Bureau of Justice Statistics. www.bjs.gov.

Scharrer, Erica. 2001. "Tough Guys: The Portrayal of Hypermasculinity and Aggression in Televised Police Dramas." *Journal of Broadcasting & Electronic Media* 45 (4): 615–34.

Sierra-Arévalo, Michael. 2019. "The Commemoration of Death, Organizational Memory, and Police Culture." *Criminology* 57 (4): 632–58.

Sierra-Arévalo, Michael. 2021. "American Policing and the Danger Imperative." *Law & Society Review* 55 (1): 70–103.

Sierra-Arévalo, Michael, and Justin Nix. 2020. "Gun Victimization in the Line of Duty: Fatal and Nonfatal Firearm Assaults on Police Officers in the United States, 2014–2019." *Criminology & Public Policy* 19 (3): 1041–66.

Silvestri, Marisa. 2017. "Police Culture and Gender: Revisiting the 'Cult of Masculinity.'" *Policing: A Journal of Policy and Practice* 11 (3): 289–300.

Skogan, Wesley G. 2008. "Why Reforms Fail." *Policing and Society* 18 (1): 23–34.

Skolnick, Jerome H. 1966. *Justice without Trial: Law Enforcement in Democratic Society.* New York, NY: John Wiley & Sons.

Skolnick, Jerome H. 2002. "Corruption and the Blue Code of Silence." *Police Practice and Research* 3 (1): 7–19.

Stoughton, Seth W. 2014a. "Law Enforcement's Warrior Problem." *Harvard Law Review* 128 (6): 225–34.

Stoughton, Seth W. 2014b. "Policing Facts." *Tulane Law Review* 88 (5): 847–98.

Stoughton, Seth W. 2016. "Principled Policing: Warrior Cops and Guardian Officers Implementing De-Incarceration Strategies." *Wake Forest Law Review* 51 (3): 611–76.

Swidler, Ann. 1986. "Culture in Action: Symbols and Strategies." *American Sociological Review* 51 (2): 273–86.

Tyler, Tom R. 2004. "Enhancing Police Legitimacy." *Annals of the American Academy of Political and Social Science* 593: 84–99.

Van Maanen, John. 1974. "Working the Street: A Developmental View of Police Behavior." In *The Potential for Reform of Criminal Justice*, edited by Herbert Jacob, 83–130. Beverly Hills, CA: Sage Publications.

Van Maanen, John. 1978. "Observations on the Making of a Policeman." In *Policing: A View from the Street*, edited by Peter K. Manning and John Van Maanen, 292–308. New York, NY: Random House.

Van Maanen, John. 1983. "The Boss: A Portrait of the America Police Sergeant." In *The Control of the Police*, edited by Maurice Punch, 275–317. Cambridge, MA: MIT Press.

Waddington, P. A. J. 1999. "Police (Canteen) Sub-Culture. An Appreciation." *British Journal of Criminology* 39 (2): 287–309.

Walker, Samuel E., and Carol A. Archbold. 2013. *The New World of Police Accountability*. Thousand Oaks, CA: SAGE Publications.

Walsh, William F. 1986. "Patrol Officer Arrest Rates: A Study of the Social Organization of Police Work." *Justice Quarterly* 3 (3): 271–90.

Way, Lori Beth, and Ryan Patten. 2013. *Hunting for "Dirtbags": Why Cops Over-Police the Poor and Racial Minorities*. Boston: Northeastern University Press.

Western, Bruce. 2006. *Punishment and Inequality in America*. New York: Russell Sage Foundation.

Westley, William A. 1953. "Violence and the Police." *American Journal of Sociology* 59 (1): 34–41.

Westley, William A. 1970. *Violence and the Police: A Sociological Study of Law, Custom, and Morality*. Cambridge, MA: MIT Press.

White, Michael D., Lisa M. Dario, and John A. Shjarback. 2019. "Assessing Dangerousness in Policing: An Analysis of Officer Deaths in the United States, 1970–2016." *Criminology & Public Policy* 18 (1): 11–35.

Wilson, James Q. 1968. *Varieties of Police Behavior: The Management of Law and Order in Eight Communities*. Cambridge, MA: Harvard University Press.

Zimring, Franklin E. 2006. *The Great American Crime Decline*. New York: Oxford University Press.

Zimring, Franklin E. 2017. *When Police Kill*. Cambridge, MA: Harvard University Press.

PART II

Use of Force

4

Soldiers and Police

MICHAEL WALZER

In the first eight months of 2018, 668 people were shot and killed by police officers in the United States. In the same period, the Norwegian police didn't shoot anyone. This is how arguments about police shootings often begin, but it isn't the right beginning. The comparison is meant to be critical (and the number 668 requires criticism), but the difference between the two countries doesn't make for an effective critique. Police in Norway don't carry guns on patrol and are therefore unlikely to shoot their fellow citizens; nor do many of those citizens carry guns. By contrast, the US is awash in guns—roughly 265 million firearms of all sorts are currently in circulation (Woods 2018, 26). This simple fact makes comparisons with countries like Norway, or even with countries like France, where police do carry guns, radically unhelpful. In the ordinary course of their work, American police are more likely to encounter armed men (and, though rarely, armed women) than are police almost anywhere else. So police work is different here; it is more dangerous. It may not be as dangerous as the police sometimes claim when justifying particular killings, but it really is dangerous. Anyone critical of police behavior, as I will be, has to acknowledge the truth of this statement.

Nor are the police responsible for the dangers they encounter. Any rational police officer would prefer to have a monopoly on the use of force, certainly on the legitimate use of force. The history of gun ownership and use in the US includes accounts of justified self-defense—on the frontier and in the "Wild West," where policing was largely absent and also in the American South, where African Americans needed guns to protect themselves and their families against vigilante mobs, which often included the local police (Cobb 2014). But most Americans live today in what I will call a "zone of peace," where the risk of violence is minimal.

The pervasiveness of guns in a society where they are rarely needed is due in large part to the gun industry and the gun lobby. These two have been amazingly successful in preventing the passage of laws, like those of most other countries, controlling the sale of guns and limiting the rights of people who aren't soldiers or police officers to carry them (Woods 2018, 16–27). That success is undoubtedly related to the history and ideology of the frontier and also to the revolutionary "right to bear arms," which has become a favorite theme of rightwing politics—so that the same people who loudly support the police are also responsible or, at least, partly responsible for the dangers of police work.

Those dangers, along with the high crime rate of the 1970s and '80s, are important reasons for what is probably the most significant change in law enforcement in the US in recent decades—the militarization of the police. But the more immediate cause of militarization is the political popularity of the "war on drugs," which led successive presidents, Democrats as well as Republicans, to spend billions of dollars arming the police with weapons designed for an army. The metaphorical character of the "war on drugs" is, in effect, denied; it's a real war, one retired officer told me; it's like Vietnam. No doubt, the drug war is more military-like than the "war on poverty," but in fact it isn't a war, and it doesn't require police forces equipped with tanks, helicopters, and machine guns. Strangely, the acquisition of weapons like these has proceeded apace despite the radical drop in criminal activity, including drug-related activity, over the last two decades (Balko 2014).

I don't mean to underestimate the violence that came with the crack epidemic of the 1980s and early '90s. In Washington, DC, in 1991 there were 485 homicides, considerably more than one a day, and murder rates were similar in cities around the country (Forman 2017, 218). Politicians everywhere, White and Black alike, were calling for more aggressive policing and for more arrests. Still, the doctrine of "broken windows," which served to justify the aggressiveness, was not a military doctrine. Rightly understood, it was a program both for intensified police work and for urban reform. Fix the broken windows, improve maintenance in the housing projects, clean and light the streets—and at the same time put more officers on the streets (Kelling and Wilson 1982). Tanks were hardly necessary for this kind of police work.

Militarization doesn't affect only the equipment of the police but also, and more importantly, the mentality of the police and then the everyday practice of policing. Along with the weapons comes a marked propensity to use them. New Haven Police Chief Nick Pastore, who opposed militarization in his city, told the *New York Times* in March 1999 that outfitting police in battle gear "feeds a mindset that you're not a police officer serving a community, you're a soldier at war" (Balko 2014, 191). Militarization blurs the line that has historically (in principle and in law) divided what police do from what soldiers do; it erases the boundary between the zone of peace and the zone of war.

The raids by SWAT teams on American homes—often with no-knock warrants, with police in full armor, guns drawn—are proof of the erasure. Radley Balko's *Rise of the Warrior Cop* explains how militarization was funded, describes its remarkable extent and, most important, provides a long list of misplaced raids, battered homes, and unnecessary killings (including of police officers shot by armed homeowners defending themselves). Balko, whose politics is libertarian, argues persuasively for alternative tactics that would be less dangerous and more effective. A similar argument is made by James Forman Jr. from a liberal/left perspective in his account of "crime and punishment in Black America" (Balko 2014, chap. 9; Forman 2017, epilogue).

Long before the militarization of the last decades, the police often conducted themselves like soldiers—in the ghetto neighborhoods of Northern cities, for example, or in Black communities in the South—acting like an occupying army, treating their fellow citizens as if they were enemies. In the labor wars of the late nineteenth century and well into the 1930s, the police were something like the army of corporate America. But they were never armed as they are today, never so openly encouraged to imagine themselves as "warriors," and these facts require us to think again about the difference between soldiers and police. Hence my purpose in this chapter: to draw a line between the two as clearly as I can.

Soldiers and Police

Any argument against militarization has to be focused on the rules of engagement for soldiers and police officers. I emphasize the rules of *engagement*; I am not concerned here with anything like the Code of Ethics adopted half a century ago by the International Association of Chiefs of Police (IACP). This is an admirable document. It commits law enforcement officers "to serve the community, to safeguard lives and property, to protect the innocent against deception, the weak against oppression" and so on (IACP 1957). There are many codes of this kind, generalized accounts of virtue adopted or endorsed by local police departments. But all of them lack the specificity required to make clear to officers on the street what they can and cannot do.

I am also not concerned with the rules that guide police conduct when they are engaged in community service. During Hurricane Sandy the basement of my home in Princeton, New Jersey, was flooded, and the house smelled strongly of gas. We called 911, and the police came very quickly. They politely told us to get out of the house because of the danger of an explosion, and then they went into the house to turn off the gas. I am sure there are rules that require both courtesy and courage, and I am grateful to the police who routinely follow the rules. But my subject here are the harder rules that govern, or fail to govern, the use of force, particularly lethal force.

Both law enforcement and war require the use of force; these are, however, very different activities, and the necessary rules have to be shaped to match the circumstances and purposes of each. Soldiering takes place in the zone of war, whose paradigmatic form is the battlefield, but which extends to all those places that are subject to attack—a munitions factory, for example, or an encampment of soldiers. The purpose of fighting in the zone of war is to win, to defeat the enemy, and the means of defeat are death and destruction. Soldiers are organized and disciplined to achieve this purpose—but also to set limits to the death and destruction they inflict. The rules of engagement require them to aim only at enemy combatants and to do their best to shield noncombatants, including the civilian population of the country with which they are at war. I will come back to the question of what "doing their best" means in the zone of war.

When soldiers act as "peacekeepers" they are by definition not acting in a war zone. They can't keep the peace unless there is peace, and if there is peace, they are, whatever their uniform says, engaged in police work. Often, however, peacekeepers are rushed into a country where the war is not quite finished and the peace is unstable. Then they are in a kind of halfway house, where all of the rules are unclear, and they must decide, minute by minute, how they ought to behave. Soldiers often don't behave well in these "in-between" conditions, but it's not clear that police would do better. Men and women need to be specially trained for engagements in places where there is neither war nor peace. This need is especially visible in conditions of colonial rule and military occupation, where we would probably prefer that the use of force be abandoned altogether. These kinds of cases lie beyond my compass here. For the purposes of this chapter, I will keep the zones of war and peace neatly separated.

Police officers operate in the zone of peace, in a country or a city where there are no battlefields. "Shootouts" between officers and, say, the members of a criminal gang may occur, but these are exceptional events; they involve few people, and they have no extensions. Police officers responding to a shooter in a school or church must act with courage, but this is more like the courage of firemen rushing into a burning building than it is like the courage of a soldier in battle; the first purpose of firemen and police is to save lives.

The police are not a force for destruction; instead, they are in every sense of the word a conservative force. They keep the peace. They act, as the IACP Code says, "to safeguard lives and property"—in principle, all lives and the property of those who have property. "The basic nature of the law and the police, from its earliest origins," writes Alex Vitale, as if he is outraged by the discovery, "is to be a tool for managing inequality and maintaining the status quo" (Vitale 2017, 15). Yes, that's what the police do. They "protect the weak from oppression" only when the oppression is, in one way or another, illegal. If the social system as a whole is oppressive, if the society is radically unequal, the police protect the oppressors and enforce the inequality.

But there is a paradox about police work in a constitutional democracy where all citizens are (supposed to be) equal under the law. The police have to honor that equality even while they defend the inegalitarian order. It is easy to be cynical about this: "The law, in its majestic equality," wrote Anatole France, "forbids the rich as well as the poor to sleep under bridges, to beg in the street, and to steal bread" (France [1894] 1992). The cynicism is justified—up to a point, as they say—and yet we hold police officers to the high standard of equal treatment, and we condemn officers who treat the poor generally, or racial minorities particularly, without respect. That condemnation implies the belief that it is possible to defend inequality while treating people of different ranks and races equally.

Often, of course, the police share the prejudices that are common in their society—in the US, that mostly means the racial prejudices. And then they are likely to choose among the laws they enforce the ones that weigh most heavily on the people they dislike or fear. Or, for similar reasons, they focus their attention on this neighborhood rather than that one. This discretionary focus had particularly malign effects during the drug crisis, where, for example, marijuana use among Black and White Americans was pretty much the same but many more Blacks, thousands more, were arrested and imprisoned for possession of the drug (Forman 2017, chap. 1). Similarly, according to the political scientist Michael K. Brown, "big city police have either enforced or not enforced the law in ways that maintain racial segregation and thus racial inequality, in response to the demands of white neighborhoods" (Brown 1988, 350).

"Enforced or not enforced" effectively describes the alternatives we face as citizens: if we don't like the laws the police enforce, we have to change the laws (legalize marijuana, for example). It makes little sense to criticize the police except for discrimination in enforcement. If we like the laws they disregard, then we have to defend the integrity of the legal order: enforce the law! Changing the race, ethnicity, and gender of the officers may also be necessary, but it is unlikely to be entirely effective. Brown argues that bringing Black men and women onto the police force probably won't make much difference. "Given the role of the urban police as protectors of wealth in a vastly unequal society, [the police] will be viewed as oppressors regardless of their ethnic makeup" (Brown 1988, 355). James Forman Jr. (2017) confirms the "won't make much difference" argument from the other side: Black police chiefs and officers are often as committed as their White counterparts to aggressive policing. Still, different personnel should make some difference: a larger role for Black Americans in law enforcement ought to make it harder for police agencies to ignore White nationalist activity, as they have commonly done in the recent past (Reitman 2018).

If you change the social order, you will change what the police do. Imagine an egalitarian, socialist society. The police would be actively engaged in repressing pro-capitalist conspiracies—and some of today's critics would be actively engaged in defending the repression. But the police themselves are not agents of change; they are agents of maintenance.

One qualification of that last sentence: the sharp reduction in the crime rate in the years since the mid-1990s is, to some extent, the product of aggressive policing (there are other causes, and fierce debate about all of them), and the chief beneficiaries of the reduction are poor people and minorities, who have always been the chief victims of crime in America (Zimring 2013; Sharkey 2018). So here is a social change for the better brought about, in part, by the police. White-collar crime has not declined, but it isn't the object of ordinary police work and, anyway, the larceny of the rich is mostly legal, aided and abetted by the government and beyond the reach of law enforcement. When criminal activity is reduced, the life of the poor is improved—but they remain poor.

Maintaining the status quo in an unequal and heavily armed society means that the police are allowed to use force—against revolutionaries, obviously, who don't expect to be patted on the head, and against radical activists who aim at disruption (and sometimes against activists who don't—an example in a moment), but also and more commonly against reckless drivers, thieves, muggers, drug dealers, violent husbands, and murderers who don't threaten the social order but only "lives and property" within it. For this purpose, police officers in the US carry guns and are authorized to use them; like soldiers, then, they require a restraining discipline. When they use force, they must do their best not to endanger the people whose lives they exist to protect—including the lives of criminals.

The fact that police work is dangerous and that too many Americans own guns does not exempt the police from this obligation or excuse them if they do less than their "best" to meet it. Soldiering is even more dangerous, and yet we require soldiers to live by the rules of engagement. Their "best" sometimes involves the acceptance of risks beyond the ordinary risks of battle in order to reduce the risks they impose on enemy civilians. And soldiers are held to account by a system of military courts, in principle and sometimes in practice, for any misuse of lethal force. Some writers have argued that the militarization of the police would be a good thing if it brought with it the kinds of training, discipline, and accountability that exist in the US Army (Tecott and Plane 2016). Balko reports that former US soldiers have told him "that military raids on residences where . . . suspected insurgents may be hiding are done more carefully and with more deference to the rights of potential innocents than some of the SWAT raids they see and read about today" (Balko 2014, 335). Yet many of the "warrior cops" think that they are acting like warriors.

Policing in the US is radically decentralized. There are some eighteen thousand law enforcement agencies, each with its own norms of police conduct, each with its own police culture. It is important to say that militarization affects only some, I don't know how many, of these agencies, and also that the incidence of police killing differs radically among them. The numbers don't correlate with crime rates; they are probably determined more by the culture of each agency. Reading media accounts of police shootings, it doesn't seem that many of these agencies have done enough to make officers accountable for the misuse of their weapons—nor have most of them done enough to define "misuse." The crimes of the police are radically under-policed; officers are almost never indicted for unnecessary or unjustified killings. Justice for soldiers is often problematic, but at least it has a visible institutional form; justice for police hardly has that (Zimring 2017, chap. 9).

A centralized system would probably be better at enforcing the rules of engagement. But the Supreme Court, interpreting the Fourth and Fourteenth Amendments to the Constitution, provides only the most general guidelines for national law enforcement, and our traditional aversion to anything that looks like a "standing army," operating at home, makes the creation of a federal police force impossible. There are good reasons for the aversion; still, opposition to a federal force shouldn't lead to the creation of a multitude of army-like and often undisciplined local forces.

So it makes sense to set out rules of engagement for the police that apply generally, even if there is no general jurisdiction within which they can be enforced. Here, then, are rules for the zone of peace, based on the assumption, which I think is true, that all the domestic "wars"—the war on crime, the war on drugs, and even the war on terror—are in fact and should remain metaphorical wars.

The Rules of Engagement

I need first to ask for whom the rules are written. In the zone of war, the most important decisions about how to engage the enemy are made by junior officers in the field. Ordinary soldiers have to know the rules, since they are told to refuse illegal orders, but they are not the ones who give the orders. The situation is very different in the zone of peace. As James Q. Wilson pointed out long ago, police departments are unlike almost every other organization in that "discretion increases as one moves down the hierarchy" (Wilson 1978, 7). The most important decision makers, those with the most discretion, are the lowest ranking police officers—the patrolmen and women working alone or in pairs, on foot or in a car. The rules of engagement are written, above all, for them. But they are most likely to obey the rules if the chief of police and other city officials are committed to them.

Junior officers on the battlefield must uphold the principles of distinction and proportionality, which are usefully joined in the doctrine of "double effect." They and their soldiers are bound to aim only at military targets (distinction) and to make sure that any collateral damage to civilian life and property is "not disproportionate" to the value of the target. An officer in the field can call in an artillery strike on an enemy position, for example, only if they are sure that the strike won't kill civilians—beyond some "proportionate" number that they have to figure out. I know how flexible "proportionality" is; still, the intended effect of the military action allows but also sets limits on the unintended or collateral effect.

The rules for police differ from the double effect doctrine in two critically important ways. First, it's not just innocent bystanders, the unintended victims, who have to be counted in proportionality calculations, but also the intended victims—fleeing suspects, say. Their death may itself be disproportionate to the value of stopping whatever crime they were (or may have been) engaged in. An old legal doctrine, enunciated by a Kentucky court in 1902, concludes differently: it doesn't matter, the judges wrote "if the suspected felon was killed in the course of capture since, in the eyes of the law, he had already forfeited his life by committing the felony" (Kleinig 1996, 112). Today it is recognized that life is not forfeited by felonious behavior—and certainly not by "suspected" felonious behavior.

The second difference from classic double effect doctrine is that, except in unusual and extreme situations, police shouldn't be making proportionality calculations at all. Using force to arrest a suspected felon may be justified (if it's not "excessive"), but killing innocent people in order to make the arrest isn't justified. The police can't say that these innocent deaths are "not disproportionate" to the value of arresting this particular suspect. In the zone of peace, innocent deaths will always be disproportionate.

The reason for the different rules governing police conduct is, most simply, the absence of the urgencies of war. If the fleeing suspect escapes, it is not a disastrous defeat for the police; nor is the danger to the general public any greater than it was an hour earlier, before the police tried to apprehend the suspected felon. The established routines of the zone of peace and the strong institutional environment within which those routines are sustained, make criminal activity an acceptable risk in a way that enemy military activity isn't. We live with it. Intermittently, citizens demand greater police control, as Black community leaders did in the 1960s and after, in defense of their neighborhoods (Fortner 2015). But we don't, and shouldn't, allow police to fight and kill the way soldiers do.

Political and legal consequences follow from the differences I have just described. When soldiers kill an enemy soldier, no investigation is warranted; when they kill civilians, an investigation is required. In the case of the police, by contrast, any killing calls for investigation—since the first responsibility of the police is the protection of life. Again, soldiers will escalate the fighting if they think they can win, while police should always aim at de-escalation; they "keep" the peace, and when peace is disturbed, they must try to restore it. When they don't do that, as in Chicago in 1968, when a massive political protest was met by a police riot—"a club swinging melee [where] police ranged the streets striking anyone they could catch" (Walker 1968, 7)—then condemnation is necessary and a strong reassertion of the rules of engagement.

The Actual Fleeing Suspect

For a concrete account of those rules, I will look at some legal cases, beginning with one of the most famous, *Tennessee v. Garner*, decided by the US Supreme Court on March 27, 1985.

John Kleinig describes the facts of the case:

> Errol Garner was a slightly built, fifteen-year-old black youth. He was shot while seeking to escape apprehension after he had apparently burglarized a vacant house ($10 was found in his possession). Although the pursuing officer did not believe that Garner was armed or even dangerous, the Memphis Police Department defended the officer's actions by appealing to the "fleeing felon" privilege. Had Garner not been shot, he would not have been apprehended. (Kleinig 1996, 114–15)

Arguing before the Supreme Court, lawyers for the State of Tennessee claimed that the public's interest in encouraging the peaceful surrender of suspects justified the shooting. But the Court ruled against Tennessee, holding that Garner's life outweighed any such interest. The ruling, however, included an exception: if "the officer has probable cause to believe that the suspect poses a significant threat of death or serious injury to the officer or others," they may shoot (Kleinig 1996, 115). It is hard to see how a fleeing suspect could pose a threat to the officer from whom they are fleeing. But if the suspect posed a danger to others, if they seized hostages, say, and threatened them, lethal force might be justified—though it would be better to let them go if they released the hostages unharmed. Mostly, the Court got it right: the presumption is in favor of life, even the life of a felon.

Eight years before *Tennessee v. Garner*, the IACP at its annual meeting had voted 4–1 in favor of laws "permitting police to shoot fleeing felony suspects" (Kleinig 1996, 114). That's a large margin, but still 20 percent of the chiefs defended what is now established law and was always morally right: don't shoot. By contrast, in the zone of war, fleeing soldiers can be shot, since they are presumed to be fleeing in order to rejoin their unit and return to the battle. Mass flight after a decisive battle might signal the end of the fighting, and then shooting the fleeing soldiers would not be justified. In effect, they would be fleeing the zone of war itself.

Don't shoot is a simple rule that would, even when we recognize necessary exceptions, greatly reduce police killings (Zimring 2017, chaps. 11–12). But there are other potentially lethal police engagements.

Hot Pursuit

According to John Kleinig, writing in 1996, pursuits "involving police cars kill and maim more people each year than police firearms." This is almost certainly not right, since police shootings in the 1990s were radically underestimated—or ignored (Kleinig 1996, 117; Zimring 2017, chap. 2). Still, high-speed chases—"hot pursuit," a favorite theme of Hollywood movies—are very dangerous. It's only in recent years that the danger has been recognized as a legal issue. Since *Tennessee v. Garner*, there have been a number of court cases in which the car chase is viewed as a "use of force." None of them has established what seems to me the necessary restraint.

One of the best-known cases, *Scott v. Harris* (2007), involved the police pursuit of a speeding motorist on a highway in Georgia. The pursuit continued for some time at very high speeds; it was finally terminated when one of the police officers rammed the motorist's car, causing it to crash. The motorist was rendered quadriplegic. He sued, claiming the ramming of his car constituted unreasonable force. On April 30, 2007, the Supreme Court reversed a District Court decision and ruled in favor of the pursuing officer: "a police officer's attempt to terminate a dangerous high-speed car chase that threatens the lives of innocent bystanders does not violate the Fourth Amendment, even when it places the fleeing motorist at risk of serious injury or death." It is certainly true that car chases like this one threaten innocent lives; the motorist did not deny this in his suit; he argued instead that everyone's safety would have been assured if the police had given up the chase. Who is responsible for the dangers of hot pursuit? In this case, obviously, the speeding motorist should have stopped and accepted his ticket, but if he doesn't stop, are the risks of police pursuit worth the goal of the pursuit?

Perhaps there is no simple answer to this question, though I suspect that there is. Surely the Court should have recognized that sometimes the rules of engagement require disengagement. A successful escape is less dangerous to life and limb, and less dangerous to law and order, than a successful pursuit.

Conclusion

The rules of engagement obviously have to extend beyond shootings and car chases to include the use of police clubs, chokeholds, no-knock raids (even with a warrant), the stop-and-frisk-policy, searches, profiling, the "third degree," and much else. Everywhere, whether officers act with force or without, the rules require them to treat everyone they encounter with equal respect. There are sure to be encounters where we will want to argue about what equal respect requires. But one principle should drive the argument and shape all the rules for all encounters: here in domestic society, in the zone of peace, there are criminals, suspected criminals, thugs, thieves, rioters, rowdy young men, hustlers, bullies, people selling drugs, people with a joint in their pocket—but there are no enemies. All these men and women have lives that the police are required to value, even if these same men and women need to be stopped from doing whatever they are doing.

I acknowledge that what they are doing is sometimes dangerous, sometimes despicable, and it is easy to think that they have forfeited their rights by their behavior. That's what enemy soldiers do in the zone of war by fighting and preparing to fight; that's why they can be killed. In the zone of peace, only someone in the act of violently breaking the peace, someone who threatens the life of an officer or anyone else—only they have forfeited their rights, and only for that moment. Once the moment passes and the threat recedes, the police are dealing, again, with rights-bearing fellow citizens or fellow humans. The most important thing they need to know is that they are not at war.

BIBLIOGRAPHY

Balko, Radley. 2014. *Rise of the Warrior Cop: The Militarization of America's Police Forces.* New York: Public Affairs.

Brown, Michael K. 1988. *Working the Street: Police Discretion and the Dilemmas of Reform.* New York: Russell Sage.

Cobb, Charles E. 2014. *This Nonviolent Stuff'll Get You Killed: How Guns Made the Civil Rights Movement Possible.* New York: Basic Books.

Forman, James Jr. 2017. *Locking Up Our Own: Crime and Punishment in Black America.* New York: Farrar, Straus and Giroux.

Fortner, Michael Javen. 2015. *Black Silent Majority: The Rockefeller Drug Laws and the Politics of Punishment.* Cambridge, MA: Harvard University Press.

France, Anatole. (1894) 1992. *Le Lys Rouge.* Paris: Gallimard.

IACP (International Association of Chiefs of Police). 1957. "Law Enforcement Code of Ethics." www.theiacp.org.

Kelling, George L., and James Q. Wilson. 1982. "Broken Windows: The Police and Neighborhood Safety." *Atlantic Monthly,* March 1982.

Kleinig, John. 1996. *The Ethics of Policing.* Cambridge, UK: Cambridge University Press.

Reitman, Janet. 2018. "State of Denial: How Law Enforcement Failed to See the Threat of White Nationalism." *New York Times Magazine,* November 11, 2018, 38–49, 66–68.

Scott v. Harris. 2007. 550 US 372.

Sharkey, Patrick. 2018. *Uneasy Peace: The Great Crime Decline, the Renewal of City Life, and the Next War on Violence.* New York: Norton.

Tecott, Rachel, and Sara Plane. 2016. "Maybe U.S. Police Aren't Militarized Enough. Here's What Police Can Learn from Soldiers." *Washington Post,* August 16, 2016. www.washingtonpost.com.

Tennessee v. Garner. 1985. 471 US 1.

Vitale, Alex S. 2017. *The End of Policing.* New York: Verso.

Walker, Daniel. 1968. *Rights in Conflict: The Violent Confrontation of Demonstrators and Police in the Parks and Streets of Chicago during the Week of the Democratic National Convention of 1968.* New York: Bantam.

Wilson, James Q. 1978. *Varieties of Police Behavior: The Management of Law and Order in Eight Communities.* Cambridge, MA: Harvard University Press.

Woods, Elliott. 2018. "Fear: How the NRA Sells Guns in America Today." *New Republic,* May 2018. https://newrepublic.com.

Zimring, Franklin E. 2013. *The City that Became Safe: New York's Lessons for Urban Crime and Its Control.* New York: Oxford University Press.

Zimring, Franklin E. 2017. *When Police Kill.* Cambridge, MA: Harvard University Press.

5

When Police Do Not Need to Kill

FRANKLIN ZIMRING

The control of police use of deadly force is a priority concern for police ethics in the twenty-first century in the United States. The frequent death of civilians from police gunfire is a major threat to public health, a chronic threat to public trust in police, and a major challenge to police administrators in the US. The first section of this chapter will provide a brief outline of the known facts on police use of deadly force, its frequency, its social and demographic distribution, the circumstances that provoke police deadly force and the rules that govern police use of deadly force in civil and criminal law and in police administration. The second section of the chapter argues that the best hope for saving civilian lives and preserving public trust is not widespread reliance on criminal law but rather clear administrative rules governing when police should use deadly force and when they should not. The third part of the analysis identifies one major explanation for inadequate controls on the use of deadly force in police administration—the failure of police chiefs to make the survival of civilians a priority concern along with officer safety in making policy choices. Police administrators can do a much better job of keeping police officers protected from life-threatening force and minimizing the number of citizens their officers kill, but only if they consider civilian lives to be an important value in determining police deadly force policy. Many current practices suggest the need to better serve this important public priority.

* * *

Until quite recently, little was known about either the volume of killings by police in the US or the circumstances that produce civilian deaths. The three attempts by the federal government to estimate the total volume of police killings in the US produced a range of estimates between four hundred and six hundred per year (Zimring 2017, chap. 2), but all these estimates were well under the true count. Both a sophisticated analysis by the Research Triangle Institute (Banks et al. 2015) and two careful counts based on searches of the Internet demonstrated that close to one thousand one hundred persons each year die in interactions with police or in police custody. The estimate of one thousand one hundred was first established for calendar year 2015, but the equivalent data for both 2016 and 2017 suggests that volume does not vary much in recent years (see e.g., *Washington Post* 2018). The vast majority of the one thousand one hundred civilian deaths each year, about 85 percent, are shootings by police officers, with 987 such deaths by shootings reported in 2017.

The high volume of civilian deaths is well above the rate of civilians killed by police in other developed nations, as shown in Figure 5.1.

While Figure 5.1 shows a much higher rate for the US than for comparison nations, it probably understates the American total by about 8 percent. Why does the American rate so overwhelmingly dominate comparisons with other developed nations?

Figure 5.2 shows us that when compared with England and Germany, the US also has a vastly higher rate of police officers killed by assaults from civilians.

While the US rate of killings by police is about one hundred times as high as in England and Wales, the US rate of police deaths from assault is also twenty-five times the English rate. German police officers are one-forty-fourth as likely to die by civilian assault as their American equivalents.

The demographics of civilians killed by police provide some clues about the reasons for US dominance. 95 percent of all persons killed by police are men; and while a slight majority of all victims are non-Hispanic Whites, both African Americans and Native Americans are twice as likely per one hundred thousand people to be killed by police as non-Hispanic White males (Zimring 2017, 45).

Since *Tennessee v. Garner* was decided in 1985, police cannot lawfully use deadly force to effect a felony arrest unless the failure to use deadly force presents risks to the lives of officers or citizens. In our analysis of reasons given by police officers for a killing, only 2.7 percent of all cases where police describe the nature of the threat that provoked the killing were said to be a risk to the lives of other civilians (Zimring 2017, 62). The overwhelming majority of all killings by police were responses by

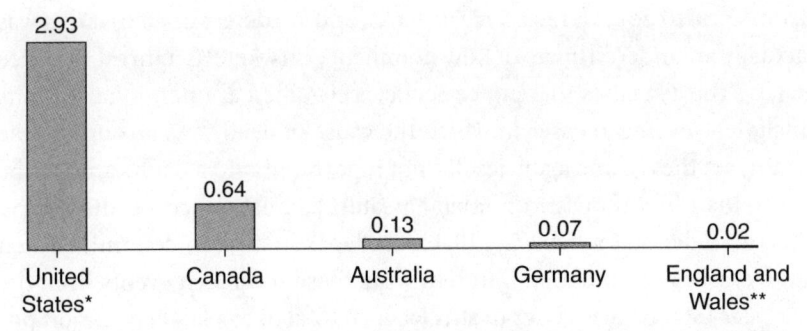

```
 2.93
┌────┐
│    │        0.64
│    │      ┌────┐         0.13         0.07
│    │      │    │       ┌────┐       ┌────┐       0.02
│    │      │    │       │    │       │    │      ┌────┐
United      Canada       Australia    Germany     England and
States*                                           Wales**
```

Figure 5.1. International Comparisons of Killings by Police with a Corrected US Rate. Source: Zimring (2017), based on data from the Centers for Disease Control and Prevention (2016). Reprinted with permission of Harvard University Press.
* Based on Research Triangle Institute Low Rate Annual Average of 920
** Shootings Only

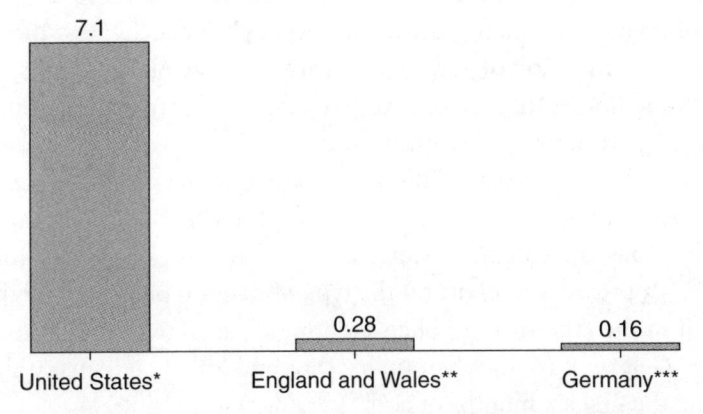

```
 7.1
┌────┐
│    │
│    │
│    │
│    │         0.28
│    │       ┌────┐        0.16
│    │       │    │       ┌────┐
United        England     Germany***
States*       and Wales**
```

Figure 5.2. Annual Risk of Fatal Assault per 100,000 Police Officers, United States, England and Wales, and Germany. Source: Zimring (2017), based on data from the Centers for Disease Control and Prevention (2016). Reprinted with permission of Harvard University Press.
* See notes on Figure 6.1 in Zimring (2017)
** Home Office estimate of 0.4 deaths per year, 144,486 police officers and constables
*** Wikipedia estimate of 243,625

police to threats to the safety of police. And this provides a clear path to the reason why police in the US kill so often and also are killed so much more often than police in other nations.

My study of police deaths from assault discovered that the FBI reported that 91.8 percent of all fatal assaults of police in the six years from 2008 to 2013 were firearms attacks, and we determined that this was actually an underestimate of how dominant guns were as a threat to police safety. The 292 cases that police agencies classified as intentional assaults included seventeen cases in which the cause of death was an automobile crash, yet these same agencies did not report *any* auto assaults among the more than fifty thousand nonfatal assaults against police. So there is no clear foundation for believing that local departments can determine when auto crashes are intended. But removing these seventeen events from the six-year total of 292 officer deaths leaves a total of 275 fatal attacks on police officers in six years. No fewer than 268 of these 275 fatal assaults were committed with firearms, which thus account for 97.5 percent of the death risk police face from intentional assault (Zimring 2017, 94–97).

This near-monopoly of guns as a threat to American police safety also tells us why US police are so much more vulnerable to fatal assault than their German, Australian, and English colleagues—the vastly higher concentration of guns, particularly concealable handguns, in the streets and homes that police patrol. A shorthand explanation of the difference between one police death from assault per year in Germany and fifty such deaths per year in the US is sixty million civilian handguns.

Does the predominance of handguns in the US also explain the three deaths a day that civilians suffer at the hands of police? Yes and no. Figure 5.3 provides a report on the type of weapon possessed by the assailant in the accounts of police shootings that were found on the web by the *Guardian* (n.d.) when police shot and killed civilians in the US during the first six months of 2015.

Over half of the threats of injury reported by police in the accounts of their shootings and killings of civilians involved the presence of a firearm (55.7 percent), but almost half of the conflicts that resulted in death did *not* involve guns. Knives, which produced under 1 percent of police deaths by assault in six years, are the weapon reported in 16.5 percent of all killings by police and no weapon is reported in more than 11 percent of civilian deaths. When the mistaken belief by police that the adversary had a gun (3.7 percent) are added to the 55.7 percent with reported guns, it still appears that more than 40 percent of the conflicts that provoke killings by police are not assaults when there is a substantial threat to the life of the officer who shoots. About four hundred times a year, police officers kill civilians when the adversary possesses

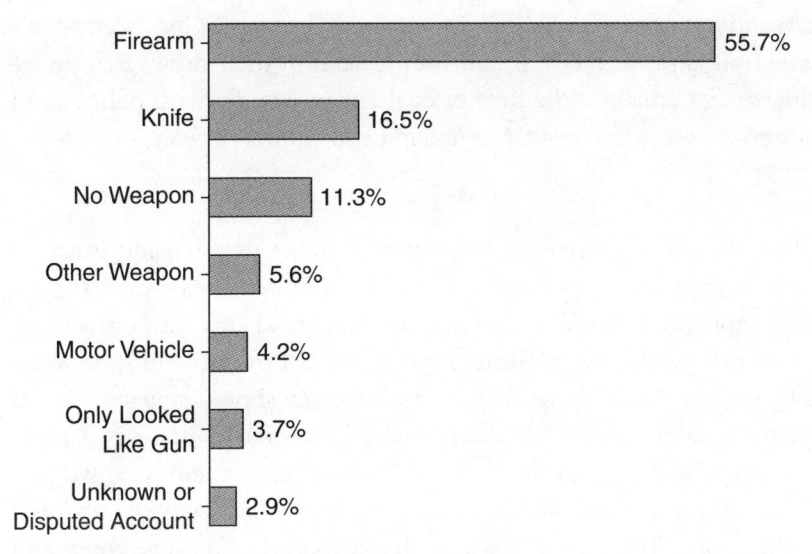

Weapon	Percentage
Firearm	55.7%
Knife	16.5%
No Weapon	11.3%
Other Weapon	5.6%
Motor Vehicle	4.2%
Only Looked Like Gun	3.7%
Unknown or Disputed Account	2.9%

Figure 5.3. Weapons Used by Targets of Police Shootings ($n = 479$). Source: Zimring (2017), based on data from the *Guardian* (n.d.) sample, January through June 2015. Reprinted with permission of Harvard University Press.

either no weapon or a weapon that produces less than 1 percent of police officer fatal attacks (Zimring 2017, 96–97).

The review of officer deaths in the US creates a sharp policy division that is necessary when considering the thousand or so times each year that police shoot and kill civilians. For the more than five hundred cases where the police say they were threatened with a gun, we need to study in detail the nature of the threat to the officer and the potential tactics available to respond to that threat. We cannot dismiss the possibility of a threat to a police officer's life as a matter of definition when guns are present. For the more than four hundred cases a year where the provocation for the shooting by police was not a gun, it is almost always true that a nonlethal response by police would not put a police officer's life at risk. These are cases where the wholesale restriction of police gunfire would be justified. But how should policies be changed? By changing the definitions in our criminal codes for when deadly force by police is justified? By increasing the number of cases where state and federal litigation produces money damages for the victims of shootings by police or their dependents? Or should the major focus be on generating and enforcing clear and consistent administrative regulation of when police can and can't fire at civilians? The next section argues for an emphasis on administrative rules. A concluding section then shows that police chiefs must consider the lives of civilians in conflict with police as an important value to consider in making and enforcing rules.

* * *

When the existing strategies for control of police use of deadly force are measured against the need to save several hundred lives every year, the only approach that offers the hope of widespread effectiveness is to set clear and specific administrative rules that tell frontline officers when they should not *start* shooting and when they should *stop* shooting if circumstances change. With a thousand killings of civilians a year, the chances of a police shooting in the US leading to a felony conviction of the officer are close to one in a thousand, for a variety of good and bad reasons. The criminal law is an appropriate response when and only when the killing involves a willful violation of a departmental rule and a criminal law standard. If the rules are vague and ambiguous, and when the training and standards in a department are quite weak, it seems inappropriate for a single officer to carry all of the blame. Money damages after the fact of a problematic shooting are both more common than criminal convictions and more suited to situations in which regulations and institutional problems contribute to an unjustified and unnecessary killing. While civil damage awards might also inspire future efforts at prevention, the award of damages comes only after the fact of an unnecessary death and the small size and modest frequency of these transfer payments are not by themselves going to be a sufficient incentive to provoke the major changes that could save hundreds of lives each year (Zimring 2017, chap. 7).

The best hope for major progress in the reduction of the number of civilians who die when deadly force is not necessary to protect police is a series of evidence-based rules that police administrators formulate and enforce. In the more than 40 percent of all circumstances where the police do not face weapons that threaten their lives, they should be told, "Don't shoot." There are currently about one hundred killings a year in the US where the victim didn't possess any weapon, more than 150 other killings a year where the victim was said to possess a knife or other cutting instrument, and many other confrontations where blunt objects, tools, or blunt implements are the perceived threat to the police. There are fifty thousand reported assaults against police each year in the US and in a typical year none of the fifty or so police deaths are a result of these instruments. In the city of Vallejo, California, in February of 2018, a police officer justified his fatal shooting by his belief that his adversary might attack him with a flashlight (Ravani and Haigney 2018). Did the officer fear for his life from a flashlight attack?

There are many other provocations of police use of deadly force where "don't shoot" protocols from commanders can serve the interests of public and police safety simultaneously. There are many other situations where a change in circumstances occurs—a combatant runs away or drops a weapon or is wounded and no longer a threat. In these cases, where the serious threat to police safety has abated, the police should be ordered to stop shooting. As a question of saving citizens' lives, this is not a small matter. One reason police kill so many civilians is that once police start shooting, they often *keep* firing. The current data on deaths by police gunfire nationally doesn't provide details on how often police shootings result in multiple wounds, but we analyzed official reports of 202 police shooting incidents over a six-year period in Chicago (for these reports, see Hing, Bordens, and Epton 2015). When we compared the death rate from shootings by police over the course of seven years in Chicago, it was more than twice as high per one hundred shootings as an earlier study had found for shootings by civilians (38 percent versus 14 percent; see Zimring 2017, 66). Reports by the Chicago police showed that a majority of all shootings by the police resulted in more than one wound being suffered by the victim. And Figure 5.4 shows that the fatality rate of police gun attacks increases substantially as the number of wounds inflicted increases.

Shootings that inflict only one wound produce a death rate of 20.8 percent—so four out of five victims survive a one-wound attack by police. But a second wound increases the death rate to one in three, and more than two wounds produces death in a majority of all cases. So inflicting multiple wounds more than doubles the death rate from shootings by police and thus becomes a critical determinant of who lives and who dies when police use firearms.

The combination of "don't shoot" and "stop shooting" rules covering weapons and unarmed assaults that do not represent a substantial

                                74.2%
                  56%   60%

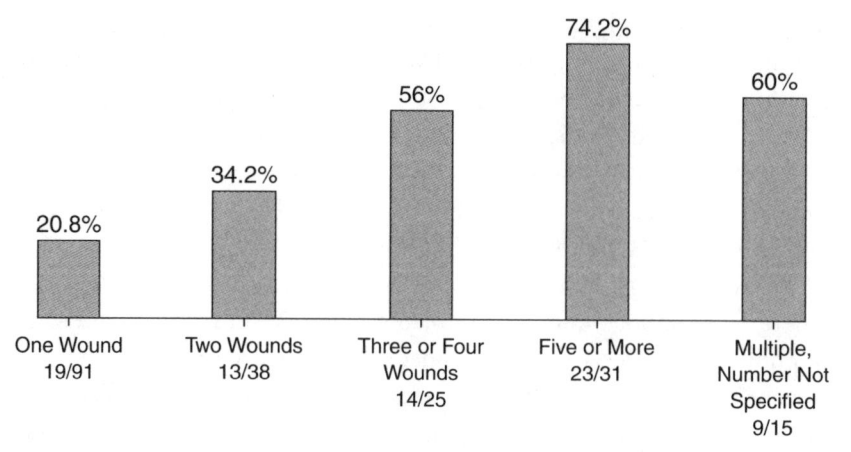

         34.2%

20.8%

One Wound   Two Wounds   Three or Four   Five or More   Multiple,
  19/91   13/38   Wounds   23/31   Number Not
                              14/25   Specified
                                                           9/15

Figure 5.4. Death Rate from Chicago Shootings by Number of Wounds. Source: Zimring (2017), based on data from Hing, Bordens, and Epton (2015). Reprinted with permission of Harvard University Press.

threat to police or innocent civilians could cut the death rate from police gunfire in half in the US if effectively enforced and obeyed. A combination of careful study of gun-present cases to determine when police can limit lethal force responses without serious risk can also over time make gun-present attacks less deadly for the civilians involved. Better rules of engagement for cases where a firearm was suspected but not evident can probably also save a large number of lives in the US.

At least half and probably more than that of all killings by police could be prevented without changing either the substance of police work or its danger for frontline officers. Then why hasn't the massive current death toll been substantially reduced by administrative rules even before the cacophony of public concern generated by Ferguson and Black Lives Matter? If my assertion is true—that the most effective strategy to reduce killings by police is simple and specific rules—then the proximate cause of the currently high death rate from unnecessary killings by police is a management failure to set such rules that is epidemic among thousands of police forces throughout the US. Part of the explanation for this is problematic decentralization of the management of law enforcement in the US. The vast majority of police in America are creatures of local government—municipal police or county sheriffs. The state level of government has highway patrol officers but very few officers with general criminal-justice responsibility. And because policing is not a major activity at the state level of government, there is very little expertise there on questions about police management that could be used to generate data on policing and to supervise municipal and county law enforcement. Local police are on their own in the American federal system within the boundaries of state government, where most other criminal justice concerns are governed. The national government has a larger policing presence than states do, with the FBI, immigration and border patrol, and drug enforcement agencies. The federal government also has some responsibility for local police in the Department of Justice with its Civil Rights Division and Office of Community Oriented Policing Services (COPS). These programs are relatively new and small but have been of substantial importance because they have made use of force, and particularly fatal force, a priority for generating investigation and consent decrees (Zimring 2017, 240–42). Whatever momentum was generated during the Obama administration, however, was swiftly terminated under the Trump administration.

*　*　*

This concluding section of my argument will cover two assertions—one obvious and the second more controversial. The obvious point is that police chiefs in democratic governments have an ethical obligation to make preserving the lives of citizens engaged in conflicts with their police officers into an important management priority, along with police officer safety, effective law enforcement and facilitating the safe use of public spaces by those who reside in the communities they police. Of course, preserving the lives of citizens is a police chief's priority, and why should that concern be in any way diminished when the citizen is in actual or apparent conflict with police on patrol? When there is no direct cost to police safety in minimizing the dangers of police use of force, saving civilian lives should be a priority.

Yet my 2017 analysis of the current circumstances of deadly force governance in American policing did not provide reassurance on this issue of key practical importance:

> How much do police chiefs care about whether the civilians their officers shoot live or die? The circumstantial evidence suggests that police

departments do not regard whether the victims of police shootings live or die as a matter of great moment, from the rhetoric used by the FBI and police departments . . . to the wide variety of non-life-threatening circumstances that nonetheless support police claims of lethal force justification. (Zimring 2017, 220)

How is it possible that the good people who become chief administrative officers of police forces in the US do not spend time and resources trying to minimize the deaths caused by their officers when they come into conflict with civilians? There are two assumptions that have inhibited police chiefs from recognizing the importance of the need to save civilian lives. The first is that the police chief regards each individual case in which police officers fire weapons as a set of unique events that should be judged only as individual events and not aggregated into any statistical patterns and examined collectively. A citizen was refusing to drop a sharp object he was brandishing when the police officer fired his gun. The chief sees each case as unique and is unwilling to study the outcome of many hundreds of "citizen displayed a knife" incidents reported by police to the FBI Law Enforcement Officers Killed and Assaulted (LEOKA) program to see whether officers were injured and if so, how seriously. Phoenix, Arizona, Police Chief Jeri Williams provides a classic statement of both the uniqueness rationale and its use to inhibit aggregation and statistical analysis: "As a 30-year veteran, I understand firsthand the challenges and split-second decision-making our officers face every day. Each analysis *is unique and cannot be compared to other situations*" (Prange 2018; emphasis added).

And the police chief seems willing to assume that anything less than maximum lethal force by police would increase the risk of death or great bodily harm to his police officers. This assumption of a zero-sum relationship between the level of deadly force that officers use and the extent to which their lives are at risk seems to mean that the chief can tolerate his six officers firing fifteen rounds at a small man who hasn't dropped a knife because their lives may have been at risk if they had stopped after two or three rounds (Zimring 2015). But why doesn't the police chief commission a statistical study of whether there were any police fatalities from knife assaults in the six years from 2008 to 2013? (See Zimring 2017, Table 5.3.) There were two deaths from concealed knives during the six-year span and no deaths from visible bladed weapons. Since the chief regards each attack as singular and unique, there is no reason to consider any attack as part of a larger statistical pattern.

Here are a few of the indications that police do not regard reducing the death toll from police use of deadly force to be a high priority:

1. The dreadful undercount of killings by police in the "official" statistics compiled by the FBI and the Bureau of Justice Statistics.
2. The failure of any call for a statistical analysis of how much the multiple-shots-fired policy of police increases the civilian death rate from these conflicts and whether there is any evidence that this policy saves police lives.
3. The widespread acceptance of allegations (with no supporting evidence) that knives brandished within twenty-one feet of a police officer put the police officer's life in serious danger and justify lethal police force (Zimring 2017, 100–2).
4. The failure of police agencies to collect and audit any data on police injuries from conflict with civilians and what weapons and circumstances put police most at risk.

This last statistical pattern is peculiar but important. Why shouldn't statistics on what injures and kills police officers be carefully collected and rigorously analyzed? Is the sloppy and unaudited LEOKA data on officer injuries and deaths evidence that the government doesn't care about police? Certainly not. That would be so inconsistent with the conspicuous embrace in public media of gratitude to "first responders" that there must be a more plausible reason why data on assaults against police is treated so sloppily and never regarded as an important data set to be audited and used to evaluate policy.

My cynical supposition is that keeping police injury data sloppy and obscure serves the interests of police and police departments by protecting the currently loose and permissive standards of police use of deadly force from any plausible scrutiny. The FBI reports an "official" data set where attacks with hands and feet are reported to be three times as likely to injure an officer as are attacks with guns (Zimring 2017, chap. 5). How serious are these "personal force" injuries? Nobody knows. But with attacks which rarely kill police dominating the official injury statistics, very few public health professionals will be tempted to place much trust in these data as an indicator of what really threatens police safety. So unreliable statistics serve as an insurance policy for the status quo—they perpetuate the wide variety of provocations that are permitted to tolerate police in the US killing three victims a day.

The first order of law reform in police use of deadly force is to deconstruct the incorrect management assumptions that have deterred police chiefs from being aggressive in saving civilians from unnecessary death. The fact patterns that produce a thousand fatal shootings each year cluster around a series of recurring enforcement issues, potential threats, weapons of concern, and alternative strategies to deadly force. Careful study produces reliable indications of whether and to what extent allowing officers only non-deadly responses put police at life-threatening risk. As soon as good empirical tests of police responses to patterns of provocation are introduced into policy consideration, the better angels of police administration can begin to care about saving civilians from police killings, where this can be done with minimal risk.

There are no alternatives in 2020 to introducing fact-based policy into police use of deadly force. The era when "every shooting is unique" can be a cover story in American policing will never return. It is time for police policy to catch up with the empirical reality of police shootings as a public health problem.

AUTHOR'S NOTE

I thank Ben Jones and Eduardo Mendieta for written suggestions to expand this paper and the participants in the Ethics of Policing Conference at Penn State on September 22, 2018, for their comments and questions. Two issues that generated questions at that conference concerned whether it was reasonable for administrative orders to prohibit police from shooting (1) when the risk to the police is the presence of a visible knife or bladed weapon and (2) in circumstances where the police officer is alone but can withdraw and request other officers to assist in resolving the safety threat. The empirical data supporting the wisdom of such policies is reported in my book *When Police Kill* (Zimring 2017, 94–102 on knives and bladed instruments and 59–61 on the high rate of "officer alone" killings in which the victim is not armed).

BIBLIOGRAPHY

Banks, Duren, Lance Couzens, Caroline Blanton, and Devon Cribb. 2015. *Arrest-Related Death Program Assessment: Technical Report*. Bureau of Justice Statistics with RTI International, March 3, 2015. www.bjs.gov.

Centers for Disease Control and Prevention. 2016. "Injury Prevention & Control: Data and Statistics (WISQARS)." www.cdc.gov.

Guardian. n.d. "The Counted: People Killed by Police in the US [2016]." Accessed October 23, 2020. www.theguardian.com.

Hing, Geoff, Alex Bordens, and Abraham Epton. 2015. "Officer-Involved Shootings." *Chicago Tribune*, July 29, 2015. http://apps.chicagotribune.com.

Prange, Rich. 2018. "Cop Union Criticizes Phoenix PD Chief over Shooting that Killed Suspect." 12 News, February 21, 2018. www.12news.com.

Ravani, Sarah, and Sophie Haigney. 2018. "Vallejo Officer Fatally Shoots Man Who Allegedly Raised Flashlight in Fight." *San Francisco Chronicle*, February 14, 2018. www.sfchronicle.com.

Washington Post. 2018. "Almost 1,000 Were Killed by Police Last Year. Here's What to Do About It." January 8, 2018. www.washingtonpost.com.

Zimring, Franklin. 2015. "Mario Woods' Unnecessary Death." *San Francisco Chronicle*, December 11, 2015. www.sfchronicle.com.

Zimring, Franklin . 2017. *When Police Kill*. Cambridge, MA: Harvard University Press.

6

Prioritization of Life as a Guiding Principle for Police Use of Deadly Force

DAVID KLINGER

When police officers in the United States opt to use deadly force against citizens in the course of their duties, they are exercising the most profound power that the state possesses—the power to take life.[1] The question of just when this fearsome warrant should be exercised has been with us since American police officers first started carrying firearms in the nineteenth century, and it has often been debated with contentious fury. Take, for example, the 1858 killing of John Hollis by police officer Robert Cairnes in New York City as Officer Cairnes chased Hollis following a brief altercation between the two. Hollis's death led to public outcry (which included an attempt to lynch Cairnes) and press condemnation of police violence in the form of a *New-York Times* editorial that lambasted Officer Cairnes and even questioned the need for police officers to carry firearms in the first place (Blumenthal 2015). Just over a century later, many of the riots and other civil disturbances during the tumultuous 1960s were sparked by incidents in which police officers fatally shot citizens (Klinger 2004, 8–9). More recently, protests and civil unrest following fatal police shootings in Missouri, North Carolina, and other states have elevated the matter of fatal police violence to a spot among our nation's most prominent social issues (Pickering and Klinger 2016, 22).

This longstanding American concern about lethal police violence is part and parcel of deeper Western concerns about the value of individual human life and the threat that governmental power poses to individual liberty. Thus, while the core function of the police in the US is to promote social order and protect life and property from criminal predation through their capacity to compel citizens to comply with the law, submit to state authority when they do violate laws, and otherwise do the state's bidding (Bittner 1970, 36–47; see more on this below), Americans have always been concerned that police officers might overstep the bounds of their coercive mandate. This tension between the desire of Americans for social order and to be protected from predation by fellow citizens, while remaining free from governmental overreach in the form of unnecessary police coercion, raises many issues about how the police should carry out their duties. Where deadly force goes, the issue boils down to this: just when should police officers use their ultimate coercive power to take life? As noted below, there are laws that set some parameters on when police officers may use deadly force, and almost all police departments have administrative guidelines addressing this issue. As highlighted above, however, the relevant rules don't always provide satisfactory frameworks for balancing the competing desires for order and safety on the one hand and protection from governmental overreach on the other. Given this situation, neither criminal law nor agency policy provides clear answers to the critical question of when police officers should use deadly force in the course of their duties.

Below, I argue that a principle that was developed decades ago to guide police decisions about whether and when to employ deadly force in one specific sort of situation provides sound ethical guidance for police decisions about the use of deadly force across the spectrum of police activities. Moreover, I will further argue that this principle is appropriate not only for guiding police decisions about employing deadly force, but also for guiding how the police should comport themselves in a wide variety of interactions with citizens that merely hold the *potential* for police gunfire to erupt.

Before discussing this ethical framework, two conceptual points are in order. The first is that the term "deadly force" in this essay is used synonymously with "gunfire." While various forms of physical force can be deadly (e.g., punches, kicks, blows with blunt instruments, slashes with edged weapons, and so on), a bullet striking flesh and bone is generally more damaging and life threatening than other forms of physical force. Police officers carry firearms to apply deadly force to defend innocent life, and research has shown that the vast majority of persons killed by police officers in the US die from bullet wounds (Fatal Encounters 2018). Second, and relatedly, not all applications of deadly force in the form of police gunfire result in death. In fact, research shows that no citizens die in most of the instances in which police officers fire their weapons; most police bullets fired at citizens either miss their mark or cause non-fatal injury (Klinger et al. 2016, 202). So when I use terms such as "the application of deadly force" and "police gunfire," they are not intended to suggest that anyone will (or did) die from the actions described. Rather, they should be understood as describing actions that hold a *high potential* to cause death (see, e.g., Illinois statute 720 ILCS 5/7.5, quoted below). This essay thus deals with police gunfire directed at citizens, an action that because it has a high potential to cause death or serious physical injury, is considered deadly force.

Because gunfire has a high potential to cause death, police use of deadly force rests within the broader conceptual matter of humans taking human life. Given this, determining when police should use deadly force begins with an overview of the legal framework that governs human life-taking in the US.

On Illegal and Legal Life-Taking

The Anglo-American social tradition that animates our nation's legal codes and under which police in the US operate includes the notion that human life is valuable and worthy of protection. Both federal and state statutes thus provide legal protection to all people within US borders via laws that forbid the taking of human life. Take, for example, the criminal laws in the state of Missouri that address murder and manslaughter in their various forms and provide for maximum penalties upon conviction that range from death for first-degree murder (Missouri Revisor of Statutes 2019, 565.020) to four years in prison for involuntary manslaughter (Missouri Revisor of Statutes 2019, 565.027).

These statutes, and similar laws around the nation, forbid the taking of human life in a wide array of circumstances and conditions, and provide citizens the protection of the state against fatal aggression by subjecting to serious penalty anyone who would fatally harm them. But the prohibition of taking life exemplified in these legal codes, and the protection that they afford to citizens, are not blanket. Rather, American law also recognizes the right of all persons to use lethal force to protect themselves and innocent third parties from attacks by others that are likely to produce serious injury or death. Take, for example, the second section of Florida Statute 776.012, which identifies when citizens in that state may use lethal force:

> A person is justified in using or threatening to use deadly force if he or she reasonably believes that using or threatening to use such force is necessary to prevent imminent death or great bodily harm to himself or herself or another or to prevent the imminent commission of a forcible felony. A person who uses or threatens to use deadly force in accordance with this subsection does not have a duty to retreat and has the right to stand his or her ground if the person using or threatening to use the deadly force is not engaged in a criminal activity and is in a place where he or she has a right to be. (Florida Legislature 2019, 776.012)[2]

The key to understanding how the same legal codes that forbid the taking of life in most instances permit the taking of life in others is that the criminal law governing the use of violence between citizens differentiates between innocent and aggressive life. As exemplified in the Florida statute above, the law's provision of an exception to the prohibition against killing is generally limited to those circumstances where an aggressor's actions threaten to seriously harm or kill innocents.[3] Implicit in this legal construction is the assumption that some life is more valuable than other life; innocent life is more valuable than criminally aggressive life, and is thus worthy of legal protection by providing innocents the right to protect themselves and other innocents from serious injury and death.

This notion of some lives being more valuable than others influences the world of policing in the form of laws that provide police officers with specific legal powers to take actions under some circumstances that may result in the death of citizens. Take, for example, the Illinois statute governing when police officers may use force to effect an arrest. 720 ILCS 5/7.5 in relevant part reads:

> A peace officer, or any person whom he has summoned or directed to assist him, need not retreat or desist from efforts to make a lawful arrest because of resistance or threatened resistance to the arrest. He is justified in the use of any force which he reasonably believes to be necessary to

effect the arrest and of any force which he reasonably believes to be necessary to defend himself or another from bodily harm while making the arrest. However, *he is justified in using force likely to cause death or great bodily harm* only when he reasonably believes that such force is necessary to prevent death or great bodily harm to himself or such other person, or when he reasonably believes both that:

(1) Such force is necessary to prevent the arrest from being defeated by resistance or escape; and

(2) The person to be arrested has committed or attempted a forcible felony which involves the infliction or threatened infliction of great bodily harm or is attempting to escape by use of a deadly weapon, or otherwise indicates that he will endanger human life or inflict great bodily harm unless arrested without delay. (Illinois General Assembly 2019, 720 ILCS 5/7.5; emphasis added)

The basics of this Illinois statute are echoed in the criminal codes of the other states, with variations in structure and emphasis, but the Illinois statute covers the twin basic notions of when police officers in the US are legally permitted to use deadly force: (1) to protect themselves and other innocents from suffering death or serious physical injury, and (2) to prevent the escape of violent felony suspects, those whose continued freedom is believed to gravely jeopardize community safety. Two matters should be noted here. The first is that the police are not permitted to shoot suspects whose actions do not pose the threat of serious injury or death. The second is that this essay will not comment any further on the legal power of the police to use deadly force against fleeing suspects; it will now focus exclusively on police gunfire to protect against threats of serious bodily injury and death that are rooted in the moment, not in a potential threat down the temporal line.[4]

The Literature on the Ethics of Killing and Its Limits for Policing

The notion that innocent life is more valuable than criminally aggressive life is consistent with major intellectual works on the ethics of using physical force in the defense of self and others. The rich literature on the ethics of using force to protect innocents focuses on defense of self (rather than third parties) and deadly (as opposed to non-lethal) force

(Coons and Weber 2016, 1). Ethicists have proffered several frameworks on which they base their assertions about when it is acceptable to use lethal force in defense of innocent life, and these frameworks provide different stances on the appropriateness of taking one life to protect another under certain circumstances (Coons and Weber 2016, 1–19). But all of them essentially agree that it is permissible for an innocent party to kill someone who intentionally seeks to take the innocent party's life through violent assault—that is, someone who is a "Villainous Aggressor" (Quong 2009, 507). Because Villainous Aggressors are engaging in criminal actions—directed either against other citizens or against police officers (or both)—the answer to the core question in the ethics literature on the right of the police to use deadly force to defeat such criminal actions in order to protect themselves and other innocents is quite clear; police officers are permitted to kill such persons to protect their lives and the lives of other innocents.[5]

But police officers are not mind readers. They never know exactly why an aggressor is attacking or otherwise threatening harm; they only know that he or she is doing so. This becomes an issue in the ethics literature because ethicists also sometimes speak and write of "Innocent Aggressors": persons who, while presenting an intentional lethal threat to another innocent person, are not morally culpable for their unjust threat (Quong 2009, 507). Among the sorts of persons classified as Innocent Aggressors are those who have different notions from potential victims and third parties about the threat they pose to victims (i.e., they don't believe their actions are fatally threatening), persons who are not culpable in the classic sense that a Villainous Aggressor is because they are acting under duress, and individuals whose consciousness is altered due to a mental defect or intoxicant (Alexander 2016, 26–32).[6]

The literature on the ethics of fatal force tends to presume that those who are threatened (and their protectors) have clear knowledge about the status of their attackers (i.e., whether they are Villainous or Innocent Aggressors). But in the real world, where police officers operate, this is simply not the case. Neither crime victims nor the police know with any certainty why someone is attacking. They merely know that an attack is underway. Thus, in the world of policing, the ethical issue boils down to this: how should police deal with the various threats (to themselves or to others) they face in the course of their duties, independent of the intent, legal culpability, or moral culpability of the aggressor? For a police officer facing a man who is hacking with a machete at a defenseless woman, for example, it matters not one whit why the attack is taking place; the officer must simply make a choice about whether to use deadly force to stop said assault. Because the intent of an aggressor is immaterial to the police mission, the rest of this essay will focus on police response to aggressive action, independent of whether the agent of the aggression is motivated by villainous intent.[7]

Another matter common in the ethics literature is worth addressing here. This literature often uses hypothetical situations to set up analyses of issues and typically frames the outcomes of these hypotheticals with certainty. Victims will certainly be killed if action is not taken against aggressors (or whatever agent or object may be presenting a threat) and the actions that victims (and protectors) take will certainly kill aggressors (or other sort of agent) if the latter category acts against the former (see, e.g., the various illustrative hypotheticals in Coons and Weber 2016). Again, this is not the case in the real world. It's impossible to know with certainty that the person assaulted will die (or even suffer serious injury; many people feloniously shot at are not hit by bullets), and we never know whether the protective deadly force an officer uses will kill or seriously injure. The police thus operate in a world of *possibilities* about death regarding both the outcome of aggressors' actions and the outcome of their own applications of deadly force. This must be considered when contemplating the ethics of police firearms use.

An Intellectual Frame for an Ethical Approach to Police Use of Deadly Force

The previously described legal powers that police possess to protect themselves and innocent citizens against threats of serious injury and death do not provide a complete ethical basis for determining when police officers should use deadly force, for they are quite broad. So where else might we look? The vast majority of police agencies have policy statements that govern when their officers are permitted to use deadly force (Terrill, Paoline, and Ingram 2012). Police department policies, however, typically do not circumscribe police powers much more than the criminal law,[8] and none specify when police officers *should* or *must* use deadly force; they merely provide direction about when officers in the employ of the relevant agency *may* use deadly force (and when they are prohibited from doing so). So, while police-agency policy can provide guidance beyond the criminal law, both law and policy merely place bounds around what the police are permitted to do; they do not ever *require* that officers use deadly force.

Theoretically, then, within the parameters of law and agency policy—and despite the fact that a major reason the police exist (and the sole reason they are armed) is to protect innocent life—the police might never use deadly force. Killing is merely a prerogative that police officers possess when certain conditions are met. Given that the police have broad powers to use deadly force but they are never required to do so, how can police effectively make sound choices about the use of deadly force? One answer lies in an ethical framework that is rooted in both the implicit notion in the law that some lives are more valuable than others and in the notion of why the police exist. After a brief detour into an expanded treatment of the purpose of the police, we will return to the question of ethics and detail the specifics of the framework just raised.

In *The Functions of the Police in Modern Society*, Egon Bittner (1970, 15) noted that the police were the last core element of municipal government to be developed in Western societies as the West shifted from rural and agrarian-dominated collectivities toward urban and industrial ones. Drawing on Weber's (1958, 78) notion that possessing a monopoly on the legitimate use of violence within its borders is the defining character of a state, Bittner (1970, 36–47) further argued (1) that the American police are the institution that holds a monopoly on the legitimate use of force in the nation's domestic life and, (2) because of this, the defining characteristic of the American police is their capacity to use force to carry out their duties. As members of that element of the state apparatus in which the monopoly to use force resides, then, police officers possess a unique mandate to use force to carry out their duties, up to and including their duty to protect innocent life, which many have argued is the ultimate duty of the police (Community Relations Service 2003, 5). The reason police are equipped with lethal firearms is that such weapons provide officers the capacity to carry out their mandate to protect life in the face of severe threats to their own lives and to the lives of innocent citizens.

Taking these twin notions, that the police have the legal authority to use deadly force to protect innocent life and the functional obligation to protect innocent life, as starting points, Ron McCarthy several years ago made explicit an ethical argument that had been implicit in some quarters of American policing from the beginning about when the police *should* use deadly force. The argument that McCarthy made was specific to one particular matter that the police are sometimes called upon to handle, but as will be detailed below, consideration of the matter shows that the principles he set forth are applicable across the spectrum of dangerous and potentially dangerous situations that officers are called upon to deal with.

McCarthy's Ethical Model

In a relatively obscure trade publication devoted to police special weapons and tactics (SWAT) teams, McCarthy (1989) articulated an argument about when and why the police should use deadly force against individuals who are holding other persons against their will (i.e., in hostage situations). McCarthy wrote about this issue from a viewpoint that included having spent a decade and a half as the assistant unit commander of the Los Angeles Police Department's SWAT team. In this capacity, he oversaw the successful resolution of numerous hostage situations—sometimes by means of a SWAT team member shooting a hostage taker—and he reviewed many other hostage situations that had been handled by both his and other agencies. His specific goal in penning the piece in question was to provide ethical guidance to police administrators, incident commanders, and SWAT team members about when they *should* use deadly force to end hostage situations.

McCarthy begins by noting that hostage situations present major challenges because hostage takers are ultimately in control of such situations. While the police may utilize crisis negotiations and other techniques to *influence* the actions of hostage takers, they cannot *control* hostage takers. Were the police truly in control of such situations, McCarthy notes, they would simply tell hostage takers to release their hostages and surrender, and hostage takers would immediately do so. Because this is not the case—because police directions to hostage takers to release their hostages and surrender do not resolve all hostage situations—the police are confronted with having to make choices about how much risk they are willing to take with the lives of various parties on scene. McCarthy asserts that hostage situations generally involve four sorts of parties: hostage taker(s), hostage(s), non-hostage citizens who are in the area of the hostage incident (e.g., bystanders), and police officers who have responded to the scene.

McCarthy argues that the risk calculus should be a simple one that views the four sorts of parties as being rank-ordered in a specific manner in terms of the priority that the police should place on their safety as they endeavor to resolve the situation. At the top of the prioritization schedule rest hostages. Second come other citizens in the area. Next come police officers who are on scene. The last priority is the hostage takers. In this construction, all human life is valuable, and the efforts of the police should be directed at resolving the situation without bloodshed if possible. But if decisions must be made about who lives and who dies (or who is exposed to heightened risk of injury or death), the police should simply follow the prioritization schedule and be willing to use deadly force against hostage takers to protect hostages, other citizens in the immediate area, and officers on scene.

McCarthy's analysis and argument focus on the risks posed to hostages when hostage takers (1) indicate or state that they will harm hostages and (2) have the means to seriously injure or kill hostages (McCarthy calls these twinned matters "the criteria").[9] He argues that when the police have established that a hostage taker has the means to harm or kill a hostage or hostages and has demonstrated a willingness to do so— in other words, when the criteria are met—police should take the first opportunity available to shoot the hostage taker. He asserts this based on two premises: first, because the prioritization of life places a higher value on the life of the hostage than on that of the hostage taker, and second, because if the police do not shoot the hostage taker when they have the opportunity to do so, the hostage taker may well act on his or her indicated intent to harm or kill the hostage at some later time during the event. In sum, McCarthy argues that police officers should, in order to protect the lives of hostages, use deadly force against hostage takers who credibly threaten to harm or kill hostages.

A brief consideration of McCarthy's life-prioritization framework shows that it is consistent with both the laws governing the use of force (by both citizens and police officers) and key works in the literature on killing. Regarding the law, as noted above, individuals (including police officers) are held to the standard of reasonableness; at the time deadly force was used, they had reasonable grounds for believing that such force was necessary to protect innocent life. A hostage is, by definition, an innocent person. And while we can never know for certain whether a hostage taker who has threatened or otherwise indicated an intent to kill such an innocent and who possesses the means to do so will, in fact, harm or kill, it certainly seems reasonable to believe that someone holding another human against his or her will, who has indicated an intent to harm or kill this other person, and who possesses the means to do so does, in fact, present a threat to the life of said innocent person.

Regarding ethics, as noted above, essentially all of the various lines of ethical argument about the use of force to protect life hold that innocent individuals have the right to protect themselves and other innocents from aggression. And while some might object to my application of the ethical principle of defensive force to protect life to hostage situations because the police on the scene of a hostage situation can never know for certain that a hostage taker who has threatened a hostage and has the means to make good on the threat will actually harm the hostage, I would simply say that the dominant ethical paradigm of defense of life does apply because (1) within the paradigm, wholly innocent life is viewed as more valuable than aggressive life, and (2) I believe that if we are to err, we should err on the side of the wholly innocent, not the aggressor.

And beyond the matter of whether it is ethically permissible for the police to kill a hostage taker when McCarthy's criteria are met, an argument can be made that the police have an obligation to use deadly force under such circumstances. In "Mandatory Rescue Killings," Cécile Fabre argues that "killing in the defense of another is sometimes mandatory at the bar of justice" (2007, 364) and asserts that police officers fall into a category of persons who have an obligation to use deadly force to protect others, even when taking such action would expose them to physical danger and other negative consequences. Fabre sets up her essay with the standard boilerplate in the ethics of self-defense literature noted above about (1) the certainty of the death of innocents at the hands of aggressors and (2) the certainty of the death of aggressors at the hands of rescuers. If we accept the previous argument that police officers' lack of capacity to definitively know whether anyone will ever be killed does not void the ethical principles that render it appropriate for them to use deadly force to protect innocent life, then Fabre's notion that the police have an obligation to shoot hostage takers fits nicely with McCarthy's arguments about life prioritization as a guiding principle for deadly force decision-making in hostage situations.

Expanding McCarthy's Framework beyond Hostage Incidents

In the decades since he developed it, McCarthy's prioritization-of-life framework has moved beyond the narrow realm of hostage situations and into some other realms of police work. As it has, others have collapsed McCarthy's two types of non-suspect citizens (i.e., hostages and other citizens in the area) into a single category of "innocent citizens." For example, many training programs include instruction on using a three-level prioritization-of-life scale that consists of (1) innocent citizens, (2) police officers, and (3) suspects as a template for how to manage active-shooter incidents. Such training often includes the tuition that, when police are called upon to deal with armed individuals who are firing at innocent citizens, responding officers should move quickly toward the attacker(s) and engage the attacker(s) with gunfire if the attacker(s) continue(s) to pose a threat to innocent citizens, or if the attacker(s) threaten(s) the police. This is because the lives of innocent citizens in the area where the gunman is shooting take priority over the life of the gunman. Note also that in this instance, the prioritization of life not only calls upon the police to use deadly force to protect innocent citizens, it also calls on them to place their lives in serious jeopardy as they seek to find the active shooter. This position is consistent with Fabre's arguments in "Mandatory Rescue Killings" that persons with a professional duty to protect innocents also have an ethical obligation to expose themselves to heightened risk when trying to protect others.

But the prioritization of life is by no means universally taught in American policing. While many police trainers (myself included) have explicitly incorporated the three-level life-priority scale into their instruction, and while some articles have been written by individuals and groups interested in law enforcement operations and use-of-force matters (Hayes 2014; Ranalli 2016), the prioritization-of-life framework has not captured the attention of American Policing writ large. For example, it can be found nowhere in the *Final Report* by the President's Task Force on 21st Century Policing (2015). This state of affairs is, in my estimation, unfortunate, because the vast majority of situations that police officers in the US face in which they have to make decisions about whether to use deadly force occur outside of the realm of hostage incidents or any other SWAT operation. For example, the vast majority of people fatally shot by American police officers from 2015 to 2018 were not killed by SWAT officers (*Washington Post* 2018).

As I noted at the outset of this essay, police in the US have come under increased scrutiny regarding the use of deadly force. With this increased scrutiny have come numerous calls from various sectors of society for officers to stop shooting so many people. Zimring (2017, 227–30), for example, asserts that police officers should almost never shoot anyone who doesn't have a gun. And Campaign Zero (2018) argues that police shootings should be eliminated altogether. But these assertions are both unrealistic and dangerous. Regarding the "don't shoot unless the citizen has a gun" argument, many police officers and (many more) innocent citizens have been killed by people who did not possess firearms. For example, more than twenty thousand Americans were murdered by wholly unarmed assailants in the two decades that ended in 2015, and eighty-three police officers were murdered by unarmed assailants during this same period (Klinger and Slocum 2017, 352).[10] To deny police officers the capacity to protect themselves and citizens from aggressors who threaten life by means other than firearms is, on its face, an ethically unsound position that would almost certainly lead to more innocent citizens being murdered and more dead police officers.[11]

Regarding the drive to entirely eliminate police use of firearms, this more extreme position is even more ethically dubious and potentially dangerous. First, to deny police officers the power to protect the lives of innocent citizens from the murderous acts of assailants is to deny these citizens the protection of the state. Were police officers to cease shootings entirely, more citizens would undoubtedly be killed while the police ignored their pleas for protection. Second, in addition to the already cited numbers in the preceding paragraph about deaths of police officers, I would simply add that more than forty-five police officers were murdered with firearms each year in the decade ending in 2017 (US Department of Justice, Federal Bureau of Investigation 2017). Again, were the police to cease shootings entirely, this number would undoubtedly increase; police officers thwart numerous potentially fatal firearms assaults against them each year by shooting their assailants (*Washington Post* 2018; and see the traffic stop shooting involving Los Angeles Police Department [LAPD] officers discussed below for an example of this phenomenon).

While these extreme positions do not offer reasonable goals, careful consideration of the matter indicates that there certainly are situations in which police officers use deadly force when it could have been avoided, and not just when they behaved in a criminal fashion. So, how can we get police officers to use deadly force in the most judicious fashion possible—one that can realistically reduce the number of citizens shot by the police without exposing police officers and innocent citizens to heightened risks? One answer is to use the prioritization of life to guide police operations across the board, not just in hostage and active-shooter situations. While the framework lists suspects as the lowest priority, their lives are still viewed as valuable, and the police should seek ways to structure encounters—when they can—in ways that will not place their lives or the lives of innocent citizens in jeopardy, for as long as no innocent citizen or police life is in jeopardy, there is no need to shoot a suspect.

Take, for example, a situation in which the police are called to deal with a suicidal individual armed with a knife and sitting alone in the family basement. If the police recognize that the person in crisis is presently threatening no one but himself, and if they think in terms of the prioritization of life, they will realize that staying upstairs and communicating with the distraught individual from a distance and with structural barriers between themselves and the subject will forestall any need to consider using deadly force as they seek to prevent the subject from carrying out the stated self-threat.[12] The patrol officers in this instance can call upon specialists, such as crisis negotiators and perhaps SWAT team members, who have proven track records of resolving such situations without bloodshed (Klinger and Rojek 2005, 13).

If, on the other hand, the responding patrol officers go down into the basement, they may well find themselves in a situation where the distraught individual attacks them with the knife that he was threatening to kill himself with. In this instance, the police—based on the law, as well as the prioritization of life—would be within their rights to shoot their attacker in order to protect themselves from death or serious harm. But shootings of this ilk are eminently avoidable by keeping in mind the prioritization of life. By explicitly valuing the life of the person in crisis, the police will prioritize their lives above time, resource, or other constraints[13] and act in ways that can preclude the need to consider their lives as a priority over the life of an aggressor (e.g., by staying upstairs and calling on specialists to address the situation).[14]

Conversely, the prioritization-of-life framework will sometimes dictate that police take actions that may actually increase the likelihood that they may have to shoot a citizen, and sometimes dictate that they simply do so. Two real-life case studies illustrate these points, starting with one describing how police officers will sometimes find themselves in situations where if they don't shoot, there exists a high probability that they will be seriously injured or killed. Links to video footage of these incidents are provided in the next two endnotes.

Two Case Studies

The first case involves two Los Angeles police officers who made a traffic stop on July 27, 2018, in the San Fernando Valley. The officer who was driving the police vehicle walked up to the driver's side front door of the stopped vehicle, while the officer who was riding with her walked up to the passenger side. After a brief conversation, the first officer asked the driver, Richard Mendoza, to step out of his vehicle. When he complied with this request, he also rapidly produced a handgun, shot the first officer, then quickly spun and shot at the second officer, who was still positioned on the passenger side of Mendoza's vehicle. The second officer drew his service pistol and fired multiple rounds at Mendoza from the other side of Mendoza's vehicle, then moved around the back of Mendoza's vehicle and fired one additional round at Mendoza. The entire gunfight, which resulted in Mendoza's death, lasted approximately five seconds (the first officer, who survived, never fired any rounds).[15]

Under McCarthy's prioritization of life, the use of deadly force by the second officer was appropriate. He was shooting to protect both himself and his injured partner from an aggressor who had both displayed an intent to injure or kill and who—quite obviously—possessed the means to deliver such harm. But there is a wrinkle in this incident. When the second officer fired his last round at Mendoza after moving around the rear of Mendoza's vehicle, Mendoza was lying on the street with no weapon visible in either of his hands, for he had already been disabled by the second officer's initial gunfire. While some may say this fact makes the last round fired ethically suspect (or even inappropriate), as there was no actual threat at the precise moment the second officer fired this last round, such a claim is not consistent with the prioritization-of-life framework, because the framework acknowledges the imperfect nature of human knowledge during stressful situations. Research on the matter demonstrates that it takes some time for police officers (as is the case for any human) to make sense of a social situation, decide on a plan of action, and then execute it (Klinger 2004, 57–202). In this instance, the last time the second officer saw Mendoza before he fell out of sight on the driver's side of the car, he was actively trying to murder the second officer (after trying to kill the first officer). When the second officer next saw Mendoza, it is logical to believe that his perception of the situation was that he was still involved in a gun battle (i.e., that Mendoza was still trying to kill him and his partner), and so he did what police officers are trained to do in gun battles with people who are trying to kill them—he shot at Mendoza. As soon as the second officer perceived that Mendoza was no longer trying to murder him and his partner, he ceased firing, for that is what police officers should do when they understand an aggressor they have taken under fire no longer presents a threat to innocent life.

Requiring police officers to accurately perceive that a threat has passed—and not fire an additional round at an aggressor who seconds before was clearly attempting to kill—places the life of the suspect above that of the officers, in this case including the officer who had already been shot by Mendoza. So the prioritization-of-life framework provides us with the ability to look at and assess the appropriateness of police use of deadly force in the light of the real-world context of policing.

Please note, however, that regarding the principle of assessing police officers' actions based on real-world performance metrics, the prioritization scheme does not give officers carte blanche. Recall that McCarthy did not assert that it is appropriate to use deadly force to resolve all hostage incidents, only those where the "criteria" were met; that is, when there is an indication that a hostage taker (1) intends to harm/kill hostages and (2) possesses the means to do so. In applying the life-priority framework to non-hostage-taking situations, McCarthy's criteria means that officers should not shoot in all situations where a citizen might be presenting some threat, but only in those where it is reasonable for the involved police officers to believe that the aggressive citizen (1) is threatening to seriously harm or kill an officer or an innocent citizen and (2) possesses the means to do so. This sets the bar for the use of deadly force under the prioritization-of-life scheme at the same place that the criminal law sets it—when it is reasonable to believe that innocent life is being threatened.

But the life-prioritization framework actually places an additional ethical restriction on police officers' use of deadly force. Recall that in this scheme, the lives of suspected criminals are a priority; that is, suspects' lives are valuable. Because this is so, officers should use deadly force against such aggressors only when employing other, less deadly, means of resolving a threatening situation would jeopardize innocent life. Relatedly, because the lives of all citizens do hold value, the prioritization scheme dictates that officers seek to manage volatile situations in ways that reduce the likelihood that any innocent life will be placed in jeopardy. Thus the prioritization framework provides a scheme for reducing the number of persons shot by the police by reminding police officers in the real-life moments when they are dealing with difficult situations that (1) they should use deadly force only when the criteria are met and (2) they should seek to act in ways that can prevent situations from evolving to the point where deadly force is needed to protect innocent life.

But this notion that the police should seek to manage situations in ways that will minimize the likelihood they will need to resort to deadly force to protect innocent life is not a hard and fast rule, for the prioritization-of-life framework will sometimes indicate that officers should use tactics that may actually *increase* the likelihood that they will need to shoot an aggressor. Such situations come along when officers face circumstances in which the lives of innocent citizens, police officers, and suspects may all be in potential (or actual) jeopardy. When situations of this ilk arise, the prioritization framework dictates that officers utilize tactics that will decrease the threat to innocent citizens, even if it increases the threat to themselves and increases the likelihood that they may need to shoot an aggressor. The second case study from Los Angeles illustrates this point.

On June 16, 2018, Guillermo Perez stabbed a citizen at a church in the Van Nuys area of the city. When LAPD officers responded, they encountered a chaotic scene in which numerous people were present in an open area adjacent to one side of the church. The officers parked their patrol vehicles and deployed quite a distance away from Perez (which is consistent with the previously noted notion of keeping distance from aggressors to avoid a shooting). An officer ordered Perez to drop the knife that he still held in his right hand, and most of the officers drew their service pistols, while at least one officer armed himself with a less-lethal shotgun (a weapon that fires bean bags designed to assist in getting dangerous noncompliant suspects into custody without having to resort to deadly force). After ignoring multiple commands, Perez began walking toward the officers with the knife in his right hand and a folding chair in his left. As Perez continued to approach the officers, the officer who initially ordered Perez to relinquish the knife issued additional verbal commands, and at least one other officer also instructed Perez to drop the knife. After Perez walked past a woman standing near the exterior wall of a portion of the church in question, bean bag rounds were fired at Perez, and he retreated away from the officers. He walked past the woman near the wall, then seized her and placed the knife he was holding to her throat. When he began to slice the woman's throat, three officers—all of whom had moved closer to Perez as he retreated and grabbed the woman—fired their service pistols at him. Perez was killed by police gunfire. Unfortunately, so was the woman whose throat he was cutting.[16]

In this instance, the involved officers worked diligently to take Perez into custody without shooting him. They initially kept their distance, they issued verbal commands, and they employed less-lethal beanbag rounds in an attempt to get him to release the knife and surrender. But their efforts were unsuccessful and actually led to the death of a wholly innocent woman, because the focus on avoiding shooting Perez placed his life above that of the now-deceased female. Had the officers been operating under McCarthy's prioritization framework, they would have immediately recognized that their number one priority was to protect the woman (and the other innocent citizens in the yard) from the threat posed by Perez, and they would have used different tactics to resolve the situation.

Alternative tactics could have entailed, for example, that once Perez walked past the woman, no officers would have fired any beanbag rounds at him until at least one officer had moved into a position past Perez (as shown in the video, there was space to flank Perez to his right) where he or she could protect the woman (and other innocent citizens in the area) should the bean bag rounds lead Perez to do what he did—move back toward the innocents. While doing this would have exposed at least some of the officers to greater danger in the form of being closer to Perez than was the case when the beanbag rounds were first employed, this added threat exposure to the officers is exactly what the prioritization framework calls for—the placing of innocent citizen life above that of the officers. And it would have also increased the degree of threat to Perez, for had Perez continued to advance toward the officers who stayed in their initial positions to a point where he presented a lethal threat to an officer (or officers), he should have been felled by police bullets. This, too, would have been consistent with the prioritization framework, for it would have placed the lives of the officers above that of Perez, the aggressor.

Alternately in my proposed example tactical plan, once the officer(s) assigned to move into a position(s) to protect the innocent citizens were in place and beanbag rounds were fired, had Perez retreated toward the woman (or any other innocent citizen in the area) the officer(s) assigned the protective task should have shot Perez to protect her (and other innocent) life. Again, this would be consistent with the prioritization framework, for it would have placed the life of the woman (and other innocents in the yard) above that of the aggressor, Perez.

As it played out, by focusing their efforts on trying to not shoot Perez instead of focusing on trying to protect the innocent citizens in the area, the officers permitted the situation to spiral out of control and created an exceedingly difficult dilemma. Once Perez grabbed the woman, placed the knife to her neck, and began to cut her, the officers had only two realistic choices: they could either let Perez murder her in front of them, or they could shoot at Perez and run the risk of striking the woman.[17] This is, tragically, precisely what happened.[18] In sum, placing the life of Perez above the lives of the innocent citizens in the area led to the death of one of the innocents.

As this example shows, there are times when the ethical thing to do is to resolve a situation by shooting an aggressor well before it can devolve to the point where innocent citizens' or police officers' lives could be taken. This approach, while explicitly rooted in McCarthy's prioritization framework, is also consistent with the core precepts of other ethical traditions, as well as the criminal laws governing the use of deadly force by police officers that permit police officers to kill people whose actions threaten innocent lives.

Discussion and Conclusion

While the foregoing section ended with the idea that increasing the odds of deadly force being used and using it under certain situations are ethically sound practices, recall that these comments were offered in a context of much ink devoted to the notion that we should seek ways to reduce the number of incidents in which police officers shoot citizens. The previous call for police officers to frame high-risk encounters in ways that lower the odds that they will find themselves in situations that justify shooting should be heeded. The prioritization-of-life framework can serve to remind officers that (1) the lives of suspects are valuable and (2) that deadly force is to be used only when the threat criteria are present. Thus, the prioritization framework and its emphasis that all life is valuable directs officers to generally comport themselves in ways that reduce the likelihood they will need to use deadly force, to use tactics that will increase the likelihood they will need to use deadly force only in the rare circumstance when doing so reduces the risk to innocent life, and to shoot only when it can be reasonably established that an aggressor seeks to seriously harm or kill an innocent and has the means to do so.

As the two case studies presented in this essay demonstrate, things can happen quite quickly in the real world of police work, and officers often don't have much time to chart optimal courses of action and to decide whether deadly force is an appropriate action or if their trigger fingers should remain still. Experience has shown, however, that using the sound tactics that the prioritization framework calls for often leads to the resolution of tense situations with no police shots fired (see, e.g., Klinger 2005 and Sherman 2018). With regard to using McCarthy's criteria to guide deadly force decisions, there is evidence from the SWAT community that officers who are steeped in the prioritization schema rarely shoot suspects, even in hostage situations (Klinger and Rojek 2005, 39). Given this evidence, it would seem reasonable that police administrators and trainers should embrace and train all officers on the prioritization framework as a means to reduce the number of people police officers take under fire without at all increasing the degree of threat to innocent citizens and only marginally increasing the threat that officers may experience. But this suggested course of action won't reduce police shootings to zero, because the job of the police is not to not shoot anyone—it is to protect innocent life. Thus, as long as there are aggressors whose actions threaten to grievously injure or kill innocents, there will be police officers whose duty calls them to shoot.[19]

And because there will always be police shootings, McCarthy's prioritization framework might serve a purpose beyond enhancing the capacity of police officers to protect innocent life when it is threatened on the one hand, and reducing the number of citizens shot by police officers on the other. This potential purpose is to ease the degree of social tension surrounding the use of deadly force by police officers. As noted in the opening of this essay, concerns about police use of firearms are perennial in America but have become heightened in recent years. The widespread adoption of the life-prioritization framework could reduce these tensions and concerns by its aforementioned potential to reduce shootings. If this potential were to be realized, social tensions might be reduced due to fewer shootings, translating into less concern. A second way it could reduce tensions is that it would clearly articulate to the citizenry the ethical platform upon which police tactics and firearms usage rest. Understanding that police place the welfare of law-abiding citizens above both their own welfare and that of suspected criminals, that the police value even the lives of individuals suspected of having committed serious criminal acts, that officers will endeavor to find ways to resolve even the most dangerous situations without gunfire, and that officers will fire their weapons only when other actions cannot be reasonably expected to resolve such dangerous situations, could ease citizens' minds in the wake of instances in which officers do shoot citizens. Finally, the prioritization framework might serve to reduce tensions by allowing police leaders and spokespersons to provide the citizenry with a logically rigorous ethical explanation for why a given police shooting was appropriate (assuming it was appropriate, of course). Instead of merely referring to the legality of a given shooting, those in the law enforcement community tasked with explaining matters in the wake of shootings could also articulate why what occurred was sound police practice—practice that is rooted in the protection of innocent life. And when officer performance in a given incident included deficiencies, police leaders and other spokespersons could explain what these matters were and what the organization will do to address them.

While all of these potential positives are just that—potential—the prioritization-of-life framework does provide a cogent ethical scheme for guiding police officers as they carry out their charge to protect innocent life in the face of the ever-present possibility that they may need to use deadly force to do so. Whether the widespread adoption of McCarthy's ethical framework would have any of the possible downstream consequences posited immediately above, it appears to be a sound idea as a stand-alone proposition, because the broad contours of laws and department policies do not provide a firm enough ethical platform for something as important as the matter of state agents taking the lives of citizens.

NOTES
1. I thank Paige Vaughn for research assistance and Lucy English, Ron McCarthy, Terry Shafer, and Susan Davis for their comments on drafts of this essay.
2. Not all state laws have "stand your ground" provisions akin to the sort contained in this Florida statute, but nearly half do, and all include some form of legal indemnity for citizens who opt to use fatal force to protect innocent life.
3. Some states permit citizens to use deadly force to protect property in some instances. See, e.g., Texas Constitution and Statutes 2019, 9.41–43.
4. The notion of using deadly force to protect against future danger by shooting a particular subset of persons who are attempting to escape apprehension is rooted in *Tennessee v. Garner* (1985), a Supreme Court decision that limited the

capacity of police to shoot fleeing suspects to those suspects for whom the police had probable cause to believe had committed felony-grade crimes that involved the infliction or threatened infliction of serious bodily injury or death.

5. Just what constitutes a life-endangering attack or situation is an important issue, but one that is largely beyond the scope of this essay. For the purposes of this essay, I am assuming that a clear-cut threat exists. But see note 7.
6. The ethics of self-defense literature includes numerous other classifications of sorts of people, such as "Innocent Threats" (Quong 2009, 508), but these would not appear to be germane to policing.
7. It is worth noting here that police officers sometimes make mistakes about whether an actual threat exists. Counted among such situations would be what Fachner and Carter (2015, 3) have dubbed "threat perception failures" (cases where officers mistake objects such as cell phones for firearms), cases where persons armed with empty firearms point them at police officers, and cases where previously threatening persons no longer posed a threat in the moment an officer fires. I will generally ignore such cases in what follows, but see the first case study below for some discussion of the third just-mentioned sort of mistake.
8. Some will place restrictions on officers' authorization to shoot in certain circumstances, such as at or from moving vehicles (see, e.g., Police Executive Research Forum 2016).
9. McCarthy actually has three criteria, the additional one not mentioned above being the initial condition that the suspect in question actually has a hostage. I am ignoring this matter here because in using the terms "hostage" and "hostage taker" in this essay, the initial criterion has been met.
10. In seventy-five of these cases, the unarmed assailant took a police firearm from an officer and killed him or her with it.
11. In addition to the more than one thousand citizens killed by unarmed assailants each year during the two decades ending in 2015 were another two-thousand-plus killed per annum by assailants who cut them with edged weapons or bludgeoned them to death with blunt objects (US Department of Justice, Federal Bureau of Investigation 2000, 2005, 2010, 2015).
12. See Fyfe (1986), Klinger (2005), and Sherman (2018) for discussions of the role that keeping distance—as well as other police tactical practices—can play in reducing the likelihood of police gunfire during interactions with citizens.
13. At some point, some officers may need to enter the basement to check on or otherwise deal with the suicidal subject, but these officers could be members of a highly trained unit equipped with protective shields (for example) and less lethal weapons that *may* be able to avert the use of deadly force.
14. Of course, the suicidal individual could come upstairs and attack the police, in which case they would again be within their rights to shoot him. But in this case, it is not the police who created the need to use deadly force.
15. For a video of this incident, see Los Angeles Police Department (2018).
16. For a video of this incident, see KSBW Action News 8 (2018).

17 Perhaps someone might argue that the officers (or an officer) could have scrambled up to Perez and sought to wrestle the knife from his grasp, but this would have taken some seconds, had no guarantee of being successful, and thus would have increased the risk that Perez would have succeeded in killing the woman. Similarly, using pepper spray (if any officers had it), a Taser, or any other less-lethal device that may have been available would have provided no guarantee of working and would have thus left the woman to Perez's devices.

18 One matter that must be addressed is the discipline of the officers on scene concerning the actual firing of shots. It is entirely possible that had fewer officers fired at Perez as he was assaulting the woman, or had the three officers who did fire taken more careful aim or fired fewer rounds, that the woman would not have been killed by police gunfire. Whatever the case, any gunfire directed at Perez once he attacked the woman would have been a risky proposition for the woman. Thus, while more discipline would have reduced the risk that the woman would have been struck by police bullets, it would not have eliminated that risk.

19 This assumes two things: (1) that there will always be police forces and (2) that police officers will always carry lethal firearms.

BIBLIOGRAPHY

Alexander, Larry. 2016. "Recipe for a Theory of Self-Defense: The Ingredients, and some Cooking Suggestions." In *The Ethics of Self-Defense*, edited by Christian Coons and Michael Weber, 20–50. New York: Oxford University Press.

Bittner, Egon. 1970. *The Functions of the Police in Modern Society*. Chevy Chase, MD: National Institute of Mental Health.

Blumenthal, Ralph. 2015. "Police Killing of Unarmed Man Agitated New York . . . in the 1850s." *New York Times*, April 24, 2015. www.nytimes.com.

Campaign Zero. 2018. www.joincampaignzero.org.

Community Relations Service. 2003. *Principles of Good Policing: Avoiding Violence between Police and Citizens*. Washington, DC: US Department of Justice.

Coons, Christian and Michael Weber. 2016. "The Ethics of Self-Defense: The Current Debate." In *The Ethics of Self-Defense*, edited by Christian Coons and Michael Weber, 1–19. New York: Oxford University Press.

Fabre, Cécile. 2007. "Mandatory Rescue Killings." *Journal of Political Philosophy* 15 (4): 363–84.

Fachner, George and Steven Carter. 2015. *Collaborative Reform Initiative. An Assessment of Deadly Force in the Philadelphia Police Department*. Washington, DC: Community Oriented Policing Services, US Department of Justice.

Fatal Encounters. 2018. www.fatalencounters.org.

Florida Legislature. 2019. The 2019 Florida Statutes. www.leg.state.fl.us/statutes.

Fyfe, James J. 1986. "The Split-Second Syndrome and other Determinants of Police Violence." In *Violent Transactions: The Limits of Personality*, edited by Anne Campbell and John J. Gibbs, 207–23. Oxford: Blackwell.

Hayes, Louis. 2014. *The Priority of Life: Problems with Oversimplification*. www.theillinoismodel.com.

Illinois General Assembly. 2019. Illinois Compiled Statutes. www.ilga.gov.

Klinger, David. 2004. *Into the Kill Zone: A Cop's Eye View of Deadly Force*. San Francisco: Jossey-Bass.

Klinger, David A. 2005. "Social Theory and the Street Cop: The Case of Deadly Force." *Ideas in American Policing*, Essay 7. www.policefoundation.org.

Klinger, David A., and Jeff Rojek. 2005. *A Multi-Method Study of Police Special Weapons and Tactics Teams*. Final report to National Institute of Justice. Washington, DC: US Department of Justice.

Klinger, David A., Richard Rosenfeld, Daniel Isom, and Michael Deckard. 2016. "Race, Crime, and the Micro Ecology of Deadly Force." *Criminology and Public Policy* 15 (1): 193–22.

Klinger, David A., and Lee Ann Slocum. 2017. "Critical Assessment of an Analysis of a Journalistic Compendium of Citizens Killed by Police Gunfire." *Criminology and Public Policy* 16 (1): 349–62.

KSBW Action News 8. 2018. "Body Camera: LA Police Fatally Shoot Hostage, Armed Man." YouTube, July 31, 2018. https://youtu.be/BGxA1y1TjgM.

Los Angeles Police Department. 2018. "Mission Area Officer Involved Shooting 7/27/18 (NRF047-18)." YouTube, September 10, 2018. https://youtu.be/-Ny7dBpqdOc.

McCarthy, Ron. 1989. "The Command Decision to Shoot a Hostage Taker: How Do We Make It?" *Tactical Edge*. Winter 1989, 10–13.

Missouri Revisor of Statutes. 2019. Missouri Revised Statutes. www.revisor.mo.gov.

Pickering, Jordan C., and David A. Klinger. 2016. "Enhancing Police Legitimacy by Promoting Safety Culture." In *The Politics of Policing: Between Force and Legitimacy*, edited by Mathieu Deflem, 21–39. Bingley: Emerald.

Police Executive Research Forum. 2016. *Guiding Principles on the Use of Force*. Washington, DC.

President's Task Force on 21st Century Policing. 2015. *Final Report*. Washington, DC: US Department of Justice.

Quong, Jonathan. 2009. "Killing in Self-Defense." *Ethics* 119 (3): 507–37.

Ranalli, Mike. 2016. "Priority of Life: Building a Better Model for PERF's First Guiding Principle." Lexipol Blog, June 8, 2016. www.lexipol.com.

Sherman, Lawrence W. 2018. "Reducing Fatal Police Shootings as System Crashes: Research, Theory, and Practice." *Annual Review of Criminology* 1: 421–49.

Tennessee v. Garner. 1985. 471 US 1.

Terrill, William, Eugene A. Paoline, and Jason Ingram. 2012. *Final Technical Report Draft: Assessing Police Use of Force Policy and Outcomes*. Washington, DC: US Department of Justice.

Texas Constitution and Statutes. 2019. Penal Code. https://statutes.capitol.texas.gov.

US Department of Justice, Federal Bureau of Investigation. 2000, 2005, 2010, 2015. Uniform Crime Reporting (UCR) Statistics Data Tool. https://ucrdatatool.gov.

US Department of Justice, Federal Bureau of Investigation. 2017. Uniform Crime Reports. Law Enforcement Officers Killed and Assaulted. https://ucr.fbi.gov.
Washington Post. 2018. *2018 Police Shooting Database*. www.washingtonpost.com.
Weber, Max. 1958. *From Max Weber*. Translated and edited by Hans Heinrich Gerth and C. Wright Mills. New York: Oxford.
Zimring, Franklin. 2017. *When Police Kill*. Cambridge: Harvard University Press.

PART III

Race, Bias, and Resistance

7

Policing Narratives in the Black Counterpublic

VESLA WEAVER

In Newark, New Jersey, a young American testified to a perfect stranger. He gripped a wrinkled paper bag in one hand with six large black numbers on it. That bag contained the items that he had on his person as his government put him into a cell at the Essex County jail. He was on his way home that day. "We're being locked up and held at a ransom," he said:

> I call that a ransom, not a bail because this is a system that's created for the rich to get richer, you understand what I'm saying? We're not the rich. . . . I feel as though that system is created, why? To generate more money for, for commissaries, for my family to spend more money on commissary food and other families for other inmates who are in there. . . . I have a four-year-old son. I don't wish to spend my money on commissaries. I don't wish [to pay] lawyer's fees, and court fees, and pawns, and things like that. No, I want to give this money to my son. You know, the summertime is coming, my son loves nature, so you know, what I thought about while I was in the cell was doing more things that involve nature with him. Taking him to the zoo. Taking him to the park. Taking him to the beach . . . that's where I wish to, to put my money at, not back into this, into this injustice system.

909 miles away in a park in Milwaukee stood another man, twenty years his senior. But distance was no matter. That man stood right in front of him with the illusion of being in the same room, connected by a digital wormhole. He responded with assurance: "Yo, your voice is supported, bro," and explained a desire that prosecutors walk a day in their shoes since they "don't know what it's like to live on the other side, and they in charge of our fate." While a stranger, he was not unknown

Figure 7.1. Example of a Portal.

to the young man. His story was one that pulled on a cord, woven from intergenerational memory.

They each stood inside a chamber like the one shown here, one that we had repurposed from a container to ship goods into a container of ideas, meant to ship our thoughts. The space inside is not unlike the young man's cell in the county jail or the many millions of cells in America's prisons, jails, juvenile detention, and pre-release centers. But instead of isolation from others, instead of confinement, this dark room was designed to liberate, connect, and amplify the testimony of America's "fourth largest city"—wards of the state (Larson 2013).

We call it a Portal.

After the pair of men left the gold chamber, a young woman entered. She spoke to a mother, this time in Chicago. And over the course of the next year and a half, two thousand others told stories, took in one another's accounts, and shared freedom dreams inside these virtual front porches.

Tracey L. Meares, Gwen Prowse, and I paired up with artist and tech entrepreneur Amar Bakshi, who had designed this gold experiment in his backyard, to locate Portals in eleven neighborhoods in five cities across the US and one in Mexico City. With the help of curators, we amassed a rich archive of narrative experiences between people who would not otherwise encounter each other. We were unaccustomed to listening at this scale. But we suspected that harnessing technology could help to build a counter-infrastructure to a media that so often compounds group stigma, and create connected political spaces out of disconnection. Our Portals collaboration began from a radical partnering of immersive technology and public art with research. We sensed the power of this combination to utterly transform both *what we know* and *how we go about knowing it*.

Their testimonies come during a time: when 21 percent of the Black population in our nation's largest city was being stopped by police; when the racial gulf in prison admissions was so vast that the Bureau stopped tabulating figures like this (Figure 7.2). When footage of Black men being felled by police set off a Black Spring that swept the US and ignited Black and Brown communities to rehearse their ancestors' pleas to "Say Her Name," and shouts of "Black Lives Matter," and "No Justice, No Peace." To which they were told to dismantle their rage and stop coming undone. To show personal responsibility. That when we protested violence by police, it was we who were violent. During a time when American government infused incredible funds into the criminal justice system, monies that would continue to soak up the resources that would have actually improved the lives of poor communities.

How are people like the young person in Newark and his older interlocutor governed? How do race–class subjugated Americans charac-

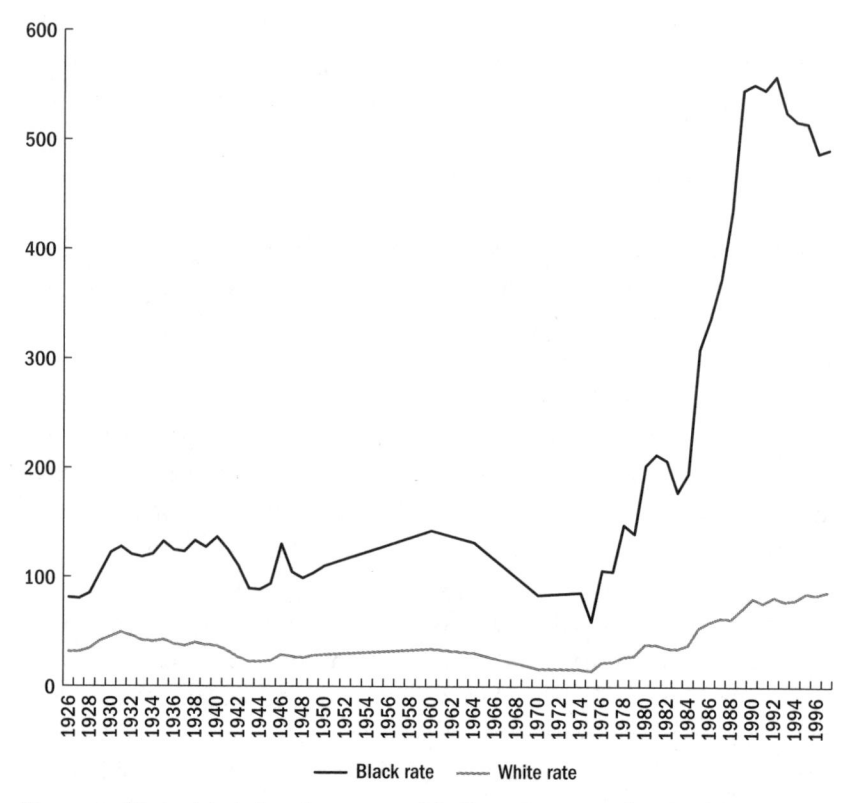

Figure 7.2. Prison Admissions (per 100,000) by Race. Source: analysis by the author of data from Historical Statistics of the United States (Carter et al. 2006, Table Aa110-124).

terize both the nature of their citizenship and logic of the state? What discourses and ideologies do they draw on to make sense of their interactions with street-level bureaucrats? How do they innovate in response to community criminalization and predatory police practices? How do they imagine liberation? And most importantly, how does their collective wisdom redefine traditional conceptions of American democracy?

We don't know. I work in a field that studies state power, citizenship, governance, and democracy—political science, that is—and we have few theories to offer or concepts to help us answer these questions. A field framed by images of representative democracy and T. H. Marshall's conception of citizenship (Soss and Weaver 2017). Where debates about what drives people's preferences and interests dominate, taking nondomination by the state as a baseline assumption. A field that is ever more concerned about the rise of inequality but seems to forget that inequality isn't just about what resources you command or not but about how the government *treats* you. A field that has mostly and unreflexively relied on a single method to understand the perceptions of the people. We don't know the answer to these questions because as social scientists we have relegated people—who the state has visited its most incredible use of state power to confine and kill—"to a class to which we do not listen" (Larson 2013, 7).

Over the past few years—maybe decades—we have learned next to nothing about the political lives of highly policed communities from orthodox methods like social surveys. This is in part because those surveys asked the wrong questions, in part because survey research rarely went into these communities or sampled in prisons and jails and halfway houses and prerelease centers (Pettit 2012), and in part because asking someone whether they strongly agree, somewhat agree, or neither agree nor disagree with this or that practice does little to shed light on the actual lived experience of the state and government authority in these places. Such methods shrink our view of policing to appreciations of whether something is more likely or less likely, controlling for such and such factor, rather than the keen political vocabularies and ideologies emerging from communities that see the police as a "legalized gang."

And yet the words of American writer James Baldwin (1966) come to mind when he spoke of policing in Harlem and so many other Black communities a half century ago, saying they were "forbidden the very air."

I study one of the largest transformations in the relationship between the American government and American citizens in the post-civil rights era. Carceral state encounters have affected the health of American democracy by creating custodial citizenship (Lerman and Weaver 2014). Criminal justice interventions structure how people engage with the state; as such, they are politically socializing experiences. Several studies have documented that criminal justice encounters have a chilling effect on political engagement, setting off political withdrawal (Burch 2013; Lerman and Weaver 2014; White 2019; c.f. Walker 2014).

In this essay, I will discuss discourses from the most extensive collection to date of first-hand accounts of the police by those who are policed. My argument is both methodological and substantive.

Methodologically, I argue that amid big data and ever more sophisticated tools of splicing it, a people's history offers the most complex accounting of the American policing regime in our time. The people are the most credible reporters we have, singular in their authority to describe modern policing to us. Their political knowledge runs deep: they know what is going on long before consent decrees, journalistic exposés, and police video footage—because they live it daily. And they are a crucial counter-narrative to statistical knowledge, media reports, and official representations. To take just one blatant example, the city I currently call home—Baltimore—reported *zero* police stops last year in Maryland's police records database.[1]

Imagine if we wanted to understand apartheid, the Holocaust, the Soviet gulag, or other state projects of control and violence only through statistics, and discounted the diary of Anne Frank, the Freedman's Bureau's interviews of newly freed slaves, the first Black prison memoir by Austin Reed in 1959, the oral histories of southern Blacks who lived under Jim Crow during the 1930s and '40s, and other firsthand witness as mere stories, secondary to statistical inquiry?

But not just that. A listening method enables substantive revelations and breakthroughs. Substantively, I argue that we mis-specify the structure and experience of the American state. If we want to theorize governance in America and beyond, racial capitalism, and citizenship, we need to understand the experience and critiques of democracy from below, how they judge how responsive authorities are, how they imagine freedom. As Joe Soss and I have argued, "if one's aim is to understand state powers to govern citizens, regulate their behaviors, revoke their freedoms, redefine their civic standing, and impose violence on them," we need to abandon scholars' preoccupation with imagining government as only a system that registers preferences and distributes uplifting material benefits, and hear their analysis of the "second face of the state," including practices of discipline, surveillance, regulation, predation, and punishment that are regularly found in race–class subjugated communities (Soss and Weaver 2017, 574).

In this essay, I describe currents that emerged from the collective narratives that challenge existing liberal-democratic framings of political life. First, I discuss what I call the state's baptism of youth and the adjacent expression of motherhood as a contested authority.[2] Second, and more broadly, I observe the ways that Portals participants characterize their relationship to government as one marked by an arrangement of distorted responsiveness.[3] Third, I show that they see policing as a mechanism (and not an outcome) where the logic that motivates the state's orientation to its citizens is to generate revenue by positioning their communities as profit sources and to keep Blacks corralled. Fourth, I find that they inhabit two distinct constitutions—the formal dictates on the book and the real rules they needed to know to stay alive. In contrast to prevailing wisdom about uninformed electorates, then, these citizens have too much knowledge of and too little power vis-à-vis state representatives.[4]

The Portals project takes the radical step of giving witness without mere spectatorship. In doing so, we depart from the academy's insistence that we only rely on statistical portrayals created by those in the *free world* to represent the ideas and experiences of those in the *unfree world* (Larson 2013). We test whether our conceptions of democratic life can withstand the glare when held up to the light of race–class subjugated communities' experience. There is an ethical obligation in formally democratic societies that contain antidemocratic institutions to heed the experiences of the state from below. Not doing so limits our understanding of both policing and American democracy.

Portals

Let me explain how Portals work since this method is unlike pretty much anything social scientists have used to date. Gold shipping containers with immersive audiovisual technology are placed in areas with high foot traffic and with community partners who see it as a benefit.

When a person comes inside, they are connected by life-size video to another person they don't know in a paired city. We ask nothing else of them but to tell us briefly about themselves and their policing interactions. Then, each participant engages in an approximately 20-minute unscripted conversation with the unknown person. Their conversation is not moderated by a researcher. Instead, Portal participants are prompted to discuss how they feel about police and their experiences with them. In practice, they can discuss whatever they like and conversations often range from thoughts on national events and the Trump presidency, local conditions and gentrification, to the more mundane small talk about the weather or the latest album. After they leave, they jot down thoughts in the Gold Book. Each of the Portals dialogues is video-recorded and transcribed. I draw on eight hundred of these conversations.

A key player is the curator, who holds events and works with other curators in the network to have formal events, cross-city discussion, and playful collaborations designed by the community and for its benefit. The Portal is a space for art and performance, a gathering spot for kids, an arena for global chess tournaments, poetry slams, town halls, and other endeavors.

Bakshi had already built a vast Portal network in fifteen countries. Conversations were taking place all over the world from Erbil, Iraq; Herat, Afghanistan; Berlin, Germany; Mumbai, India; Seoul, South Korea; and many other global cities. He had them in refugee camps, college campuses, at NGOs, and in museums.

We located Portals in communities experiencing police interventions—almost half of participants had been stopped by police over seven times and a large share had been stopped in the last week or month—but they captured a broad part of America. They stretch across distinct policing regimes—from one reformist regime after high-profile scandals (Los Angeles) to one in the midst of oversight by the federal government (Baltimore) after it planted toy guns on residents and severed the spinal cord of a local teen to one whose police force is predominantly White policing a predominantly Black community (Milwaukee).

Within cities, we moved the Portal to different neighborhoods with very different local histories, police presences, and social relations. For example, a Portal could be eliciting conversations between an upwardly mobile working-class Latino student population at California State University, Dominguez Hills, founded after the Watts riot and the Amani neighborhood in Milwaukee, one of the country's most impoverished and distressed neighborhoods (with a poverty rate of 48 percent) in a city that is the most racially segregated in the nation. The 53206 zip code where the Amani neighborhood is located has the highest share of incarcerated Black men in America; by age 30–34, only 38 percent of them have *not* spent time in a correctional facility. Another Portal sat in an equally impoverished site that contained another important source of variation—it is politically activated, founded in opposition to police torture at the infamous Homan Square "black site" in Chicago. Portals also capture differences not just in city spaces, but in the same neighborhood over time. For example, we observe communal dialogues and oppositional frameworks in Milwaukee before, in the midst of, and just after the uprising surrounding the police killing of Sylville Smith in August of 2016.

Around a single Portal, there is also dynamism. A Portal will draw in second-generation immigrants, former gang members, budding activists, college students, working-class people on their daily commute, sex workers, and police officers, as well as ex-inmates on ankle monitors. Sites encompassed a bus stop, an open-air drug market, a housing project or halfway house, a homeless encampment, a law library, a community market, and a workers' co-op.

And the dyadic nature of the Portals involves yet another source of variation—that of the participant pairings themselves, which span generations, race and class position, and gender. Conversations between Chicago and Los Angeles, for example, could be between two young Latinas, between a working-class Black man and a retiree, or a number of other combinations.

My approach here is not one of hypothesis testing but is, rather, interpretive, seeking to locate what Cathy Cohen (1999) has called an oppositional ideology—the frameworks that marginal groups use to understand the political world, contest dominant ideologies, and interpret their positioning. So, instead of asking whether people think police are fair or whether they trust police all the time, sometimes, or never—what a survey might ask—we ask how they "define the limits of the permissible" of police and residents (Dawson 2001). Instead of asking whether a police encounter *causes* a particular attitude or behavior—as those analyzing surveys might do, with some difficulty—we instead listen to hear their "causal story" of state action in their communities. Instead of trying to measure mere mentions of topics, or distributions of antipolice attitudes, we seek to explore *how people reason through their experiences*, the ways they frame and don't frame problems with the threat of violence and lack of security. By doing this, we can locate the various strands of political discourse structured by personal and communal experience with the state.

Age of First Police Stop Among Those Stopped by Police

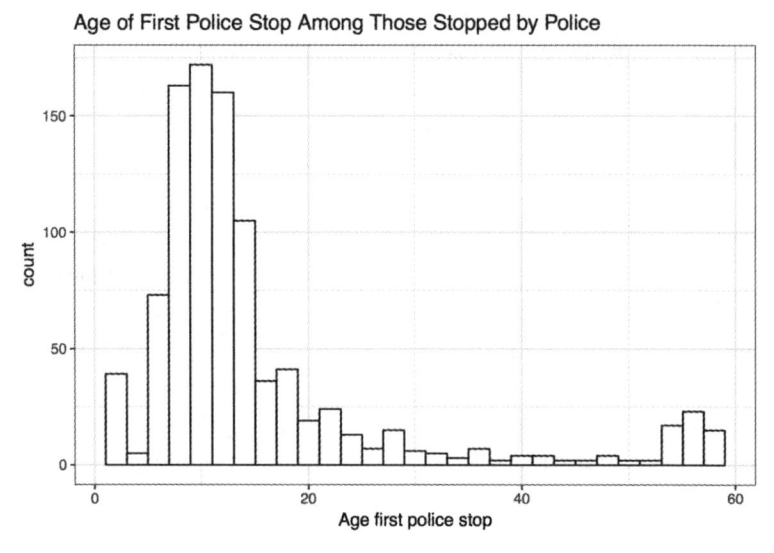

Figure 7.3. Age of First Reported Police Encounter among Portals Participants. Source: Weaver, Meares, and Prowse (n.d.).

I offer four arguments here that derive from the discursive patterns in Portals conversations: state baptism, distorted responsiveness, policing as constructive, and subjugated knowledge. The following sections explain each of these findings.

State Baptism

Policing, in America at least, is a childhood intervention. When we think of police practices, we should conjure up an image of a 12-year-old or an 8-year-old. Figure 7.3 documents the age distribution of those in our study who had been first stopped by police. Most were under 14. And the "dosage" of contact was strong: of those who were stopped before adulthood, many reported being stopped over seven times.

This is consistent with other studies. One of the largest studies of American children born in twenty US cities in the late 1990s and followed to their fifteenth birthday documented that 45 percent of Black boys reported being stopped by police by this young age (compared to

23 percent of all kids) (Geller 2017). The average age of their first police encounter was between twelve and thirteen years old. The findings of a divergent experience for Black and White youth remained robust after controls for family background and other circumstances.

I call these early encounters a *state baptism*. They are not simply early memories the way some would recall a first dance, bar mitzvah, or even first loss of a loved one. The emotional force of youths' first experiences of the police baptizes them, supplying a visceral memory of the state's potential for violence, the humiliation of being spread-eagle up against the hood of a police car for onlookers to see, and more broadly, of learning one's place in the political and racial order. This memory may confirm communal experiences, the state's taking of innocence and conferring of status.

Many of the dialogues began with childhood memories:

I've been having problems with them since I was 12. I've . . . I will remember this day because it was my first police interaction. They ran past us and the police just came and just grabbed up me and my cousin. We like, we not with them. We don't even know them . . . And I remember this officer. He was Officer [name removed], yep that was his name, Officer [name removed]. He a real big dude, like, I was scared as shit. I was twelve years old. I thought I was gon' die. [18-year-old Black woman in Milwaukee]

At a young age, like twelve years old, I, I experienced the police, they come in, into my house, they lookin' for one person but still they feel the need to put a gun to the head of a twelve-year-old, and I'm, that's my first time seeing a gun, and it's like, wow, this is what I'm exposed to, like just predetermined by who knows what, but not me being a young person. 'Cause, I just, I just hit nineteen, I just finished high school, and I'm, I'm tryin' my best to be a positive influence on my, my community and really do something big. [19-year-old Black man in Milwaukee]

When I was about 14 and 13, I always been a full-figured girl. The police would stop me when I was walking outside with my friends at night, "Are you a prostitute?" Ask me questions like that. I'm a 13-year-old girl at the time. [18-year-old Black woman in Milwaukee]

> When I first got locked up man, and put in a jail cell, I was eight years old. I was, I was in second grade. And after that bro I was like 10, 11, 12, 13, each one of those years the police called me. . . . They used to pick me up and drop me off on the other side of the motherfucking tracks. [59-year-old Black man in Chicago]

But we've known that policing is a childhood intervention for some time. In his widely cited 1993 article, Lawrence Sherman describes how young minority males were heavily exposed to "police disrespect and brutality, both vicariously and in person, *prior* to their peak years of first arrest and initial involvements in crime" (464). We might have recognized it given the early longitudinal cohort studies, in which one-third of those in the 1979 cohort stopped by police were stopped at age fifteen or younger, before the rise of broken windows policing (Bureau of Labor Statistics 2014). And it's been in plain view in virtually every national riot commission—that found that the cities that went up in flames revolted because of police violence *toward a Black kid*. It was thus fitting that Childish Gambino's recent viral video of his "This is America" featured police violence in the backdrop of Black kids dancing in school uniforms.

The violence of those early encounters is not just a momentary disruption. The legal scholar Devon Carbado (2005), drawing on his own experience, calls it a "racial naturalization." More concretely, sociologist Amanda Geller has found high levels of PTSD among children who have police encounters, which remain even after controlling for factors that select people into police contact in the first place (Geller 2017). In another study, children who lived in a high-policing zone had their test scores drop (Legewie and Fagan 2019). And we are beginning to find out that stops themselves are criminogenic: a recent study of policing in New York City found that boys who were stopped and had *not* broken the law were much more likely to later commit a crime (Del Toro et al. 2019). Police stops—instead of targeting crime-prone youth—create their own self-fulfilling prophecy.

Why are Black and Brown kids having their first encounters with government this way? Perhaps it is because police evaluate Black boys as older—four years older in fact, than they actually are, according to a study by Philip Goff and colleagues (2014). Indeed, that study confirmed that they are only seen as innocent until about age 10. The state may also be commandeering oversight normally entrusted to parents. I once sat next to a renowned criminal justice expert who told me confidently that we policed Black communities more heavily than White ones even though drug offending was similar in both places because "we can't trust the parents to handle those kids."

Portals participants who were women often spoke of how the boundaries of maternal authority were encroached on by police. They recounted their labors to keep their children safe, wishing they wouldn't age or grow tall too soon. The possibility of state violence or targeting of their children surrounded them. Motherhood was a contested authority.

> WOMAN 1: Anyway, the police have stopped my son twice coming from the train.
> WOMAN 2: Why?
> WOMAN 1: Because he was walking too fast. Yeah, that was recently. That pisses me off. I'm like, "what the hell? You supposed to walk slow, dragging?" I don't allow him to wear his pants down and none of that. . . . I cannot let the police dictate to me how to control my household. I cannot let the police dictate to me how to raise my kids. . . . Now they want to tell us we can't put our kids outside. . . . It's too much.

Another exchange between two mothers analogizes the police as usurping a father's role, to which her conversation partner elaborates that the state's "fatherly" support is distorted—quick to do harm for a stolen car but not big enough to secure them in the face of violence:

> WOMAN 3: You can't even raise your children properly, you know, with someone else [the police] trying to be their dad. I mean, you're not even a part of my family. How are you, how are you providing for me? It's as if they're giving us family support.
> WOMAN 4: How are you even being supported? I can't even get you to come to my neighborhood if somebody gets shot. . . . But for our stolen car, you can. You can do seventy and eighty down a one-way street and all these children playing on it.

Distorted Responsiveness

My second argument is different. It concerns the nature of government responsiveness. Democracy is predicated on political equality, on the notion of an "equal distance of all citizens to government." The democratic ideal, as Robert Dahl enunciated, was for "continued responsiveness of the government to the preferences of its citizens, considered as political equals" (Dahl 1971, 1). The state must give equal weight to all citizens' views. Political scientists have been keen to document how rising inequality has translated into a government skewed to the rich (Bartels 2016; Gilens 2012; Hacker and Pierson 2010), where the preferences of the poor and middle class rarely get translated into policy outcomes. This represents a decided step toward oligarchy (Winters and Page 2009). You can hardly round a corner in our discipline without coming across permutations of that argument. "Inequality is a threat to democracy" goes the refrain in a chorus of studies.

But a more basic reading of state responsiveness goes beyond the link between public preferences and policy. It's the idea that when citizens need and summon government action from frontline bureaucrats in their neighborhoods, they are responded to, and that when they step onto the sidewalk to go to church, work, or school, they claim noninterference from governing authorities.

Scholars of American political development have done better to recognize that the state is more than whether it registers preferences or not. They tell us that the American state is submerged, delegated, fragmented, private, delegated, and—most of all—weak (Mettler 2011; Hacker 2002; Morgan and Campbell 2011). The state is generally beneficent, if aloof. This is mostly right if race–class subjugated communities are outside your field of vision (Soss and Weaver 2017). It pretty well describes White Americans' experience of government, or as one scholar puts it: "In fact, the mark of middle-class living is a reduced contact with the public sector" (Fernandez-Kelly 2015, 115). This highly salutary view of the American state comes under strain once we look to the bottom, where involvement with government is not the unalloyed good supposed by liberal framings (Soss and Weaver 2017).

These questions about the health of American democracy have focused on its responsiveness to preferences and portrayed the state as distant and submerged. They have overlooked that the state has increasingly turned to, deepened its commitment to, and expanded its "second face"—coercion, containment, surveillance, regulation, predation, and discipline. High levels of state control exist alongside formal political freedom in the US—a duality Rousseau famously described as "being born free but everywhere in chains."

One of the most common narrative themes in Portals conversations is what we call *distorted responsiveness*. Instead of responsive government agents, people experienced state authorities as both everywhere and nowhere. Police authority was most energetic where it didn't matter for their lives—busting people for selling loose squares or hounding them for other minor transgressions—but withholding and out of reach when they were "steady dyin.'" Aggressive patrolling was yoked with ambivalence. This meant participants saw the police as both useless *and* harmful and saw themselves as vulnerable to the state on both flanks—to abandonment ("they give you time to die") and aggressive intervention ("Police get out they body with it.").

Not being heard, not being cared for when you are a victim, not being taken seriously is a form of nonresponsiveness and disregard by the state. It is painful in its own right. But being treated harshly *in the company of perceived abandonment* is what distorted responsiveness refers to.

These contradictory framings of the police occurred in the same breath, two sides to the same coin. A few examples will reveal its logic:

> Now with that being said, when they don't have nothing else to do, they'll go to certain neighborhoods and just pick at you. You know what I'm saying? Now when you really are needed in that neighborhood, they might have never come. But if you go like places, like crimes being committed or have been committed in Beverly Hills, Bel-Air, Brentwood, uh West Hollywood, uh anywhere in the western part of LA. Something happen there, they immediately are there and the reason for that, is because those neighborhoods is a very rich, you know what I'm saying? And it caters to the rich. A poor man wouldn't have a chance concerning the law in LA. You know what I'm saying? [21-year-old Latino, Los Angeles]

> [T]he police where I live at, they just take a long time to get there. Like, you can call them for anything. It don't matter what it is. And they be

talking like, like they don't got enough force out here to come and help you when you really need them. But they be harassing people who ain't got nothing. Absolutely nothing. Yeah, they do shit when they ready to do it. When it's beneficial to them. They really don't give a fuck about how you is. [31-year-old Black woman, Milwaukee]

I really don't like the police. Like, they don't respond fast enough when you really need them. They rude as ever, they stop you for no apparent reason at all. Like, they just. . . . I feel like they do too much. . . . Your mission is to serve and protect, but we see you as threats now. Me and my son, we scared to walk down the street. We go home, we shut all the doors, let all the blinds down. We go to bed. [18-year-old Black woman, Milwaukee]

That's like when you a child, your dad tell you, son, I got your back. Anything happen to you, son, I'm here. But instead your father is the one that's abusing you and beating you. Why is you protecting me? You the one harming me. You know what I'm saying? It's the same way with the police and the higher authority here, you know. And we go through this every day. I just got pulled over by the police last week. Not even three to four days ago. . . . Man, I got a good driving license. I'm a high school graduate. I'm not a felon, you know what I'm saying. I don't smoke, but you still wanna search my car and, and, and harass me like I murdered someone, you know. So. Yeah, bro. [Black man, Baltimore]

With these accounts in view, it seems awkward to theorize unequal democracy as just about one's preferences not being heard by officials or political exclusion—as my political science colleagues would have it; rather, we consistently observe the dual position of being not heard and crushed on a lark.

We tend to think people want greater connection to government—troves of theses in academia have been penned on how to make the connection tighter, how to bring government more fully into the lives of citizens, and citizens' voices more fully into the halls of power. But when we listen to the lived experience depicted in Portals conversations, a theory of the logic of the state and governance that is altogether different emerges. Government authorities were vigilant, penetrating, and "Johnny-on-the-spot" for slip-ups but oblivious, reticent, and unheeding to their victimization and pain.

Their government did too little *and* too much—which meant they saw it as both an obstacle and an adversary. It was neither a public good that could be had in times of duress nor an appropriately accountable representative of the state in its capacity to surveil, maim, and even kill. The furthest thing from their minds was a tighter connection to it.

They were suspended between being stateless *and* stateful. "Police didn't defend us but put the hurt on us," the logic went. Portals participants reasoned that police didn't view them as principals that could direct government action, but as subjects. Aggressive intervention alongside a state that was out of reach at other times is a lived reality that springs from disregard. People who are easy to abandon are also easy to target. But distorted responsiveness was also designed by policy, supported by legal institutions, and grounded in a theoretical justification.

On the heels of one of our nation's biggest challenges to police power during the resistance of the 1960s, a few pages by two academics in an American literary magazine— Wilson and Kelling's (1982) "Broken Windows" in the *Atlantic Monthly*—would utterly transform the logic of policing in our nation and more importantly warrant a vast expansion of state authority into race–class subjugated communities. Under the broken windows theory, policing pivoted sharply toward minor violations of order, targeting not serious threats to public safety but rather seeking out the possibility of crime by enforcing codes against disordered people and places (Camp and Hetherton 2016). As a result, high-volume stops, petty arrests, and profligate citations for misdemeanors were weakly correlated with crime but showed a strong connection to race, poverty, and place.

Policing also had a friend in our nation's highest court through its landmark policing cases, which have encouraged police stops of citizens based on the thinnest of reasons—reasons that can include "furtive movements," "they just didn't look right to me at the time," or simply "being in a high crime area." It was also bolstered by the hundreds of civil ordinances that invite police to make contact with Americans for virtually any or no reason at all, based on the criminalization of ordinary behaviors. Michael Brown of Ferguson in 2014 was violating a "manner of walking" law, a law making a crime out of gait.

> In due course, police training manuals began to take advantage of this new discretion. One read: "1) Develop suspicion (or, typically, merely

curiosity) about a driver; 2) Discover a legal justification to stop the driver (typically this justification is some minor violation of the traffic laws or vehicle code), and make the stop; 3) Decide, after making the stop, whether to seek to search the vehicle based on the close observation of the vehicle . . . 7) Seek 'bonus benefits' (forfeiture of vehicles, cash, etc.; information about additional criminal offenses)" (quoted in Epp, Maynard-Moody, and Haider-Markel 2014, 36–37).

But on the other side of this expanded discretion is a collapsing of citizen rights to claim police protection (Kennedy 1998). In ruling on a case when police ignored calls for hours from a woman that her spouse had kidnapped her children, who ultimately died, the court ruled in *Town of Castle Rock v. Gonzales* (2005) that not responding to calls for help does not violate the due process clause. Reports have documented that calls to police from these communities took much longer to generate a police response (ACLU Illinois 2014).

Distorted responsiveness has echoes elsewhere. In writing of the twinned "abuse of legal power and the withholding of laws to protect Blacks," Wendy Brown-Scott (1994) has called this "state lawlessness." The political scientist Lisa Miller (2015) describes Blacks as living in a "failed state." More recently, the sociologist Monica Bell (2017, 2057) has theorized it as "legal estrangement," describing race–class subjugated communities as "essentially stateless, unprotected by the law and its enforcers." And long before her, James Baldwin (1964) bluntly concluded that the police "certainly do not protect the lives or property of Negroes."

"Stateless" implies the absence of the state. Instead, I think it is more akin to the term political scientist Robert Mickey (2015) uses, "authoritarian enclaves"—areas within a federal polity that are marked by the absence of free assembly, association, and speech, along with extensive state violence.

Distorted responsiveness as an institutional arrangement (with the broken windows theory of policing as its rationale) has had a result that few have noticed. The wide berth given to police to ask people where they were going and to make contact began to register in a rising share of Americans who were innocent having encounters with the justice system. Criminal justice scholars have well documented rising exposure to criminal justice interventions of all sorts in the US. Terms like "mass incarceration," once a provocative and disputed notion, are now *de rigueur* and books with titles like *Misdemeanorland* have emerged to describe the extensiveness of this face of the state in citizens' lives (Kohler-Hausmann 2018).

But what actually happened over time was not just an *expansion* of exposure to the state's coercive apparatus, but a *decoupling*. Imagine a 2 x 2 typology. On one side is having run afoul of the law by committing an offense and the other is having involuntary contact with police. One would want most Americans to fall in the yes–yes or no–no quadrants (yes I offended and yes I was arrested or, conversely, no I have not committed a crime and no I have never been arrested). We examined a representative longitudinal survey of youth and found that exposure to arrest is now conditioned less on patterns of behavior than it had been in prior generations (Weaver, Papachristos, and Zanger-Tishler 2019). In other words, in 1979, young Americans were mostly in the "correct" quadrants; by 1997, they were not. Our system slipped from one where criminal justice involvement was a relatively good proxy for offending to one where a bigger share of Americans fell in the yes-arrest, no-crime quadrant. And this transformation in the relationship between crime and criminal justice contact changed dramatically in just one generation. Figure 7.4 shows predicted probabilities of arrest at different levels of criminal offending for two generational cohorts on either side of the rise of broken windows policing. For example, committing few to no crimes, one had close to a zero probability of arrest in 1979; in 2002, one had a 20-percent probability of arrest. This relationship also became racially inflected over time—Blacks had a much higher probability of arrest than both Blacks of generations prior and Whites of the same generation.

Think about that for a second: my child has a much higher risk of arrest than I did because he is a Black male. And my child has an even higher risk than his own father, who is also a Black male, just by dint of when he happened to be born.

Policing as Constructive

Academic and legal scholarship has mostly taken as its starting point that policing is an *outcome to be explained* or merely described, asking what predicts police violence, what share of police encounters are

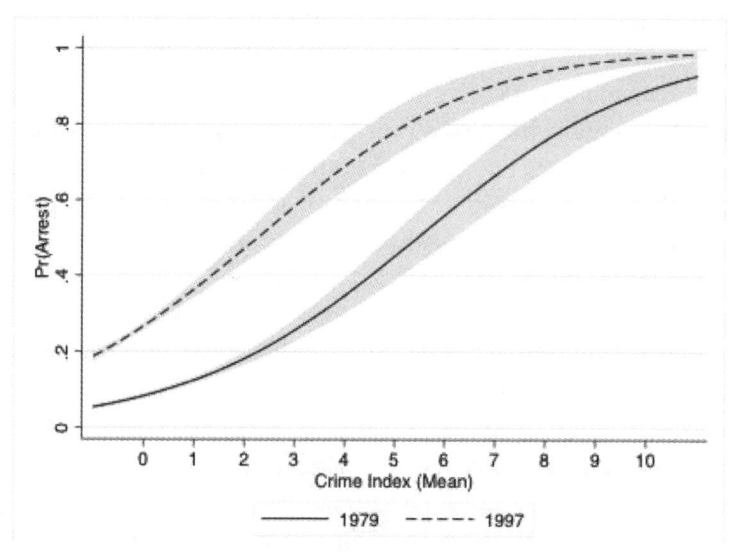

Figure 7.4. Predicted Probability of Reported Arrests, by Self-reported Offending 1979 Cohort and 1997 Cohort. Source: Weaver, Papachristos, and Zanger-Tishler (2019). Reprinted with permission of the Russell Sage Foundation, 112 East 64th Street, New York, NY 10065.

unconstitutional, how police stops correlate with social context, and so on. These are important, to be sure, and a natural starting point given that some of these academic disciplines are more focused on interpersonal violence than state violence, more on social relations than state/citizen relations, and more attuned to bureaucratic procedure than state power. But by positioning policing as an *outcome*, we deny its ability to be a crucial *input* into political life, racial order, and lived citizenship.

Portals testimonies demand that we also conceive of *policing as a mechanism*.[5] The stated function of policing is to control crime and ensure the safety of the public. But most Portals participants saw it as a means to achieve something else. Their narratives conceive of police as loyal foot soldiers of a racialized state, gentrification projects, capitalism, keeping them poor and others rich, and as central to the reproduction of violence and control. The state had broad warrants to approach them, demand from them, fleece them, assault them. This was easily accomplished because the point was not public safety but control of groups and resources.

This logic was especially pronounced in conversations where people described being positioned as potential profit sources and the redistribution of resources away from their communities. Participants commonly articulated how the system made money off of them, how their communities endured disproportionate taxation and financial drain, and how their limited resources were often seized. Phrases like "we're nothing but a check to them," "they lock people up to make money," "jailing is big business here," and "we're cheaper to imprison than educate" littered the conversations. Many dialogues also described the system as functioning primarily to generate profits and revenue that flowed out of their communities and into the coffers of municipal government agencies. But the costs they paid were no investment in their communities.

> Peace is not attractive to them, because it does not make them any money. They do not make money off peace, they make money off chaos. [19-year-old Black man, Milwaukee]

> You Black man and you young, they don't care about you . . . ya dig? They want to keep you behind the walls so they can get paid. See they get paid from you good money, man, you know, good money. That's how they sending they kids to college and all that stuff man. Buying houses and Mercedes Benz, you know. See, we can't have that, they don't want us to have it, so they kill us, they kill up all our Blacks. [53-year-old Black man, Chicago]

> So, are you all really here to serve and protect your people or are you all here to collect a dime for the city and the government? [36-year-old Black woman, Chicago]

> A lot of these police departments and criminal justice systems, they all about the money, the dollars and stuff. They like to invest in private prisons and make money off of people getting arrested rather than, like, uh, put them back in the community on a positive path. [Black man, Newark]

> It's funny because the police, we're nothing but a check to them. When we do stuff bad, we get sent to jail and they get a paycheck while we just sit in there. None of that money is going to us, they just a paycheck for it. [19-year-old Black male, Milwaukee]

Financial extraction of the poor has indeed become central to many municipal budgets (Gordon and Hayward 2016). A recent example: Ferguson police generated an average of three arrest warrants *per household*, and imposed prohibitive fees enough to support one-fifth of the city budget. Beyond policing, most jail systems charge their wards "user fees" for room and board. And then not paying those fees becomes justification for a revocation of parole or probation, and in some states one is ineligible to vote until the fees are paid, leading to large numbers of Black men being unable to cast ballots (Meredith and Morse 2017).

Consider the dramatic fact that when a man is sent to prison, he is considered voluntarily unemployed, and must continue to make child support payments or have the debt accrue (Katzenstein and Waller 2015). In addition, court fees, victim restitution, room and board, and other mechanisms saddle incarcerated people—those mostly without the means to pay—with enormous financial liabilities. As a result, the average Black man leaves prison with $17,000 of debt (Harris, Evans, and Beckett 2010).

In other words, the system is not only characterized by expanded oversight across a dizzying array of institutions but by the seizure of financial assets of justice-involved families. We don't know how extensive these are or what the cumulative extraction is or how much redistribution from the poor to the state is happening in a given year.

Subjugated Knowledge

More evidence that we have mis-specified the American state comes in exploring political knowledge in race–class subjugated communities.

For most Americans, there is one political system, one legal system, one set of rules to follow. They need only concern themselves with basic, widely accepted understandings of the law—the formal law as written. Even then, political scientists show that the average citizen is pretty ill-informed about politics and government and pays little attention to it (Delli Carpini and Keeter 1996). Scholars bemoan the lack of "citizen competence"—saying they lack the political knowledge necessary to form preferences. The public, it could be said, has "too little knowledge and too much power."

But in race–class subjugated communities, the political world is not some distant or abstract picture formed in grade school by reciting the

Bill of Rights of the US Constitution. It is a vivid image born of experience. Portals exchanges demonstrate that people had extraordinary stores of political knowledge and sophisticated theories of power and local democracy. They exhibited high-level reasoning about state actions and their meaning. They didn't have to imagine the political world, they could simply recall it from the last time they were in handcuffs.

But their political knowledge was contradictory. They understood two bodies of law—one that was the official law on the books and one that was for them—what scholars term the "hidden curriculum" (Justice and Meares 2014). The official law said they had Miranda rights, couldn't be arbitrarily beaten or killed by the state, told them they would be tried by a jury of their peers, and that they were equal before the law. They knew that was *someone's* reality in America. But the unofficial rule book, or hidden curriculum, was the one they actually lived by: it stipulated that they would never see a jury of peers, that riding "in your car four deep" constituted probable cause to be stopped and searched and handcuffed, that police shoot first and ask questions later, that if they had money they could get better adjudication, that certain mundane behaviors were forbidden, like not having your ID on you at all times. "It may not be written policy," one person said, "but that's what they do."

At the same time as they understood these two sets of rules, they patently knew there was no mechanism of redress—another layer of distorted responsiveness: "But then we have nowhere to turn. We look to the media, 'Oh you guys just complaining.' We go to City Hall, they're going to tell you what you want to hear to get out of there. . . . The politician is not going to listen because we're not affecting the bottom line, which is money." Another person described their expendability more pointedly:

> In all Black communities, you find the same policing issues . . . where the officers come in and they treat our neighborhood, our communities as an armed camp where they can come in and stormtroop, do whatever they want to do because nobody is able to complain, and if you complain, no one's there to listen to you . . . many times people simply walk away from the matter and take the abuse and move on. . . . "We're above the law, you're our subjects, and we can do whatever we want do whatever we want to do with you."

They had too much knowledge and too little power.

In the conversations, we see both their recognition of how the state should operate according to formal dictates (and their aspiration that it would someday) and the real rules they must adhere to. Engaging the state, then, was like playing an elaborate game but one where officials not only cheat or deviate from the rules occasionally, but operate by a separate rulebook. Justice, they quipped, means "just for us."

They saw the state constantly as both what it said it did and what it was actually capable of. Contradictory, yes—but also essential. This sophistication reflects what F. Scott Fitzgerald famously called intelligence: "the test of a first-rate intelligence is the ability to hold two opposed ideas in mind at the same time and still retain the ability to function." They had this knowledge *in order to* function.

The utility of such knowledge is not that it tightens the link between what the state does and one's "preferences." It is to have relief from state intrusion. Failing to know the unofficial rulebook could be the difference between life and death. Because of this, some communities could be said to have extraordinarily well-developed citizen competence.

But this knowledge was not liberating. It was labor. It meant "looking through the eyes of others"—what W. E. B. Du Bois called double consciousness, except that it was through the eyes of state authorities, and to assimilate into what the state demanded, a whole different program than what was expected of other Americans. Citizenship was a matter of navigating this fact on a constant basis. Such interactions with police may have increased their knowledge, but not their status. At best, knowledge leads to behaviors that are stopgap measures, decreasing the probability of violence in individual encounters without influencing group stigma, policy, or practice. As one participant put it, "it's not a justice system. It's a justice system to the point, it's just for us—to go through. It's nothing for us to get anything out of, but for us to go through." Thus, knowledge is not an intrinsic good but a necessary evil.

* * *

Audre Lorde (1988) once asked: "How does a system bent upon our ultimate destruction make the unacceptable gradually tolerable?" A necessary step I would think is to misidentify what a group experiences as fundamentally democratic. Even as subjugated communities say otherwise. Even as we enjoy the art of Childish Gambino's "This is America."

This essay has emphasized modes of state action from a bottom-up perspective—the way policing affects childhood and disrupts maternal authority, police aggression for petty things exists alongside the absence of police protection (a distorted responsiveness), custodial socialization flows from the hidden curriculum, and communities serve as sources of profit for the state. These potent new storylines borrow from the past. The country that is Black has been theorizing the American state in its sermons, memoirs, reporting, and poetry. But those schooled on T. H. Marshall and Robert Dahl saw pluralism and political equality everywhere. They seemed to discover new threats to democracy that have long been the state of play in race–class subjugated communities. Black intellectual and folk traditions have been contesting and reframing this view of America for at least a century.

These narratives unsettle framings of American democracy and recast how we understand the role of the state in Americans' lives. Marginalization or unequal citizenship is not simply a story of material inequality or lack of responsiveness to policy preferences. Instead, it is a broad difference in *the way the government—especially the police—orients itself toward its residents.* It is not only that people in communities like Amani in the northside of Milwaukee are exposed to a different set of material deficits concentrated in particular spaces or have their policy wishes registered less that make them vulnerable. People in these locales experience distorted responsiveness from the state's most present authority. Seeing protection as a hoax, police reprisals as a mainstay of life, and innocence as no protection, they needed to thread a tight needle where matters of government were concerned, developing extraordinary political knowledge.

I also wanted to upend the conventional approach through a new civic and counter-public infrastructure. We can learn about each other through the news media—a medium that often exacerbates our stereotypes of distant communities—or we can learn from each other through interaction. We can try to understand what Ferguson, West Baltimore, and Sherman Park meant to its residents and beyond by asking people neat dichotomous survey items on whether they disagree with this or that policy, or we can actually hear people describe their own ideas and dreams for reform and see what policing *is* through the eyes of those who experience it most directly. We can try to promote understanding and accountability between police and residents through mandating new codes of conduct, but we can also promote understanding by coming to know highly policed communities. We can lament the conditions of many American neighborhoods, or we can build a space where people and groups across cities can employ their local wisdom to strengthen Black and Brown liberation.

Midway through our "data collection," we realized something that wasn't part of the plan. The Portal had become a spark. In Milwaukee, the Portal had ignited bottom-led projects. Rival gangs in the neighborhood dropped their colors and had formed a single group to keep the area safe. A new neighborhood council was formed. Violence had ebbed. The district attorney, local sheriff, and alderman were all regularly making visits to the Portal, an area they rarely noticed before. It had become a rallying point for groups in the community—even those that normally opposed each other, police officers and the policed. People began to call it "our Portal." And community-led projects were happening every day. Kids without passports were travelling to distant places. Residents explored their neighborhood's mass loss of men to gun violence, police violence, and incarceration with Tutsis, who told them about their mass loss during genocidal state campaigns in Kigali, Rwanda. They used the Portal to reclaim space that had been in severe decline. The community pulsed with a new sense of opportunity and connectedness.

The Portal wasn't just a medium for listening, as we had originally thought, it had become a platform for building power, collaborating, and enacting redefinition. An unlocking of agency through trauma. When his partner asked, "what would you like to see changed with the interaction with the police department?" one Portals participant, a young person just out of high school said: "That's a tough one. . . . I would want them to try to give, instead of just believing everything that the police say, give people a chance to be heard."

NOTES

This essay is based on remarks delivered at the 2018 Ethics of Policing Conference at the Rock Ethics Institute at Penn State. I thank Ben Jones and Eduardo Mendieta for their helpful comments. The essay draws on qualitative, discursive evidence from a project with Tracey L. Meares and Gwen Prowse, both of Yale University. See Weaver,

Meares, and Prowse (n.d.). This essay also draws on previous work of mine with other colleagues: Prowse, Weaver, and Meares (2020); Soss and Weaver (2017); Weaver and Geller (2019); Weaver, Papachristos, and Zanger-Tishler (2019); and Weaver, Prowse, and Piston (2020).

1 I thank Frank Baumgartner for this observation.
2 This substantive argument is elaborated in Weaver and Geller (2019).
3 See Prowse, Weaver, and Meares (2020) for a further elaboration of the concept of distorted responsiveness.
4 This argument is fleshed out in Weaver, Prowse, and Piston (2019).
5 I am grateful to Darrick Hamilton for this observation.

BIBLIOGRAPHY

ACLU Illinois. 2014. "Newly Released Data Shows City Continues to Deny Equitable Services to South and West Side Neighborhoods." March 13, 2014. www.aclu-il.org.

Baldwin, James. 1964. "Fear of the Police." *Pageant Magazine*, December 1964: 188.

Baldwin, James. 1966. "A Report from Occupied Territory." *Nation*, July 11, 1966. www.thenation.com.

Bartels, Larry M. 2016. *Unequal Democracy: The Political Economy of the New Gilded Age*. Princeton, NJ: Princeton University Press.

Bell, Monica C. 2017. "Police Reform and the Dismantling of Legal Estrangement." *Yale Law Journal* 126 (7): 2054–2150.

Brown-Scott, Wendy. 1994. "The Communitarian State: Lawlessness or Law Reform for African-Americans?" *Harvard Law Review* 107 (6): 1209–30.

Burch, Traci. 2013. *Trading Democracy for Justice: Criminal Convictions and the Decline of Neighborhood Political Participation*. Chicago: University of Chicago Press.

Bureau of Labor Statistics, US Department of Labor. 2014. National Longitudinal Survey of Youth, 1979 cohort, 1979–2012 (rounds 1–25). Columbus, Ohio: Center for Human Resource Research, Ohio State University.

Camp, Jordan T., and Christina Heatherton, eds. 2016. *Policing the Planet: Why the Policing Crisis Led to Black Lives Matter*. New York: Verso Books.

Carbado, Devon W. 2005. "Racial Naturalization." *American Quarterly* 57 (3): 633–58.

Carter, Susan, Scott Sigmund Gartner, Michael R. Haines, Alan L. Olmstead, Richard Sutch, and Gavin Wright. 2006. Historical Statistics of the United States Millennial Edition Online. New York: Cambridge University Press, 2006. http://hsus.cambridge.org/.

Cohen, Cathy J. 1999. *The Boundaries of Blackness: AIDS and the Breakdown of Black Politics*. Chicago: University of Chicago Press.

Dahl, Robert. 1971. *Polyarchy: Participation and Opposition*. New Haven, CT: Yale University Press.

Dawson, Michael C. 2001. *Black Visions: The Roots of Contemporary African-American Political Ideologies*. Chicago: University of Chicago Press.

Del Toro, Juan, Tracey Lloyd, Kim S. Buchanana, Summer Joi Robins, Lucy Zhang Bencharit, Meredith Gamson Smiedt, Kavita S. Reddy, Enrique Rodriguez Pouget, Erin M. Kerrison, and Phillip Atiba Goff. 2019. "The Criminogenic and Psychological Effects of Police Stops on Adolescent Black and Latino Boys." *Proceedings of the National Academy of Sciences* 116 (17): 8261–68.

Delli Carpini, Michael X., and Scott Keeter. 1996. *What Americans Know about Politics and Why It Matters*. New Haven, CT: Yale University Press.

Epp, Charles R., Steven Maynard-Moody, and Donald P. Haider-Markel. 2014. *Pulled Over: How Police Stops Define Race and Citizenship*. Chicago: University of Chicago Press.

Fernández-Kelly, Patricia. 2015. *The Hero's Fight: African Americans in West Baltimore and the Shadow of the State*. Princeton, NJ: Princeton University Press.

Geller, Amanda. 2017. "Policing America's Children: Police Contact and Consequences among Teens in Fragile Families." Princeton University, Woodrow Wilson School of Public and International Affairs, Center for Research on Child Wellbeing. Working Papers: wp18–02-ff.

Gilens, Martin. 2012. *Affluence and Influence: Economic Inequality and Political Power in America*. Princeton, NJ: Princeton University Press.

Goff, Phillip Atiba, Matthew Christian Jackson, Di Leone, Brooke Allison Lewis, Carmen Marie Culotta, and Natalie Ann DiTomasso. 2014. "The Essence of Innocence: Consequences of Dehumanizing Black Children." *Journal of Personality and Social Psychology* 106 (4): 526–45.

Gordon, Colin, and Clarissa Hayward. 2016. "The Murder of Michael Brown." *Jacobin*, August 9, 2016. www.jacobinmag.com.

Hacker, Jacob S. 2002. *The Divided Welfare State: The Battle over Public and Private Social Benefits in the United States*. New York: Cambridge University Press.

Hacker, Jacob S., and Paul Pierson. 2010. "Winner-Take-All Politics: Public Policy, Political Organization, and the Precipitous Rise of Top Incomes in the United States." *Politics & Society* 38 (2): 152–204.

Harris, Alexes, Heather Evans, and Katherine Beckett. 2010. "Drawing Blood from Stones: Legal Debt and Social Inequality in the Contemporary United States." *American Journal of Sociology* 115 (6): 1753–99.

Justice, Benjamin, and Tracey L. Meares. 2014. "How the Criminal Justice System Educates Citizens." *Annals of the American Academy of Political and Social Science* 651 (1): 159–77.

Katzenstein, Mary Fainsod, and Maureen R. Waller. 2015. "Taxing the Poor: Incarceration, Poverty Governance, and the Seizure of Family Resources." *Perspectives on Politics* 13 (3): 638–56.

Kennedy, Randall. 1998. *Race, Crime, and the Law*. New York: Vintage.

Kohler-Hausmann, Issa. 2018. *Misdemeanorland: Criminal Courts and Social Control in an Age of Broken Windows Policing*. Princeton, NJ: Princeton University Press.

Larson, Doran, ed. 2013. *Fourth City: Essays from the Prison in America*. East Lansing, MI: Michigan State University Press.

Legewie, Joscha, and Jeffrey Fagan. 2019. "Aggressive Policing and the Educational Performance of Minority Youth." *American Sociological Review* 84 (2): 220–47.

Lerman, Amy E., and Vesla M. Weaver. 2014. *Arresting Citizenship: The Democratic Consequences of American Crime Control*. Chicago: University of Chicago Press, 2014.

Lorde, Audre. 1988. *A Burst of Light: Essays*. Ithaca, NY: Firebrand Books.

Meredith, Marc, and Michael Morse. 2017. "Discretionary Disenfranchisement: The Case of Legal Financial Obligations." *Journal of Legal Studies* 46 (2): 309–38.

Mettler, Suzanne. 2011. *The Submerged State: How Invisible Government Policies Undermine American Democracy*. Chicago: University of Chicago Press.

Mickey, Robert. 2015. *Paths out of Dixie: The Democratization of Authoritarian Enclaves in America's Deep South, 1944-1972*. Princeton, NJ: Princeton University Press.

Miller, Lisa L. 2015. "What's Violence Got to Do with It? Inequality, Punishment, and State Failure in US Politics." *Punishment & Society* 17 (2): 184–210.

Morgan, Kimberly J., and Andrea Louise Campbell. 2011. *The Delegated Welfare State: Medicare, Markets, and the Governance of Social Policy*. New York: Oxford University Press, 2011.

Pettit, Becky. 2012. *Invisible Men: Mass Incarceration and the Myth of Black Progress*. New York: Russell Sage Foundation.

Prowse, Gwen, Vesla M. Weaver, and Tracey L. Meares. 2020. "The State from Below: Distorted Responsiveness in Policed Communities." *Urban Affairs Review* 56 (5): 1423–71.

Sherman, Lawrence W. 1993. "Defiance, Deterrence, and Irrelevance: A Theory of the Criminal Sanction." *Journal of Research in Crime and Delinquency* 30 (4): 445–73.

Soss, Joe, and Vesla Weaver. 2017. "Police Are Our Government: Politics, Political Science, and the Policing of Race–Class Subjugated Communities." *Annual Review of Political Science* 20 (1): 565–91.

Town of Castle Rock v. Gonzales. 2005. 545 US 748.

Walker, Hannah L. 2014. "Extending the Effects of the Carceral State: Proximal Contact, Political Participation, and Race." *Political Research Quarterly* 67 (4): 809–22.

Weaver, Vesla M., and Amanda Geller. 2019. "De-Policing America's Youth: Disrupting Criminal Justice Policy Feedbacks that Distort Power and Derail Prospects." *Annals of the American Academy of Political and Social Science* 685 (1): 190–226.

Weaver, Vesla M., Tracey L. Meares, Gwen Prowse. n.d. "Portals Policing Project." www.portalspolicingproject.com.

Weaver, Vesla M., Andrew Papachristos, and Michael Zanger-Tishler. 2019. "The Great Decoupling: The Disconnection between Criminal Offending and Experience of Arrest across Two Cohorts." *RSF: Russell Sage Foundation Journal of the Social Sciences* 5 (1): 89–123. Kristin Turney and Sara Wakefield, eds.

Weaver, Vesla M., Gwen Prowse, and Spencer Piston. 2019. "Too Much Knowledge, Too Little Power: An Assessment of Political Knowledge in Highly Policed Communities." *Journal of Politics* 81 (3): 1153–66.

Weaver, Vesla M., Gwen Prowse, and Spencer Piston. 2020. "Withdrawing and Drawing In: Political Discourse in Policed Communities." *Journal of Race, Ethnicity, and Politics* 5 (3): 604–47.

White, Ariel. 2019. "Misdemeanor Disenfranchisement? The Demobilizing Effects of Brief Jail Spells on Potential Voters." *American Political Science Review* 113 (2): 311–24.

Wilson, James Q., and George L. Kelling. 1982. "Broken Windows." *Atlantic Monthly* 249 (3): 29–38.

Winters, Jeffrey A., and Benjamin I. Page. 2009. "Oligarchy in the United States?" *Perspectives on Politics* 7 (4): 731–51.

8

Police Ethics through Presidential Politics and Abolitionist Struggle

Angela Y. Davis and Erica Garner

JOY JAMES

Policing in the United States is officially regulated by three levels of governance: federal, state, and local or city, as police forces are directed by executive branches or "chiefs." On the national level, the director of the Central Intelligence Agency (CIA) and the head of the Federal Bureau of Investigation (FBI) directly or through their superior—for example, for the FBI, the Attorney General—report to the President of the United States (POTUS); as does the Secretary of the Department of Homeland Security who oversees Immigration and Customs Enforcement (ICE). On the state level, under combined federal and state control since 1933, National Guard commanders receive instructions and (un)ethical mandates from their governor and/or the POTUS. On the local level, city mayors (or city government) appoint and oversee their chiefs of police. From the 1790s Carolina plantations' use of slave catchers to and beyond the 2018 police murder of Botham Jean in Dallas and the 2019 police murder of Atatiana Jefferson in Fort Worth, Texas, police violence has been a controversy and tragedy in US democracy, particularly in Black communities.

Regulating US policing with enforceable ethical standards to mitigate excessive force and violence disproportionately inflicted on Black, Indigenous, impoverished, or differently abled people has proven to be a difficult task. The political demand is for such ethics to be operational throughout the nation. In the absence of elected officials standardizing non-racist or anti-racist procedures into policing—procedures that protect the civil rights of the racially fashioned, the differently abled, and the poor and working classes—activists and academics work to shape police ethics that reduce bias and the use of illegal tactics. Reforms and advocacy are sometimes led by professional elites, at other times by the Black/Brown/Indigenous and working-class and impoverished activists most vulnerable to police malfeasance and violence. The focus on police reform and ethical mandates usually scrutinizes local or city police actions. The majority of people are surveilled, disciplined, and punished by local police—for example, the New York City Police Department (NYPD) when it monitors subway fare evasion, "quality-of-life" infractions, or violent crime or suppresses anti-police violence demonstrations. However, federal, state, and city police agencies share intelligence, communicate standards and protocols, monitor or ignore malfeasance and deviations, and coordinate policing activities.

The ability to influence the politics of policing includes rhetoric and advocacy surrounding presidential campaigns. Abolitionists Angela Y. Davis and Erica Garner sought to influence executive branches or candidates to shape twentieth-first-century abolitionism traceable to the antebellum legacies of the US Constitution's three-fifths clause, which shaped the electoral college and augmented the powers of enslavers; and the Thirteenth Amendment, which "emancipated" Blacks while legalizing slavery in prison.

The analysis below contrasts and compares two prominent Black women intellectual-activists—one, a living political celebrity, Angela Y. Davis, the other, a largely unknown militant, Erica Garner. Both Black women activists, who differ in class status and strategy and came of age in different generations, have shaped ethical standards concerning policing and human rights, with complementary and contradictory political analyses. Davis was the victim of blowback from COINTELPRO and prison repression that sought to neutralize rebellions led by the Black Panther Party (BPP) and the imprisoned Soledad Brothers whom she defended. Her longevity in civil rights activism, and a productivity that has circulated through elite academia and publishing houses, led her to become an international icon in academe and human rights advocacy. In contrast to Davis, Erica Garner struggled with poverty and later, grief, following the police murder of her father, Eric Garner. Her militant creativity and political leadership led her and her allies into activist confrontations with police and government. One of the most militant of the Black Lives Matter (BLM) leaders, Garner used the radical parlance of the BPP—which Davis shunned after her 1972 acquittal—to condemn the 2014 murder of her father and her family's inability to obtain justice from executive officials at the local, state, and federal levels. The progressivism and militancy, respectively, of each activist offer critiques of and correctives for unethical state violence and indifferent governance.

Angela Y. Davis: Abolitionist Mentor

During her November 2019 keynote at the Refounding Conference of the National Alliance Against Racist and Political Repression in Chicago, IL, Angela Y. Davis reflected on the meanings of abolitionism, citing the late Rose Braz who had formally led Critical Resistance to define the organization: "Critical Resistance seeks to abolish the prison–industrial complex; the use of prisons, policing and the . . . system of the prison–industrial complex as an answer to what are social, political and economic problems." According to Davis, the prison–industrial complex is larger than the prison, and Braz "urge[s] us to think about all the connections, the connection with the police, the connection with the politicians who always scream 'law and order,' the connection with the corporations who profit from the soaring numbers of people in prison" (Davis 2019). Recalling Braz's contributions, Davis highlighted political objective and method: "abolition defines both the goal we seek and the way we do our work today." Davis argued for the visionary aspects of the movement:

> Abolition means . . . that . . . we put in place the things that would reduce incidence of harm at the front end and address harm in a non-punitive manner when harm does occur. Abolition means that harm will occur far less often and that when harm does occur we address the causes of that harm rather than rely on the failed solutions of punishment. (Davis 2019)

On face value, the definitional norm does not appear to offer a template for dealing with police violence. As with the concept "restorative justice," this abolitionism emphasizes internal harm done to communities by community members. Outsiders hostile to community—policing has functioned with anti-Black animus since the colonial slave patrols—are difficult to locate within Davis's definitions:

abolition is taking a harm-reductionist approach to our society's problems. . . . . abolition means creating sustainable, healthy communities, empowered to create safety and accountability instead of relying on police, courts and imprisonment, which are not creating safe communities. . . . I think it's important for us to reflect deeply about what that means. And as we call for community control of the police, we should also have a larger vision that allows us to understand that we're actually moving toward new forms of safety and security. (Davis 2019)

On a primary level, the call asserts that communities need not rely on police "protections" from local violence. The function of police in political repression is missing in this analysis. If the function of police is simply to protect communities and societies writ large then the ethical mandates to improve policing are more easily catalogued. Davis became a fugitive in 1970 because she believed that the police—local police, FBI, CIA—functioned through political repression to maintain racial capitalism. That function of policing, or police repression as a political phenomenon, dissipates in Davis's contemporary political analyses.

Davis joined the Communist Party USA (CPUSA) in 1968, through the Che-Lumumba Club (an all-Black formation that sought to attract young Black radicals). Che-Lumumba introduced her to the Soledad Brother Defense Committee for three Black prisoners: George Jackson, Fleeta Drumgo, and John Clutchette, who were accused of killing a prison guard in retaliation for the deaths of three Black prisoners shot by a prison guard sniper and left to bleed to death in a recreation yard. Jackson's seventeen-year-old brother Jonathan served as Angela Y. Davis's bodyguard and, with guns registered in her name, attempted an ill-fated Marin County Courthouse hostage-taking attempt, on August 7, 1970, to free his brother George. Following protocol to prevent all escapes, prison guards and/or the district attorney taken hostage fired shots into or inside the van driven by Jonathan: they killed the teen, two Black prisoners, and judge Harold Haley, who had also been taken hostage. The surviving wounded prisoner, Ruchell Magee, briefly became Davis's co-defendant in 1971, before their cases were severed.

Fearing the police, Davis became a fugitive, and one of the first women on the FBI's Most Wanted list. She was captured several months later in New York and extradited to California to stand trial on charges of conspiracy in kidnapping and murder. While she was imprisoned, in August 1971, George Jackson was shot and killed in San Quentin Prison, in what Michel Foucault and other French intellectuals and radical Americans referred to as an "assassination." Davis penned and dedicated to George Jackson the essay "Reflections on the Black Woman's Role in the Community of Slaves," written from her jail cell in Marin County (Davis 1971b). After a trial monitored around the world, Davis was exonerated of all charges on June 4, 1972. Following her acquittal, the National United Committee to Free Angela Davis was transformed, in 1973, into the National Alliance Against Racist and Political Repression (NAARPR). It closed in 1986. The Alliance was refounded in 2019 in Chicago at a conference for which Davis provided the keynote.

Angela Y. Davis's political genealogy in prison abolitionism is traceable to Black revolutionary struggles shaped by George Jackson and the BPP. She became the public face and head of the Soledad Brother Defense Committee at age 27. From her acquittal to the present day, Davis's political speech and alliances—with (neo)liberals such as President Barack Obama and feminist Gloria Steinem—elide her lineage to Black militants that introduced her to abolitionism in favor of progressive evolution, one positioned as the logical path for a political revolution.

As a former political prisoner, Davis wields credibility in theories of social policing that encompass political repression. During the era of militancy that brought her fame and notoriety, the title "political prisoner" was reserved for rebels against the state—communists imprisoned under the House Un-American Activities Committee, civil rights activists held captive in Mississippi's Parchman Farm, and Black Panthers framed and imprisoned through COINTELPRO. By the time of the emergence of the NAARPR in 1973, membership in a racially stigmatized group and class (Black and impoverished) qualified one as a "political prisoner" if one were accused, convicted and incarcerated for a crime. Ethical or political acts of rebellion against injustice were no longer the primary metric. Agitation for socialism/communism, anti-imperialism/racism, dedication to a liberation movement—all were irrelevant for this classification. As anyone or everyone overly policed due to subjugated identities—gender, racial minority, stigmatized sexuality, impoverished, immigrant—became a "political prisoner," progressives increasingly ceased attributing to police the specific function of political repression, that is, punishing ideologies and movements (e.g., socialism, Black liberation, Indigenous sovereignty) that challenged the state.

The NAARPR, which worked on cases for Joann Little, Eddie Carthan, Assata Shakur, and American Indian Movement leader Leonard Peltier, folded in 1986. A decade later, Davis received external funding from foundations to form Critical Resistance (CritResist). Amplified by the resources of first-tier public universities, the project prototype was launched in March 1998 at the "Unfinished Liberation" conference, attended by two thousand people, at the University of Colorado, Boulder. Davis, the conference keynote, selected many of the attendees who would go on to co-lead CritResist for nearly a decade. In September 1998, CritResist was launched at the University of California, Berkeley.

Through decades of labor and writings, and prominent platforms—the academy proved to be a key organizational structure that replaced the CPUSA—Davis defined the "abolition" movement. The NAARPR's Chicago refounding, attended by eight hundred people from twenty-eight states in the "house" built by the Chicago Teachers Union (CTU) (the opening greeting by Union leadership welcomed conference attendees to a home constructed with Black women's labor), was shaped in part by the leadership of Black women and multiracial cadres, which had recently and triumphantly settled a strike to force the city to address the needs of impoverished, homeless, and differently abled children through city restrictions on aggressive policing. At the conference, without discussing the existence of radical activist political prisoners and repression of US dissidents, Davis addressed the discourse of "public safety" as a pretext for mass incarceration: "the contradictions in the whole prison–industrial complex and the punitive institutions that are embraced by it cannot create safety by putting people in very unsafe conditions." Deprivation and violence in prisons and jails prevent rehabilitation and healing, according to Davis: "We try to address violence by turning them [community members] over to institutions that are responsible for the continued production and reproduction of violence." Her solution is pragmatic activism:

> People often assume that when you say you're an abolitionist, it means that you are totally opposed to any kind of reform, as if somehow or an-

other, you know, at the strike of midnight, we're going to get rid of the police and get rid of prisons and then we'll be somewhere else. The question is: how do we get there without constantly reproducing the very idea[s] that have put us in the grip of prisons and police in the first place? (Davis 2019)

At the Saturday gathering, after the Friday evening keynote, Davis attempted to recall a slogan chanted the night before by friends and families who lost kin and children to police violence and police torture to obtain false confessions, asking: "[Y]esterday everybody really responded to 'Indict the cops . . .' What was it? 'Indict the killer cops?'" The audience, in a call-and-response, chanted: "INDICT! CONVICT! SEND THESE KILLER COPS TO JAIL! THE WHOLE DAMN SYSTEM IS GUILTY AS HELL!"

Chuckling, Davis offered an instructive corrective:

OK. OK. That's it. And I totally understand why we say that, because it makes us feel powerful. It makes us feel as if we can really accomplish something. But, you know, sometimes we also at the same time have to ask ourselves, where is the impulse coming from? And how is it that we are using the very structure and the very strategies that are responsible for what we are fighting against? Do you understand what I'm saying? And I think, you know, sometimes you might think of that as a contradiction. I don't think of it as a contradiction because . . . it's OK to say that, but then you have to realize, "Why am I saying that? Why does that make me feel so good?" (Davis 2019)

Davis emphasized the chant's first stanza, which concerns individual punishment. The second stanza, which points to structural malfeasance and corruption, she ignored. Ultimately, oppressed communities might be less interested in individual police officers than in the structures that permit oppressive conditions to be maintained by police forces. As the leading or most iconic proponent of contemporary abolitionism, Davis asked the gathering to reflect on how "the very structures of imprisonment and policing" are embedded in their emotional reactions. That was an important opportunity for reflection. She argued to the crowd that "abolition urges us to become aware of that and to think deeply about the ways in which we often accomplish the goal of the state even as we are attempting to challenge it."

The "goal" of the state, though, is not to punish its employees hired to police dissidents and racially or sexually nonconforming working-class and impoverished communities. The state protects the police despite their lethal aggressions; hence the structural difficulty of disciplining police forces. Cops and their kin and supporters mockingly chant "Blue Lives Matter" not just because shouting "White Lives" evokes White nationalism and supremacy but because "blue lives" represent a uniform(ed) system, a regime of power in which the hierarchy of lives (excluding wealthy Whites) places police of all ranks and character in an upper tier. Urging the gathering "not to be afraid of contradictions," Davis left unspoken any acknowledgment of the ethical contradictions that one will encounter with the hypothetical assumption that police forces and executive branches of governance believe in true equality, and that disenfranchised communities can control police behavior to conform to civil rights.

As will be discussed more fully below concerning abolitionist Erica Garner, NYPD Officer Daniel Pantaleo consistently denied that he had applied a chokehold to Eric Garner's neck, although forensics experts and coroners testified that he did. "Guilty as hell." Still, Pantaleo did not need abolitionists to ensure that he would never be incarcerated. He was only fired when the police commissioner who terminated his employment was ready to retire into lucrative employment in private security industries. The commissioner thus retired, vilified by his (White) NYPD rank and file and the Police Benevolent Association, but was well compensated. Mayor Bill de Blasio while campaigning for president had denounced racist violence from police and reassured agitated activists who called on him to use his executive powers to fire Pantaleo that, although the mayor would not directly act, justice would be served (Southall 2019; NBC New York 2019).

Davis did not deal with the specific contradictions of restorative justice with "soulless" bureaucracies in part because of her advocacy for Black feminists as a leadership cadre and a corrective to ills in the community and in the police forces that monitor and discipline the community. (In 2020, Davis would campaign for Kamala Harris [and Joe Biden] arguing that a nuanced feminism dictates voting for the former

California prosecutor. See Reuters 2020.) Black feminist strategies are essential, Davis told the gathering, because "they teach us that we can inhabit contradictions." She added that to be "at the center of contradictions" could lead to "something very powerful"; noting that it is not necessary to "assume that either we're abolitionist and want to tear the whole damn system down or over here we're reformists" (Davis 2019).

Davis urged the crowd to "recognize that activism produces knowledge" and that collectively "we're producing new ways of looking at the world. We wouldn't be where we are today if people hadn't done that before us. But let me end by saying let's move toward community control of and then abolition of [the] police state." The charge for community control over the police had been a constant demand at the conference. Control by the community indicated that the mass did not trust the executive branches, including newly elected Chicago Mayor Lori Lightfoot, a Black lesbian feminist. When asked, "Should we consider community patrol groups to help to search, to surveil police as well as criminals or predators to our neighborhood?" Davis responded by referencing the 1966 Black Panther Party for Self-Defense in Oakland, California, formed in response to a police killing of an unarmed Black teenager who fled from them.

> I remember when Huey Newton and Bobby Seale began the process of patrolling the community with a gun and with the law book. And I think community control can be very important. Nowadays, everybody has cell phones. So often it is the case when some form of police violence happens, someone is there to capture it. . . . I just don't want us to always think only about defensive measures. . . . How can we engage in community control of the police in order to guarantee that certain kinds of actions do not take place? (Davis 2019)

Small organizations such as the Malcolm X Grassroots Cop Watch, and large organizations, such as the American Civil Liberties Union, provide apps that allow observers of police misconduct to download images directly to nonprofit "watch dogs." By 1968, displaying weapons to "educate" Black communities that they had the right to self-defense was no longer useful; the Panthers considered the police to be an occupying colonial force. That lens is generally not applied to police forces today. Those organizing surveillance and digital observations of police also advise that one should have legal defense available. (As a case in point, Ramsey Orta, who took the cell phone footage of Garner's murder was later harassed, arrested, and incarcerated on unlicensed weapon charges.)

Davis pointed toward progress, stating that decades prior it was nearly impossible to have police charged for killing a Black person. Today, she observed, "The police are now in a position of defense in many places. And I think we need to take advantage of that." Davis included in her analyses the victories that had been secured for political prisoners: "The FOP [Fraternal Order of Police] used to be able to make decisions regarding everything, including people like [former Panther and MOVE member] Mumia Abu-Jamal." According to Davis, although FOP malfeasance placed Abu-Jamal on death row in Pennsylvania, "a possibility of freeing Mumia" exists. Davis linked mass policing and incarceration with traditional "political prisoners," arguing that "doing work around community control of the police" requires organizing around cases similar to Abu-Jamal's. Abu-Jamal's case (he maintains his innocence) involves the killing of a White Philadelphia police officer; the militarized retributive norms of contemporary police posit that anyone convicted of killing an officer should die in prison.

Davis chastised the audience at the NAARPR Refounding Conference that European foreigners are more familiar with Abu-Jamal's case than Americans: "people all over Europe know Mumia Abu-Jamal, there are streets named after him in Germany and France. But here in the US, we're still struggling to enlighten people about the conditions that have left this amazing brother to spend half of his life or more behind bars" (Davis 2019). Davis failed to note the role of class, literacy, and leisure as well as European/White intense interests in rebel American Blacks and Panthers. Abu-Jamal became an international political celebrity due to his writings, such as *Live from Death Row*, and his initial death sentence galvanized international movements. For some, there is a presumed ethical lapse on the part of a (Black) working class/laboring poor cadre that might have limited time for reading, or might be preoccupied with the trauma and violence closer to home, for example, for decades the Chicago Police Department (CPD) ran a torture ring that garnered over one hundred false confessions largely from Black men and women who pled guilty to crimes they did not commit and were sentenced to lengthy prison sentences.

The 2019 NAARPR gathering mapped out a strategy for controlling the CPD. This was explained by the organization's newly elected executive director, Frank Chapman, who had suffered for decades in prison until the NAARPR won his exoneration and freedom in the 1980s. For the NAARPR, the infusion of ethical mandates in policing would be achieved through gaining power in local government. First, the focus would be on the election of progressive alder(wo)men who would pass local legislation to curb the power of the CPD (notorious for torture rings, corruption, and police murders). The alder(wo)men would then shape the mayor's agenda for policing; from that level of executive power, they would repeat the necessary steps to move to the state and national levels of executive power. This strategy aligns with Davis's analysis.

Davis embraced the academic, political persona that promoted the Black radical tradition as compatible with academic traditions and advocacy democracy, projecting a network that could enable ethical mandates to control police malfeasance:

> The new field formation—critical prison studies and its explicitly abolitionist framework—situates itself within the Black Radical Tradition, both through its acknowledged genealogical relation to the period in US history we refer to as Radical Reconstruction and, of course, through its relation both to the work of W. E. B. Du Bois and to historical Black feminism. (Davis 2017a)

The BPP, a party which Davis supported but never joined, was largely comprised of activists twenty-five years old and younger who were recruited from among, or identified with, the working class (proletariat) or impoverished (lumpenproletariat) that was over-policed by White governance. Of that cadre, Davis wrote in 1971, "society has objectively reduced their possibilities of subsistence and survival," leading to an "urgent need to organize the unemployed and lumpenproletariat" (Davis 1971a). Years later, Davis translated the imperative to advocate for the most repressed and underserved sector into the validation of leadership mandates tied to a Black feminist tradition; she asserts that the article she wrote in prison, "Reflections on the Role of the Black Woman's

Role in the Community of Slaves" (Davis 1971b), dedicated to George Jackson three weeks after his death, is actually a feminist manifesto for Black female leadership. The feminist mandate eclipses the slain revolutionary's relevance to contemporary abolitionism—Jackson introduced Davis to the experiential knowledge of prison torture and rebellion; her traumatic seventeen months in a county jail are adjacent and personally derived knowledge. At some point, for Davis, police/prison accountability shifts from rebellion to electoral politics and influencing the middle class.

Davis's admonition to vote for "Her" (Hillary Clinton) in September 2016 was practical and pragmatic politics (West Savali 2016). Davis noted the "super predator" language that Clinton affixed to Black children and the FLOTUS's implicit support of Bill Clinton's 1996 Omnibus Crime Bill. By 2016, though, Clinton had embraced and leveraged Black feminists as campaign supporters for her centrist police reforms and iconic embodiment of feminists as governmental leaders. "Mothers of the Movement"—Black women who had lost their children in high-profile incidents to White police or vigilante violence—became political surrogates for Clinton. In a 2016 interview expressing support for some of Bernie Sanders's policies, Davis states that she prioritized "independent, more radical politics" such as tuition-free public education and single-payer or universal healthcare. She adds, however, that "there are larger questions about the prison industrial complex that have not been sufficiently raised. We not only need to bring about an end to mass incarceration, we need to question the racism that is embedded in the whole history of punishment in this country" (Huggins Salomon 2016). Elsewhere Davis states that Sanders "seemed to be just learning how to incorporate a critique of racism" (Dukmasova 2016).

While an undergrad at the University of Chicago, Sanders assisted a 1963 school boycott of two hundred thousand mostly Black children, who with their parents protested the use of trailers on the South and West Sides of Chicago to keep Black students from integrating White public schools that had empty desks and the capacity for more students (Felsenthal 2016). Sanders later marched with Martin Luther King, Jr. King lived for months in a Chicago tenement with Coretta Scott King to gain experiential knowledge for the "poor people's campaign." The photo of Sanders's arrest by aggressive police was printed on 2020 election swag t-shirts. Despite his history of anti-racist *activism*, Davis suggested that Sanders take a "crash course on intersectionality" (Dukmasova 2016). The concept of intersectionality here supplants actual activism for Black freedom. Sanders's activism with Black families led to his arrest, at a time when Davis, a minoritized but privileged student at Brandeis, was a non-activist student in Frankfurt, Germany. The "intersectionality" by which Davis finds Sanders lacking itself lacks vectors for *ideology* (did Black feminist leaders of abolitionism publicly advocate socialism in contrast to Obama's embrace of imperial capitalism?); and *alliances* (does the agency of nonelite working-class parents share peerage with elite academics or celebrity activists?).

A former third-party vice-presidential candidate in 1980 and 1984 on the CPUSA ticket against Reagan, Davis opposed the duopoly of the mainstream parties and unbridled violent policing in US domestic and foreign affairs—until Barack Obama's election in 2008. BLM emerged during the Obama administration, as police killings of unarmed Blacks continued amid the tepid response from the government. (The federal investigation of Daniel Pantaleo's violations of the civil rights of Eric Garner sat on the desks of Attorney Generals Eric Holder and Loretta Lynch until after Trump's election; only then did the Department of Justice begin an investigation of the police—an investigation that would be conducted by an administration whose president encouraged the NYPD to rough up suspects in police custody.) For Davis, Obama served in the "Black radical tradition," although POTUS 44 embodied centrist and corporate policies. Advocating an "independent politics" or "new party" that supported labor unions and worked against racism, sexism, homophobia, and transphobia, Davis recommended that the re-founded NAARPR "develop mass movements that can create the kind of pressure that will force whoever is elected . . . to progressive directions" (Davis 2017b). Davis does not articulate how Black elites—protecting their interests and theoretically Obama from a White backlash—shielded 44's centrist politics from legitimate critiques about his government's inefficacy in protecting Black communities vulnerable to police and racist and political repression.

Davis's pragmatism mixes reformism into a Black radical lineage, blurring distinctions and strategies of how to achieve a world without prisons. Repression of both pacifists and militarists is central to policing that prevents governmental evolution toward a mass reduction in incarceration. The function of police repression is to intimidate and inflict harm in order to prevent redistributive power. Executive branches of both political parties are amenable to authorizing police forces to repress dissent and disclosure. The Obama administration prosecuted more whistleblowers under the Espionage Act than previous administrations combined. By offering no clemency for Edward Snowden and commuting the sentence of Chelsea Manning, Obama sent mixed messages on "political prisoners" (here, middle-class Whites engaged in the political act of publicly disclosing government malfeasance and war crimes). Whereas the Clinton administration offered clemency to some Puerto Rican *independentistas*, Obama's Attorney General and FBI director placed Assata Shakur on an international terrorist list with Al Qaeda. While increasing the bounty on the Black exile fugitive to $2 million, the Obama administration did commute the sentence of *independentista* Oscar Lopez Rivera. Davis, who has publicly defended Shakur since 1973 as innocent of killing a New Jersey trooper, does not publicly reconcile or rationalize these contradictions.

In progressive media Davis castigates the US government for endangering the life of former Black Panther Assata Shakur by placing her on an international terrorist list, yet fails to note that this occurred during the Obama administration. Davis does not note that BLM put police racism on the agenda so that even Barack Obama had to speak about it. Yet, the explicit policies of the Obama administration to expand community control over policing and curtail anti-Black aggression in US policing require more scrutiny. Davis was a mentor to female BLM leaders who enjoyed celebrity status, representing what was a mercurial mass movement until tens of millions of dollars from the Ford Foundation and anonymous donors brought the "Movement for Black Lives" (M4BL) into the fold of conventional or electoral politics (see Ferguson 2018). Elite funding provided definitional norms and an aspirational template for nonelites bearing the brunt of police violence and malfeasance and community decay. Davis would mentor the BLM women who became celebrities (*Teen Vogue* 2019). Black militants known as a fierce fighters, however, would remain outside the fold of conventional and profitable platforms.

The ideological differences in abolitionist struggles have been downplayed likely since the 1998 inception of Critical Resistance, originally housed in academic formations led by bourgeois women and men of color. There "abolitionism" and the definitional norms of police ethics would be defined in ways compatible with host structures. As we will see below, Erica Garner's lack of a college degree and lack of influential speaking and publishing platforms restricted her resources to her own under-resourced and over-policed Black community in public housing or the New York City Housing Authority (NYCHA). Garner could not be leveraged as an icon from a well-endowed industry. However, in the span of only two years, she became an architect of abolitionism. Though not as prominently known as Davis, she still left a significant imprint on political thought and activism.

Erica Garner and Unruly Hope

Erica Garner did not wield a public platform prior to the NYPD homicide of her father, Eric Garner, in 2014. Her family tragedy led her to build a political movement without the backing of a political party, donor funding, or academic network. Garner's political imagination and vocabulary invoked the imaginative, disruptive politics of the Panthers, whom FBI Director J. Edgar Hoover designated the "number one threat to the internal security" of the US (Lieberman 2020, 241). Garner's familial loss deepens the political ideology that fuels her militancy. Her ideological ties to the BPP are theoretical and inspirational. A political "wild card"—as were the Panthers' social programs, armed self-defense, and militarism—Garner's street-based leadership was often deemed too loud, unruly, and impractical for mainstream abolitionism.

Garner was associated with BLM as a young leader when the movement emerged after the 2013 acquittal of George Zimmerman for the murder of Trayvon Martin. The following year, the tragedies of Eric Garner and Michael Brown killed by police in New York City and Ferguson, Missouri, dominated media news cycles. A rebel, Garner appeared sporadically on varied platforms, largely using them to denounce conventional politics and coalitions in abolitionist movements. Unlike Davis, Garner avidly turned her ire on the Democratic Party and bluntly criticized powerful politicians. She repeatedly mourned, criticized, and raged against the NYPD homicide of her father and lack of police accountability at every level of executive power: the president, governor, and mayor.

Eric Garner was killed on July 27, 2014, on Staten Island by NYPD Officer Daniel Pantaleo, who applied a banned chokehold while other White officers applied chest compression and White female paramedics watched without intervening. Garner—who had asked police to leave him alone after they tried to arrest him for allegedly selling loose cigarettes—panted, protested, and pleaded eleven times, "I can't breathe." Then he died. In late 2014, the Staten Island grand jury declined to indict Pantaleo. He stayed on the police force, collecting merit raises. The civil rights case then went to Obama's Attorney General Loretta Lynch, whose office "sat on it" for over two years, finally deciding to prosecute only one week before the inauguration of Donald Trump. In late 2019, Attorney General William Barr ordered the Justice Department to drop all civil rights charges against Pantaleo. He was fired in August 2019 by NYPD Commissioner James P. O'Neill, five years after Eric Garner's death (see Benner 2019; Southall 2019).

Just twenty-four years old and a single mother when her father died, Erica Garner fought to collect herself following this tragedy, and to repurpose herself. She grew up in public NYCHA housing with her family and spent time in foster care. She navigated personal circumstances as an impoverished outlier with a rebel comportment. From the July 2014 NYPD homicide of her father Eric Garner to her own death in December 2017 following complications after the birth of her second child and asthma, Garner became a highly visible disruptor of conventional politics and conventional progressive abolitionism. By 2016, she had national if not international recognition as an alternative to the activism practiced by nonprofits, academics, and progressive politicians.

Garner's radicalism organically differentiated itself from liberalism and managerial or advocacy democracy (for more on advocacy democracy, see Sokolova 2006). Her militancy was an expression of her community, her cadre, and her grief. There were no platforms, networks (other than street and underground) to leverage her critique of the NYPD as an organized "gang" of "killer cops." So, she used her body in weekly "die-ins" at the site where her father had died from chest compression and choking. Davis, in contrast, seeks to influence liberalism and turn it toward a radical ideology with the least offensive critiques of powerful democratic elites and funders. The crassness of political discourse wielded by Garner is starkly clear. Yet, so too is the convolutedness in the political discourse of Davis, whose inoffensive offense is the opposite of the language of revolutionary abolitionism she embraced in the early 1970s, and today is possibly an impediment to clear communication about political struggle. Garner's callouts to politicians and political organizations that betrayed struggling Black communities were uncivil. The verbal rudeness was a jarring contrast to abolitionist speech emanating from the academy and well-funded nonprofits. Garner was channeling the discourse and tactics of the lumpen that Marx wrote about and Davis admired.

Ideologies deemed too radical by the mainstream can be popularized if the "rabble" is persuasive and persistent. Speaking for the disposed and violated and becoming a media "magnet," Erica Garner loudly defended her father's memory and her family. One way she did this was through her powerful campaign ad for Bernie Sanders, a democratic socialist who had argued in 2012 that Obama should be "primaried" to push him toward progressive reforms. Garner also condemned Mayor de Blasio with vulgarity for caring too little about Black people.

After Erica Garner's death, journalist Ben Norton (2017) wrote: "New York City Mayor de Blasio was one of the most shameless figures trying to co-opt Erica Garner's memory—even though Erica had relentlessly criticized de Blasio and the impunity he has guaranteed for police who kill Black people." Garner's rebel politics were clearly expressed through her social media accounts. The comments that were expressed before and after the 2016 election made it clear to her readers that both parties had failed. After the 2016 presidential victory, Garner dismissed "high net worth democrats [who] deconstruct the election . . . they are no allies of mine" (@es_snipes November 22, 2016). She asserted that Blacks were neither true Democrats nor Republicans: "WE are Black in America which means we will NEVER be American. Cant u tell 300 yrs later?" (@es_snipes February 6, 2017). During the Democratic primary elections, her critique of capitalism led her to support Sanders, the independent, over Clinton: "when i think about capitalism I think about slavery, share cropping, bank scandal wall street donors . . . #HillaryClinton's people" (@es_snipes October 13, 2015).

Erica Garner stormed out of ABC's 2016 "The President and the People: Race in America" forum because she felt that the event profited in ratings off of her father's death while offering no solutions to police abuse and violence. She recounts her controversial exit: "They lied to me and my family getting us to travel to DC to participate. . . . They promised me that I and Patrice Cullors could ask [questions]." A video clip shot from a cell phone temporarily appeared online after Garner's death. It showed President Barack Obama and presidential advisor Valerie Jarrett speaking with Garner in the hall and attempting to calm her after the taping. Obama begins to chastise her about political decorum, then stops to offer his condolences for her loss, and then resumes instructing her on political messaging that can reach the broadest base. In interviews that Garner released later, she maintains that she was invited only for ratings on the anniversary of her father's death. Garner's "ABC, fuck you" selfie and comments that it was unfortunate that Black people had to be loud in order to be heard were heard by networks and politicians who sought forums to demonstrate responsiveness and efficacy in rhetoric that failed to substantively address racist and lethal policing. Garner's abrasive critiques led her to be excluded from prestigious platforms; she wasn't a good "look" for the more well-heeled (Jackson 2016). Her unruly hope and despair were seen as liabilities by those who could adjust to unspoken but established guidelines for acceptable protest. Even the most prominent Black mothers who had lost children to police or vigilante violence deflected their rage away from Democratic officials who did not deliver tangible gains against police violence.

At the July 2016 Democratic National Convention in Philadelphia, the first night of speakers included President Bill Clinton, who had helped fuel mass incarceration with the 1994 Omnibus Crime Bill. Also on stage that night were "Mothers of the Movement," surrogates for Hillary Rodham Clinton. Among the Black parents-turned activists whose unarmed children had been killed by police or died in police custody were the mothers of Trayvon Martin (Sybrina Fulton), Sandra Bland (Geneva Reed-Veal), Michael Brown (Lesley McSpadden), and Eric Garner (Gwen Carr). Leaked emails from the hacked account of John Podesta, former White House Chief of Staff and 2016 chair of Clinton's presidential campaign, informed the public that the Democratic National Committee counseled staff to cheer every time "Black Lives Matter" was chanted but not to speak to media or activists of specific policies to regulate police violations and enforce ethical mandates within policing. Although Erica Garner's grandmother, Gwen Carr, participated in campaign appearances for Clinton, Garner herself remained adamant that only one presidential candidate, an outlier, actually took reforms in policing and imprisonment seriously.

Garner's ire and despair over the Democratic Party increased after Trump's victory: "Who is organizing to put these corporate democrats the fuck up out of your community?" (@es_snipes February 6, 2017). For Garner, the Democrats failed to win the presidency because they had failed to enforce ethical policing in Black and Brown communities: "My dad was killed under democrats and had democrats in a liberal city cover it up" (@es_snipes January 22, 2016). Disparaging the Democratic Party and the Congressional Black Caucus in tweets, Garner evokes the unethical policing practices used against the BPP as highly relevant: "i wonder sometimes are we setting ourselves up to be stamped out like the panthers" (@es_snipes September 12, 2016). Pointing to the communal care or captive maternal aspects of the panthers, she tweets: "The Panthers were a threat because they had the largest 'school lunch' program in the nation" (@es_snipes December 12, 2017). That the Panthers were uniformly depicted as terrorists—even those framed or acting in self-defense—was included in Garner's analysis: "#Hillary on the death penalty—must be reserved for terrorists . . . remember they called the panthers enemies of the state #DemDebate" (@es_snipes February 4, 2016).

Several months before her death, Garner entertained the idea of running for office—"If I run . . . [it's] because the #democrats there have failed us" (@es_snipes October 23, 2017). (Davis herself ran as a vice presidential candidate on the CPUSA ticket against presidential candidate Ronald Reagan in 1980 and 1984; Reagan as governor used his executive powers to have the UC Regents fire Davis from UCLA for being a member of the Communist Party, and later advocated the death penalty for her when she was on trial.) Garner's visibility shrank as she became more politically combative. Her politics were not assimilable to mainstream tastes and she consistently challenged the authority of all executive branches: President Obama, New York Governor Andrew Cuomo, and New York City Mayor Bill de Blasio. Garner's personal loss of her father led her to militancy that linked Black victimization with Black rebellion and street protests.

Months after her father's death, without funding or platforms, Garner gained media attention by staging demonstrations at the exact site where Pantaleo killed her dad. Those "die-ins" were filled with chants of "I Can't Breathe!" Needing more activists, Garner sought the support of Al Sharpton, whose National Action Network (NAN) brought three busloads of protestors to Staten Island. Conflicts with NAN and other organizations existed, yet Garner continued to organize and the splinter groups NYC Shut It Down and Millions March emerged. Negative, conservative press featured Garner criticizing Sharpton, yet the street protests grew. Garner confronted elected officials and filed a Freedom of Information Law (FOIL) request for civilian complaints against Pantaleo (it was blocked by the NYPD and the mayor). However, despite the activism, her despair grew: "I pursued every lead and exhausted every option to find justice for my father. Nothing worked—and every time I'd hit a dead end, I'd hear about another terrible story like my father's. Reality set in: I live within a system that regularly kills black people. My will to fight started to fade" (Garner and Alabi 2015). Garner never trusted government to provide social justice; hence her activism was uncivil and persistent, but without most mainstreamed allies, chasms of vulnerability became the norm for her.

Garner described the toll her trauma had taken: "When you deal with grief, when you talk about grief and you talk about how regular families deal with it, you know, families have problems, trouble coping with it." She went on, "Mental health is very important. . . . For families that's put in my position, black families that's on public assistance, that doesn't have the income to get therapy is $300 an hour, and I don't think that's fair, and it's not made for the black population, because how are we supposed to cope with this if we don't have someone to talk to, someone professionally to talk to?" She ended by saying, "I'm constantly reading articles and doing the research on my dad's case. But I'm not taking care of me" (Garner 2018).

According to Reggie Harris, a close friend of and co-activist with Erica Garner, public officials postured as supporters of the Garner family and Black communities but sided with city, state, and national bureaucracies: "She got empty words and promises. . . . de Blasio called himself a progressive but sided with the police unions. . . . Cuomo . . . appoint[ed] a special prosecutor, but only for one year. . . . Erica took her fight all the way to a Democratic White House to no avail" (Harris 2018).

Political confrontations increased precarity and diminished health: "The stresses of fighting for three years became too much for one person to bear. The fact that her death took place mere weeks after she took a year off and a few months after having her child is not lost" (Harris 2018). Heartfelt tributes to Garner highlight the vulnerability of families. Garner grew up partly in foster care, shaped by poverty and state domination (Wang 2017). She publicly shared that her three-year-old niece "bashed a boy in the head with a book at school and said that 'I'm angry the cops killed my grandfather. That's the reason why I did it'" (Garner 2018). Referencing the lack of sufficient mental health services for grief, she raised the issue of childhood trauma, which receives less attention given that adult women have become the face of movements. In the Garner apartment, Alyssa (Erica's daughter) would turn her back to the television whenever news flashes used the images of her grandfather being choked to death as a stand-in for Black death or trauma during police encounters. Watching and making eye contact with her mother, the child would only turn back to the cartoons after the footage of their (grand)father dying disappeared, her need for comfort outweighing her desire for entertainment. Four generations of Garner captive maternals protested and grieved: Gwen Carr, Esaw Garner, Erica Garner, Alyssa (on captive maternals, see James 2016).

Erica Garner's despair led not to suicide but to a breakdown of the body that led to collapse. An asthma attack precipitated a major heart attack that led to brain damage and a medically induced coma on December 23, 2017. She died at Brooklyn's Woodhull Medical and Mental Health Center on December 30, 2017. At the age of 27, she left behind two sisters, two brothers, grandmother Gwen Carr and mother Esaw Snipes, and two children: seven-year-old Alyssa who appears in the Sanders's ad and four-month-old Eric (her father's namesake). Garner had acknowledged in an interview with Ben Dixon: "I'm struggling right now with the stress and everything. This thing, it beats you down. The system beats you down to where you can't win" (@BenjaminPDixon December 28, 2017).

New York City had settled in 2015 with Eric Garner's family for $5.9 million but distributed funds only after Erica Garner's death. The 2016 philanthropic donations of tens of millions for a Black-led movement for Black lives included dozens of organizations, yet that financial support never likely reached Garner, who died in poverty (Ferguson 2018). For activist commentator Kirsten West Savali, Garner was politically unique: "Erica stood, unshakable, as an emerging, powerful voice of the radical black left. . . . Erica Garner was an intentional revolutionary" (West Savali 2017).

Conclusion

At the February 2019 State of the Union Address, President Donald Trump promoted the First Steps Act by showcasing two African Americans released under the Act after years of incarceration for drug trafficking. Presidential pardons, clemencies, and signings of reform bills offset anti-Black animus and draconian policing of the poor and racialized, but only to degrees. Celebrities such as Kim Kardashian had successfully lobbied Trump, gaining access to the oval office through First Daughter Ivanka Trump. For some, this highlighted the importance of celebrities in social reforms; for others, it underscored the capriciousness of politics dependent on celebrity advocates. Neither Angela Y. Davis nor Erica Garner would have uncritically championed the reforms passed by Trump: as a presidential candidate, Trump campaigned on police violence against arrestees and detainees in immigration centers, jails, and prisons. Trump's attorneys general and FBI directors avidly criminalized Black dissent against police violence by labeling protestors "Black Identity Extremists," while banning access to abortion and reproductive rights, which placed girls and women in medical and legal jeopardy. Some abolitionists have described Trump as a "uniter-in-Chief" (@VanJones68 November 14, 2018). Davis is not among them; she does not applaud reactionary politicians. Still, a powerful, charismatic centrist executive caught her political imagination. President Obama's lament that he could not "federalize" the police to control or limit their anti-Black animus followed his castigation of a street insurrection in the aftermath of Freddie Gray's death in police custody. All paths for ethical reforms of police forces lead to the executive branches where indifference, claims of incapacitation, or White nationalism block reforms and radical advocacy for community control of police.

Erica Garner—the "disruptor"—sought transformative change through critique and confrontation of a mayor, governor, and president—all who refused to meet the needs of the working class and poor. Angela Y. Davis—the nexus between historical Black rebellions and contemporary well-funded platforms—promotes visionary ideals and conventional politics as the path for radical goals. Garner's "unruly hope" distanced her from elite corridors of power shaped by academia, nonprofit corporations, and progressive media. Davis's confident faith in evolutionary politics solidifies the stature of political celebrities in human rights advocacy. Although Erica Garner's platforms were small, rickety stages built by un(der)funded outsiders, her militancy and that of her cadre helped spark a twentieth-first-century movement that believes in a Manichean divide between police violence and democratic (Black) freedom. Longevity was not on her side. It remains to be seen whether a continually challenged democracy, with or without decorum, can achieve the benchmark of her ethical demands and commitment to justice.

BIBLIOGRAPHY

Benner, Katie. 2019. "Eric Garner's Death Will Not Lead to Federal Charges for N.Y.P.D. Officer." *New York Times*, July 16, 2019. www.nytimes.com.

Davis, Angela Y. 1971a. "Political Prisoners, Prisons and Black Liberation." History Is a Weapon. www.historyisaweapon.com.

Davis, Angela Y. 1971b. "Reflections on the Black Woman's Role in the Community of Slaves." *Black Scholar* 3 (4): 2–15.

Davis, Angela Y. 2016. Keynote, Black Matters: The Futures of Black Scholarship and Activism Conference, University of Texas-Austin, September 29, 2016.

Davis, Angela Y. 2017a. "Angela Davis: An Interview on the Futures of Black Radicalism." Verso Blog, October 11, 2017. www.versobooks.com.

Davis, Angela Y. 2017b. "Inauguration 2017 Special Coverage." Interview by Amy Goodman. *Democracy Now!*, January 20, 2017. www.democracynow.org.

Davis, Angela Y. 2019. NAARPR Keynote and Panel Address at Chicago Refounding Conference of National Alliance Against Racist and Political Repression (NAARPR), November 22–24, 2019. [Quotations from this source are my own transcription.]

Dukmasova, Maya. 2016. "Advice from Angela Davis in the Aftermath of the Election." The Bleader, November 17, 2016. www.chicagoreader.com.

Felsenthal, Carol. 2016. "The Story behind Bernie Sanders's 1963 Arrest." *Chicago Magazine*, March 15, 2016. www.chicagomag.com.

Ferguson, Karen. 2018. "The Perils of Liberal Philanthropy." *Jacobin*, November 26, 2018. www.jacobinmag.com.

Garner, Erica. 2018. "Erica Garner Was 'Unbought and Unbossed' in Push for Justice after her Father Died in NYPD Chokehold." Interview by Amy Goodman. *Democracy Now!*, January 3, 2018. www.democracynow.org.

Garner, Erica, and Kemi Alabi. 2015. "Conflict Can Destroy Movements: We Need to Fight the System, Not Each Other." *Guardian*, December 9, 2015. www.theguardian.com.

Harris, Reggie. 2018. "Garner Way Political Director: Erica Garner 'Put Her Entire Life in This Fight.'" *Time*, January 3, 2018. https://time.com.

Huggins Salomon, Sheryl. 2016. "Angela Davis Talks Black Liberation, History and the Contemporary Vision." *Ebony*, February 17, 2016. www.ebony.com.

Jackson, Jenn M. 2016. "Erica Garner Walked Out of Obama's Town Hall on Police Violence." *Black Youth Project*, July 15, 2016. www.blackyouthproject.com

James, Joy. 2016. "The Womb of Western Theory: Trauma, Time Theft, and the Captive Maternal." *Carceral Notebooks* 12: 253–96.

Lieberman, Robbie. 2020. "The Black and Red Scare in the Twentieth-Century United States." In *The Palgrave Handbook of Anti-Communist Persecutions*, edited by Christian Gerlach and Clemens Six, 225–43. Cham: Palgrave Macmillan.

NBC New York. 2019. "James O'Neill to Lead Visa's Global Security after Resigning from NYPD." November 6, 2019. www.nbcnewyork.com.

Norton, Ben. 2017. "Erica Garner Was a Revolutionary. Don't Let Neoliberal Democrats Whitewash and Exploit Her." Ben Norton Blog, December 30, 2017. https://bennorton.com.

Reuters. 2020. "U.S. Political Activist Angela Davis Says Harris Makes Democratic Ticket 'More Palatable.'" August 13, 2020. www.reuters.com.

Sokolova, Marina. 2006. "Advocacy Democracy Modes: Benefits and Limitations." *Informacijos Mokslai*, 37: 110–21.

Southall, Ashley. 2019. "Daniel Pantaleo, Officer who Held Eric Garner in Chokehold, Is Fired." *New York Times*, August 19, 2019. www.nytimes.com.

Teen Vogue. 2019. "Black Lives Matter Co-Founder Patrisse Cullors Talks Prison Abolition, Therapy as Reparations, and Teaming Up with Angela Davis and Yara Shahidi." February 22, 2019. www.teenvogue.com.

Wang, Vivian. 2017. "Erica Garner, Activist and Daughter of Eric Garner, Dies at 27." *New York Times*, December 30, 2017. www.nytimes.com.

West Savali, Kirsten. 2016. "Angela Davis: 'I Am Not So Narcissistic to Say I Cannot Bring Myself to Vote for Hillary Clinton.'" The Root, September 30, 2016. www.theroot.com.

West Savali, Kirsten. 2017. "Erica Garner: 'I'm in This Fight Forever.'" The Root, December 31, 2017. www.theroot.com.

PART IV

Policing's Past and Future

9

Police and Slave Patrols

A History of State-Sponsored White-on-Black Violence

SALLY HADDEN

Though current police training emphasizes a color-blind approach to law enforcement, it will hardly come as a shock to learn that, in earlier times, men paid to uphold the law were actually encouraged, indeed, required to target specific groups based on their genetic profiles. Systematic racialized patterns of enforcement and harassment in the name of law, as well as violence, targeted minority communities for centuries in America, and in the process have created a deep reservoir of distrust toward the police among African Americans. Their enslaved ancestors (as well as those freed in the Civil War era) were repeatedly subject to state-sponsored violence by White slave patrollers and their successors, the Ku Klux Klan. That slave patrols preceded or were, in many cases, precursors to city and county police forces across the South is a poorly understood part of law enforcement history. The mistrust that many African Americans feel today about modern police is not merely a reflection of current-day policing methods, but also derives from a long, violent history of American law enforcement that was far from color-neutral, was focused on controlling slave behavior, and persisted for generations. Understanding this history of violent and discriminatory law enforcement, teaching it, and instructing modern officers how to overcome a legacy of distrust are themes this essay explores.

* * *

Most modern histories of American police start in the early nineteenth century, but that omits whole sections of colonial and early national American law enforcement that merit closer examination. As familiar as some readers may be with Robert Peel and his centralization of London police in 1828–29, there is a corresponding lack of awareness about the paid watch forces that existed prior to that time. Keeping "watch throughout the night" is a response to human anxiety experienced for centuries, as threats hidden by day became sources of danger after dark. Fear of attack by robbers, kidnappers, and worse kept many indoors after sunset. Those who stirred out of doors at night might be considered lawful or lawbreakers, depending on circumstance. "Suspicion was not distributed equally": "reputation, location, class, and gender" were used to "evaluate nocturnal activities" in the early modern period, and in America at least, one might add race to that evaluative list (Koslofsky 2011, 8). Upper-class men might walk through a village undisturbed at night, but the presence of a Native American or a stranger generated far more ambiguous reactions among White colonists. In early America, the potential harm posed by hostile Native Americans disturbed many newly arrived Europeans in regions inhabited by both groups. Meanwhile, runaway debtors became desperate when they had no money and their numbers were swelled by indentured servants seeking to elude their would-be masters; debtors and servants joined the "usual suspects" accused when crimes were committed. To control nighttime activity, colonial curfews became commonplace in towns and cities on both sides of the Atlantic. In addition, shopkeepers paid men to watch over their stores to prevent theft.

As settlements became towns, and towns grew in size and diversity, the care taken to protect homes and merchandise gradually developed into a broader mandate: to protect individuals at night via prevention that extended to all. This need became more urgent as ships arrived carrying sailors and Africans who spoke unfamiliar languages and whose very differentness could portend danger. The expanding number of strangers in the midst of colonial settlements—be they Indians, Africans, runaway servants, debtors, sailors—created a rising tide of anxiety in settlements gaining in population. The growth of city size, labor disputes, urban riots, and increasing immigration (particularly German and Irish) in the nineteenth century have all been explored as causes for the creation of American police, but community-sponsored peacekeeping existed well before the mid-nineteenth century, as studies from the 1960s and '70s uncovered (Lane 1967; Richardson 1970; Miller 1976).[1] The earliest forces, whether called the night watch, city guard, or town marshal, functioned as preventative (to deter offenses from taking place) rather than detective (to detect criminals, apprehend them, and punish wrongdoing after the fact). In the seventeenth and eighteenth centuries, fear of the stranger led to the formation of night watch forces in many locations and, in places where slave numbers were growing, to the development of slave patrols.[2]

At the same time as constables and night watchmen were active, colonial assemblies turned their attention to controlling slaves. Their intervention would not have been necessary had slaves voluntarily given their perfect and undivided loyalty to their masters' wishes—but of course no slave ever did. In the seventeenth century, legislatures in Barbados and elsewhere in the Caribbean developed laws to curb unwanted slave behaviors, whether that was walking abroad at night or selling foodstuffs in the markets by day. Initially, responsibility for enforcement was placed on overseers, but their inadequacy quickly led in the 1650s to the use of hired slave catchers. This weak patchwork system of enforcement caused Barbadian lawmakers to try again: in 1661 they created a comprehensive slave code that mandated that all Whites must share responsibility for apprehending runaway slaves. This system, too, failed to restrict slave movement enough for Whites. In the late seventeenth century, White islanders shifted responsibility from all Whites to the colony's militia, which was expected to enforce the laws on weekends and holidays. This model of militia-led patrolling spread to Jamaica, Antigua, and eventually to the North American mainland (Hadden 2001, 12–14).

White Barbadians emigrated to South Carolina in the seventeenth century, bringing much of their cultural and legal backgrounds with them, along with their slaves. Geographic differences demanded new solutions: on Barbados, the ocean provided a restrictive boundary that few slaves attempted to transgress, but the sheer size of North America and scattered nature of settlement there meant that in South Carolina runaway slaves might evade recapture and travel great distances in the process. To combat these tendencies, South Carolina's legislature instituted curfew restrictions (1687) that all Whites were to enforce, but South Carolina was no more successful than Barbados at making all Whites responsible for monitoring and controlling slave behavior. This shared responsibility soon led to the development of regular slave patrols (1704), which were colony-wide forces dedicated to the control of enslaved individuals. Meanwhile, in Charleston, the first urban watch groups appear to have come into existence in 1701: the two groups evolved side by side in Charleston, but outside of that city, patrols remained the primary form of law enforcement, targeting African Americans (Hadden 2001, 14–20).

In South Carolina, slave patrols were drawn from the militia, as in Barbados, but their functions soon made them distinct. In Barbados, all militia men served as patrollers; in South Carolina, the patrol functioned as a subset of the militia. In South Carolina, the militia might be marched to a distant frontier to fight against Native Americans or to the shore to ward off pirates. However, patrollers were designated to remain in the district from which they were drawn and were not to leave that area for any reason. In effect, Carolinians created two paramilitary groups capable of confronting two different enemies (foreign and domestic) simultaneously. Slave patrols in South Carolina were, for a brief time in the 1730s, paid for their service. This experiment ended and did not resume, despite the occurrence of the Stono Rebellion in 1739 (Hadden 2001, 14–24). Mandatory enlistment in the unpaid militia provided South Carolina its patrollers without additional cost. South Carolina's laws for slave patrols were copied and spread widely as White settlement expanded away from the earliest colonies, first to Georgia and then elsewhere across the Deep South as settlers moved into the interior of North America (Crane 1999).

Two other versions of patrols developed that did not entirely follow South Carolina's lead. In 1705, Virginians also crafted their own comprehensive slave code. The law provided rewards for private individuals who recaptured runaways but did not create a formal body charged to do so. In 1727, Virginia's burgesses called for their militia to patrol on specific holidays (Christmas, Easter) as well as from "time to time." In their earliest incarnation, patrollers could not use physical punishment on slaves, but were required to take a slave to a local constable for corporal punishment (this requirement soon fell away). Slave patrols were paid if they stayed on duty for more than two days, which suggests that they initially did not receive payment very often. In 1738, Virginians revised their patrol law in a significant manner: men appointed to patrol duty were exempted from service in the militia, and they were paid for each night of service they performed. Moreover, patrollers were exempted from taxation during their period of service, meaning that they received an additional indirect form of payment for controlling slaves (Hadden 2001, 24–32). These patrols existed long before their police counterparts: the earliest police in Richmond, Virginia, banded together as a public guard in 1801.

Meanwhile, in North Carolina, a third method of creating slave patrols developed in the eighteenth century. Slower to grow in population than its neighbors, North Carolina only enacted a comprehensive slave code in 1715, introducing a slave pass system and authorizing all Whites to "take up" any slave they discovered without a pass. The first formal slave patrol groups, called "searchers," came into existence in 1753 following an insurrection attempt. County courts had the power to appoint searchers, and the men were drawn from the rolls of potential jurors and taxpayers. Appointment as a searcher came with a tax exemption, as in Virginia, such that the men who became known as slave patrollers may be discovered through examination of early county tax reports. Patrols were paid additional sums if they discovered stolen goods or barrels. Their work increased to the point that the North Carolina legislature granted them additional forms of indirect compensation in 1779: patrols did not have to serve on juries, perform road work duty, or attend militia musters (Hadden 2001, 32–38).

The very earliest slave patrols from the seventeenth and eighteenth centuries evolved as cities and slave populations expanded. Rural patrols were managed by militia (as in South Carolina and Virginia) or county courts (the North Carolina example). Meanwhile, city patrols remained under the jurisdiction of town councils. As such, the development of police forces in urban areas like Charleston, South Carolina, or Alexandria, Virginia, was intertwined with the existence of local slave patrols. As towns became incorporated, town officials requested and received power from their legislatures to institute their own urban patrols. Politicians in Columbia, South Carolina, asked for power to regulate their own patrol due to the "inefficiency" of the surrounding county patrol. Virginia cities gained this power in 1832 in "An act concerning patrols" which specified that incorporated towns might supervise their own patrols (but unincorporated towns could not) (Commonwealth of Virginia 1832, 19–20). Fear of urban slaves and their nighttime activities prompted local Whites from Danville, Virginia (near the mountains), to

Georgetown, South Carolina (at the seashore), to establish civic patrol groups. Savannah likewise had an armed, uniformed city guard by 1796, which patrolled first on foot and later on horseback. The town council of Alexandria, Virginia, finally paid regular patrols a few years after 1800 (Caton 1933, 80–82). But no matter how much or how little city patrols were paid, enslaved men and women knew that patrollers were more likely to be active at night, attempting to restrict slave movement (Hadden 2001, 51–63).

Limiting slave and free Black movement was one task assigned to slave patrols, but hardly the only one. By the early nineteenth century, laws directed patrollers to "visit the negro houses . . . as often as may be necessary" to search for weapons and for individuals who should not be present; they were to "be vigilant and endeavor to detect all thefts" paying particular attention to individuals who traded alcohol to slaves for stolen goods; and they were to go anywhere that slaves were suspected of hiding or gathering, particularly to secret religious gatherings that were thought to be places where insurrections could be planned (Cantwell 1860, 377). Patrols could enter any building, slave cabin, or business, searching for slaves without a warrant. Their work granted them immunity from the requirements that policemen otherwise had to follow when searching the property of suspicious individuals. Their activities drew them to the farms and plantations where Whites were known to be absent, elderly, or infirm; in areas where Whites were few, patrols attempted to provide additional supervision, even though this practice was difficult to sustain in coastal South Carolina where White absenteeism was high every year during the so-called "sickly season." Patrol regulations in Louisiana parishes like St. Tammany insisted that every slave cabin had to be visited once a month by patrollers and that any man failing to perform his duty could be fined between ten and twenty-five dollars for the infraction—a significant sum when twenty dollars might constitute a month's wages (Williams 1972, 406). Changes in St. Tammany Parish coincided with reforms happening in New Orleans in 1836, where the city instituted around-the-clock patrolling by men on the beat, breaking up the squads of individuals who worked in groups and instead assigning patrolmen to work on a rotation of beats around the city (Rousey 1996, 35).

Dispersing slave gatherings of any type and any size was a designated slave patrol duty, for these meetings were considered potentially dangerous and even insurrectionary, but it would take scrutiny by a slave patroller to determine whether a slave was traveling for legitimate or illegitimate purposes. Former slave Fannie Moore recalled in her old age that slave patrollers beat to death a slave they discovered at an illicit dance (Rawick 1973, 132). Ex-slave narratives, such as those collected by the Works Progress Administration (WPA) in the 1930s, are replete with examples of patrol violence directed at slaves discovered away from their masters' plantations for dances, secret religious meetings, or simple truancy. Slaves traveling from one plantation to another on sanctioned business for their masters, however, typically carried passes, documents that were supposed to provide freedom of movement to individuals otherwise restricted to one plantation or farm. Slaves who were married "abroad" (meaning, their spouse lived on a different farm) often had weekly passes that permitted regular movement for the purposes of conjugal and familial visits.

Passes granted by masters to their slaves should have provided immunity from any sort of patrol harassment, but personal animosity and vindictiveness could override that protection. Patrollers might beat individuals whom they saw dressed nicely or who simply offended them by refusing to be deferential. Such indiscriminate beatings could produce conflict between slave masters and patrols, but slave patrols were insulated from countermeasures like lawsuits or fines; the very nature of their work, authorized by state law, granted them protection if other Whites thought their violence had gone too far (Crane 1999, 123–24). Stories persist of slaves who attempted to bargain with or bribe patrols to turn a blind eye to their truancy or stolen goods. More often, enslaved men and women had to contend with the limits patrols placed on their patterns of movement (Hadden 2001, 105–20). On rare occasions, slaves struck back, using the routines of patrol behavior—repeatedly traveling down the same road going in order from house A to house B—to lay ambushes where patrollers could be attacked (Hadden 2001, 133–35). Most slaves did not choose reprisal but attempted to become invisible to the eyes of patrollers, either by complying with their dictates, or by leaving the zones of their control entirely and turning runaway.

Not all slave patrols worked by moving from point to point. Stationary patrolling, much like the modern stakeout, was also used to intercept slaves moving along secret paths and near the homes of individuals suspected of trading liquor to slaves illegally. Farmers who suffered repeated losses due to slave theft might invite patrols to work near their property to prevent future incursions. Poor Whites, whose circumstances and sympathies might lead them to barter liquor for stolen foodstuffs, sometimes also found their property under surveillance by slave patrols. Nothing prevented patrols from entering the homes of Whites to look for slave-supplied goods, but surveillance outside might catch the slaves trading illicit goods (Hadden 2001, 122).

Paid by their governments (either directly or indirectly) and limited in movement to their town or county region, slave patrols have sometimes been confused with slave catchers, like those immortalized in the fictional *Uncle Tom's Cabin* (Stowe 1852). Slave catchers sought reward money from slave masters for capturing runaways who had traveled long distances from the plantations of their masters. Effectively, they worked as independent agents, being paid only for their successes in retaking runaway slaves who had already successfully evaded patrols. While slave catchers worked all over the South, they mostly concentrated near rivers or in cities with sizeable free Black populations (like St. Louis or New Orleans). Slave catchers also operated in the North, where long-distance runaways might flee (Meaders 1995, 47–65; Foner 2015). Slave catchers sometimes worked by commission for specific slave owners, to retake a specific runaway known to have traveled hundreds of miles into states where slavery was not legal. By contrast, slave patrollers were always local men, rooted in their communities and operating among slaves who they frequently knew well. Patrollers' work might be considered largely preventative, while slave catchers' activities tended more toward detection and retrieval.

The 1830s saw heightened patrol activity in many parts of the South, although in some regions that was a result not of threatened insurrection but simply growing populations of enslaved men and women. Lewis County, Missouri, the northernmost county of the state and directly across the Mississippi River from the free state of Illinois, only came into existence in 1833: White slave owners tended to settle elsewhere in the state to put some distance between their slave property and the lure of freedom across the river (Lee 1971, 294–95). In 1836, the first Lewis County slave patrol formed and was ordered to go out nightly for a total of twenty-four hours each month. By 1840, the county had 1,075 slaves living in Lewis County, and their numbers continued to rise, reaching one thousand two hundred in 1850. In the wake of John Brown's daring raid on military supply stores at Harpers Ferry, Virginia—thought by many to be a harbinger of pan-southern race war—Lewis County residents wanted a more active patrol. A month after Brown's raid, the *La Grange National American* (published in Lewis County's largest city) advocated that the county patrol should have the power to detain any African American they encountered after 8pm, whether free or enslaved.[3]

Widespread White fear of slave insurrections reached dizzying heights in 1859 and 1860, and slave patrols responded with vigorous enforcement. In Washington County, North Carolina, patrols were augmented by an additional fifty armed men after reports circulated of a threatened slave revolt in the vicinity. Fires in cities like Charlotte, North Carolina, led to increased manpower on slave patrols to try to find the culprits responsible. Local areas that had allowed patrolling to lapse formed new patrol groups, like the one in Vicksburg, Mississippi. Across the South, anxiety caused by Brown's raid and plans to distribute weapons to enslaved African Americans reanimated slave patrols in places where patrolling had become lax (Hadden 2001, 170–71; Crane 1999, 126–27).

Once the American Civil War commenced in 1861, White southerners faced new problems in staffing slave patrols. The demand for able-bodied men to join the Confederate Army drained the pool of available men who could also serve in local patrols. Although some areas increased the number of patrols in the first year of the war, such a sustained effort became virtually impossible once the Confederacy introduced conscription in the spring of 1862. At that point, men between eighteen and thirty-five, sound in mind and body, became subject to the army's demands. Exceptions to conscription existed—exempting teachers, hospital and railroad workers, ministers, and state officials—and among the most detested was the exemption granted to men who owned twenty or more slaves, introduced in October 1862. This left some White adult men in each community who could continue to patrol at night, though their numbers were significantly diminished. As the Union Army captured more and more territory, enslaved men and women escaped the watching eyes of patrollers and fell under the jurisdiction of northern commanders. Should a Confederate Army unit be in the vicinity, slaves might find their movement even more restricted, as the local patrol received reinforcement from roving bands of cavalry. Fluctuating restrictions near the scenes of battle could paradoxically create greater or lesser amounts of surveillance from patrol groups over African Americans. In cities like Richmond, Virginia, capital of the Confederacy, slave patrols continued to operate in tandem with military provost marshals each night until the war's conclusion. In smaller towns, some of which abandoned patrolling in the middle of the war, the approaching victory by northern forces led to the reintroduction of patrols, utilizing old men and young boys, in 1865 to subdue slaves and prevent them from acting as they pleased (Crane 1999, 172–87).

Emancipation, whether it occurred in 1863 with President Abraham Lincoln's proclamation or as the result of General Grant's victory over Robert E. Lee in 1865, officially ended slave patrols. However, many southern Whites refused to accept the end of slavery and directed their hostility to former slaves in a variety of ways. Foremost among these hostile acts was the introduction, postwar, of laws to control and punish nighttime travel by African Americans, the reintroduction of a pass system, and roving bands of White vigilantes that searched the homes of former slaves looking for weapons or other contraband. In the winter of 1865, rumors circulated that emancipated African Americans intended to rise up and slaughter Whites across the South at Christmas. Though the rebellion never materialized, fears of insurrection caused some Whites to band together as patrols or extralegal groups to continue monitoring African American behavior. Some postwar governors simply ignored the Thirteenth Amendment and called for their militia to continue to function as patrols (Hadden 2001, 194–99).

Lawmakers in southern states responded to the Thirteenth and Fourteenth Amendments by introducing Black Codes, which were intended to reintroduce slavery in everything but name. Black Codes listed all forbidden behaviors by African Americans, which included everything from not having a job to being disrespectful to White people. The compulsive desire Whites had to control African Americans, even in freedom, generated wide support for these new laws in the South and an opportunity for southern police forces—new in some cities—to reintroduce patrol activities under the guise of police work. Anti-vagrancy laws (which featured prominently in all state Black Codes of this period) were effectively a return to the pass system that enabled all patrols to ask for papers from African Americans—only now the papers would have to show the name of a freed slave's employer. Without papers, "strolling" or "idle" African Americans were subject to incarceration. Their court and jail fees would often be paid off by a local White who could force the African Americans to work until those funds had been "repaid." This system forced all African Americans to find a White employer or face the prospect of being jailed and then sold off for a period of time to a White who wanted unfree workers (Wilson 1965; Richardson 1969; Williamson 1965). Backlash against the Black Codes in Congress (dominated by northerners) delayed the readmission of southern states into the Union and forced repeal of those laws in the 1860s.

The continued military occupation of the South by Union troops forced the Black Codes into abeyance, but southern Whites did not need laws on the books to continue their centuries-long intimidation tactics against African Americans. Though slave patrols may have been formally disbanded and Black Codes disallowed, southern Whites in the 1860s and '70s found new ways to use violence and terror to keep African Americans from fully using their civil and political rights. White vigilante groups like the Ku Klux Klan, the Knights of the White Camelia, and other unnamed bands took up the nighttime activities of slave patrols with a similar objective: to intimidate African Americans with the threat of violence. The Klan and other White supremacist groups broke up religious and social gatherings, took away weapons belonging to African Americans, and engaged in other actions that ranged from pranks to systematic brutality directed at former slaves. The Klan's increasing power after 1865 drew on the legacy of slave patrols but with added urgency: they believed that African Americans, now freed, must be forcefully reminded that the South continued to be controlled by Whites. Whatever name these southern White groups used, their actions were similar: they worked primarily at night, as patrols had done, using the cover of darkness to surprise and terrify their victims. Freedom brought changes to their actions, however. The property rights that Whites had in their slaves prevented slave patrols from engaging in the strongest forms of brutality, for to do so risked retribution from slave-owning neighbors who had seen their valuable (human) property damaged. Slave owners routinely participated in patrols, thus restraining the impulse toward the greatest violence. Where slave patrols had been somewhat restrained in their brutality toward slaves—a slave with a broken arm could not work the next day—there were no financial disincentives to extreme violence in the postwar, post-emancipation world. The Klan could beat, maim, or even kill an African American, and no southern White would protest the brutality.

There was a second difference between the Ku Klux Klan and the slave patrols that preceded them, aside from the increased violence the Klan could inflict. Slave patrols operated within the law, with the support and legal imprimatur of state and community. Southern White men who rode on patrol had no reason to mask their identities, for they had nothing to fear from going about openly. In the postwar period, however, violence against African Americans was subject to retaliation by Union army officers or local branches of the Freedmen's Bureau. The continuing and increasing use of violence directed at African Americans inspired Congress to pass the Enforcement Acts of 1870 and 1871, which criminalized violence against African Americans; the Third Enforcement Act specifically permitted the suspension of habeas corpus to prosecute men who attacked former slaves while hooded. As federal protection of African Americans escalated, southern Whites who wished to participate in the Klan but avoid detection took the precaution of wearing hoods to disguise themselves. The white sheets became distinctively tied to Klan activities, while also presenting the White men beneath them as terrorizing ghosts to the African Americans who encountered them. Where slave patrols had never needed disguises, postwar White supremacists like the Klan robed themselves in sheets to prevent detection and increase the psychological terror their victims experienced when they were attacked (Hadden 2001, 207–20; Trelease 1971; Wade 1988; Fry 1991).

Slave patrols have been absent from the American scene since 1865, but long shadows continue to be cast by their human imitators. The all-too-obvious legacy lives on in the modern-day Klan and other White supremacist groups, who use masks and false identities to shield their actions from discovery—even as they continue to target African Americans for physical and psychological intimidation.[4] The intermittent use by Whites of lynching spread terror in the nineteenth and twentieth centuries. Less obvious, yet clearly related to slave patrols, are the modern-day police forces of America; contemporary law enforcers cannot entirely escape the legacy of White-on-Black violence that inflected southern law enforcement even before the American Civil War. Police forces from Baltimore to New Orleans maintained tight racial restrictions on both free and enslaved African Americans, restrictions that persisted after emancipation occurred. Racist attitudes combined with support from local White community leaders encouraged police commanders like Bull Connor in the 1960s to terrorize Civil Rights leaders in Birmingham, Alabama. As Birmingham's Commissioner of Public Safety, Connor allowed groups like the Klan to brutalize Freedom Riders intent on desegregating public transit in 1961, actions that smacked of the racial control envisioned by creators of the slave patrols (Nunnelley 1991). Recurrent violence between White officers and African American citizens, though less obviously driven by race hatred than by ingrained indifference to Black lives, has extended the ugly inheritance patrols bequeathed to American society into the twenty-first century.

* * *

If one knows that an organization has a history of immoral and violent behavior, what is the ethical individual to do—should she join such a group? In the case of modern-day police departments, upholding law and order seems a noble calling. Yet police departments developed from groups like slave patrols, as this essay has demonstrated, that engaged in what most Americans today would consider to be reprehensible behavior: race-based violence. In the years that followed the end of slavery, other organizations across the South, like the Klan or Knights of the White Camelia, continued to terrorize African Americans by the systematic use of racial violence—a pattern of behavior that police officers at best tolerated and at worst participated in. Once Reconstruction ended and the few African Americans who served on police forces were removed from their posts, Jim Crow-era police forces continued to use their powers across the South to victimize African Americans and target them for rigorous enforcement of the law, with arrest and conviction rates that far outstripped comparable rates for Whites guilty of the same offenses. What actions, therefore, can a recruit or a leader of a police department take in order to behave in an ethical fashion toward African Americans, in light of this history of systemic racial discrimination and violence?

Teaching the history of patrols is an initial step. Courses on criminal justice and introductions to law enforcement should instruct students about these episodes from the American past that reveal patterns of brutality and White-on-Black violence. They should learn that slavery consisted not of individual masters choosing to become slaveholders with the right to harm slaves (a private decision, set within an institution that officially ended in 1865) but that slavery included state-sponsored and paid-for acts of domination (a publicly funded choice, with consequences that outlasted the institution's 1865 demise). Officers training in police academies and new recruits receiving continuing education on peacekeeping should learn about the activities of slave patrols that worked in their locality, state, or region; for those living outside of the American South, this material might be supplemented by information about the various African American diasporas and their timing in history, to make clear the connection between African American experiences of patrols or the Klan and African American internal migration from the South to other parts of the United States. This education effort could include texts as well as documentaries about patrols, such as *Slave Catchers, Slave Resisters*, which was broadcast on the History Channel (Aponte-Rios 2005). Focusing on pre-Civil War history and the Klan may cause some students to respond with claims of "those groups were illegal or only existed before the Civil War." Educators and ethicists should also insist upon the study of post-Civil War policing, to have students explore how the justice system was perverted during the regime of Jim Crow that prevailed well into the twentieth century. Some literature should be required reading: Dennis Rousey's study of the police department in antebellum and postwar New Orleans demonstrates clearly that while that city briefly had an integrated police force from 1865 to 1877—and one that was a model for the entire nation—the end of Reconstruction changed everything. After 1877, African American officers were expelled from the force, and city police adopted brutality toward African Americans as the norm by 1889. What had once been a national model for integration and good policing turned into a venal and violent force of racial oppression (Rousey 1996).

Another step in this ethical engagement with the past could move beyond the education of current-day law officers. In America, we might take as our model the South African Truth and Reconciliation Commission, instituted in 1996 in the wake of apartheid, to promote national unity in a severely racially divided country. The Commission encouraged victims to come forward and give name and voice to the human rights violations perpetrated against Black South Africans by their White oppressors. In the case of South Africa, these offenses were still within living memory and in many instances the criminals were still alive—yet the purpose was not to retroactively criminalize behaviors that had previously been considered just and legal, though reparations were an option. The intention was also to make public the harms and hold open the possibility for true repentance on behalf of the wrongdoers.

In America, justice could not be done to victims now long dead, but recording, acknowledging, and remembering our history of repeated and systematic White-on-Black violence could make significant inroads into the mistrust that African Americans typically experience when they think of modern police. This process might be limited to the pre-Civil War period, but a more productive local experience might be to explore all periods of the American past for White-on-Black state-sponsored violence through testimony, newspapers, court and local records, and then to find ways to memorialize and recognize that history. This could be accomplished through some combination of television broadcasts, museum exhibits, public works of art, permanent markers, or other means. The historical marker and soil collection projects sponsored by the Equal Justice Initiative's (2019) Community Remembrance Project engages the public in this type of memorialization effort, and it offers a model for how acknowledging and educating the public can broaden the collective memory of racialized violence in society.[5] Working locally to remember this past of racialized violence would personalize this endeavor—the local context would, one suspects, make the process of recording and remembering less abstract and more "real" for the participants.

As a historian, I am more comfortable interpreting the past than prescribing for the future. Yet the topic of White-on-Black state-sponsored violence is one that continues to be an unhealed wound in our nation's shared experience, a deep scar that is reopened with each new outrage that ignores how Black Lives Matter. Rather than whitewash this violence with its twin legacy of resentment and mistrust, hoping that all of it will "just go away," perhaps the healthiest way to rebuild communities and foster greater trust in law enforcement, one community at a time, is to understand, teach, and remember the slave patrols of the past, in hopes that all will benefit from knowing about and remembering that experience in times to come.

NOTES

1 For a summary of early literature, see Monkkonen (1981, 4–15).
2 The long-running debate between those focused on the development of police as a response to working-class unrest, anxiety about social change and immigration versus those fixated on the new police as a manifestation of expanded national state authority (both phenomena being largely associated with the late eighteenth or early nineteenth centuries) has overlooked the critical role that social anxiety, particularly social anxiety about "the other," played in early America. For an overview of the historiographic divide in police literature, see Harris (2004, 7).
3 November 19, 1859, article, cited in Lee (1971, 301).
4 The Klan has gained new members at various points in its history. For the 1920s, see Maclean (1995).
5 I am grateful to the editors for bringing the valuable work of this foundation to my attention.

BIBLIOGRAPHY

Aponte-Rios, Miguelangel. 2005. "Slave Catchers, Slave Resisters." Northern Light Productions, A&E Home Video.

Cantwell, Edward. 1860. *The Practice of Law in North Carolina*. Vol. 1. *Legislative and Executive Powers*. Raleigh, NC: Strother and Marcum.

Caton, James R. 1933. *Jottings from the Annals of Alexandria: Legislative Chronicles of the City of Alexandria*. Alexandria, VA: Newell-Cole.

Commonwealth of Virginia. 1832. *Acts Passed at a General Assembly of the Commonwealth of Virginia, Begun and Held at the Capital, in the City of Richmond, on Monday, the Fifth Day of December, in the Year of Our Lord, One Thousand Eight Hundred and Thirty-One, and of the Commonwealth the Fifty-Sixth*. Richmond, VA: Ritchie.

Crane, J. Michael. 1999. "Controlling the Night: Perceptions of the Slave Patrol System in Mississippi." *Journal of Mississippi History* 61 (2): 119–36.

Equal Justice Initiative. 2019. Community Justice Initiative. https://eji.org.

Foner, Eric. 2015. *Gateway to Freedom: The Hidden History of the Underground Railroad*. New York: Norton.

Fry, Gladys-Marie. 1991. *Night Riders in Black Folk History*. Reprint ed. Athens, GA: University of Georgia Press.

Hadden, Sally E. 2001. *Slave Patrols: Law and Violence in Virginia and the Carolinas.* Cambridge, MA: Harvard University Press.

Harris, Andrew T. 2004. *Policing the City: Crime and Legal Authority in London, 1780–1840.* Columbus, OH: Ohio State University Press.

Koslofsky, Craig. 2011. *Evening's Empire: A History of the Night in Early Modern Europe.* Cambridge, UK: Cambridge University Press.

Lane, Roger. 1967. *Policing the City: Boston 1822–1885.* Cambridge, MA: Harvard University Press.

Lee, George. 1971. "Slavery and Emancipation in Lewis County, Missouri." *Missouri Historical Review* 65 (3): 294–317.

Maclean, Nancy. 1995. *Behind the Mask of Chivalry: The Making of the Second Ku Klux Klan.* New York: Oxford University Press.

Meaders, Daniel. 1995. "Kidnapping Blacks in Philadelphia: Isaac Hopper's Tales of Oppression." *Journal of Negro History* 80 (2): 47–65.

Miller, Wilbur H. 1976. *Cops and Bobbies: Police Authority in New York and London, 1830–1870.* Chicago: University of Chicago Press.

Monkkonen, Eric. 1981. *Police in Urban America 1860–1920.* Cambridge, UK: Cambridge University Press.

Nunnelley, William. 1991. *Bull Connor.* Tuscaloosa, AL: University of Alabama Press.

Rawick, George. 1973. *The American Slave: A Composite Autobiography*, vol. 15: *North Carolina Narratives*, part 2. Westport, CT: Greenwood Press.

Richardson, James. 1970. *The New York Police: Colonial Times to 1901.* New York: Oxford University Press.

Richardson, Joe M. 1969. "Florida Black Codes." *Florida Historical Quarterly* 47 (4): 365–79.

Rousey, Dennis. 1996. *Policing the Southern City: New Orleans, 1805–1889.* Baton Rouge, LA: Louisiana State University Press.

Stowe, Harriet Beecher. 1852. *Uncle Tom's Cabin: Or, Life among the Lowly.* Boston: J. P. Jewett.

Trelease, Allen W. 1971. *White Terror: The Ku Klux Klan Conspiracy and Southern Reconstruction.* New York: Harper & Row.

Wade, Wyn C. 1988. *The Fiery Cross: The Ku Klux Klan in America.* New York: Simon and Schuster.

Williams, E. Russ, Jr. 1972. "Slave Patrol Ordinances of St. Tammany Parish, Louisiana, 1835–1838." *Louisiana History* 13 (4): 399–412.

Williamson, Joel. 1965. *After Slavery: The Negro in South Carolina During Reconstruction, 1861–1877.* Chapel Hill, NC: University of North Carolina Press.

Wilson, Theodore B. 1965. *The Black Codes of the South.* Tuscaloosa, AL: University of Alabama Press.

10

From Protection to Predation

Policing as the Pursuit of War by Other Means in the Third Reich

NICOLAS DE WARREN

Rather than consider the ethics of policing in the United States, Europe, or further afield in a contemporary context, I shall propose to address this theme from an historical vantage point, more specifically, from a case study of the transformation of the police into an indispensable institution and instrument for a totalitarian regime. My aim in this chapter is to chart a logic of transformation that reveals the significance of biopower and governmentality—notions drawn from Michel Foucault's thinking—for the analysis of the multiple configurations of policing under the Third Reich. I am especially interested in exploring the volatility of the distinction between the police and the military in the theoretically instructive context of Nazi Germany. From this admittedly distant perspective vis-à-vis the ethics of policing in our own social, cultural, and political contexts, I hope to address a broader set of questions regarding the shifting relationship between the military and the police, as driven by the intensification of bio-political diffusions of power, to the point that the radical transformation of both, as illustrated with the Third Reich, leads to emergence of a novel form of state-organized violence: *the predator*.

This analysis is situated within an overarching interest in the evolution or, more accurately stated, the devolution or splintering of organized violence in the twentieth and twentieth-first centuries. Rather than consider this "splintering" of warfare,[1] in concept as well as practice, solely within the current debates of the "New Wars" (see Kaldor 2012), my secondary aim in this chapter is to extend our understanding of the phenomenon of "New Wars" to include what might be termed

"New Policing": transformations in the ethics, or as shall be the case with Nazi Germany, the *unethics* of policing.

My claim (for which this contribution is meant to offer motivation and illustration) is that any reflection on the transformations subsumed under the heading of "New Wars" must take into consideration the double transformation of the militarization of the police *and* the "policification" of the military—if I may coin this term. Whereas the employment of professional military forces for policing tasks in the context of peacekeeping, cosmopolitan law enforcement, and anti-terrorism are often discussed in debates about the "New Wars," the analogous phenomenon of the militarization of the police within nation-states remains neglected (e.g., Kaldor 2012, 132–34). This militarization of the police takes on varied forms (one thinks of the deployment of militarized police forces against drug networks in Brazil and the Philippines) and often involves the influx of ex-military personnel (often with combat experience abroad), military training and equipment, and, most critically, a mode of perception and speaking in which police actions are framed as *war*.

As I hope to illustrate with the example of totalitarianism in the German context, within this double transformation, the organization, function, and mentality of "the military" as well as "the police" becomes transformed, and by no means in terms of a reciprocal exchange of roles and responsibilities. This transformation of the police and the military leads to the emergence of new forms of organized violence that are no longer recognizable as either "the police" or "the military," to wit, as either a militarized police or a policing military. The double transformation of the police and the military cannot be conceptualized without an analysis of the transformation of the schemas of space and time in which organized violence becomes deployed.

As I shall argue, the (territorial) border and the (conceptual and institutional) boundary becomes the site for the normalization of the exception or, as is strikingly apparent with Nazi Germany, the normalization of the "unethical." In the particular context of the Third Reich, this new figure of violence, as I shall conclude this argument, is the *predator* or *hunter* as a state-organized, supported, and sustained form of violence. The production of this new form of state-organized violence—the predator—operates within the produced in-between of the border and the boundary.

Modern Sovereignty, the Police, and the Military

Given that my interest is not merely historical, but theoretical—specifically, historically informed theoretical reflection—let me first delineate in broad strokes the contours of a conceptual framework in which I shall examine policing in Nazi Germany. Ever since the seventeenth and eighteenth centuries, the police have become indispensable for the modern nation-state in Western Europe and North America. Not fortuitously, the historical origins of the modern police coincide with the parallel establishment of modern military institutions, as professional, state-organized national armies. Beginning with transformations in warfare toward the end of the sixteenth century and into the Thirty Years War, nation-states increasingly employed the service of trained, standing armies, which required a sophisticated degree of training, organization of economic resources, centralized bureaucracies, hierarchical administration, taxation and levying, and, most significantly, concentration of power (see Tilly 1985, 1992). Both of these forms of organized violence—the police and the military—are integral to the modern conception of sovereignty, as influentially defined by Max Weber in terms of the monopolization of violence. In Weber's conception, the state is "a human community that (successfully) claims the monopoly of the legitimate use of physical force within a given territory" (Weber 1958, 78).

This definition of the absolute sovereignty of the state and foundational principle of *raison d'état* extends back to the political thought of the late sixteenth and early seventeenth centuries. In Jean Bodin's *Six livres de la république*, often considered as a foundational statement of the concept of modern state sovereignty (along with Thomas Hobbes's *Leviathan*), we find a marked accent on the violent origins of the state. As Bodin writes: "The Republic establishes itself through the violence of those who are strongest [*La Republique s'establit par la violence des plus forts*]" (Bodin 1576, IV, 1, 7). Within the state, the citizen is likewise constituted as the subject of violence, namely, as subjected to authority of the sovereign, or, as Bodin writes, "by the majesty of the person to whom allegiance and obedience is due [*par la majesté de celuy auquel il doit obeisance*]" (Bodin 1576, I, 6, 114). Bodin distinguished five "marks" or features of sovereignty: the right to appoint magistrates and their legal empowerment; the right to establish and overturn laws; the right to declare war as well as peace; the authority to which magistrates can appeal; and the power over the life and death of individuals.

Within the republic, sovereignty is absolute, indivisible, and "perpetual," and as Thomas Hobbes would clarify more distinctly, sovereignty is neither the king nor the people nor any given institution, but the state itself, which, like the image of Leviathan, transcends in thus unifying its integral parts, or elements. Leaving aside any further consideration of these respective political philosophies, it is interesting to note Bodin's usage of the term "police" in the sense of *gouvernement*, the "form of government of the polis, of a state [*forme de gouvernement d'une cité, d'un État*]," and the rule of "the soul over the body and reason over greed [*l'âme sur le corps and raison sur la cupidité*]" (Becker 2014). In Bodin's understanding, the term *police* does not signify the enforcement of public law and control over citizens, but expresses, more broadly, the governing of the "soul" of the city and state. Already with the conceptual foundations of modern state-sovereignty, the police become conceptualized not just in terms of enforcement and protection, but as productive of social order.[2]

This connection between the genealogy of modern sovereignty and the origins of the modern police is central to Michel Foucault's analysis of the shifting forms and manifestations of power since the fifteenth and sixteenth centuries. Throughout Foucault's writings, from his work on madness to his celebrated lectures at the *Collège de France*, the police represent a constant, if developing and varied, theme of inquiry. In *Discipline and Punish*, the police are conceptualized as an institution of the modern state within a narrative of the transformation of power as sovereignty (as with Jean Bodin) to disciplinary power. The establishment of the police proves critical for the formation of what Foucault calls the "carceral society" of disciplinary power. The institutions of police and the prison are strictly correlated; both form a state-administered "police-prison system" operating both "inside" and "outside" prison walls (Foucault 1995, 297–98).[3]

Foucault's notion of a "carceral society" suggests that "outside" the prison walls remains nonetheless "inside" (and likewise, that "inside" prison walls is not "outside" the public sphere, but inside the inside, namely, where the deployment of disciplinary power achieves its most spectacular and concentrated locus). This becomes reinforced with the further insight that disciplinary power operates along with the formation of the "Panopticon," again, both inside and outside the prison. The term *police* broadly designates an institution of disciplinary and surveillance techniques. As Foucault proposes, "the organization of the police apparatus in the eighteenth century sanctioned a generalization of the disciplines that became co-extensive with the state itself" (Foucault 1995, 215). In this conception, the police are an indispensable instrument and institution for the "generalization of discipline," that is, the formation of a disciplinary society, as well as for the generalization of visibility, that is, the formation of a panoptic society. Both of these generalizations, or operations of policing, encroach on non-disciplinary spaces as well as "invisible spaces." As Foucault writes, "this power had to be given the instrument of permanent, exhaustive, omnipresent surveillance, capable of making all visible, as long as it could itself remain invisible. It had to be like a faceless gaze that transformed the whole social body into a field of perception: thousands of eyes posted everywhere" (Foucault 1995, 214).

In addition to this conception of the police in its disciplinary and surveillance functions, Foucault identifies another essential function of police in the genealogy of modern power and the state. In the lectures grouped under the title *Security, Territory, Population*, Foucault turns his critical attention to what he dubs "the secret history of the police" in regulating social welfare, economic markets, urbanization, and health. Under the heading of governmentality, not to be confused with the state, the object of power is the control and maintenance of populations. Governmentality, in this argument, operates through two essential institutions: the police as "internal array of forces" and the "military-diplomatic apparatus" as external array of forces. As Foucault remarks,

> From the seventeenth century "police" begins to refer to the set of means by which the state's forces can be increased while preserving the state in good order. In other words, police will be the calculation and technique that will make it possible to establish a mobile, yet stable and controllable relationship between the state's internal order and the development of its forces. (Foucault 2009, 313)

In identifying the police and the military as the primary institutions of governmentality, Foucault echoes Weber's definition of the state, even as the notions of "sovereignty" and "power" have been reformulated into "governmentality" and "biopower." Nonetheless, a formal spatial, institutional, and conceptual division subtends both conceptions: police is the array of *internal* force whereas the military is the array of *external* forces. Whereas the military (in the modern sense of the professional institution of the state) organizes and operates legitimate violence projected outside of national territory (against other states or external political actors on the international stage), the institution of the police organizes and operates the monopoly of legitimate violence within the territorial boundaries of the state. In Weber's definition (much as in Foucault's), what underpins this distinction between the police and the military is the clarity and stability of territorial borders in terms of the conceptual and institutional boundaries projected in contrasting spaces of possible reach. Within the monopoly of violence of the modern state, the police have no jurisdiction beyond national boundaries, while the military cannot be deployed within national boundaries (unless under the exception of civil war). A spatial border is not only a territorial marker. It also becomes a set of conceptual boundaries delineating a space of legality, a cultural-psychological marker of the difference between criminal and enemy, and a political situation of conflict between friend and foe.

This distinction between police and military in terms of territorial borders and conceptual boundaries is implied in Carl von Clausewitz's seminal (unfinished) treatise *On War*. If Weber's conception of the modern nation-state implies a theoretical foundation for modern police, as the legitimate employment of violence *within* national territory, Clausewitz explicitly codified the modern conception of nation-state in terms of its legitimate employment (and hence monopolization, that is: private armies or militias cannot fight in the name or in lieu of the nation-state) of violence *outside* national borders. Only the nation-state can claim both the rationality and legitimacy of organized violence outside its territory in the pursuit of its political interests (Clausewitz's term *Politik* can be read narrowly as policy, or interest of the state, or as the political—I shall not enter into this debate here).[4] In Clausewitz's formula, "war is the continuation of politics by other means," politics can exercise either a moderating or accelerating role on organized violence, as either curbing the intrinsic progression of war to an absolute pitch of violence or adopting the means of violence for the pursuit of determinate political ends. Whereas the aim (*Ziel*) of war is the destruction of enemy forces, the goal (*Zweck*) and hence *the point* of war is political. Clausewitz's critique of war is to show that reason is self-limiting; it must set limits on its use of violence, and this is the power of reason in two senses: legitimate employment of violence and power for self-critique, that is, limitation of its own employment of violence.

In one of many striking images found in *On War*, Clausewitz characterizes war as a "total phenomenon," or what he calls "the paradoxical trinity" of the military, the people, and government (the state). A distant echo of Plato's tripartite structure of the *polis* and the individual soul, this Trinitarian conception allows for both objective and subjective readings, that is, as social institutions and psychological (cultural) dispositions. A theory of war, as organized violence, operates between these three tendencies, as he writes, "like an object suspended between three magnets." In this image, the state can employ violence against another state, against its citizens in enforcement of law, or against the disintegration of the social. Viewed through this prism, these three forms of organized violence correspond to intra-state warfare, state violence (disciplinary power), and public order (governmentality).[5] These three forms of organized violence become distributed along the basic distinction between the military and the police. When conceived along these lines, war is a "total phenomenon" (in Clausewitz's sense) with its mobilization of the three elements of the "holy trinity." By contrast, policing, in its functions as enforcement of law and production of social order, is only a partial phenomenon, that is, it does not require, as a regulative ideal, the total mobilization of the nation-state (as would prove historically to be the case with the great wars of the twentieth century), or engage the military.

This demarcation between the police and the military is thus not only drawn across a national border defining inside and outside. When conceptualized in this Clausewitzian manner, it is a line of demarcation internal to the *polis*, insofar as the military, as an element of the nation-state, remains impartial and unengaged to the deployment of violence within. This boundary between police and military also delineates different zones of peace and war. Whereas the condition of the polis internally is peace (excepting, of course, civil war), the condition of the state in relation to the outside remains at peace under the threat of war, and hence, in the absence of perpetual peace. The temporality of warfare is future directed. The state must continually prepare itself for future wars, develop new technologies, study the militaries of other nations, imagine different possible wars (the invention of *Kriegspiel*, or war games, is contemporaneous with Clausewitz's time), and decode the intentions of other nations. Not surprisingly, Clausewitz himself lectured (and wrote his treatise) as an instructor at the newly created *Allgemeine Kriegsschule* that had been established under von Scharnhort's reforms after the Prussian defeats in 1806. History, or the past, is also important, since, as with Clausewitz, there are no laws of war (in the way that there are laws of physics or geometry); only through a study of past wars can one prepare for future wars.

By contrast, the temporality of policing is conservative.[6] It is conservative in the sense of enforcing laws and guarding against social disorder, or, in other words, productive in a conservative manner. Unlike the stage of international relations, which is a state of intermittence of war that should rationally become guided, if we follow Kant's vision for perpetual peace (in contrast to more "realist" interpretations of Clausewitz), the zone of peace is a condition of peace with intermittent irruptions of criminal and social violence. The function of the police is to enforce laws and hence maintain peace as well as produce social order (and, as importantly, to pervade society with the symbolic presence of the state). The police represent organized patterns of violence or schemas within a basic condition of peace; even when the police are employed for the production of social order, as with campaigns against proliferation of social violence (drugs, for example), strictly speaking, one cannot speak of a "war against drugs" since the aim of war is to *establish* peace through violence, whereas the aim of police is to *ensure peace through violence*. This means, critically, that there is a necessary end to war for, in Clausewitz's conception, war begins with a speech act—a declaration—and terminates with a speech act. The aim of war is peace: to compel the will of the other party to one's own demands. War has a finality that policing does not. Since policing is an organized violence within a time of peace, this means that there cannot be a final end to policing—unless, of course, as we shall see when we turn to policing under the Nazi regime, war is declared against criminality and the production of social order becomes also characterized as war, such that policing becomes transformed into organized violence in pursuit of utopic peace. The demarcation between zones of peace and zones of war correlates to a demarcation between criminals, agents of social unrest, whose deviance cannot cause them to be characterized as enemies of the state and, by the same logic, enemies of the state, who cannot be deemed criminals. The Clausewitzian formula cannot be inverted (policing cannot be war continued by other means nor can police wage war, not even metaphorically) and war cannot be the pursuit of politics—if by politics one means the remit of policing, governmentality and disciplinarity—by other means.[7]

This Clausewitzian framework with its implied distinction between the police and the military already becomes blurred, however, during the Napoleonic wars in which Clausewitz himself participated and for which he became one of its keenest observers. Even as *On War* provides a broad theoretical articulation of the transformation of war and its rational implementation as the pursuit of the political by other means for the modern nation-state, it proved to be this very same European conflagration—a veritable world war—that revealed multiple challenges and complications to this theoretical outlook. If we consider the Napoleonic wars from 1805 to 1815 (from Austerlitz to Waterloo), we recognize three different forms of organized violence: campaigns of national armies centered around set-piece battles (the 1805 Campaign culminating with Austerlitz; the defeat of the Prussian armies in 1806; the 1813 "War of Liberation," etc.); what we would now call "counterinsurgency" campaigns against irregular troops, "guerillas" (a termed coined during the Peninsular Campaigns from the Spanish *guerrilleros*); and asymmetrical warfare against partisans in Spain, Russia, Tyrol, and Calabria (see Esdaile 2004; Finley 1994; Tone 1995); as well as Napoleon's "other war" against banditry and brigands in France and throughout French occupied territories and possibly also his maritime blockade of Continental Europe after 1806 (Broer 2010).

The pervasiveness of brigands and banditry in early modern Europe represents a now forgotten background condition for the consolidation of the modern nation-state, governmentality, the modern police, and the military (bandits and banditry appear not to play a role in Foucault's work, for example). As Eric Hobsbawm argued in his classic study *Bandits*, "social banditry of this kind [those who are *not* or not only regarded as simple criminals by public opinion] is one of the most universal social phenomena known to history, and one of the most amazingly uniform" (Hobsbawm 2000, 21).⁸ A glance at notable works of the eighteenth century amply attests to the presence of bandits and banditry: David Hume's *History of England* (Hume routinely evokes the scourge of "bands of robbers" and "thieves" in the countryside since Anglo-Saxon times), Friedrich Schiller's *Die Räuber*, and the popularity in Germany around 1800 of a distinctive genre of literary works of robbers, serial killers, and thieves (see Jäger 2013). The mobility of the poor, seasonal agrarian labor, the absence of centralized control, and institutions of the state outside cities contributed to the periodic outbreak of social violence in rural territories. The consolidation of the modern nation-state developed, in part, through the "extrusion" of violence from domestic societies to the international stage as a consequence of the pacification of society by state power and governmentality (see Giddens 1985). This disarming of bandits, brigands, and local warlords represents one of the principal achievements of modern nation-states in the eighteenth and nineteenth centuries. Napoleon's innovation consisted of the militarization of the *gendamerie* and the assigning of policing and pacification duties to military units against insurgency as well as local banditry (the distinction was not always clear, as with Napoleon's own roots in Corsica and affiliation with Pasquale Paoli).⁹ Given these considerations, the relationship between police and military must be examined through the prism of these three forms of organized violence (war, counterinsurgency, banditry), as "three magnets" (to borrow Clausewitz's metaphor) in which state-organized violence is suspended, taking on different forms. An examination of the relation between the military and the police, in other words, should not be reduced to a simplistic opposition between "war" and "peace."

Roughly contemporaneous with the Napoleonic Wars, the modern police emerged within the modern nation-state. Historians of the police in the nineteenth century have examined different conceptions and genealogies. As Mark Finnane (2016) has argued, three main genealogical lineages feed into the formation of the "modern" police:¹⁰ the establishment in 1829 of Robert Peel's London Metropolitan Police; Julien Alletz's (1823) *Dictionnaire de police moderne pour toute la France*, where the function of the police, construed as governmentality, includes arresting criminals, supervision of economic markets, street traffic, and public health, but also, among its diverse duties, the regulation of mushrooms;

and the militarized *gendarmerie*, drawing from French innovations before the Revolution and under Napoleon, and which provided the model for paramilitary police forces in nineteenth-century Europe for the purpose of internal state security (see Emsley 1999). One should also note the German discourse of *Polizeiwissenschaft*, Fichte's "passport police" (see Chamayou 2013), and Hegel's understanding of the police as a visible embodiment of the state in civil society and as a supporting institution for civil society ("caring for the common interest") (see Neocleous 1998). As Foucault likewise recognizes, the term *police* has possessed different meanings since the seventeenth and eighteenth centuries, and it is this multiplication of polices and functions of policing—economic, surveillance, governmentality, biopower—that characterizes the modernity of the police (Foucault 2009, 312–14.).

Policing the Reich

With its ascension to power in 1933, the Nazi regime undertook a profound and systematic transformation of the police forces and legal institutions.[11] Under the Third Reich, we find a complex set of cultures and institutions that attest to the pluralization of policing agencies and functions, as well as an increased level of hierarchical bureaucratization:

Kripo: *Krimminalpolizei*
Sipo: *Sicherheitspolizei*
SD: *Sicherheitsdienst*
Orpo: *Ordnungspolizei*
Gestapo: *Geheime Staatspolizei*
SS: *Schutzstaffel* (divided into the *Allgemeine SS* and the *Waffen SS*, the latter
    forming militarized units deployed in combat alongside the *Wehrmacht*)
Feldgendarmerie: *Wehrmacht* military police

These various agencies map onto different functions of policing (criminal, state security, military police, governmentality, military units, surveillance and intelligence) and thus provide a striking example of the multiple conceptions of "the" police within a highly bureaucratic and totalitarian state. There is, strictly speaking, no *one* all-embracing conception of the police, but a multiplicity of policing agencies within a unified, *saturated* police state. This multiplication of agencies produced, on the one hand, a thicket of inter-institutional rivalry and centers of power, all bound by loyalty to Hitler, and, on the other hand, an occultation of responsibility, such that any *ethical* accountability or conscience for particular policies and actions could be dissipated across a division of functional tasks.[12]

This apparatus of police institutions developed in conjunction with an equally radical transformation of the German legal system. The institution of the police cannot be understood without its relation to the institution of the law *as well as* its relation to the deployment of biopower and governmentality. In Foucault's genealogy of power and, more specifically, his analysis of the police, law remains a neglected dimension in this thinking.[13] In the particular case of Nazi Germany, the circuit between the police and the state cannot be understood without including the transformed Nazi legal system. The biopower-political and -governmental dimensions of the Nazi police operated within a legal framework predicated on dismantling the traditional legal structures of the Weimar Republic and the Prussian state.

Central to this Nazi dismantling of German law was an aggressive rejection of what it described as the "liberalism" of established legal thought and institutions. The Criminal Code in Germany was established under the Hohenzollern Empire shortly after unification in 1871 and was based on classical jurisprudence, with its legal definitions reaching back to Napoleon's Penal Code of 1810. During the nineteenth century, a "humanitarian jurisprudence" had lessened cruel punishments and incorporated the principle of *nulla poena sine lege*, equality of citizens before the law, freedom from unlawful arrest, and other civil rights.[14] Within the first years of the Nazi regime, such civil rights were abolished, including, the principle of *nulla poena sine lege*. As of 1935, German law "permitted the punishment of acts offending the 'sound feeling of the people' even though no existing law was violated" (Hoefer 1945, 386). This dismantling of basic civil rights, due process, equality before the law, and other hallmarks of "liberal" legal thinking reflected an obsessive effort to establish a distinctive "German" frame of legal thinking and political thought, which would undo the "corrupting foreign" influence of ideas from the French Revolution. Already a pronounced theme during the First World War, Nazi legal reforms sought to replace the "Idea of 1789" with a German idea of freedom and Nation. Critical to this process was the dismantling of any juridical independence and replacement of civil servants and judges with Nazi party members. This *politization* of the judiciary mirrors the *militarization* of the police. In 1937, all personnel serving in the judiciary were required to swear an oath of loyalty to Hitler (much as with the police and the military).

For Nazi legal thinkers, liberalism was identified with the notion of individual rights and liberties, and that laws protected individuals from each other, but just as significantly, from the state (see Müller 1992; Steinweis 2013).[15] This emphasis on the individual as bearer of rights and the law as protecting individuals from society and the state was connected to the presumption of innocence, and therefore, the presumption that guilt had to be established in a public court of law with due process, where the individual was protected by rights. The Nazi reform of the legal system explicitly rejected these basic notions in arguing that the law is not meant to protect individuals or private property, but serves instead as an instrument for the development of *Kultur* and formation of the nation.

This shift of the object of law from the individual to the people (*das Volk*) assigns to law an emphatic socio-culturally productive function; the aim of law is not the protection of individuals (or groups of individuals), but the constitution and maintenance of social body and spirit. In this scheme, the status of the criminal changes from an individual who retains rights and must be proved guilty (presumption of innocence) to the status of an enemy who endangers the social body. The rhetoric of *contamination* becomes deployed to produce political affects within the German population in support of such a changed frame of perception. The law has the main purpose of protecting the people-nation from the criminal, rather than protecting the criminal from the state or the people: the criminal code protects the nation, not the individual endangering it (Chapoutot 2018, 198). As explicitly declared by the Nazi jurist Reinhardt Höhn: "National Socialism has changed the police in its essence. From a mere administrative institution functioning by a set of rules, it was made into a reactive body serving the community of the people" (Chapoutot 2018, 210). As Hitler proclaimed to the Reichstag in 1942: "I expect the German justice system to understand that the nation is not there for it, but that it is there for the nation." Hitler reverses the maxim: *pereat mundus, fiat justitia* ("let justice be done, though the world perish") into "let the Third Reich be accomplished, though justice perish" (Chapoutot 2018, 214).

This transformation is apparent in a changed conception of arrest. The power to detain and arrest, as a fundamental power of the police, is determined within a legal framework of authority and empowerment. As implemented by the Gestapo, "protective custody" (*Schutzhaft*) gave legal authority for arrest, imprisonment, and execution of any German citizen (or Germans disbarred of citizenship, Jews, who were legally stripped of citizenship in 1935) for any or no cause, without juridical oversight. The arbitrariness of identifying and declaring *who* is the criminal is no longer based on the actual violation of a law, and hence, a deed, but on the absolute arbitrariness of police authority. "Protective custody," which traditionally served as the means of police protection for criminals from the people or from state authority without juridical oversight, became transformed into a means of exposing "the criminal" to the institutional violence of the police. This "duplicity" of the Nazi legal system proved integral to its practice in policing: representing the rule of law while acting within extra-juridical spaces *within* a juridical space such that these non-places would seem not only "normal" but also "legal" by proxy (Chapoutot 2018, 205–7; Hoefer 1945, 390). Policing within such a legal framework thus produces a normalization of the extra-juridical by inscribing such practices—detentions and arrests—within the juridical space of legality.

This transformation of the criminal into an enemy of the people and the functioning of the police within extra-juridical spaces within a juridical space operates through a transformation of the border and the boundary.[16] Within a Clausewitzian–Weberian model, methodologically employed in this analysis as an ideal type, the distinctions between zones of peace and zones of war as well as between the police and the military were materialized with territorial borders (inner and outer) and conceptualized with symbolic, functional, and institutional boundaries (the police and the military). The organized violence of the police operates *internally*; the organized violence of the military operates *externally*. During the Third Reich, the identity of the police and its function in policing became discursively encoded and symbolically represented in terms of *war*. Judges and police officers were understood as waging "a war against parasites, harmful elements, and brigands." As Roland Freisler (State Secretary of the Reich Ministry of Justice and President of the People's Court) declared: "We are waging a war of eradication, and we shall most energetically make sure that it is the criminal, not the state... that is left to hang" (Chapoutot 2018, 203). This bellicose aggressiveness and intent of the law transformed the law and the police into a means to pursue war by other means: law and policing—"politics" in these combined senses—is the pursuit of war by other means. This implicit inversion of Clausewitz's formula, in fact, had already been achieved during the First World War (see de Warren 2019). In the Nazi ideologue Günther Stier's *Das Recht als Kampordnung der Rasse* (The Law as Battle-Order for the Race), this conception of law as war is connected to a vision of human existence as a struggle among races (Chapoutot 2018, 204).[17]

The campaign against criminality, construed broadly and racially as an enemy of the people, becomes inscribed within a semantics of war *within* the ostensible zone of peace. War becomes the matrix for the intelligibility of social and cultural relations. This internalization of war within the social body becomes the locus of an "inner front" of struggle. In the words of Reinhardt Höhn: "the mission of the German police is to combat the enemy within" (Chapoutot 2018, 210). The notion of "inner front" (*innere Front*) designated a "frontline experience" *within* the nation, not against "external" enemies, but against enemies within.

This interjection of the semantics of "frontline experience" already became established in the latter years of the First World War and became increasingly entrenched during the 1919–20 German Civil War and the clashes of paramilitary units during the Weimar Republic. The collapse of Germany in 1919, with the German devolution into a fractious landscape of internal violence, further traumatized and brutalized German collective consciousness (see Mosse 1990). During the Weimar Republic, demoralized and unemployed soldiers swept back into Germany after the war, with many finding a continuation of their life of violence in the units of the *Freikorps*, but as significantly, in the civilian police force.

The militarization of the police occurs through the increasing employment of battle-hardened—traumatized—veterans, who often inclined toward association and sympathy with right-wing *Freikorps* units. The police are thus seen (psychologically and culturally) as engaged in a struggle "on the front lines" of "combat" against the internal enemy, much as the military is engaged in struggle "on the front lines" against external enemies. This internalization of war is not a mirror image of military warfare against external enemies in one critical regard: paranoia. Paranoia of the enemy within (mostly associated with Jews and Communists) made the police into an institution for the policing of collective social paranoia.

Assigned with producing social order and defending the people, police became understood as "caretakers of the health" of the nation and its population. We witness the collapse of any boundary between the public and the private.[18] Even sleep was not immune to this absolute encroachment of biopower and governmentality (see Beradt 1985). Indeed, every aspect of "life" corresponded to a policing agency, as is evident from the organization of both the SD (*Sicherheitsdienst*, the intelligence branch of the SS) and the Gestapo (the Nazi state's secret police).

The SD (as of 1942) contained four sections with different subsections:

Section A: Legal order and structure of the Reich.
Section B: Nationality
Section C: *Kultur*
Section D: Economics (Avalon Project 2008)

The Gestapo (as of 1943) was organized into six sections with different subsections:

Section A: Enemies, sabotage, and protective service
Section B: Political churches, religious sects, and Jews[19]
Section C: Card files, protective custody, and matters of press and Party
Section D: Regions under German occupation
Section E: Security
Section F Passport and foreign police (Avalon Project 2008)

We should not imagine, as is often portrayed in contemporary cultural representations of the Nazi "police-state," that Nazi Germany was policed by a network of informants and the specter of "Big Brother." The situation was in fact more complex. There existed a self-policing dimension of the population, supported by propaganda, as well as a network

Figure 10.1. *Die Polizei: Dein Freund, Dein Helfer* (The Police: Your Friend, Your Helper). Reprinted with permission of the Bundesarchiv.

of informants (*Vertrauensleute*) that took on a proactive dimension (see Gellately 2002). Policing against criminality, political dissent, and the like was aggressively proactive (see Hall 2009). Through propaganda organized and disseminated by the state, we also have what we might term the policing of the *image* of the police, such that shaping the image of the police itself becomes an object of a certain policing function, or

Figure 10.2. *Die Polizei im Fronteinsatz* (The Police in Service at the Front). Reprinted with permission of the Landesarchiv Baden-Württemberg, Staatsarchiv Freiburg (145/2 Nr. 213).

function of governmentality. Images of the police portrayed the police in two different types: as "friend and helper" and in military service at the (external) front.

These two contrasting images did not form a contradiction, but expressed the transformed function of the police as employed within ter-

Figure 10.3. Poster for *Tag der Deutschen Polizei* (Day of the German Police). Reprinted with permission of the Bundesarchiv.

ritorial borders as well as outside territorial borders at the front lines, or to secure and administer occupied territories. The two contrasting images of the police as "helper" at home and "soldier" *im Fronteinsatz* (in service at the front) allow for the subtle psychological image of the police as defined by *Geschlossenheit und soldatische Pflichttreue* (resoluteness and soldierly loyalty to duty). In making the connection between the "martial loyalty to duty" of the police, the image of the police as helper to the people in time of ordinary, "natural" calamity, transferred itself into an appeal to the population to sacrifice itself in time of exceptional calamity: *war*.

As the motto chosen for the annual *Tag der Deutschen Polizei* (Day of the German Police) in 1937 makes clear, obedience to the laws and the people is the *condition* for the having a "friend" and "helper" in the *entire* police: "Be obedient to the laws and be loyal to your people/nation, then you always have the entire police as your friend [*Sei gehorsam den Gesetzen und Deinem Volke treu, dann hast Du stets zu Freunden die ganze Polizei*]." By implication, much as the police are a friend and helper to the people in time of need, on the condition of duty and obedience to the people, ordinary individuals must exercise their duty and obedience to the people, the nation, in time of calamity.

The development in Nazi Germany of the science of "criminal biology" (*Krimminalbiologie*) and eugenics are an apparent manifestation of what Foucault (1990) calls biopower. The attempt was made to establish "scientifically" a proactive and preventive knowledge in terms of which the police became proactive; and the legal notion of "preventive detention" (*Vorbeugungshaft*)—literally, bending before or forward—also developed in conjunction with systematic racial profiling. Surveillance was thus extended in time into the future with and, much as with the scenario in Philip K. Dick's "The Minority Report," the ideal was to not just prevent crime but to arrest and detain *future* criminals based on scientific means. We have here an example of a crude "crime anticipation system" and "crime prediction" as a science. These "sciences" provided the "scientific" basis for the transformation of the police into a form of "preemptive power" (see Massumi 2015). As Kurt Daluege (Chief of the *Ordnungspolizei*) stated in 1933: "The reprehensible acts of professional criminals should be prevented in an a priori manner mechanically."[20]

The deployment of units from the *Ordnungspolizei* (civilian police units) to the occupied areas with assigned roles in the elimination of local Jewish populations represents one of the more significant uses of police outside both national borders and conceptual boundaries. As Christopher Browning (1992) has examined in detail for Reserve Police Battalion 101, such deployments proved critical in the *mobile* dimension of the Final Solution, where, in fact, most of the wanton killing of Jews, NKVD officers (People's Commissariat of Internal Affairs, the Soviet secret police), local administrators, and others took place. A rationale for the deployment of police units in occupied territories emerged early in the war with the campaign in Poland. Partly, the rationale stemmed from the necessity of protecting local German populations (*Volksdeutsche*, a minority) from "Polish violence." The *Einsatzgruppen* considered their "policing mission" to be protection of the home as well as protection of the occupied territories within an ideological image of "race war" as vital for the "struggle of existence" of the German people (Chapoutot 2018, 223). This deployment of units from the *Ordnungspolizei* is not outside the national border, but outside the distinction between "inside" and "outside," territorially as well as conceptually. Most of these deployments occurred in the Eastern Front, and, more specifically, in what the historian Timothy Snyder (2010) has dubbed "the bloodlands," in which killing on mass scale reached unprecedented intensity and ferocity.

What this represents is how the extreme becomes the normal in such a "borderland" or space that is neither within the nation-state (and hence not within the function of police) nor without, or outside, since these territories possess a different legal status. The borderland in which such units operated is neither inside nor outside. Likewise, in concentration camps, inmates were called *Häftlinge*—"detainees"— neither enemy nor criminal. As the historian Johann Chapoutot observes: "German police activity was completely unconstrained by borders [*Grenzen*] or distinctions [*Trennungen*] either geographical or legal" (Chapoutot 2018, 230). This produces the borderlands of permissibility for the exception that becomes normalized. "Intersectionality" and "inbetweeness" serve as the locus and as the inversion of the relation between legality and ethics: the legalization of the unethical, in which the police play a central function. Extermination of the Jews as the state of exception falling under the governance of the police renders this extreme situation "normal" and mundane, as it coincides with "daily life" and the protection of the social body, and allows for the normalization to *invisibility*, even as everyone "knows" what occurs in the borderlands.

Undoubtedly, the most extreme and telling example of this transformation of policing within the borderlands, where the meaning (and distinction) of "the police" and "the military" becomes transcended and dissolved into a new figure of organized violence, is with the notorious

"Black Hunters" of the SS Dirlewanger Brigade (see Ingrao 2011). Named after Otto Dirlewanger—a veteran of the First World War deemed mentally unstable, a drug addict, a fighter in the *Freikorps* units, and a PhD in political science, who led this unit during the war on the Eastern Front—this brigade was recruited from ex-convicts, criminals, and poachers. In one day alone, this unit killed an estimated thirty-five thousand men, woman, and children during the Warsaw Uprising. Reporting directly to Heinrich Himmler, the conduct and operations of the "Black Hunters" were a cause of concern to local German police units and administrators in occupied territories as well as to the Germany Army.

The formation of military units from hunters and poachers was in itself not an unusual feature of European armies since the eighteenth century (*Jäger* in German or *chasseur* in French). Such units were composed of soldiers with excellent marksmanship and training in open-border skirmishing and reconnaissance. The Dirlewanger Brigade, however, was unique in that poachers and criminals, that is, those outside the law and outside the police, were recruited into a "policing" unit, which became especially prized for its counterinsurgency actions against Soviet partisans in addition to its participation in mass killings of civilians in occupied territories. The recruitment was controlled legally: convicted criminals were selected through a judicial process, thus effectively creating an extra-judicial unit by judicial means. A talent for hunting and invisibility was particularly sought after, thus maximizing the exposure of the victim and the non-exposure of the hunter, and, in this manner, creating a fighting unit that broke with the reciprocity of warfare. The conduct of this *Sondereinheit* was approved at the higher echelon, but local administration and even the police received reports of unacceptable conduct and investigated members of this unit. This unit participated in the emergence of what Christian Ingrao (2011) calls the "cynegetic model" of killing in war: the assembling of victims for killing or the stealthy ambushing of partisan forces. In this dual function against civilians and partisans, in the mode of cynegetic violence, the Dirlewanger Brigade transcended the distinction between discrete functions of a militarized police and policing military. The "policing" and the "military" become overtaken by the cynegetic organization of violence: "war" is "hunting," or, rather, politics becomes the pursuit of predation by other means much as predation becomes the pursuit of politics by other means. In operating in a liminal space in between the police and the military, a new figure of violence emerges that roams in pursuit of its quarry: *the predator*.[21]

NOTES

1 For this notion of the "splintering of war," see Münkler (2004, 2016).
2 For the historical development of policing that emphasizes this productive function of policing, see Campensi (2009). With an emphasis on eighteenth-century political and economic thought, see Neocleous (2000).
3 This police-prison system includes, in Foucault's analysis, a third element: delinquency, such that each forms an element in a circuit (Foucault 1995, 271–92).
4 For my reading of Clausewitz, see de Warren (2015).
5 For these three patterns of violence along Clausewitzian lines, see Kraus (2009).
6 On this point, see Chapter 4 in this volume: "Soldiers and Police" by Michael Walzer.
7 For a reading of Clausewitz that stresses this rationality of political constraints on war, see Aron (1976). For an eloquent contemporary statement of this distinction between zones of peace and zones of war, see Chapter 4 in this volume: "Soldiers and Police" by Michael Walzer.
8 For a comparative study, see Jackson (1970).
9 On Napoleon's gendarmes, see Broer (2016).
10 On the colonial dimension of the development of modern police, see Brogden (1987).
11 For a detailed account of the establishment of the Nazi police state during the 1930s, see Browder (1990).
12 This proved especially important for the psychological burden of mass and indiscriminate killing at the ground level. As Christopher Browning observes in his study of Reserve Police Battalion 101: "the psychological alleviation necessary to integrate Reserve Police Battalion 101 into the killing process was to be achieved through a twofold division of labor. . . . This change would prove sufficient to allow men of the Reserve Police Battalion 101 to become accustomed to their participation in the Final Solution. When the time came to kill again, the policemen did not 'go crazy.' Instead, they became increasingly efficient and calloused executioners" (Browning 1992, 77).
13 See Hunt (1992) and Hunt and Wickham (1994). For a critique of this claim, see Beck (1996).
14 For these details, I rely on Hoefer (1945).
15 For the lasting impact of these transformations for postwar German legal institutions and practices, see Stolleis (1998).
16 I shall omit here any discussion of the establishment (in 1934) and function of the "people's court" or *Volksgerichtshof*. See Sweet (1974).

17 For Foucault's own inversion of Clausewitz's formula and his genealogy of the concept of "race wars," see *Society Must Be Defended* (Foucault 2009).
18 Giorgio Agamben (1998, 147) perceives a connection between the "Nazi Schutzstaffel" with its encroachment on privacy and Johann Heinrich Gottlob von Justi's eighteenth-century conception of *Polizei* and *Polizeistaats*.
19 Adolf Eichmann headed this office.
20 Nazi law had already established a "three strikes you're out" policy of its own: Otto Thierack, Minister of Justice, in 1942: "If he has violated the law repeatedly and consistently . . . a single new violation even if it cannot be counted as criminality of the gravest kind suffices as the last straw to isolate criminal from community forever" (Chapoutot 2018, 214).
21 For the anthropology of "man the hunter," see Chamayou (2012). For the contemporary replacement of war and policing with predation/hunting, see Chamayou (2015).

BIBLIOGRAPHY

Agamben, Giorgio. 1998. *Homo Sacer: Sovereign Power and Bare Life*. Translated by Daniel Heller-Roazen. Stanford, CA: Stanford University Press.

Alletz, Julien. 1823. *Dictionnaire de police moderne pour toute la France*. Paris: Lottin de St. Germain. https://gallica.bnf.fr.

Aron, Raymond. 1976. *Penser la guerre, Clausewitz*. Paris: Gallimard.

Avalon Project. 2008. "Nazi Conspiracy and Aggression Volume 2, Chapter XV, Part 6." Yale Law School Lillian Goldman Law Library. https://avalon.law.yale.edu.

Beck, Anthony. 1996. "Review: Foucault and Law: The Collapse of Law's Empire." *Oxford Journal of Legal Studies* 16 (3): 489–502.

Becker, Anna. 2014. "Jean Bodin on Oeconomics and Politics." *History of European Ideas* 40 (2): 133–45.

Beradt, Charlotte. 1985. *The Third Reich of Dreams: The Nightmares of a Nation, 1933–1939*. New York: Aquarian Press.

Bodin, Jean. 1576. *Six livres de la république*. Chez Jacques du Puys, Libraire Juré. https://gallica.bnf.fr. [All translations from this source are my own.]

Broer, Michael. 2010. *Napoleon's Other War: Bandits, Rebels and their Pursuers in the Age of Revolutions*. Oxford: Peter Lang.

Broer, Michael. 2016. "The Napoleonic Gendarmerie: The State on the Periphery Made Real." *Crime, Histoire & Sociétés / Crime, History & Societies* 20 (1): 91–105.

Brogden, Mike. 1987. "The Emergence of the Police—The Colonial Dimension." *British Journal of Criminology* 27 (1): 4–14.

Browder, George. 1990. *Foundations of the Nazi Police State: The Formation of the Sipo and SD*. Lexington, KY: University Press of Kentucky.

Browning, Christopher. 1992. *Ordinary Men: Reserve Police Battalion 101 and the Final Solution in Poland*. New York: Harper Books.

Campensi, Giuseppe. 2009. *Genealogie della pubblica sicurezza: Teoria e storio del moderno dispositivo poliziesco*. Verona: Ombre Corte.

Chamayou, Grégoire. 2012. *Manhunts: A Philosophical History*. Princeton, NJ: Princeton University Press.
Chamayou, Grégoire. 2013. "Fichte's Passport Police: A Philosophy of the Police." *Theory and Event* 16 (2): n.p.
Chamayou, Grégoire. 2015. *Drone Theory*. London: Penguin.
Chapoutot, Johann. 2018. *The Law of Blood: Thinking and Acting as a Nazi*. Cambridge, MA: Harvard University Press.
de Warren, Nicolas. 2015. "A Rumor of Philosophy: On Thinking War in Clausewitz." *Russian Sociological Review* 14 (4): 12–27.
de Warren, Nicolas. 2019. "Dilthey's Dream and the Struggle of World-Views." In *Interpreting Dilthey: Critical Essays*, edited by Eric Nelson. Cambridge: Cambridge University Press.
Emsley, Charles. 1999. *Gendarmes and the State in Nineteenth Century Europe*. Oxford: Oxford University Press.
Esdaile, Charles. 2004. *Fighting Napoleon: Guerrillas, Bandits and Adventurers in Spain, 1808–1814*. New Haven, CT: Yale University Press.
Finley, Milton. 1994. *The Most Monstrous of Wars: The Napoleonic Guerrilla War in Southern Italy, 1806–1811*. Columbia, SC: University of South Carolina Press.
Finnane, Mark. 2016. "The Origins of 'Modern' Policing." In *The Oxford Handbook of the History of Crime and Criminal Justice*, edited by Paul Knepper and Anja Johansen, 497–518. Oxford: Oxford University Press.
Foucault, Michel. 1990. *History of Sexuality, Volume 1: An Introduction*. New York: Vintage Books.
Foucault, Michel. 1995. *Discipline and Punish: The Birth of the Prison*. Translated by Alan Sheridan. New York: Vintage Books.
Foucault, Michel. 2009. *Security, Territory, Population: Lectures at the College de France, 1977–1978*. Edited by Michel Senellart and translated by Graham Burchell. New York: Palgrave Macmillan.
Gellately, Robert. 2002. *Backing Hitler: Consent and Coercion in Nazi Germany*. Oxford: Oxford University Press.
Giddens, Anthony. 1985. *The Nation-State and Violence*. London: Polity Press.
Hall, Claire. 2009. "An Army of Spies? The Gestapo Spy Network 1933–45." *Journal of Contemporary History* 44 (2): 247–65.
Hobsbawm, Eric. 2000. *Bandits*. New York: The New Press.
Hoefer, Frederick. 1945. "The Nazi Penal System." *Journal of Criminal Law and Criminology* 35 (6): 385–93.
Hunt, Alan. 1992. "Foucault's Expulsion of Law: Toward a Retrieval." *Law and Social Inquiry* 17 (1): 1–38.
Hunt, Alan, and Wickham, Gary. 1994. *Foucault and Law: Towards a Sociology of Law as Governance*. London: Pluto Press.
Ingrao, Christian. 2011. *The SS Dirlewanger Brigade: The History of the Black Hunters*. New York: Sky Horse Publishing.

Jackson, Bernard. 1970. "Some Comparative Legal History: Robbery and Brigandage." *Georgia Journal of International and Comparative Law* 1 (1): 45–103.
Jäger, Christian. 2013. "Robbers and Lady-Killers." In *Gender, Agency and Violence: European Perspectives from Early Modern Times to the Present Day*, edited by Ulrike Zitzlsperger, 87–95. Newcastle upon Tyne: Cambridge Scholars Publishing.
Kaldor, Mary. 2012. *New and Old Wars: Organized Violence in a Global Era*. Stanford, CA: Stanford University Press.
Kraus, Keith. 2009. "War, Violence and the State." In *Securing Peace in a Globalized World*, edited by Michael Brzoska and Axel Krohn, 183–202. London: Palgrave Macmillan.
Massumi, Brian. 2015. *Ontopower*. Durham, NC: Duke University Press.
Mosse, Georg. 1990. *Fallen Soldiers*. Oxford: Oxford University Press.
Müller, Ingo. 1992. *Hitler's Justice: The Courts of the Third Reich*. Cambridge, MA: Harvard University Press.
Münkler, Herfried. 2004. *Die neuen Kriege*. Frankfurt: Rowohlt Verlag.
Münkler, Herfried. 2016. *Kriegssplitter: Die Evolution der Gewalt im 20. und 21. Jahrhundert*. Frankfurt: Rowohlt Verlag.
Neocleous, Mark. 1998. "Policing the System of Needs: Hegel, Political Economy, and the Police of the Market." *History of European Ideas* 24 (1): 43–48.
Neocleous, Mark. 2000. *The Fabrication of Social Order: A Critical Theory of Police*. London: Pluto Press.
Snyder, Timothy. 2010. *Bloodlands: Europe Between Hitler and Stalin*. New York: Basic Books.
Steinweis, Alan, and Robert Rachlin, eds. 2013. *The Law in Nazi Germany: Ideology, Opportunism, and the Perversion of Justice*. New York: Berghahn Books.
Stolleis, Michael. 1998. *The Law under the Swastika: Studies on Legal History in Nazi Germany*. Chicago: University of Chicago Press.
Sweet, William. 1974. "The Volksgerichtshof: 1934–45." *Journal of Modern History* 46 (2): 314–29.
Tilly, Charles. 1985. "War Making and State Making as Organized Crime." In *Bringing the State Back In*, edited by Peter Evans, Dietrich Rueschemeyer, and Theda Skocpol, 169–91. Cambridge: Cambridge University Press.
Tilly, Charles. 1992. *Capital, Coercion and European States*. Oxford: Blackwell.
Tone, John. 1995. *The Fatal Knot: The Guerrilla War in Navarre and the Defeat of Napoleon in Spain*. Chapel Hill, NC: University of North Carolina Press.
Weber, Max. 1958. "Politics as a Vocation." In *From Max Weber: Essays on Sociology*, edited by H. H. Gerth and C. Wright Mills, 77–128. New York: Oxford University Press.

11

Police, Drones, and the Politics of Perception

LISA GUENTHER

In 2011, a county sheriff in North Dakota borrowed a Predator drone from a local Air Force base to track down three suspected cattle thieves. This was the first time a drone had been used to assist in the arrest of United States citizens, although US Customs and Border Protection has been using Predator drones to monitor the border with Mexico since 2005 (Grossman 2013), and police departments in Houston and Las Vegas began experimenting with drones in 2007 (Wall and Monahan 2011, 245). Today, police forces across the US and Canada use drones to track suspects, document crime scenes, reconstruct traffic accidents, assist in search-and-rescue operations, and monitor public protests. According to the director of the Miami-Dade Police Department, the use of drones gives police "a good opportunity to have an eye up there . . . a surveilling eye to help us to do the things we need to do, honestly, to keep people safe" (quoted in Neocleous 2014, 162). A 2012 survey found that 67 percent of Americans supported the use of police drones to pursue "runaway criminals" and 64 percent supported their use to control "illegal immigration" (Wall 2013, 45). So far, the drones used by domestic police have been not been armed. But from 2004 to 2011, drones used in US military operations killed over two thousand five hundred people in Pakistan alone (*Economist* 2011). More than 160 of these people were children (Woods 2011).

Advocates and apologists for drone warfare claim that it is a "smart" and even "virtuous" weapon, given its alleged capacity to target specific threats without putting one's own soldiers' lives at risk (Der Derian 2009, xxi). But, as critics point out, the necropolitical fantasy of putting "warheads on foreheads" obscures the actual practice and impact of drone warfare. Drone operations do not always target specific individuals. Some begin by mapping what is called the "pattern of life" of anonymous individuals and groups in a certain area, then identifying aberrations in this pattern as potential threats. This practice has resulted in countless mistakes where civilians are blown to smithereens for behaving in ways that seem suspicious to drone operators sitting in trailers on the other side of the globe. And even when a specific target is correctly identified, the weapons mounted on drones, such as AGM-15 Hellfire missiles, have a "kill zone" of fifteen meters (forty-nine feet) and a "wound radius" of twenty meters (sixty-six feet) (Chamayou 2015, 141–42). The other people killed in so-called "surgical strikes" are often retroactively constituted as militants, insurgents, or combatants in order to shore up the boundaries of this virtuous warfare (Chamayou 2015, 144–49).

Even if the technical problems with targeted killing could be sorted out, the shift from a battlespace where combatants confront one another on a plane of shared vulnerability to a vertical space of radically asymmetrical surveillance, tracking, and incapacitation implies a shift in the political logic of armed conflict that many scholars have compared to policing. For example, Mark Neocleous calls drone warfare "a continuation of the police logic inherent in air power since its inception" (Neocleous 2014, 156), and Grégoire Chamayou argues that "as soon as one leaves behind a 'relationship of mutual risks' and the 'requirement of reciprocity' is broken, war is no longer war: it turns into a kind of police action" (Chamayou 2015, 163).

In recent years, there has been much discussion and debate about the militarization of police in the US, most of which has focused on the mindset of the "warrior cop" and the use of conventional military-grade equipment such as tanks, grenade launchers, and assault rifles. But as the logic of war shifts toward global policing, the militarization of domestic police is also shifting. For example, while military drones are busy mapping the "pattern of life" in Pakistani villages, domestic police forces are using algorithmic software like PredPol to create maps of crime "hotspots," based on established patterns of arrest that both reflect and compound the dynamics of racial profiling. The use of air power to police and/or terrorize racialized groups has historical roots in British colonial campaigns of the 1920s, which deployed a combination of aerial bombardment and predatory taxation schemes to destroy villages and disrupt subsistence economies in India, forcing colonial subjects into the wage labor economy (Neocleous 2014, 142–52). I will return to the connection between state racism, algorithmic calculation, and the extraction of wealth from the poor later in this chapter.

According to Lieutenant General David Deptula of the US Air Force, "The real advantage of unmanned aerial systems [or drones] is that they allow you to project power without projecting vulnerability" (quoted in Chamayou 2015, 12). In other words, they allow the hunter to pursue its prey without being exposed to reciprocal danger. In addition to his work on drones, Chamayou has traced a philosophical history of "manhunts" back to Plato and Aristotle, developing a concept of *cynegetic power* to account for "the technologies of predation indispensable for the establishment and reproduction of relationships of domination" (Chamayou 2012, 7). Chamayou identifies three main forms of cynegetic power in European history: hunting Indigenous peoples (to appropriate their land), hunting Africans (to appropriate their labor power), and hunting the poor (to clear the way for capitalist development).[1] He traces the emergence of urban police forces in Europe to the third form of cynegetic power, although in the North American context, slave patrols and paramilitary forces like the North-West Mounted Police played at least as important a role in the history of policing. However you parse the relationship between hunting Indigenous peoples, Africans, and the poor, cynegetic power produces, reinforces, and naturalizes a radical asymmetry between two kinds of human beings: hunters and prey. For Chamayou, "the manhunt appears as a means of *ontological policing*: a violence whose aim is to maintain the dominated in correspondence with . . . the concept that the dominant have imposed on them" (Chamayou 2012, 12). By imposing this concept through asymmetrical force, the hunter, in effect, "produces the game that it is supposed to hunt down," providing its own theoretical justification for the justice and/or natural inevitability of predation (Chamayou 2012, 56). The history of drones is, for Chamayou, a chapter in the history of manhunts. The generic and proper names of drones celebrate this cynegetic power: "hunter-killer" drones are called Predators or Reapers; they are equipped with surveillance systems called ARGUS or Gorgon Stare; and Mid-Altitude Long-Endurance drones are known by the acronym MALE.

Drones are useful for the expansion and development of cynegetic power because they enable perception and action at a distance. A military drone operator in rural Nevada can observe, track, and attack human targets on the other side of the world without exposing himself or his fellow soldiers to harm. Chamayou calls this the "history ... of an eye turned into a weapon" (Chamayou 2015, 11). In a sense, there is nothing radically new about this effort to weaponize perception. What is the panopticon, if not an architecture for (re)producing an asymmetrical division between seeing and being seen? What is the story of Gyges in Plato's *Republic*, later analyzed by Emmanuel Levinas as the epitome of murderous subjectivity, if not a fantasy of seeing without being seen, "project[ing] power without projecting vulnerability"? And yet, drones both intensify the asymmetry of surveillance and power and mobilize a broad array of technologies and methods that challenge conventional accounts of perception.

If drones were simply flying cameras (as they were in the early 1970s when the Israel Defense Force first invented them [Chamayou 2015, 27–8]), then it might be possible to account for them by expanding and modifying a subject-centered account of perception, as if the "eye" in the sky were essentially an "I" in the sky: a singular, autonomous subject who steers his drone like a pilot in a ship. In this model of perception, first-person consciousness is both the initiator of the process (I decide to look, therefore I see) and also a neutral apprehender of data about what there is to see (I collect information about the world through my eyes, with the help of my flying camera).

But today's drones are not just flying cameras, and the notion of a single drone operator following his target like a homunculus in a tiny plane misconstrues how drone perception actually works. As Wall and Monahan (2011) explain, a drone is not a single entity, it is an "assemblage of aircraft, cameras, missiles, communication technology, and distant pilots" through which "people 'down below,' whether migrants, insurgents, or citizens, are abstracted from their local social, political, and geographical contexts" (249–50). Military drone operations require the collaboration of a whole network of advisors, analysts, commanders, ground forces, and drone operators, all of whom are constantly interfacing with the sensory apparatus and data processing software of one or more drones tracking emergent patterns that may or may not become threats. According to Derek Gregory, these operations are "executed onscreen through video feeds and chat rooms (displays show as many as thirty different chats at a time) that bring a series of personnel with different skills in different locations into the same zone" (Gregory 2012, 195).

Far from simply extending the consciousness of a single drone operator into a distant field of perception and action, the networked structure of drone perception *organizes the sensory and cognitive capacities* of a multiplicity of differently situated and differently embodied agents (on the ground and in the air, fleshy and metallic, high-ranking and low-ranking, etc.), and it also *organizes the perceptual field* into "patterns of life" and their aberrations, which may or may not be targeted as potential threats. Brian Massumi calls this the logic of preemption, which does not wait for actual threats to appear, but actively produces them by "flushing out" potential dangers and retroactively constructing them as legitimate targets. At the same time that drones render military operations more like police raids, the "green to blue pipeline" (Wall 2013, 35) funnels military weapons and technology to police forces, putting tanks, anti-aircraft missiles, drones, and other equipment in the hands of domestic police departments. But it's not clear that police need drones, let alone weaponized drones, to participate in the logic of hunting or cynegetic power that organizes drone perception and action in the militarized battlespace of algorithmically mapped hotspots.

In what follows, I will address a set of questions that stretch between the ethical-political and the epistemic. To what extent does the use of drones by police extend and intensify a logic of predation that is already operative in the perceptual practices of neoliberal policing, both in the "soft power" of broken windows policies and in the "hard power" of militarized SWAT team raids? Does the use of drones by domestic police introduce a new and unforeseen danger, or does it intensify the danger that is already operative, and to some degree normalized, in police training and practices of the past forty years? And what is the particular role of *perception* in the ethics and politics of policing? Furthermore: to what extent does the logic of cynegetic power also organize other, more mundane practices, such as the impulse of white people to call the police when a Black man wades into a pool in his socks (Mervosh 2018), or a Black woman tries to use a coupon in a CVS drugstore (Stevens 2018), or two Black men wait for their friend in a Starbucks (Horton 2018), and so on? How is it that some white people feel empowered to move from a perception of (what they take to be) abnormality and a feeling of discomfort to the identification of a threat and the summoning of state violence to eradicate that threat?

My larger argument is that it's not just drones, and not just military or police forces, that process information by picking out "patterns of life" and identifying deviations from these patterns as potential problems or threats. This is a core feature of embodied perception, as analyzed by phenomenologists like Maurice Merleau-Ponty, Gestalt theorists like Kurt Koffka, philosophers of mind like George Lakoff and Mark Johnson, dynamic systems theorists like Susan Oyama, cognitive scientists like Andy Clark and David Chalmers, and neurologists like Francisco Varela. This insight is crucial for acknowledging the continuity between racist perception by individual citizens, racial profiling by police, and the racist targeting of "common people with beards" by the US military (Chamayou 2015, 51).[2] Drone technology intensifies social dynamics and power relations that are already operative in the distributed cognition of embodied perception in the contemporary US, widening the range of collaborators and increasing their capacity for vertical or asymmetrical division. In order to challenge and transform the logic and practice of what Chamayou calls "inter-human predation," both at the level of police drone warfare and in everyday civilian life—we need to build a capacity for critical perception that interrupts the kill-chain,[3] not only at the moment of pressing the button, but also in everyday practices of solidarity and reciprocity that resist cynegetic priming.

Police Perception

The displacement, extension, and collectivization of human perception through the distributed cognition of drone technology raises epistemic, and even ontological, questions about the nature of perception. At what point does the extended cognition of a human agent "primed" by racial ideology become the autonomous cognition of a hunter-killer drone? And at what point does the drone's own capacity to gather and process data, using algorithms to solve problems and navigate unpredictable terrain, give rise to an emergent sense of intelligence, to the point where we might say that the drone "perceives" its own targets?

My engagement with these questions begins from the premise that perception is always already political; there is no such thing as a value-neutral intake of sensory information about the world, not even by drones. The perceptual practices of human beings are embodied and situated in a world that is deeply contoured by relations of force and resistance in the past, present, and even the future (to the extent that collective aspirations shape the interpretation of the past and the mobilization of present capacities). Perception is both receptive and constitutive of meaning; by picking out a determinate figure on an indeterminate ground, perceivers identify emergent patterns that become more or less stable and "truthy" through continuous feedback loops.

A core function of policing is to mobilize perceptual practices to surveil, track, and apprehend other human beings through a use of force that is, within certain limits, sanctioned by the state. The etymology of the word *cop*, understood as a slang term for police officer, bears a trace of this connection between perception and violence. The term emerged in mid-nineteenth century England, soon after the establishment of a professional police force in the city of London. *Cop* is short for *copper* (or "one who cops"), which is derived from the verb, *to cop*, meaning "to capture, grasp, lay hold of, 'nab.'" The Latin root is *capere*, meaning to take or seize, but also to "take in" in the sense of understanding. *Capere* gives us words such as capture and captivity, but also concept and perception (from *concipere* and *percipere*).[4]

Until recently, police theory and practice has focused mainly on the patrolling officer who walks his "beat" on a horizontal plane shared with residents and potential suspects. For example, in his 1968 book *Varieties of Police Behavior*, Harvard professor James Q. Wilson described the perceptual practice of urban policing as follows:

> The patrolman confronting a citizen is especially alert to two kinds of cues: those that signal *danger* and those that signal *impropriety*. A badly dressed, rough-talking person, especially one accompanied by friends and in his own neighborhood, is quickly seen as a potential threat—he may, out of his own hot temper or because of the need to "prove himself" in front of his buddies, pull a knife or throw a punch. A teenager hanging out on a street corner late at night, especially one dressed in an eccentric manner, a Negro wearing a "conk rag" (a piece of cloth tied around the

head to hold flat hair being "processed"—that is, straightened), girls in short skirts and boys in long hair parked in a flash car talking loudly to friends on the curb, or interracial couples—all of these are seen by police officers as persons displaying unconventional and improper behavior. (Wilson, quoted in Harcourt 2001, 39–40)

In other words, the patrolling officer is trained to scan the streets for (highly gendered and racialized) norm violations, and to perceive these abnormalities as potential signs of danger and criminality.

The theory of "broken windows," which Wilson developed in collaboration with Rutgers criminologist George Kelling in 1982, also affirms the perceptual attunement of police to "visible cues of public disorder," sanctioning the removal of what Wilson and Kelling (1982) call "disreputable or obstreperous or unpredictable people" from public space, and their containment elsewhere, lest they turn middle-class neighborhoods into "an inhospitable and frightening jungle."[5] This is clearly an example of what Chamayou calls cynegetic power: the broken windows model deploys police to hunt the racialized, poor, queer, and/or genderqueer, for the sake of removing them from public space and enforcing an asymmetrical social order and a tidy, homogeneous aesthetic order. The core claim of broken windows theory is that the perception of aesthetic disorder, such as graffiti or vandalism, erodes "the informal control mechanisms of the community itself," triggering both a fear of crime among "regulars" or "decent folk" and a license to commit crime among "undesirable persons," and even among some regulars (Wilson and Kelling 1982). Broken windows grants police both a theory of prey and a theory of the flock whose perceptual and affective habits render them vulnerable to other predators. And yet, for all this asymmetry, the patrolling officer who polices the social and aesthetic order of neighborhoods, stopping and frisking potential sources of disorder, still walks his beat at street level. What happens when police power goes vertical?

In 1996, Princeton professor John DiIulio developed a theory of the "super-predator" which, in spite of its name, is also a hunter's theory of its prey. According to DiIulio, a new generation of young Black and Latino men was emerging: a lost generation without empathy or mercy, which had to be incapacitated before it had a chance to destroy the rest of us. In her 2018 book *Carceral Capitalism*, Jackie Wang critically analyzes the theory of the super-predator as a biopolitical construction of racialized youth as "a *calculable risk that must be preemptively managed*" for the sake of protecting a heteronormative, white, middle-class body politic (Wang 2018, 197). Even if the threat never materializes—and even if young Black men become the *targets*, not the *agents* of predation, as in the case of the Central Park Five—the image of the super-predator primes both the police and the public to anticipate monstrous violence from racialized youth. Wang shows how the shift from a tax state or welfare state to a predatory debt state has affected the theory and practice of policing in the US. As the Department of Justice's report on Ferguson revealed, some municipalities have turned to fines and fees to generate revenue, in effect hunting the poor—not merely to remove them from public space, but also to fund the maintenance of public amenities. Thanks to the 1033 program (signed into law by Bill Clinton in 1996, the same year as "The Coming of the Super-predators" was published), local police departments received $5.1 billion in military equipment from the US Department of Defense, making the business of hunting the racialized poor more radically asymmetrical (Lamothe 2015).

But the militarization of policing is not just a matter of heavy equipment like tanks and grenade launchers. Wang offers a detailed analysis of the predictive software program PredPol, which generates:

> maps that are covered with red square boxes that indicate where crime is supposed to occur throughout the day. Officers are supposed to periodically patrol the boxes marked on the map in the hopes of either catching criminals or deterring potential criminals from committing crimes. The box is a kind of *temporary crime zone*: a geospatial area generated by mathematical models that are unknown to average police officers who are not privy to the algorithms, though they may have access to the data that is used to make the predictions. (Wang 2018, 241)

While the average police officer cannot "see" crime hotspots without the prosthetic device of a map that is algorithmically generated by PredPol, the map both concretizes past police practice (since it relies on data from previous arrests) and primes patrolling officers to look for criminal activity in specific areas that have already been targeted by police in the past. The red boxes or "temporary crime zones" of a PredPol map find their military correlate in the so-called "kill box," which Chamayou describes as "a temporary autonomous zone of slaughter" in which a three-dimensional geographic area for drone strikes is "opened, activated, frozen, and then closed" based on the identification of an emergent threat (Chamayou 2015, 54–5). The effect of these "temporary lethal microcubes" (Chamayou 2015, 56) is to allow for more decentralized operations to unfold autonomously and simultaneously, based on data that is continuously gathered and processed by both drones and ground forces. While PredPol's "red boxes" are not the same as the military's "kill boxes," the algorithms used by PredPol were developed by researchers at the University of California with funding from the Army, Navy, and Air Force, and they were first used in Iraq "to track insurgents and predict casualties in war zones overseas" (Wang 2018, 232).

Even when lethal force is not used, people whose everyday lives happen to unfold in spaces marked as red boxes or kill boxes are more likely to be perceived as potential criminal and/or terrorist threats, given the "frame of war" that organizes their appearance in this space (Butler 2009). As Sabeen Ahmed argues in her phenomenological analysis of "living under drones," race becomes "a signifier applied not to bodies per se, but to spaces from which certain bodies are presumed to have emerged, a data point among an assemblage of characteristics used to locate and identify supposed 'threats'" (Ahmed 2018, 384). The extended, enactive, and distributed cognition of predictive policing has turned impoverished and racialized neighborhoods into what Wang calls "zones marked for looting" through the extraction of predatory fines and fees for norm violations such as one's "manner of walking" (Wang 2018, 41). And, as we saw in Ferguson, a police officer's perception of a young Black man's manner of walking can be lethal, even if that zone is not explicitly marked as a "kill box."

We have now arrived at the central claim of my paper: the militarized perception of neoliberal policing is a form of predatory or cynegetic power that shares core features with the perceptual practices of drone warfare. Both are radically asymmetrical, algorithmically driven, technologically and socially extended, and structured by racist state violence.

To see how this is the case, we must take a closer look at the perceptual dimension of drone warfare, with a particular focus on priming and preemption.

Drone Surveillance

What is a drone, anyway?

Wall and Monahan (2011, 240) call drones "an actuarial form of surveillance," given the degree to which drone operators rely on algorithmic software to detect patterns and anomalies that might warrant further investigation. Derek Gregory describes the process as follows:

> First, archived images are scanned to filter out "uneventful footage" and distinguish "normal activity from abnormal activity." Ideally this forensic monitoring—which is a sort of militarized rhythmanalysis, even a weaponized time-geography—would be based on cultural knowledge, but the image bank is so vast that experiments are under way with automated software systems for "truthing" and annotating video imagery, and new TV technologies are being explored to tag and retrieve images. (Gregory 2011, 195)

Or, as Ross McNutt, President and CEO of Persistent Surveillance Systems, explains more succinctly: "What we essentially do is a live version of Google Earth, only with a full TiVo capability. . . . It allows us to rewind time and go back and see events that we didn't know occurred at the time they occurred" (Alderton 2018).

But the drone assemblage's powerful capacity for "knowledge capture" is also its pitfall (Neocleous 2014, 148). As Lieutenant General David Deptula admitted already in 2010, "We're going to find ourselves in the not-too-distant future swimming in sensors and drowning in data" (Magnuson 2010). In order to remain useful for hunting human beings, the data collected by drones must be processed in a way that aligns with the interests of cynegetic power. In his 2015 book *Drone Theory*, Chamayou describes this data processing in a way that resonates with James Q. Wilson's description of police perception, but with a few key differences. Drawing on Derek Gregory's research, Chamayou argues that the main function of drone surveillance is to map what the military calls "patterns of life," and to alert military analysts to abnormalities or deviations from these patterns. Chamayou describes this drone cartography as "a superimposition, on a single map, of Facebook, Google Maps, and an Outlook calendar. This would be a fusion of social, spatial, and temporal particulars, a mixed mapping of the socius, locus, and tempus spheres—in other words, a combination of the three dimensions that, not only in their regularities but also in their discordances, constitute a human life" (Chamayou 2015, 48).

This identification and analysis of "patterns of life" generates anonymous profiles that can be tracked without ever identifying the target as an individual. As with the pattern-based software of PredPol, Chamayou explains that, in the military context, "Predicting the future is based on knowledge of the past. The archives of lives constitute the basis for claims that, by noting regularities and anticipating recurrences, it is possible both to predict the future and to change the course of it by taking preemptive action" (Chamayou 2015, 43). But unlike the resident who is stopped and frisked by a patrolling officer, the military drone operator "*will never see his victim seeing him doing what he does to him*" (Chamayou 2015, 118). In drone warfare, the phenomenological structure of seeing and being seen is fractured and dislocated by tens of thousands of miles. This dislocation creates a "moral buffering" effect that allows some drone operators to take pleasure in "squashing bugs" without ever having to face their victims or be exposed to the risk of reciprocal harm (Chamayou 2015, 119; see also 1–9, 106–13). As one Reaper drone operator explains, "We can develop those patterns of life, determine who the bad guys are, and then get the clearance and go through the whole find, fix, track, target, attack cycle" (quoted in Chamayou 2015, 47).

This process of determining "who the bad guys are" is also a process of *producing* them. In his 2015 book *Ontopower*, Brian Massumi develops an intricate analysis of the ontological, epistemic, and political dimensions of network-centric warfare in recent US military theory. Network-centric warfare is a counter-insurgency model of war, the dynamics of which are by no means restricted to global military operations.[6] Massumi's analysis of network-centric warfare is rich and multifaceted, and I will not do it justice here. My aim is only to show in more depth how the hunter produces its own prey, and to suggest that there is already something dronelike in the structure of cynegetic power, whether or not it makes use of actual drone technology.

Massumi takes great care to unpack the claim in a 2003 Department of Defense publication called *Power to the Edge* that "information is now literally the pointy end of the spear" (p. 174, quoted in Massumi 2015, 126). For Massumi, information becomes "pointy" when it operates in the interval between the imperceptible emergence of a threat and the action that will have preempted that threat by flushing it out and annihilating it in advance of the damage it might have done. In the age of network-centric warfare, sluggish delays between perception, cognition, communication, and action can mean death for the soldier and failure for the military operation. Rather than being trained to follow specific orders from central command, soldiers in the age of "pointy" information must be primed to "enter into the no-time of the decision that is one with perception, where perception is already in action before reflection. Making information pointy means making it fit back into the cut of forming experience" (Massumi 2015, 126). In other words, the ideal soldier is like a drone plugged into a decentralized network or assemblage, but with its own autopoietic capacity to navigate unforeseen circumstances and even to produce events that are in greater conformity with what the military apparatus is equipped to handle.

Rather than passively waiting for threats to arise, the preemptive power of network-centric warfare "actualizes the potential [threat] in a shape to which it hopes it can respond" (Massumi 2015, 14). For Massumi, *priming*—understood as "the making active in the present of an inheritance from the past, brought forward in the habitual form of a reflex or a learned response" (Massumi 2015, 107)—is a key component of this process. Priming functions as a kind of "push-notification" that alerts the networked soldier to a threat that will have been perceptible by the time he has disabled it, but that need not (and even *should* not) be perceptible as such prior to the use of force. Massumi explains: "The trigger-action is not a decision, if by that is meant an implemented conclusion. It is more like a cue given to a future to unfold itself, while enfolding a modulation consequent to its having been cued. It is the future itself, not reflection, that processes the decision. Here decision is a performative forwarding" (Massumi 2015, 119).

Massumi argues that "Truth, in this new world order, is by nature retroactive. Fact grows conditionally in the affective soil of an indeterminately present futurity" (Massumi 2015, 14). In other words, *by the time they shoot you, you will have become a threat.*

Police (as) Drones

In their essay, "Leave our Mikes Alone," Stefano Harney and Fred Moten call Darren Wilson a "drone" whose "genocidal instrumentalization in the state's defense" attacks the "jurisgenerative fecundity" of insurgent Black life (2017, 19, 22). In another conversation, with Robin Kelley, Moten explains:

> We need to understand what it actually is that the state is defending itself from and I think that in this respect, the particular instances of Michael Brown's murder and Eric Garner's murder are worth paying some attention to because what the drone, Darren Wilson, shot into that day was insurgent Black life walking down the street. I don't think he meant to violate the individual personhood of Michael Brown, he was shooting at mobile Black sociality walking down the street in a way that he understood implicitly constituted a threat to the order he represents and that he is sworn to protect. (quoted in Wang 2018, 192)

If this is what's happening, then the use of drones by police—or the deployment of police *as* drones—is not a new frontier in the technology of policing, but rather the entrenchment and intensification of very old frontiers of racist and colonial state violence.

Police forces need not use actual drones—and if they do, these drones need not be armed with weapons—for the logic of preemption and predation that structures the drone assemblage to be at work in local policing. What do police do, if not track "patterns of life," identify abnormalities as potential threats, and seek to arrest or preempt them? But if drones function as assemblages, then it would be reductive to see Darren Wilson as a kind of robot deployed remotely by a white supremacist command center. Rather, we need to interrogate the logic of preemption and predation that divides the world into hunters and prey, or the hyper-protected and hyper-exposed, and that aggregates the perceptual, affective, analytical, and practical capacities of human and non-human actors in a way that normalizes and intensifies this division.

Predatory policing is a collective practice; it networks the potentially lethal force of police officers with the percepts and affects of neighbors who call the cops, real estate developers who invest in gentrification, city councilors who vote for increased fines and court fees, journalists who report on local crime, academics who accept military funding for their research, and so on. Just as military drones are embedded in an assemblage without which they would not be able to perform their current functions, so too is Darren Wilson part of an enabling assemblage of gated communities designed to prevent the redistribution of wealth through taxation, municipal budget shortfalls in low-income communities, fines and fees to make up for these shortfalls, arrest quotas to harvest fines and fees from the most vulnerable residents, and so forth. While there is ample evidence that Wilson, as a single individual, engaged in racist perception, this is just part of the story. A whole network of institutions, relations, needs, and demands both identify Ferguson as a hunting ground for the racialized poor and prime police to look for socially vulnerable residents to fill their quotas.[7] But if this is the case—if the drone assemblage is collaborative and interactional—then it would take collaborative interactions and relationships to dismantle it.

Chamayou asks: "And what if drone psychopathology lay not where it is believed to be, in the possible traumas of the drone operators, but in the industrial production of compartmentalized psyches, immunized against any possibility of reflecting upon their own violence, just as their bodies are already immunized against any possibility of being exposed to the enemy?" (Chamayou 2015, 123). In the context of domestic policing, we could rephrase this question as follows: What if racist police officers are not the only, or even the primary problem? What if the slow violence of everyday investments in whiteness as property, and the immunization of propertied persons from critical reflection and ethical responsibility, were the fundamental source of the harm to which racialized subjects, both near and far, are exposed? How would we begin to unmap the pattern of life that values the protection of private property more highly than the lives of other people?[8] What would it take not only to disarm the drone as a distinct entity, but also to dismantle the whole drone assemblage, and with it the logic of cynegetic power?

Critical Perception

The possibility of ethical policing—or, at least, the possibility of less unethical policing—lies in the interruption of normalized and naturalized habits of racist perception, both horizontally and vertically. A drone can identify "patterns of life" more quickly and efficiently than human cognition. But a drone cannot question the meaning of these patterns or interrogate the hermeneutic frame of its own program. It cannot practice what Alia Al-Saji calls critical-ethical vision, which arises through the interruption of perceptual habits (akin to the phenomenological *epochē*) and the cultivation of a capacity to hesitate, to slow down the movement from perception to judgment, and from judgment to action, long enough to allow for other possible futures to emerge beyond one's initial gut reaction (Al-Saji 2009, 2014).

This is what police who kill unarmed Black men, women, and children fail to do, and it is what drone operation teams who have been staring at screens for days, weeks, or even months with nothing to do but wait for a kill shot sometimes refuse to do, preferring to yield to the momentum of something finally happening. It is also what ordinary citizens fail or refuse to do when they call the cops on people who annoy them or make them feel uncomfortable. The aim of critical perception is neither to transcend perceptual habits (say, through the use of reason or the operationalization of better data), nor to ontologize perceptual habits (as if they were "hardwired" and therefore impossible to change), but rather to acknowledge both the power and the limits of patterned and patterning perception, and to slow down long enough to be troubled by what one feels and perceives.

Chamayou also reflects on the use of time lags by people living under drones to hold open a synapse of evasion or resistance to vertical domination: "There is a time lag between what happens on the ground and when the drone operators see the image of that on their screen.... The *New York Times* reports that targets now make the most of this asynchrony: when individuals think that they are being hunted by a drone, they adopt zigzag movements" (Chamayou 2015, 74–5). This practice of resistance is important, but it is not sustainable as a solution to the problem of globalized cynegetic power. Chamayou argues that new forms of protection *from* interhuman predation, rather than *through* interhuman predation, must be invented, and he calls for a "new conception of fraternity" in which "people become brothers—or sisters—not by filiation or birth, but by the simple fact of recognizing their own situation in that of the other" (Chamayou 2012, 69). But it's not at all clear how to realize this "simple fact" in the face of such deeply entrenched divisions between the hyper-protected and the hyper-exposed.

Jackie Wang argues that social movements like Black Lives Matter are promising "experiments in creating new modes and rhythms of being and material social networks rooted in the reproduction of everyday life" (Wang 2018, 12). Perhaps the shared existential situation of (inter)human vulnerability, even in a world where social and material support for one's vulnerability is so unequally distributed, is most deeply felt when people march and sing in the streets together, blocking traffic with their bodies and co-creating rhythms that contest the order of racial capitalism.[9] In "Leave our Mikes Alone," Harney and Moten ask readers "to imagine jurisgenerative black social life walking down the middle of the street—for a minute, but only for a minute, unpoliced, another city gathers, dancing" (Harney and Moten 2018, 15). They suggest, in a way that resonates with both Wang and Chamayou, that "love is the undercommon self-defence of being-incomplete" (Harney and Moten 2018, 8). While these suggestions may not solve the problem of cynegetic power, they offer much-needed inspiration for imagining and feeling our way toward the possibility of a world beyond interhuman predation.

NOTES

1 More precisely, hunting Indigenous people is based on a theory of the right to conquest (exclusion/displacement), hunting Africans is based on a theory of the slave's responsibility for his own enslavement (coercive inclusion/captivity), and hunting the poor is based on a theory of police power (incarceration/confinement). All are examples of primitive accumulation.

2 Chamayou relays the testimony of "a young Pakistani man, a victim, together with his family, of a drone strike, when he was asked why he thought they had been attacked: 'They say there were terrorists, but it was my home. . . . There are no terrorists. It's just common people with beards'" (Chamayou 2015, 51).

3 "The kill-chain can be thought of as a dispersed and distributed apparatus, a congeries of actors, objects, practices, discourses and affects, that entrains the people who are made part of it and constitutes them as particular kinds of subjects" (Gregory 2011, 196).

4   Oxford English Dictionary. See my paper, "Seeing Like a Cop" (Guenther 2019), for a more extended discussion of perception and policing.
5   See also criminologist Edward Banfield's concept of class, based on "patterns of perception, taste, attitude, and behavior" (quoted in Harcourt 2011, 28).
6   For more on the historical and political connection between police and counterinsurgency, see Owens (2015) and Dubber (2005). One need only look at the brutal and insidious COINTELPRO campaign against Black radical political movements to see how the logic and tactics of counter-insurgency have shaped policing in the domestic US as well (Churchill and Vander Wall 2001).
7   See the Department of Justice report on Ferguson: "Partly as a consequence of City and FPD [Ferguson Police Department] priorities, many officers appear to see some residents, especially those who live in Ferguson's predominantly African-American neighborhoods, less as constituents to be protected than as potential offenders and sources of revenue" (US Department of Justice 2015, 2).
8   See Razack (2002) on "unmapping."
9   See also Berardi (2012, 54–5) for an account of "the pleasure of sharing the breath and space of the other" as the basis of solidarity in social movements. For Berardi (or Bifo), "The perception of time by a society is shaped by social refrains" (Berardi 2012, 130–1). Anti-capitalist social movements contest the social refrain of global financial markets, in which all value is fungible, and they "concatenate" or co-create new refrains and new collective rhythms that allow us "to enter into relation with entities not composed of our matter, not speaking our language, and not reducible to the communication of discreet, verbal, or digital signs" (Berardi 2012, 121). For Bifo, "Social solidarity is not an ethical or ideological value: it depends on the continuousness of the relation between individuals in time and in space. The material foundation of solidarity is the perception of the continuity of the body in the body, and the immediate understanding of the consistency of my interest and your interest" (Berardi 2012, 128). These suggestions also seem promising in the face of a naturalized, normalized "pattern of life" based on the elimination of threats to propertied personhood.

BIBLIOGRAPHY

Ahmed, Sabeen. 2018. "From Threat to Walking Corpse: Spatial Disruption and the Phenomenology of 'Living under Drones'" *Theory & Event* 21 (2): 382–410.

Al-Saji, Alia. 2009. "A Phenomenology of Critical-Ethical Vision: Merleau-Ponty, Bergson, and the Question of Seeing Differently." *Chiasmi International* 11: 375–98.

Al-Saji, Alia. 2014. "A Phenomenology of Hesitation: Interrupting Racializing Habits of Seeing." In *Living Alterities: Phenomenology, Embodiment, and Race*, edited by Emily Lee, 133–172. Albany, NY: State University of New York Press.

Alderton, Matt. 2018. "To the Rescue! Why Drones in Police Work are the Future of Crime Fighting." Redshift by Autodesk, April 13, 2018. www.autodesk.com.

Berardi, Franco "Bifo." 2012. *The Uprising: On Poetry and Finance*. Los Angeles: Semiotext(e).

Butler, Judith. 2009. *Frames of War: When is Life Grievable?* New York and London: Verso.
Chamayou, Grégoire. 2012. *Manhunts: A Philosophical History.* Translated by Stephen Rendall. Princeton, NJ: Princeton University Press.
Chamayou, Grégoire. 2015. *Drone Theory.* London: Penguin Random House.
Churchill, Ward, and Jim Vander Wall. 2001. *The COINTELPRO Papers: Documents from the FBI's Secret Wars Against Dissent in the United States.* New York: South End Press.
Der Derian, James. 2009. *Virtuous War: Mapping the Military-Industrial-Media-Entertainment Network.* New York: Routledge.
Dubber, Mark. 2005. *The Police Power: Patriarchy and the Foundations of American Government.* New York: Columbia University Press.
Gregory, Derek. 2011. "From a View to a Kill: Drones and Late Modern War." *Theory, Culture & Society* 28 (7–8): 188–215.
Grossman, Lev. 2013. "Drone Home." *Time,* February 11, 2013. http://time.com.
Guenther, Lisa. 2019. "Seeing Like a Cop: A Critical Phenomenology of Whiteness as Property." In *Race and Phenomenology: Between Phenomenology and Philosophy of Race,* edited by Emily Lee, 189–206. Lanham, MD: Rowman and Littlefield.
Harcourt, Bernard E. 2001. *Illusion of Order: The False Promise of Broken Windows Policing.* Cambridge, MA: Harvard University Press.
Harney, Stefano, and Fred Moten. 2017. "Leave Our Mikes Alone." Unpublished paper. https://static1.squarespace.com/static/53a0503be4b0a429a2614e8b/t/59d81c2eedaed84653048f0d/1507335215476/Harney-Moten.pdf.
Horton, Alex. 2018. "Starbucks CEO Apologizes after Employee Calls Police on Black Men Waiting at a Table." *Washington Post,* April 15, 2018. www.washingtonpost.com.
Lamothe, Dan. 2015. "How the Pentagon's Distribution of Military Gear to Police Is about to Tighten Again." *Washington Post,* August 13, 2015. www.washingtonpost.com.
Magnuson, Stew. 2010. "Military 'Swimming in Sensors and Drowning in Data.'" *National Defense,* January 1, 2010. www.nationaldefensemagazine.org.
Massumi, Brian. 2015. *Ontopower: War, Powers, and the State of Perception.* Durham, NC: Duke University Press.
Mervosh, Sarah. 2018. "A Black Man Wore Socks in the Pool. After Calling the Police on Him, a Manager Got Fired." *New York Times,* July 9, 2018. www.nytimes.com.
Neocleous, Mark. 2014. *War Power, Police Power.* Edinburgh: Edinburgh University Press.
Owens, Patricia. 2015. *Economy of Force: Counterinsurgency and the Historical Rise of the Social.* Cambridge, UK: Cambridge University Press.
Razack, Sherene, ed. 2002. *Race, Space, and the Law: Unmapping a White Settler Society.* Toronto: Between the Lines.
Stevens, Matt. 2018. "CVS Fires 2 for Calling Police on Black Woman over Coupon." *New York Times,* July 9, 2018. www.nytimes.com.
Economist. 2011. "Out of the Blue." July 30, 2011. www.economist.com.

US Department of Justice. 2015. *Investigation of the Ferguson Police Department.* www.justice.gov.

Wall, Tyler. 2013. "Unmanning the Police Manhunt: Vertical Security as Pacification." *Socialist Studies/Études socialistes* 9 (2): 32–56.

Wall, Tyler, and Torin Monahan. 2011. "Surveillance and Violence from Afar: The Politics of Drones and Liminal Security-Scapes." *Theoretical Criminology* 15 (3): 239–54.

Wang, Jackie. 2018. *Carceral Capitalism.* Semiotext(e) Intervention Series 21. South Pasadena, CA: Semiotext(e).

Wilson, James Q., and George L. Kelling. 1982. "Broken Windows." *Atlantic,* March 1982. www.theatlantic.com.

Woods, Chris. 2011. "Drone War Exposed—the Complete Picture of CIA Strikes in Pakistan." Bureau of Investigative Journalism, August 10, 2011. www.thebureauinvestigates.com.

12

Predictive Policing and the Ethics of Preemption

DANIEL SUSSER

The American justice system, from police departments to the courts, is increasingly turning to information technology for help in identifying potential offenders; determining where, geographically, to allocate enforcement resources; assessing flight risk and the potential for recidivism among arrestees; and making other judgments about when, where, and how to manage crime. In particular, there is a focus on machine learning and other data analytics tools, which promise to accurately predict where crime will occur and who will perpetrate it. Activists and academics have begun to raise critical questions about the use of these tools in policing contexts. In this chapter, I review the emerging critical literature on predictive policing and contribute to it by raising ethical questions about the use of predictive analytics tools to identify potential offenders. Drawing from work on the ethics of profiling, I argue that the much-lauded move from reactive to preemptive policing can mean wrongfully generalizing about individuals, making harmful assumptions about them, instrumentalizing them, and failing to respect them as full ethical persons. I suggest that these problems stem both from the nature of predictive policing tools and from the sociotechnical contexts in which they are implemented. Which is to say, the set of ethical issues I describe arises not only from the fact that these tools are predictive, but also from the fact that they are situated in the hands of police. To mitigate these problems, I suggest we place predictive policing tools in the hands of those whose ultimate responsibility is to individuals (such as counselors and social workers), rather than in the hands of those, like the police, whose ultimate duty is to protect the public at large.

From Reactive to Preemptive Policing

Law enforcement has always utilized a mixture of reactive and proactive strategies, but several historical factors have conspired over the past few decades to give proactive approaches pride of place. First, rising crime rates in the 1960s and '70s led American police departments to question the largely reactive approaches of the middle part of the twentieth century, and shift toward what came to be known as "community policing" (Uchida 2005; Walsh 2005). Developments such as "broken windows" theory and problem-oriented policing in the 1980s and 1990s represented a change in "the definition of policing from one of crime control to one of community problem-solving and empowerment" (Uchida 2005, 36). That is, police departments began to focus their efforts on working with community members to transform the social and environmental conditions that encourage crime—in order to prevent it—rather than merely responding to criminal behavior.[1]

The second historical factor was the rise of Compstat. Throughout the 1990s, William Bratton led the development of an approach to policing—first at the New York City Police Department, and then widely adopted elsewhere (Willis, Mastrofski, and Weisburd 2004)—which "builds upon the police organizational paradigms of the past and blends them with the strategic management fundamentals of the business sector" (Walsh 2005, 206). Central to that enterprise was the incorporation of huge amounts of data into law enforcement practice.[2] While the Compstat model retained community policing's bottom-up orientation, allowing precinct commanders to determine local enforcement strategies, it introduced strict accountability from on high (Walsh and Vito 2004; Walsh 2005). To do so, the Compstat system required highly formalized data collection and processing to provide managers reliable, up-to-date information with which to conduct "relentless assessment" of their subordinates (Walsh and Vito 2004, 59; Willis, Mastrofski, and Weisburd 2007). But this turn to data-driven policing did more than facilitate new management processes; it enabled a change in focus from individual cases to larger crime patterns now visible in the data (Willis, Mastrofski, and Weisburd 2004), and a further entrenchment of the idea that policing is about preventing crime rather than merely controlling it (Walsh 2005).

Finally, the terrorist attacks of September 11, 2001. Understood by many as being, at bottom, a failure of information sharing among intelligence and law enforcement agencies, 9/11 resulted in an even greater emphasis on data-driven approaches to crime control and the rise of "intelligence-led policing" (Ratcliffe 2008). As Sarah Brayne (2017) argues, after 9/11 local police came to be viewed as "actors on the front lines of the domestic war against terror," leading local and federal law enforcement organizations to work together "to assess the viability of a more predictive approach to policing" (981). The emphasis on prediction and prevention over reaction and response was cemented in the process.

Alongside this historical and organizational background, in which police departments increasingly prioritized proactive policing strategies over reactive ones, one also finds the emergence of specific predictive tools in law enforcement practice. Although much of the emerging public discourse around predictive policing treats it as a fundamentally new phenomenon, police departments have long collected crime data, and they have long used it to make decisions about where limited resources ought to be devoted (Pearsall 2010; Perry et al. 2013).[3] Until the advent of big data–driven analytics tools, this generally took the form of "crime mapping"—using information about where and what kinds of crimes have occurred in order to identify patterns useful for making forward-looking predictions about where criminal activity is likely to take place in the future. According to a report from the National Institute of Justice (NIJ) (the research arm of the US Department of Justice), this kind of "crime analysis" has been in use since at least the turn of the twentieth century, and perhaps longer (Harries 1999, 1), and was central to early iterations of Compstat (Willis, Mastrofski, and Weisburd 2004).[4] Many will recognize the pre-digital form of this strategy in the physical maps on police department walls, with push-pins or other markers designating recent police activity, from films and television police procedurals.

As the NIJ report argues, crime mapping techniques developed piecemeal until the 1990s, when two concurrent trends marked a shift in their evolution: first, the incorporation of computers (especially geographic information systems, or GIS) into mapping and visualization practices, and second, the professionalization of crime analysis, including the introduction of insights from academic criminology, geography, and cartography (Harries 1999, 3–6). Computerizing crime mapping offered several obvious advantages—it made it possible to analyze more information, to keep better track of trends (since old maps could be easily retained for comparison as new information was added, unlike what was possible with physical maps and push-pins), and as the cost of computers declined, more departments gained access to the tools and techniques of digital crime analysis (Harries 1999, 3–6). The professionalization of crime mapping, or what is sometimes called "crime forecasting" (Perry et al. 2013)—especially the incorporation of academic research into its ongoing development—meant that it could be driven by more than tacit knowledge (e.g., the beat cop's familiarity with his or her route) and intuition, as social scientific theories designed to explain when, where, and why crime occurs were used to refine the analyses (Eck et al. 2005).[5]

Today, advanced crime mapping tools have been packaged into off-the-shelf products available for purchase by law enforcement agencies, without the need for in-house experts. PredPol and HunchLab are, perhaps, the most widely adopted and frequently discussed. Developed by anthropologist Jeffrey Brantingham and computer scientist George Mohler, PredPol analyzes data about when, where, and what kinds of crimes have occurred (focusing mainly on non-violent crime), in order to predict where hotspots are likely to emerge. As of early 2019, the software had been purchased and deployed in "dozens" of US municipalities (Haskins and Koebler 2019). HunchLab works in a similar way, though it implements an allegedly more advanced method of hotspot prediction known as "Risk Terrain Modeling," which incorporates information about environmental factors, such as the presence of pawnshops and public transportation (which are correlated, for example, with higher burglary rates) into the predictions (Caplan and Kennedy 2011; Chammah 2016).

Crime mapping is fundamentally spatiotemporally oriented or place-based, the aim being to use information about historical crime patterns to identify "hot spots"—places and periods of time prone to above-average criminal activity (Eck et al. 2005; Perry et al. 2013). In addition to trying to predict where and when crime will occur, however, law enforcement agencies have also long attempted to understand *who* is likely to be involved in criminal activity—either as a perpetrator or a victim. According to Andrew Ferguson (2016), such "person-based"[6] predictive policing strategies developed independently of the spatiotemporally oriented varieties described above, emerging from public health research focused on crime. "For decades," he writes, "sociologists identified the reality that a small subset of individuals in any community committed the vast majority of crimes. Police recognized that targeting those individuals could result in a disproportionate reduction of crime rates" (Ferguson 2016, 713).

This idea—that specific people, and groups of people, not just specific places and times—are statistically more likely to be implicated in criminal activity, led to the introduction of social network analysis into crime prediction. The premise of social network analysis is that sociological phenomena (such as crime) can be explained and predicted in part by the types and structures of social relationships that connect individuals (Borgatti et al. 2009). In the context of criminology, the relevant relationships or networks of interest have largely been gangs, drug dealing operations, and the mafia, all understood to be nexuses of crime. By analyzing the social networks of known offenders, police can identify others statistically likely to be involved in future criminal activity (Ferguson 2016; Tayebi and Glässer 2016).

As with crime mapping, the rise of cheap, powerful data-driven technologies meant new possibilities for social network analysis, as well as new insights into the correlations between other empirically observable phenomena and the potential for involvement in criminal activity. Contemporary person-based modeling "creates risk profiles for individuals in the criminal justice system on the basis of age, criminal record, employment history, and social affiliations" (Shapiro 2017). These profiles are then used to identify potential offenders and score their risk of involvement in future crimes. The Chicago Police Department, for example, maintains a "Strategic Subjects List" (or "heat list") which contains information on thousands of citizens (Rosenblat, Kneese, and boyd 2014; Dumke and Main 2017). Although the vast majority of people on the list have some kind of criminal record, not all do, and many (13 percent) have never been charged with a violent crime (Dumke and Main 2017). Person-based predictive policing technologies like Chicago's heat list are, at the moment, less prevalent in the field than place-based tools

(Degeling and Berendt 2018), but their use is growing, having already been adopted by police departments in New Orleans, Los Angeles, Kansas City, and Rochester, New York (Ferguson 2017b).

These tools are changing how police perceive and interact with the public in important ways. First, as Sarah Brayne (2017) argues, data-driven policing means the police are able to effectively surveil an unprecedentedly large number of people. Network analysis, as we just saw, leads to people who have never had any contact with the police appearing in databases of potential offenders. And datasets from across public sector institutions are being integrated into police surveillance systems, meaning any contact with the state can potentially bring individuals to law enforcement's attention. Police officers no longer have to "actively search" for persons of interest, either. Instead, "passive alerts" notify officers whenever individuals matching certain profiles are found in the system. As Elizabeth Joh writes, "new technologies have altered surveillance discretion by lowering its costs and increasing the capabilities of the police to identify suspicious persons" (2016, 15).

In addition to preemptively identifying people for police scrutiny, predictive policing tools increasingly mediate encounters between individuals and police through risk assessments and threat scores. Intrado's "Beware" system, for example, claims to "help first responders understand the nature of the environment they may encounter during the window of a 9-1-1 event."[7] Using information collected from public crime data, social media, and commercial data brokers, the system issues color-coded assessments—green, yellow, red—designed to indicate how dangerous an individual is to law enforcement (Robinson and Koepke 2016). As Ferguson argues, such assessments obviously

> distort the day-to-day police decisions about use of force and reasonable suspicion. After all, once police have information that a person has a high threat score, this knowledge will color criminal suspicion and increase perceived danger, resulting in more frequent and more aggressive interactions with people the algorithm deems "high risk." (Ferguson 2017c)

Taken together, the historical trajectory of American law enforcement away from reactive and toward proactive approaches, and the introduction of increasingly data-driven, predictive tools into the everyday work of police, represent what Brayne calls "a migration of law enforcement operations toward intelligence activities" (2017, 986). "[L]aw enforcement," she writes, "typically becomes involved once a criminal incident has occurred. . . . Intelligence, by contrast, is fundamentally predictive. Intelligence activities involve gathering data; identifying suspicious patterns, locations, activities, and individuals; and preemptively intervening based on the intelligence acquired" (Brayne 2017, 986). Obviously, such intelligence-driven, preemptive policing creates different risks and, when it goes wrong, threatens different harms than traditional, reactive law enforcement (Maguire 2000). And so this migration toward predictive, preemptive policing brings with it different ethical challenges.

Critical Responses to Predictive Policing

Activists and academics have raised a number of concerns about data-driven predictive policing techniques. First, many watching the emergence of predictive policing technologies and their integration into everyday policing practice worry, above all, about the lack of transparency around how these technologies work (what data they collect, the statistical methods used to analyze that data, etc.), how they are being deployed, and the concomitant absence of accountability (Dumke and Main 2017; Robinson and Koepke 2016). As Ferguson argues, this is in part simply the latest iteration of an old problem, given that "police accountability has long been a fraught issue" (2017a, 1168). But predictive technologies introduce new problematic dynamics: the tools are extremely complex, requiring special expertise to audit them; they are generally powered by proprietary algorithms, owned by private firms reluctant (and, so far, uncompelled) to reveal their inner workings; and they are still nascent technologies undergoing constant innovation and change (Ferguson 2017a). Such problems notwithstanding, calls for increased transparency around predictive policing technologies are growing (Robinson and Koepke 2016; Schmidt 2018; Zarsky 2013), mirroring concerns about algorithmic opacity in other contexts, such as credit scoring and search (Pasquale 2015).

Second, critics have raised questions about accuracy and bias. Worries about bias in predictive policing technologies are a special case of concerns about "algorithmic bias" more generally, an issue stemming from realizations—beginning in the mid-1990s—that computers can encode and perpetuate discriminatory effects on their users and others impacted by their operations (Friedman and Nissenbaum 1996). More recently, it has become apparent that the class of computational techniques known as machine learning—which drives a majority of predictive tools—is especially vulnerable to this problem.[8] Because machine learning tools "learn" to make predictions from patterns latent in the data they are trained on, their predictions carry forward any biases or other effects of discrimination reflected in that data. Given the history of discrimination against Black and minority populations in the United States, predictive policing algorithms trained on historical data are likely to perpetuate and reinforce racial biases (Ferguson 2017a; Kutnowski 2017; Selbst 2017; Shapiro 2017). And indeed, that is what we have already begun to see. An algorithm for predicting potential recidivism, commonly used in courts around the US to make bail, sentencing, and parole decisions, is more likely to erroneously flag Black offenders as dangerous than White offenders (Angwin et al. 2016), and place-based predictive algorithms used by police departments to determine where and when to deploy officers results in the disproportionate over-policing of majority Black neighborhoods (Lum and Isaac 2016).

A third—related—strand of critique looks not at bias in training data, but rather at the feedback loops and multiplier effects that can result from putting predictive algorithms into practice. When predictive policing tools are deployed in the field, they continue to collect data, which is then used to update and refine their predictive models. As a result, the models become trained over time on a disproportionate amount of information about the people and places they directed law enforcement to in the first place, producing feedback loops (Ensign et al. 2018). People and places historically discriminated against thus become targets of police attention (leading to more arrests, etc.), which leads to data that appears to confirm the original predictions. As Kristian Lum and William Isaac write, "newly observed criminal acts that police document as a result of these targeted patrols then feed into the predictive policing algorithm on subsequent days, generating increasingly biased predictions. This creates a feedback loop where the model becomes increasingly confident that the locations most likely to experience further criminal activity are exactly the locations they had previously believed to be high in crime: selection bias meets confirmation bias" (2016, 16; see also Ferguson 2017a).[9]

Finally, some have asked not about the predictions of predictive policing, nor about the enforcement dynamics the predictions produce, but rather about how predictive technologies change the way people think about and understand the role of law enforcement generally. Bernard Harcourt articulated an early version of this worry in *Against Prediction* (2007). Tracing the history of what he calls "actuarial approaches" to policing (meaning predictive approaches grounded in statistical methods), he argues that beyond concerns about the accuracy of statistical models or the utility of such models for actually preventing crimes (concerns he also raises), a more fundamental problem with incorporating predictive tools into law enforcement practice is the effect it has on our conception of the law enforcement enterprise. Just as holding a hammer makes everything look like a nail, reliance on statistical methods for structuring the work of law enforcement reshapes our understanding of that work in its actuarial image. "We have come to associate the prediction of future criminality with just punishment," Harcourt writes. "This seems intuitively obvious, even necessary.... But, the fact is, we have chosen this conception of just punishment.... We chose it as against a rehabilitative model and as against a more strictly retributivist model" (2007, 31–32). As the work of law enforcement has come to be understood fundamentally in terms of predicting and mitigating risk, the rationale for subjecting people to law's coercive force has likewise reoriented toward people's predicted riskiness.[10]

In what follows, I continue in the vein of this last strand of critique, raising questions about the effects of predictive technologies on the treatment of individuals by the state. Specifically, I attempt to shed light on some ethical ramifications of person-based predictive policing—law enforcement officials singling out individuals for investigative scrutiny on the basis of algorithmically generated predictions. I leave questions about the ethics of place-based predictive policing to the side.

Problems with Profiling

As we've seen, person-based predictive policing is, in effect, a data-driven form of profiling. Unlike the beat cop evaluating someone's suspicious behavior in the moment, predictive policing tools evaluate individuals on the basis of whether they are a certain type—the *kind of person* who is likely to commit a crime.[11] Using information about who has committed past crimes[12] (their age, employment history, social networks, and so on), law enforcement generates "risk profiles"—assessments of how similar individuals are to past perpetrators, and thus how likely they are to engage in future criminal activity (Shapiro 2017). While the technology driving this kind of profiling is new, the underlying idea is not. Law enforcement has long engaged in low-tech forms of profiling, and scholars and advocates have raised concerns about the ethical ramifications of such strategies. To understand the ethics of person-based predictive policing, it therefore helps to consider arguments about the ethics of profiling more generally.

Profiling and Generalization

First, it is perhaps important to distinguish the sort of profiling at issue here from what has traditionally been referred to as "criminal profiling"—i.e., the use of crime scene evidence to infer the perpetrator's personality in order to guide an investigation (Gregory 2005; Turvey 2012). Such profiling works backward from an actual crime to an actual criminal (rather than a potential crime and potential criminal). Though data analytics tools are today frequently used to aid criminal profilers, and such tools are sometimes described using the umbrella term "predictive policing," they raise substantially different ethical questions than those raised by the predictive tools that identify individuals likely to commit future crimes (Perry et al. 2013).[13] My argument in what follows does not bear on criminal profiling, at least directly.

A more familiar and more relevant strategy is *racial profiling*—selecting people for differential treatment on the basis of their race. Racial profiling, especially in the context of law enforcement, has long been a subject of controversy. Discussions about whether it is morally acceptable for law enforcement to engage in racial profiling are relevant to debates about the ethics of predictive policing for at least two reasons. First, both racial profiling and person-based predictive or algorithmic profiling involve *preemptive* interventions by law enforcement. For reasons discussed above, police departments have become increasingly focused on preventing crime, rather than merely responding to it. The purpose of both racial profiling and predictive profiling is to determine in advance of any outwardly suspicious behavior whether or not particular individuals are especially likely to commit a crime, and to intervene before they do. Second, in both cases the *method* of making such determinations is statistical inference. Which is to say, in the absence of outwardly suspicious behavior, judgments about individual risk are made by examining the statistical correlations between an individual's group memberships and criminality more generally.

Examples of racial profiling by law enforcement abound. Customs agents have disproportionately subjected African American women to invasive treatment at US airports (Schauer 2003). In cases of so-called "pretext stops," Black drivers have been disproportionately stopped and searched on US roads (Hosein 2018). Arab and Muslim people in the US—especially after 9/11—have been targeted with suspicion simply because of their race or religion, and they have been singled out for questioning and other forms of differential treatment by law enforcement and intelligence agencies (Hosein 2018). Such practices are so prevalent that in 2009 the American Civil Liberties Union reported that "the practice of racial profiling by members of law enforcement at the federal, state, and local levels remains a widespread and pervasive problem throughout the United States, impacting the lives of millions of people in African American, Asian, Latino, South Asian, and Arab communities" (American Civil Liberties Union and The Rights Working Group 2009).

Like the predictive or algorithmic profiling described above, racial profiling is a form of "statistical discrimination" (Lippert-Rasmussen 2014; Schauer 2018). Which is to say, it involves sorting or classifying people on the basis of observable traits assumed to be statistically correlated with some target characteristic. In the case of intelligence and law enforcement agencies racially profiling Arab Americans, for example, it is assumed that race or ethnicity is meaningfully statistically correlated with the propensity for terrorist acts. Because what law enforcement is interested in—the disposition to terrorism—is not easily observable, race is used as a proxy. Person-based predictive policing tools work the same way. What law enforcement wants to know—whether someone is especially likely to commit a crime—cannot be directly observed, so proxy attributes are used instead. Age, employment status, past criminal charges, and other characteristics statistically correlated with criminality are used as the basis for discriminating between those who pose the least and those who pose the greatest risks for future criminal behavior.

"Discrimination" has a pejorative connotation, and racial profiling has often been criticized for being discriminatory. As Frederick Schauer argues, however, discrimination cannot itself be the problem, because acting on the basis of statistical inferences of the sort just described is unavoidable. At a basic level, to discriminate simply means to make value-laden distinctions. We discriminate when we choose to eat tasty rather than bland foods, when we go for walks on clear rather than rainy days, and when we hire charismatic rather than lackluster job candidates. And making these kinds of distinctions almost always requires statistical inferences. Having previously found a certain brand of food bland, we infer that it is very likely the same brand will be bland this time. Because we found that previous job candidates who lacked charisma during their interviews were ultimately unmotivated in their positions, we assume that this uncharismatic job candidate would be unmotivated in this position too. Inductive reasoning—*making generalizations*—is fundamental to human judgment (Schauer 2003).

That racial profiling seems to many intuitively morally unacceptable therefore cannot be explained simply by the fact that it involves statistical discrimination.[14] Rather, for Schauer, racial profiling is ethically suspect because it involves *bad statistics*. In most cases of profiling on the basis of race (or, equally, gender, sexual orientation, or other social categories), the alleged correlations between such categories and most target characteristics simply turn out to be spurious (Schauer 2003).[15] Even though some people think women, as a group, lack business acumen, or gay men lack physical courage—to take Schauer's examples—there is no justification for those beliefs (Schauer 2003). Such generalizations (or "stereotypes") about social groups are just wrong. They are *prejudices*, not sound inductive inferences. Judging individuals on the basis of false generalizations about the social groups of which they are members is wrong, because it is highly likely that the judgments will be mistaken. As Schauer writes, "much of the history of unfortunate discrimination is a history of the erroneous belief in statistical relationships that turn out to have no basis in fact" (Schauer 2018, 47).

Picking Proxies

But false generalizations are an easy case. What should we make of statistically well-grounded profiling? Is it acceptable to judge individuals on the basis of *nonspurious* correlations between group membership and target characteristics? If, in theory, race really was correlated with rates of criminality, would racial profiling be justified? Is it reasonable to assume that someone poses an especially high risk for future criminal behavior just because they share certain traits in common with criminals? Some argue that the answer is categorically no. Even in cases where there is a high degree of certainty that a generalization about someone will turn out to be true, it is wrong to make consequential decisions about them on that basis, because the chance that the judgment is mistaken—however small—denies them the right to individualized treatment (see Schauer 2003, 20–22; Lippert-Rasmussen 2011, 2014, 275). The moral intuition behind this categorical rejection of statistical discrimination—that individuals ought not to be judged using generalizations about groups to which they belong, but rather only on the basis of their own particular characteristics—is powerful and widely shared.

As Schauer (2003) argues, the idea of individualized or particularized judgment is implausible when taken to its extreme, because even judgments that seem on the face of it highly individualized are usually, at bottom, grounded in statistical inferences.[16] However, critics of racial profiling need not argue that all profiling is unacceptable to demonstrate that racial profiling is. They only need to show that it is unacceptable to use race, specifically, as a proxy variable when making certain kinds of judgments, such as whom to single out for police attention. Kasper Lippert-Rasmussen (2014) adopts this strategy, arguing that using race as a proxy for criminality is wrong—even if it is sometimes statistically sound—because the history of discrimination against racial minorities is likely an important cause of disparate crime rates between races, and using that statistical disparity as a justification for burdening minority groups offends norms of fairness. Adam Hosein (2018) argues it is wrong because using race as a proxy for criminality contributes to a sense of inferior political status among targeted racial minorities.

Returning to the question of predictive policing, Schauer's argument (that race is usually a poor proxy for other traits) and Lippert-Rasmussen's and Hosein's arguments (that even when race is a sound proxy it is probably wrong to use it) demonstrate that while statistical inference may be unavoidable, there are important ethical questions to consider about *how such inferences are made*. At the very least, information about race should be excluded from the datasets predictive policing algorithms analyze when generating risk scores. Moreover, since such arguments likely apply equally to other important "socially salient groups" or "protected attributes" besides race—such as gender, sexual orientation, and ability—we can reasonably conclude that data about membership in those groups ought to be excluded too (Lippert-Rasmussen 2014). And to some extent, this is what we find. Although, as we've seen, there is insufficient transparency around most existing predictive policing algorithms, some law enforcement agencies—such as the Chicago Police Department—insist that they do not use data about race to generate their scores (Dumke and Main 2017; Stroud 2014).

There is reason to worry, however, that this solution—excluding certain kinds of information from predictive policing algorithms—while laudable, is insufficient. Namely, it is a feature of machine learning algorithms (which are, again, the computational technique underlying most predictive policing systems) that they will find proxies for meaningful variables regardless of whether or not those variables are explicitly introduced into the system. As Solon Barocas and Andrew Selbst write: "Even in situations where data miners are extremely careful, they can still effect discriminatory results with models that, quite unintentionally, pick out proxy variables for protected classes" (2016, 675). Indeed, the veneer of mathematical objectivity offered by algorithmic assessments can in fact serve to mask the ways such assessments further entrench racial bias in policing. "Mathematized police practices," writes Brayne, "serve to place individuals already under suspicion under new and deeper forms of surveillance, *while appearing to be objective*, or, in the words of one captain, 'just math'" (2017, 997, emphasis in original). Thus, predictive profiling doesn't merely raise similar ethical questions to those raised by racial profiling, it threatens to reintroduce racial profiling in a new guise.[17]

Past as Prologue

Social group membership is not the only kind of proxy variable deserving of critical scrutiny. The language of "predictive policing" evokes a sense of futurity, an orientation toward what has yet to come. But, of course, predictions must be generated out of something, and that something is data about the past.[18] The people on the Chicago Police Department's heat list are there not because of anything they are doing in this moment; the list is updated frequently, but not in real time. They are on the list because they have been charged with crimes in the past, or because they have been the victims of crime, or because they have been associated with known offenders, or because they are a certain age (Dumke and Main 2017). They may not have done anything remotely indicative of potential criminality in some time—for those on the list simply because they were the victims of crime, they may *never* have acted suspiciously—and yet the Strategic Subjects List indicates to law enforcement that they are a risk, a potential threat, and that they ought to be treated as such.

As we've seen, this is part of a larger trend away from reactive policing postures, toward preventive or preemptive ones. Prior to the emergence of intelligence-led policing, individuals were generally singled out for police attention because they were engaged—in the moment—in suspicious acts (Brayne 2017). Racial profiling is an exception to that rule, and person-based predictive policing technologies encourage another. Chicago's Strategic Subjects List and other systems like it enable police to identify purportedly "high-risk" individuals by comparing them with known criminals who have similar biographies—similar criminal records, similar histories of criminal victimization, past associations with similar people. Which is to say, they allow the police to generalize about individuals using not race but history as a proxy for potential criminality. Once high-risk individuals are identified, they are subjected to differential treatment. In the Chicago case, this means visits from teams of police officers warning that they are under extra scrutiny (Gorner 2013; Stroud 2014). As we saw above, it can also mean police officers in the field approaching purportedly high-risk individuals with greater vigilance (Ferguson 2017c).

This kind of predictive strategy—using information about people's past associations, past behaviors, past run-ins with the law to make predictions about their risk of future criminality—freezes people, Medusa-like, in their pasts, suspending them, condemning them to permanent stigmatization. Once identified by the system as a potential threat (a "strategic subject"), a person's history is set in stone and they are marked by the state as inalterably suspicious. As Bonnie Sheehey argues, the predictive system

> codifies and stabilizes the past, turning it both into something that is bound to repeat in the future and into something that can be securely acted on in the present. This codification of the past in the form of data functions to close the past off from possibilities of what could have been. No longer open or negotiable, the past gets preformed and packaged in the shape of data as something already given. (Sheehey 2018, 8)

Using a person's history to mark them as suspicious in the present renders them the "type" of person who would, of course, have the kind of historical record they do. (As we saw in the case of place-based predictive policing: "selection bias meets confirmation bias.") In doing so, their very identity becomes cause for suspicion—they become *suspicious people*. They need not engage in any overtly suspicious behavior to attract attention from law enforcement, and, indeed, there is nothing they can do (or abstain from doing) to avoid such attention.[19]

These considerations suggest additional ethical concerns about police profiling, beyond those raised in the previous section. First, by marking individuals as suspicious people, regardless of any overtly suspicious behavior, predictive technologies rob them of the presumption of innocence. Legally, in the US, that presumption is only formally required in court once someone has been charged with a crime.[20] Morally, however, the right to be presumed innocent is broader than that. As Ian Kerr and Jessica Earle (2013) argue,

> If the legal universe has a prime directive, it is probably the shared understanding that everyone is presumed innocent until proven guilty. . . . [T]he presumption of innocence and related private sector due process values can be seen as wider moral claims that overlap and interrelate with core privacy values. (Kerr and Earle 2013)

The kind of "preemptive predictions" (to use Kerr and Earle's term) predictive policing technologies generate—which is to say, predictions that serve to anticipate and constrain people's behavior—undermine bedrock moral and legal values designed to "provide fair and equal treatment to all by setting boundaries around the kinds of assumptions that can and cannot be made about people" (Kerr and Earle 2013). Once someone is flagged by a person-based predictive policing algorithm, the police are authorized to make assumptions about them that they are forbidden from making about others.

At a deeper level, this treatment demonstrates a failure to recognize targeted individuals as full moral subjects. A hallmark of moral personhood is the capacity for agency—the ability, precisely, to thwart predictions, to surprise. Presuming to know how individuals will behave in the future, and preemptively, punitively intervening on the basis of that assumption suggests one of two things: either that law enforcement is sure they are right about how targets will act in the future, or they think the benefits of guessing correctly outweigh the costs of getting it wrong. If the former is true, then the deployment of predictive policing technologies treats individuals as rigid, mechanical automata, rather than as dynamic, agential beings—that is, as moral subjects. If the latter is true, then the deployment of predictive policing technologies acknowledges that its targets are moral subjects but then proceeds to *instrumentalize* them, treating their interests as subservient to the interests of others. Whether the truth is closer to the former or the latter, its ethical prospects are poor.

Of course, some will object that given the existence of predictive profiling tools, and the significant threat of crime, it would be negligent for the police *not* to use them. As I suggest in closing, however, there is, in fact, a third option: the power of predictive profiling technologies could be harnessed by others besides the police.

Conclusion: Just Preemption

Philosophers and science and technology studies scholars have long argued that in order to evaluate the social and ethical implications of new and emerging technologies, it is not enough to investigate the technologies themselves; one must explore the broader sociotechnical contexts in which technologies are developed and used (see, e.g., Latour 2005; Pinch and Bijker 1984; Winner 1980). The question is not simply, "Is this technology good or bad? Does it promise to make things better or worse?" Rather, the question must be, "What does it mean for this technology to be developed and used in this way, in this context, by these particular social actors?"

I want to conclude by suggesting that the problems I have pointed to throughout this essay arise not simply from the predictive dimension of predictive policing technologies, but also from the fact that these technologies are situated in the hands of police. The duty of police officers is not only to individuals, but also to the public at large, and as a result, the work of policing is not fundamentally oriented to the *interests* of individuals, but rather to the public interest. Scholars of policing have shown that police work is far more complex and multifaceted than merely "enforcing the law," and many police officers spend much of their time aiding individual citizens (see Bittner 1970; Goldstein 1977). But the principal goal of policing, its basic function, is ensuring public safety.[21] Advocates of community policing attempted to "rearrange priorities" among various police functions in the 1990s, de-prioritizing crime fighting and elevating individual assistance (Eck and Rosenbaum 1994). As we saw above, however, the trend over the last two decades has been to reestablish crime prevention as law enforcement's primary mission.[22]

It is in this context that the outputs of predictive policing algorithms—risk assessment scores, strategic subjects lists—are interpreted and acted upon. To be designated "high-risk" or a "strategic subject" *means* that one is a threat, a potential obstacle standing in the way of public safety. And it is this understanding that shapes the particular preemptive interventions made on the basis of such designations. Being identified as high risk or a strategic subject means facing heightened vigilance on the part of police (which can be dangerous to the person deemed a threat), or a visit from police officers warning that one is under heightened scrutiny (which can be embarrassing and demeaning, and a dangerous signal to others).[23] The worries discussed in this chapter, about individualized judgment and racial stigmatization and the presumption of innocence and potential instrumentalization, all carry normative force because it is police officers—people duty bound to promote the public interest over and above the interests of individuals, and authorized to use coercive force in carrying out that duty—who are making decisions on the basis of these predictions.

That these worries are in part a function of context suggests that they might be diffused if predictive profiling technologies were otherwise situated.[24] It is easy to imagine such tools driving the work of social services agencies, for example, rather than law enforcement.[25] In such a context, the prediction that someone was likely to commit a crime would mean something very different. Since the work of those who provide social services—such as social workers, counselors, and job placement officers—is oriented primarily toward the needs and interests of individuals (and only indirectly toward the public interest), to them a person appearing on a strategic subjects list is not, in the first place, a threat, but rather someone in need of assistance.

If predictive profiling technologies were placed in the hands of social workers, or anyone else whose work is fundamentally oriented to each individual's needs and interests, consider how the ethical questions raised throughout this essay would change: Is it unfair to generalize about someone in order to determine whether or not they need extra care? Are we comfortable treating someone as an underserved person, irrespective of any outwardly observable demonstrations of need, and to intervene preemptively to provide them with services? Is it acceptable to preemptively offer a person extra services, even at the risk that our predictions about their needs are proven wrong? By shifting the context in which predictive technologies guide people's work, we shift the moral calculus. Rather than asking if and when it is right to make individuals absorb the costs of erring on the side of public safety, we ask if and when it is right to make the public absorb the costs of erring on the side of individual welfare.

The answer to this last question is not obviously "yes, always." A world in which predictive profiling tools were given to social workers rather than the police would bring with it its own ethical tradeoffs and complexities. But that hypothetical world will likely strike many as more plausibly just than our own world, where such tools are controlled by the police.

NOTES

1. Community policing "seeks to turn patrol from a reactive to a proactive function" (Walsh 2005, 205).
2. Willis, Mastrofski, and Weisburd refer to Compstat as a "data-saturated environment" (2007, 148).
3. Perry et al. (2013, xiv) write: "We found a near one-to-one correspondence between conventional crime analysis and investigative methods and the more recent 'predictive analytics' methods that mathematically extend or automate the earlier methods."
4. Jennifer Bachner (2014) points to examples of crime visualization from as far back as 1829 in France, and claims that crime analysis of this sort was in regular use in mid-nineteenth century England, predating the establishment of formal police forces in the United States.
5. A number of theoretical frameworks have been used to support place-based crime forecasting, from "repeat victimization theory" to "routine activity theory" to "broken windows theory," each pointing to a different set of environmental factors correlated with criminal activity. See Eck et al. (2005).
6. This is sometimes referred to as "offender-based predictive policing." I prefer to follow Robinson and Koepke (2016) in calling it "person-based," as many of those identified by such tools turn out not to be offenders at all.
7. From Intrado's website (www.intrado.com/beware), quoted in Joh (2016, 24).
8. An entire field has quickly emerged in response to the problem of bias in machine learning algorithms. Work presented at its flagship conference, FAccT: ACM Conference on Fairness, Accountability, and Transparency, gives a sense of the scope of the problem and methods for remedying it. See http://facctconference.org.
9. Bernard Harcourt (2007) locates this dynamic in pre–machine learning predictive tools as well; he calls it the "Ratchet Effect."
10. Sheehey (2018) raises related questions.
11. A different class of automated technologies, which Michael Rich (2016) calls "Automated Suspicion Algorithms," do in fact examine behavior in real time, in addition to historical, demographic, and social network information.
12. Or more precisely, who has been *charged* with committing past crimes.
13. For a discussion of ethical issues in criminal profiling, see Boylan (2011) and Turvey (2012).
14. For a qualified defense of racial profiling, see Risse and Zeckhauser (2004).
15. However, Schauer defends the use of profiling in many cases where the statistical correlation between the proxy attribute and the target attribute holds.
16. Even judgments based on direct observations of individuals are usually made by comparing what one is observing, probabilistically, with previous, similar observations.
17. Hanni Fakhoury, a staff attorney at the Electronic Frontier Foundation, said about this: "It ends up being a self-fulfilling prophecy. The algorithm is telling you exactly what you programmed it to tell you. 'Young black kids in the south side of Chicago

are more likely to commit crimes,' and the algorithm lets the police launder this belief. It's not racism, they can say. They are making the decision based on what the algorithm is, even though the algorithm is going to spit back what you put into it. And if the data is biased to begin with and based on human judgment, then the results the algorithm is going to spit out will reflect those biases" (Llenas 2014).

18 According to the *New York Times*, the Chicago Police Department's Strategic Subjects List "draws, the police say, on variables tied to a person's past behavior, particularly arrests and convictions, to predict who is most likely to become a 'party to violence'" (Davey 2017).

19 Interestingly, this dynamic arguably exhibits the logic of racialization. Beyond the fact that the machine learning algorithms driving these systems very likely identify and incorporate proxies for race in their calculations—i.e., despite best efforts, race is likely an *input*—race is also, in some sense, an *output*. These systems create classificatory hierarchies of relative risk and they subject members of the different classificatory groups to systematically different treatment. Those deemed unthreatening are left alone; those deemed risky are subjected to heightened surveillance and the promise of more severe punishment if found engaging in criminal behavior.

20 Predictive policing is not "pre-crime"—the law enforcement bureau from Philip K. Dick's "Minority Report," that incarcerates people for crimes they are predicted to, but have not yet, committed—though some argue that predictive policing moves us in that direction (see McCulloch and Wilson 2016).

21 Jerome Hall writes that "organized police forces have functioned everywhere and at all times to maintain order principally by preventing crimes and apprehending offenders" (1953, 139). Walsh and Vito claim that "Police departments are created to provide public safety for a defined governmental jurisdiction" (2004, 51).

22 Indeed, as Johnny Nhan writes, it is characteristic of contemporary "police culture" that "Most officers marginalize activities that are not oriented toward law enforcement as not 'real' police work and consider such peacekeeping activities as a form of 'social work'" (2013, 5). See also Sierra-Arévalo's contribution in this volume.

23 A *Chicago Tribune* article describes one person's reaction to being identified as a strategic subject: "Interviewed at his Austin home, McDaniel said he was offended at being singled out by West, commander of the Austin police district. All the attention made him nervous because his neighbors noticed, leading them, he feared, to wonder if he was a police snitch. Two officers waited outside on the porch while the commander and a criminal justice expert spoke to McDaniel in his home. 'Like I said, I have no (criminal) background, so what would even give you probable cause to watch me?' said McDaniel, a high school dropout. 'And if you're watching me, then you can obviously see I'm not doing anything'" (Gorner 2013).

24 Kutnowski (2017) makes a similar suggestion about place-based predictive policing tools, arguing that they should reside not with police but rather with policy makers and urban planners. But he offers a different rationale.

25 Indeed, in Chicago, the police often bring social workers with them when they visit strategic subjects, or they provide them with information about how to access social services. Because the overall context is law enforcement, however, the goal of treating the underlying causes of criminal behavior necessarily takes a back seat to the goal of deterring it. For example, as Ferguson points out (quoting Andrew Papachristos and David Kirk), when Chicago police and prosecutors visit gang members on the Strategic Subjects List, "the point of the message stresses the deterrent aspect of the program," and informs the target that, if they are caught misbehaving, "you will be punished harder because you were warned" (Ferguson 2016, 718–19).

BIBLIOGRAPHY

American Civil Liberties Union and The Rights Working Group. 2009. *The Persistence of Racial and Ethnic Profiling in the United States: A Follow-up Report to the U.N. Committee on the Elimination of Racial Discrimination*. www.aclu.org.

Angwin, Julia, Jeff Larson, Surya Mattu, and Lauren Kirchner. 2016. "Machine Bias." *ProPublica*, May 23, 2016. www.propublica.org.

Bachner, Jennifer. 2014. "Predictive Policing: Preventing Crime with Data and Analytics." IBM Center for the Business of Government.

Barocas, Solon, and Andrew D. Selbst. 2016. "Big Data's Disparate Impact." *California Law Review* 104 (3): 671–732.

Bittner, Egon. 1970. *The Functions of the Police in Modern Society: A Review of Background Factors, Current Practices, and Possible Role Models*. Chevy Chase, MD: National Institutes of Mental Health.

Borgatti, Stephen P., Ajay Mehra, Daniel J. Brass, and Giuseppe Labianca. 2009. "Network Analysis in the Social Sciences." *Science* 323 (5916): 892–95.

Boylan, Michael. 2011. "Ethical Profiling." *Journal of Ethics* 15 (1–2): 131–45.

Brayne, Sarah. 2017. "Big Data Surveillance: The Case of Policing." *American Sociological Review* 82 (5): 977–1008.

Caplan, Joel M., and Leslie Kennedy W., eds. 2011. *Risk Terrain Modeling Compendium: For Crime Analysis*. Rutgers, NJ: Rutgers Center on Public Security.

Chammah, Maurice. 2016. "Policing the Future." *The Verge*, February 3, 2016. www.theverge.com.

Davey, Monica. 2017. "Chicago Police Try to Predict Who May Shoot or Be Shot." *New York Times*, December 21, 2017. www.nytimes.com.

Degeling, Martin, and Bettina Berendt. 2018. "What Is Wrong about Robocops as Consultants? A Technology-Centric Critique of Predictive Policing." *AI & SOCIETY* 33 (3): 347–56.

Dumke, Mike, and Frank Main. 2017. "A Look Inside the Watch List Chicago Police Fought to Keep Secret." *Chicago Sun-Times*, May 18, 2017. https://chicago.suntimes.com.

Eck, John E., Spencer Chainey, James G. Cameron, Michael Leitner, and Ronald E. Wilson. 2005. *Mapping Crime: Understanding Hot Spots*. Washington, DC: National Institute of Justice.

Eck, John E., and Dennis P. Rosenbaum. 1994. "The New Police Order: Effectiveness, Equity, and Efficiency in Community Policing." In *The Challenge of Community Policing: Testing the Promises*, edited by Dennis Rosenbaum, 3–24. Thousand Oaks, CA: SAGE Publications.

Ensign, Danielle, Sorelle A. Friedler, Scott Neville, Carlos Scheidegger, and Suresh Venkatasubramanian. 2018. "Runaway Feedback Loops in Predictive Policing." *Proceedings of Machine Learning Research* 81:1–12.

Ferguson, Andrew Guthrie. 2016. "Predictive Prosecution." *Wake Forest Law Review* 51 (3): 705–44.

Ferguson, Andrew Guthrie. 2017a. "Policing Predictive Policing." *Washington University Law Review* 94 (5): 1109–89.

Ferguson, Andrew Guthrie. 2017b. *The Rise of Big Data Policing: Surveillance, Race, and the Future of Law Enforcement*. New York: New York University Press.

Ferguson, Andrew Guthrie. 2017c. "Police Are Using Algorithms to Tell Them If You're a Threat." *Time*, October 3, 2017. http://time.com/

Friedman, Batya, and Helen Nissenbaum. 1996. "Bias in Computer Systems." *ACM Transactions on Information Systems* 14 (3): 330–47.

Goldstein, Herman. 1977. *Policing a Free Society*. Cambridge, MA: Ballinger.

Gorner, Jeremy. 2013. "Chicago Police Use 'Heat List' as Strategy to Prevent Violence." *Chicago Tribune*, August 21, 2013. www.chicagotribune.com.

Gregory, Nathan. 2005. "Offender Profiling: A Review of the Literature." *British Journal of Forensic Practice* 7 (3): 29–34.

Hall, Jerome. 1953. "Police and Law in a Democratic Society." *Indiana Law Journal* 28 (2): 133–77.

Harcourt, Bernard E. 2007. *Against Prediction: Profiling, Policing, and Punishing in an Actuarial Age*. Chicago: University of Chicago Press.

Harries, Keith. 1999. *Mapping Crime: Principle and Practice*. Washington, DC: National Institute of Justice.

Haskins, Caroline, and Jason Koebler. 2019. "Dozens of Cities Have Secretly Experimented with Predictive Policing Software." *Motherboard*, February 6, 2019. https://motherboard.vice.com/

Hosein, Adam Omar. 2018. "Racial Profiling and a Reasonable Sense of Inferior Political Status." *Journal of Political Philosophy* 26 (3): e1–e20.

Joh, Elizabeth E. 2016. "The New Surveillance Discretion: Automated Suspicion, Big Data, and Policing." *Harvard Law & Policy Review* 10 (1): 15–42.

Kerr, Ian, and Jessica Earle. 2013. "Prediction, Preemption, Presumption." *Stanford Law Review Online* 66 (September): n.p. www.stanfordlawreview.org/

Kutnowski, Moish. 2017. "The Ethical Dangers and Merits of Predictive Policing." *Journal of Community Safety & Well-Being* 2 (1): 13–17.

Latour, Bruno. 2005. *Reassembling the Social: An Introduction to Actor-Network-Theory*. Clarendon Lectures in Management Studies. New York: Oxford University Press.

Lippert-Rasmussen, Kasper. 2011. "'We Are All Different': Statistical Discrimination and the Right to Be Treated as an Individual." *Journal of Ethics* 15 (1–2): 47–59.

Lippert-Rasmussen, Kasper. 2014. *Born Free and Equal? A Philosophical Inquiry into the Nature of Discrimination*. New York: Oxford University Press.

Llenas, Bryan. 2014. "Brave New World of 'Predictive Policing' Raises Specter of High-Tech Racial Profiling." *Fox News*, February 25, 2014. www.foxnews.com/

Lum, Kristian, and William Isaac. 2016. "To Predict and Serve?" *Significance* 13 (5): 14–19.

Maguire, Mike. 2000. "Policing by Risks and Targets: Some Dimensions and Implications of Intelligence-Led Crime Control." *Policing and Society* 9 (4): 315–36.

McCulloch, Jude, and Dean Wilson. 2016. *Pre-Crime: Pre-Emption, Precaution and the Future*. London: Routledge.

Nhan, Johnny. 2013. "Police Culture." In *The Encyclopedia of Criminology and Criminal Justice*, edited by Jay S Albanese, 1–6. Oxford, UK: Blackwell Publishing.

Pasquale, Frank. 2015. *The Black Box Society: The Secret Algorithms that Control Money and Information*. Cambridge, MA: Harvard University Press.

Pearsall, Beth. 2010. "Predictive Policing: The Future of Law Enforcement?" *NIJ Journal* 266: 16–19.

Perry, Walt L., Brian McInnis, Carter C. Price, Susan C. Smith, and John S. Hollywood. 2013. *Predictive Policing: The Role of Crime Forecasting in Law Enforcement Operations*. Santa Monica, CA: RAND Corporation.

Pinch, Trevor J., and Wiebe E. Bijker. 1984. "The Social Construction of Facts and Artefacts: Or How the Sociology of Science and the Sociology of Technology Might Benefit Each Other." *Social Studies of Science* 14 (3): 399–441.

Ratcliffe, Jerry. 2008. *Intelligence-Led Policing*. Cullompton, UK: Willan Publishing.

Rich, Michael L. 2016. "Machine Learning, Automated Suspicion Algorithms, and the Fourth Amendment." *University of Pennsylvania Law Review* 164 (4): 871–929.

Risse, Mathias, and Richard Zeckhauser. 2004. "Racial Profiling." *Philosophy and Public Affairs* 32 (2): 131–70.

Robinson, David, and Logan Koepke. 2016. *Stuck in a Pattern: Early Evidence on 'Predictive Policing' and Civil Rights*. Upturn. www.upturn.org/

Rosenblat, Alex, Tamara Kneese, and danah boyd. 2014. "Predicting Human Behavior." Data & Society Research Institute. https://datasociety.net.

Schauer, Frederick F. 2003. *Profiles, Probabilities, and Stereotypes*. Cambridge, MA: Belknap Press of Harvard University Press.

Schauer, Frederick F. 2018. "Statistical (and Non-Statistical) Discrimination." In *The Routledge Handbook of the Ethics of Discrimination*, edited by Kasper Lippert-Rasmussen, 42–53. London: Routledge.

Schmidt, Christine. 2018. "Holding Algorithms (and the People Behind Them) Accountable Is Still Tricky, but Doable." Nieman Lab, March 21, 2018. www.niemanlab.org.

Selbst, Andrew D. 2017. "Disparate Impact in Big Data Policing." *Georgia Law Review* 52 (1): 109–95.

Shapiro, Aaron. 2017. "Reform Predictive Policing." *Nature News* 541 (7638): 458–60.
Sheehey, Bonnie. 2019. "Algorithmic Paranoia: The Temporal Governmentality of Predictive Policing." *Ethics and Information Technology* 21 (1): 49–58.
Stroud, Matt. 2014. "The Minority Report: Chicago's New Police Computer Predicts Crimes, but Is It Racist?" The Verge, February 19, 2014. www.theverge.com.
Tayebi, Mohammad, and Uwe Glässer. 2016. *Social Network Analysis in Predictive Policing*. New York: Springer.
Turvey, Brent E. 2012. *Criminal Profiling: An Introduction to Behavioral Evidence Analysis*, 4th ed. Burlington, MA: Academic Press.
Uchida, Craig. 2005. "The Development of the American Police: An Historical Overview." In *Critical Issues in Policing: Contemporary Readings*, 5th ed., edited by Roger G. Dunham and Geoffrey P. Alpert. Long Grove, IL: Waveland Press.
Walsh, William F. 2005. "Compstat: An Analysis of an Emerging Police Managerial Program." In *Critical Issues in Policing: Contemporary Readings*, 5th ed., edited by Roger G. Dunham and Geoffrey P. Alpert. Long Grove, IL: Waveland Press.
Walsh, William F., and Gennaro F. Vito. 2004. "The Meaning of Compstat: Analysis and Response." *Journal of Contemporary Criminal Justice* 20 (1): 51–69.
Willis, James J., Stephen D. Mastrofski, and David Weisburd. 2004. *Compstat in Practice: An In-Depth Analysis of Three Cities*. Washington, DC: Police Foundation.
Willis, James J., Stephen D. Mastrofski, and David Weisburd. 2007. "Making Sense of COMPSTAT: A Theory-Based Analysis of Organizational Change in Three Police Departments." *Law & Society Review* 41 (1): 147–88.
Winner, Langdon. 1980. "Do Artifacts Have Politics?" *Daedalus* 109 (1): 121–36.
Zarsky, Tal. 2013. "Transparent Predictions." *University of Illinois Law Review* 2013 (4): 1503–69.

ACKNOWLEDGMENTS

The Rock Ethics Institute hosted a conference entitled "The Ethics of Policing" at the Penn State University Park campus September 20–22, 2018. To our knowledge, the conference was the first dedicated to police ethics since high-profile killings by officers in Ferguson and elsewhere sparked large-scale protests and put the topic of policing at the center of national debate in the United States. The conference was also unique in its broadly interdisciplinary approach to the ethical challenges that face policing today. We are grateful to the many scholars, as well as law enforcement officials and community members, who participated in the conference and embraced its vision of examining police ethics through an interdisciplinary lens. The conference brought various perspectives in dialogue with one another and resulted in incredibly rich discussions. This volume aims to share more broadly the research and insights from that conference.

Neither the conference nor the resulting volume would have been possible without generous support from the Rock Ethics Institute, Criminal Justice Research Center, Social Science Research Institute, Penn State Law, Penn State University Libraries, and Departments of African American Studies, Philosophy, and Sociology and Criminology all at Penn State. In particular, we thank Amy Allen, Eric Baumer, Eleanor Brown, Andrew Dudash, Derek Kreager, Hari Osofsky, Ted Toadvine, and Cynthia Young for their belief in and contributions to this project. We also are grateful to the Penn State College of the Liberal Arts for providing funding for indexing and to Joshua Wretzel who created the index. Special thanks goes to Christopher Moore for his insightful feedback on the introductory chapter. We are indebted to our editor Ilene Kalish at New York University Press for her enthusiastic support for this project and sage advice from start to finish. Two anonymous reviewers offered valuable feedback that undoubtedly improved the book. Finally, an amazing team at Penn State—Toni Auman, Rebecca Bennitt, Whitney Chirdon, Joanne Nash, and Betsy VanNoy—handled many of the details involved in organizing the conference that led to this book. We deeply appreciate their skill, patience, and passion, which helped turn the vision for this project into a reality.

ABOUT THE EDITORS

BEN JONES is Assistant Director of the Rock Ethics Institute at the Pennsylvania State University and has a PhD in political science from Yale University. He does research in moral, legal, and political philosophy and the history of political thought.

EDUARDO MENDIETA is Professor of Philosophy at the Pennsylvania State University. He has a PhD in philosophy from the New School for Social Research. He does research in moral, legal and political philosophy as well as on post-Second World War German philosophy, twentieth-century Latin American philosophy, and Latinx philosophy.

ABOUT THE CONTRIBUTORS

NICOLAS DE WARREN is an Associate Professor of Philosophy at the Pennsylvania State University and received his PhD from Boston University. He has written more than sixty articles, and is the author of *Husserl and the Promise of Time: Subjectivity in Transcendental Phenomenology* and coeditor of *New Approaches to Neo-Kantianism* (with Andrea Staiti). He is the recipient of a European Research Council grant for a project on the impact of the First World War on twentieth-century philosophy. He is currently writing two books: one on evil and forgiveness, the other on German *Kriegsphilosophie* during the First World War.

LISA GUENTHER is Queen's National Scholar in Political Philosophy and Critical Prison Studies at Queen's University. She is the author of *Solitary Confinement: Social Death and its Afterlives* and *The Gift of the Other: Levinas and the Politics of Reproduction*, as well as a coeditor of *Death and Other Penalties: Philosophy in a Time of Mass Incarceration* (with Geoffrey Adelsberg and Scott Zeman). As a public philosopher, her work appears in *The New York Times*, *The Globe and Mail*, *Aeon*, and CBC's *Ideas*. She is a member of the P4W Memorial Collective and has previously worked with the REACH Coalition in Nashville, Tennessee.

SALLY HADDEN is an Associate Professor of History at Western Michigan University. She researches law in early American history and is author of *Slave Patrols: Law and Violence in Virginia and the Carolinas* and *Traveling the Beaten Path: Charles Tait's Charges to Federal Grand Juries, 1822–1825* (with David Durham and Paul Pruitt). She also coedited *Signposts: New Directions in Southern Legal History* (with Patricia Minter) and *A Companion to American Legal History* (with Al Brophy). Currently, she is working on projects that examine eighteenth-century lawyers in colonial American cities and the earliest US Supreme Court.

JOY JAMES is the Francis Christopher Oakley Third Century Professor of Humanities at Williams College. She is author of *Shadowboxing: Representations of Black Feminist Politics, Transcending the Talented Tenth: Black Leaders and American Intellectuals*, and *Resisting State Violence: Radicalism, Gender and Race in US Culture*. Among her edited books are *Warfare in the American Homeland, The New Abolitionists: (Neo)Slave Narratives and Contemporary Prison Writings, Imprisoned Intellectuals*, and *The Angela Y. Davis Reader*. Numerous organizations have recognized and supported her research, including the Fletcher Foundation, the Rhode Island Council for the Humanities, the Rockefeller Foundation, and the Ford Foundation.

BEN JONES is the Assistant Director of the Rock Ethics Institute at the Pennsylvania State University and has a PhD in political science from Yale University. He does research in moral, political, and legal philosophy and the history of political thought. His research appears in *Political Research Quarterly, Ethical Theory and Moral Practice, Journal of Applied Philosophy, Journal of Criminal Law and Criminology, Washington Post*, and other venues. Previously, he was the Executive Director of the Connecticut Network to Abolish the Death Penalty and a Campaign Strategist at Equal Justice USA.

DAVID KLINGER is a Professor of Criminology and Criminal Justice at the University of Missouri–St. Louis and received his PhD in Sociology from the University of Washington. Previously, he worked as a patrol officer for the police departments of Los Angeles, California, and Redmond, Washington. His research interests span the field of crime and justice, with an emphasis on the organization and actions of modern police. He received the American Society of Criminology's inaugural Ruth Cavan Young Scholar Award and is author of *Into the Kill Zone: A Cop's Eye View of Deadly Force*, as well as numerous academic articles.

TRACEY L. MEARES is the Walton Hale Hamilton Professor and a Founding Director of the Justice Collaboratory at Yale Law School. Before joining Yale, she was a professor at the University of Chicago Law School from 1995 to 2007. She was the first African American woman granted tenure at both law schools. Meares is a nationally recognized expert on policing in urban communities and has worked extensively with the federal government, including as a member of President Barack Obama's Task Force on 21st Century Policing. In 2019, Meares was elected a member of the American Academy of Arts and Sciences.

EDUARDO MENDIETA is a Professor of Philosophy at the Pennsylvania State University. He has a PhD in philosophy from the New School for Social Research and MA in systematic theology from Union Theological Seminary. His research interests include Frankfurt School Critical Theory, Latin American philosophy, Liberation Philosophy, and Latino/a Philosophy. He also has done work on and with Angela Y. Davis. He is author of *Adventures of Transcendental Philosophy: Karl-Otto Apel's Semiotics and Discourse Ethics* and *Global Fragments: Globalizations, Latinamericanisms, and Critical Theory*, as well as the editor of numerous books, including *The Cambridge Habermas Lexicon* (with Amy Allen).

JAKE MONAGHAN is an Assistant Professor of Philosophy at the University of New Orleans and received his PhD in philosophy from the University of Buffalo. His research focuses on normative justifications of realized institutions and the moral norms that govern our roles within them. He particularly is interested in institutions of law enforcement. His research has appeared in the *Journal of Political Philosophy, Philosophical Quarterly, Journal of Medicine and Philosophy, Philosophy and Public Affairs*, and *Environmental Values*. Currently, he is working on a project about what legitimate policing looks like when there are failures in adjacent components of our political and criminal justice systems.

MICHAEL SIERRA-ARÉVALO is an Assistant Professor in the Department of Sociology at the University of Texas at Austin. His research focuses on policing in the United States and uses quantitative and qualitative methods to understand police culture, behavior, and legitimacy. His current book project examines how contemporary police behavior is shaped by policing's structural and cultural preoccupation with danger and the threat of violence. His research has appeared in *Criminology, Proceedings of the National Academy of Sciences, Law & Society Review, Crime & Delinquency, Annual Review of Law and Social Science*, and other outlets.

DANIEL SUSSER is an Assistant Professor in the College of Information Sciences and Technology and a Research Associate in the Rock Ethics Institute at the Pennsylvania State University. A philosopher by training, he works at the intersection of technology, ethics, and policy. His research aims to highlight normative issues in the design, development, and use of information technology, and to clarify conceptual issues that stand in the way of addressing them through law and policy. He earned a BA in computer science and philosophy from The George Washington University and a PhD in philosophy from Stony Brook University.

MICHAEL WALZER is a Professor Emeritus of Social Science at the Institute for Advanced Study. One of America's foremost political thinkers, he has written on a wide variety of topics in political theory and moral philosophy: political obligation, just and unjust war, nationalism and ethnicity, economic justice, and the welfare state. He is the author of over thirty books, which include *Just and Unjust Wars, Spheres of Justice, On Toleration, Arguing about War*, and *The Paradox of Liberation*. For more than three decades, he served as co-editor of *Dissent*. His current work includes research on the history of Jewish political thought.

VESLA WEAVER is the Bloomberg Distinguished Associate Professor of Political Science and Sociology at Johns Hopkins University. She writes on the lived experience of policing and incarceration, how citizens understand state power, and the reproduction of racial inequality in the US. She is coauthor of *Arresting Citizenship: The Democratic Consequences of American Crime Control* (with Amy Lerman) and *Creating a New Racial Order* (with Jennifer Hochschild and Traci Burch). She has been an Andrew Carnegie Fellow and her research has been supported by the Russell Sage Foundation, National Science Foundation, Ford Foundation, and Brookings Institution.

FRANKLIN ZIMRING is the William G. Simon Professor of Law at the University of California, Berkeley. He is the co-winner of the Stockholm Prize in Criminology for 2020.

INDEX

abolitionism, 181–182, 189, 193, 194
abolition of slavery, 35
Abu-Jamal, Mumia, 188
Acapulco police department, 42
accountability norm, 50–53, 61n14
advocacy, 18
advocacy democracy, 194
Against Prediction (Harcourt), 276
AGM-15 Hellfire missiles, 249
Ahmed, Sabeen, 257
Alletz, Julien, 231
Al Qaeda, 192
Al-Saji, Alia, 263
alxiety, 206
American Civil Liberties Union (ACLU), 187, 278
American Medical Association, 54, 60n5
American Police, 93
apartheid, 219
arrests, 73, 77, 168 fig., 235
asymmetrical warfare, 230
automobile crashes, 110
autonomy, 54, 58, 59
awards, 67, 74–80
Axon, 14

Bakshi, Amar, 151, 156
Baldwin, James, 153, 166
Balko, Radley, 95
Baltimore Police Department, 48
bandits, 230–231
Bandits (Hobsbawm), 230–231
Barocas, Solon, 281
Barr, William, 194

Bayley, David, 26
Bell, Monica, 166
Bellaire, Ohio Police Department, 52
"Beware" system, 273
Biden, Joe, 186
Biehl, Richard, 59
biopower, 222, 227, 233, 241
Bittner, Egon, 127
Black Codes, 214–215
"Black Hunters," 243
"Black Identity Extremists," 200
Black Lives Matter, 54, 70, 180–181, 192, 193, 196–197, 220, 264
Black Panther Party (BPP), 180, 193, 197
Black Radical Tradition, 189
Black Reconstruction (Du Bois), 33, 35
Blackstone, William, 43
Bland, Sandra, 196
Bloomberg, Michael, 45, 47
Blue Lives Matter, 186
"blue wall of silence," 51, 58
Bodin, Jean, 224
body cameras, 13, 14, 85
Bonaparte, Napoleon, 230–232
borderlands, 242
borders, 242
Brantingham, Jeffrey, 271
Bratton, William, 269
Brayne, Sarah, 270, 273, 274, 281
Braz, Rose, 181
brigands, 230–231
"broken windows," 94, 160, 252, 254, 269
"Broken Windows" (Wilson and Kelling), 165

Brown, John, 213
Brown, Michael, 1, 3, 14, 165, 193, 196, 261
Browning, Christopher, 241, 244n12
Brown-Scott, Wendy, 166
Buffalo Police Department (BPD), 48, 52
Butler, Paul, 33

Cairnes, Robert, 120
Campaign Zero, 132
capitalism, 195
captive maternals, 199
Carbado, Devon, 160
Carceral Capitalism (Wang), 256
"carceral society," 225
Carr, Gwen, 196, 199
Castile, Philando, 1
Central Intelligence Agency (CIA), 179
Central Park Five, the, 255–256
Challenge of Crime in a Free Society, The, 26
Chalmers, David, 253
Chamayou, Gregoire, 249, 250–251, 253, 255, 257, 258–259, 262, 263
Chapman, Frank, 188
Chapoutot, Johann, 242
Che-Lumumba Club, 182
Chicago Police Department (CPD), 188–189, 272, 281
Chicago Teachers Union (CTU), 184
childhood trauma, 199
Childish Gambino, 160, 173
citizen, 224
citizenship, 34, 152, 172
civic patrol groups, 210
Civilian Complaint Review Board, 51
civilian lives, 107
Civilizing Security (Walker and Loader), 33
civil rights, 233
civil rights movement, 11, 35, 69
civil society, 232
Civil War, the, 11, 213
Clark, Andy, 253
Clausewitz, Carl von, 227–230
Cleveland Police Department, 51

Clinton, Bill, 196
Clinton, Hillary, 190, 195, 196
Clutchette, John, 182
Cohen, Cathy, 157
COINTELPRO, 180, 183, 265n6
Communist Party USA (CPUSA), 182, 191, 197
Community Oriented Policing Services (COPS), 27, 115
community policing, 269
compassion, 80
competence norm, 61n14
COMPSTAT, 27, 69
Compstat, 269, 270
Confederate Army, the, 213
Connor, Bull, 11, 216
constitutional law, 27
contradictions, 187
"cop," 254
counterinsurgency, 230
crack epidemic, 94
crime, 29
crime fighting, 68–70, 72
crime forecasting, 271
crime mapping, 270–271
crime reduction, 26–27, 99
criminal biology, 241
criminal justice interventions, 153, 166
criminal law, 112, 123, 139
criminal profiling, 277
criminology, 272
critical perception, 263
critical prison studies, 189
Critical Resistance, 181, 184, 192–193
Crutcher, Terence, 1
Cullors, Patrice, 196
Cunningham, Terrence, 12
custodial citizenship, 153
cynegetic power, 250, 252, 255, 262. *See also* cynegetic violence
cynegetic violence, 243. *See also* cynegetic power
cynicism, 50

Dahl, Robert, 160, 173
Daluege, Kurt, 241
danger, 70–71, 80
Das Recht als Kampordnung der Rasse (The Law as Battle-Order for the Race), 236
Davis, Angela, 2–3, 18, 180, 181–193, 195
de Blasio, Bill, 186, 195
debt, 170
delinquency, 244n3
democracy, 154, 162
democracy theory, 34–35
Democratic Party, 193, 197
Department of Justice, Civil Rights Division, 115
Deptula, David, 250, 258
de Warren, Nicolas, 18
Dick, Philip K., 241
Dictionnaire de police moderne pour toute la France (Alletz), 231
Dilulio, John, 255
Dirlewanger, Otto, 243
Discipline and Punish (Foucault), 225
discretion: abuse of power and, 7; legitimacy and, 52; place in the police hierarchy and, 101; unavoidability of, 42
discrimination, 279
distorted responsiveness, 163–167, 171
diversification, 59
Dixon, Ben, 199
doctrine of double effect, the, 101–102
"don't shoot" protocols, 113
double consciousness, 172
drone perception, 251–252
drones, 19, 248, 250–251, 253, 258
Drone Theory (Chamayou), 258
drone warfare, 249
drug abuse, 56
Drumgo, Fleeta, 182
Du Bois, W. E. B., 33, 35, 172, 189
DuBose, Samuel, 1

Earle, Jessica, 283
effective policing: crime fighting and, 26; defined, 25; lawful policing and, 28–29; legitimacy and, 31; procedural justice and, 31
Elmont Police Department (EPD), 67, 74
Ely, Sheriff Sherman, 11
emancipation, 214
enforcement activity, 70, 85n2
Enforcement Acts of 1870 and 1871, 216. *See also* Third Enforcement Act, the
epistemic norms: deficiencies in, 45; knowledge acquisition and, 44, 57; knowledge production and, 44, 57; law enforcement policy and, 48–49; professional ethics and, 44
epoche, 263
equality: democracy and, 162; legitimacy and, 43–44, 52; police having to honor, 97; stop, question, and frisk (SQF) and, 46
Equal Justice Initiative, 12, 219
Espionage Act, the, 192
ethical policing, 263
ethics of policing: historical context and, 10; historically informed approaches to, 12; historical understandings of, 6; individuals and, 41; institutions and, 41; nonideal theory and, 8; political philosophy and, 44; technology and, 15
ethics of profiling, 268
eugenics, 241
euthanasia, 54
extended cognition, 253

Fabre, Cecile, 130, 131
Fassin, Didier, 5–6
Federal Bureau of Investigation (FBI), 179
felonies, 77–78, 101–102
femininity, 71–72
Ferguson, Andrew, 272, 273
Ferguson Police Department, 3
Fichte, Johann Gottlieb, 232

Final Solution, the, 241
financial extraction, 170
Finnane, Mark, 231
First Steps Act, 200
Fitzgerald, F. Scott, 172
fleeing suspects, 103–104
Flint Police Department, 55
Floyd, George, 1, 2
Floyd v. New York City, 29
Forman Jr., James, 10, 95, 98
Foucault, Michel, 183, 222, 225, 232
Fourteenth Amendment, the, 100
Fourth Amendment, the, 28, 43, 100, 104
France, Anatole, 97
Frank, Anne, 154
Fraternal Order of Police, 13, 188
Freedmen's Bureau, 216
freedom, 29
Freedom of Information Law (FOIL), 198
Freedom Riders, 216
Freikorps, 236, 243
Freisler, Roland, 236
French Police, 93
French Revolution, the, 233
Fulton, Sybrina, 196
Functions of the Police in Modern Society, The (Bittner), 127

Garner, Alyssa, 199
Garner, Eric, 1, 186, 191, 193, 196, 261
Garner, Erica, 18, 180, 193–200
Garner, Errol, 103–104
Garner, Esaw, 199
Geller, Amanda, 160
Gelman, Andrew, 45–46
gendamerie, 231–232
gender, 71–72, 75–80, 82–83
German Civil War, 236
German Criminal Code, the, 233
Gestapo, the, 235, 237
Goff, Philip, 160
gouvernement, 225
governance, 179

governmentality, 226–227, 231, 233
governmental overreach, 121
Grant, Ulysses, 214
Gray, Freddie, 1, 200
"great American crime decline," 70
Gregory, Derek, 251, 258
"guardian" policing, 72–73, 80, 82, 84
Guenther, Lisa, 19
guerillas, 230
gunfire, 121
gun recovery, 77–78
guns, 93–94, 110. *See also* weapons
Gyges, 251

Hadden, Sally, 10, 18
Haftlinge (detainees), 242
Haley, Harold, 182
Harcourt, Bernard, 276
hard power, 252
Harmon, Rachel, 28
Harney, Stefano, 261
Harris, Kamala, 186
Harris, Reggie, 198
harshness, 43, 47
Hegel, Georg Wilhelm Friedrich, 232
hidden curriculum, 171
Himmler, Heinrich, 243
history, 12, 283
History of England (Hume), 231
Hitler, Adolf, 233
Hobbes, Thomas, 5, 225
Hobsbawm, Eric, 230–231
Hohenzollern Empire, 233
Hohn, Reinhardt, 234, 236
Holder, Eric, 191
Hollis, John, 120
Holocaust, the, 154
Homan Square, 157
homicides, 94
Honig, Bonnie, 33
Hoover, J. Edgar, 193
Hosein, Adam, 280
hostages, 128–130

hostage situations, 128–130
hostage takers, 128–130
hot pursuit, 104–105
House Un-American Activities Committee, 183
humanitarian jurisprudence, 233
Hume, David, 231
HunchLab, 271
Hurricane Sandy, 96

ice cream stops, 56–57
Immigration and Customs Enforcement (ICE), 179
implied consent, 39
improvement norms, 49, 52, 57
incarceration, 56
individual, the, 234
inductive reasoning, 279
inequality, 162
informal norms, 40
information, 260
Ingrao, Christian, 243
"inner front," 236
Innocent Aggressors, 125
innocent citizens, 131
innocent life, 123, 128, 140, 141
institutions, 60n1
intelligence, 172, 274
intelligence-led policing, 270
International Association of Chiefs of Police (IACP), 13, 54, 96, 103
international relations, 229
intersectionality, 191, 242
Intrado, 273
Israel Defense Force, 251

Jackson, George, 182, 183, 190
James, Joy, 18
Jarrett, Valerie, 196
Jean, Botham, 179
Jefferson, Atatiana, 179
Jim Crow laws, 11, 154, 217
Joh, Elizabeth, 273

Johnson, Mark, 253
justice, 172
just war theory, 16

Kaba, Mariame, 32
Kant, Immanuel, 229
Kardashian, Kim, 200
Kelley, Robin, 261
Kelling, George, 254
Kelly, Ray, 53
Kerr, Ian, 283
"kill boxes," 257
killings by police, 1–2, 109 fig., 117, 130
King, Coretta Scott, 190
King, Martin Luther, Jr., 190
Kleinig, John, 104
Klinger, David, 17
Knemeyer, Franz-Ludwig, 4
Knights of the White Camelia, 215, 217
knives, 110, 116–117. *See also* weapons
knowledge acquisition, 44, 49, 57
knowledge production, 44, 49, 57
Koffka, Kurt, 253
Ku Klux Klan, 18, 205, 215–216, 217
Kultur, 234

La Grange National American, 213
Lakoff, George, 253
law, 233, 234
Law Enforcement Assistance Act of 1965, 69
Law Enforcement Officers Killed and Assaulted (LEOKA), 116
law enforcement policy, 42, 48
law enforcement strategy, 42, 269
lawful policing: constitutional law and, 27; defined, 25; effective policing and, 28–29; procedural justice and, 31; vigilantism and, 27. *See also* policing
"Leave our Mikes Alone" (Harney and Moten), 261, 264
Lee, Robert E., 214
legal codes, 122–123

legal estrangement, 166
legitimacy (political): aggressive policing strategies and, 66; bad law enforcement and, 41; defined, 41; epistemic norms and, 57; guardian policing and, 82; improvement norms and, 52, 57; informal norms and, 40; as normative, 41; requirements for, 57; stop, question, and frisk (SQF) and, 42
legitimacy (psychological), 29–31
lethal force, legitimacy and, 43
Levinas, Emmanuel, 251
liberalism, 194, 233–234
liberation, 174
liberty, 29
life prioritization, 123, 127, 131–132, 133, 135–137, 139–141
life-taking, 122–124
Lightfoot, Lori, 186
Lincoln, Abraham, 214
Lind, Allan, 30
Lippert-Rasmussen, Kasper, 280
Live from Death Row (Abu-Jamal), 188
Loader, Ian, 33
Locke, John, 42
Locking Up Our Own (Forman), 10
Loehmann, Timothy, 52
logic of preemption, 252
London Metropolitan Police, 231
Lorde, Audre, 172
Los Angeles Police Department (LAPD), 84–85, 128, 134–139
Lum, Kristian, 275
Lynch, Loretta, 191, 194
lynching, 216

machine learning, 19, 275
Magee, Ruchell, 182
Malcolm X Grassroots Cop Watch, 187
"Mandatory Rescue Killings" (Fabre), 130, 131
manhunts, 250
Manning, Chelsea, 192
marijuana, 98

Marshall, T. H., 152, 173
Martin, Trayvon, 196
Marx, Karl, 195
masculinity, 71–72
mass incarceration, 166, 184, 188, 196
mass policing, 188
Massumi, Brian, 252, 259–261
McCarthy, Ron, 128, 136
McNutt, Ross, 258
McSpadden, Lesley, 196
Meares, Tracey, 15, 151
medical ethics, 54
Memphis Police Department, 103–104
Mendoza, Richard, 134–135
mental health, 198
Merleau-Ponty, Maurice, 253
Miami-Dade Police Department, 248
Mickey, Robert, 166
militarized policing, 223; in Black communities, 9; causes of, 94; cynegetic power and, 257; equipment of police and, 94; mentality of police and, 95; PredPol and, 256; training and, 100; the War on Drugs and, 94
military, the, 228, 230, 237
"military-diplomatic apparatus," 226
militias, 207–208
Miller, Lisa, 166
"Minority Report, The" (Dick), 241
Misdemeanorland (Kohler-Hausmann), 167
Mohler, George, 271
Monaghan, Jake, 16
"Monday-morning quarterbacking," 52
Moore, Fannie, 211
Moten, Fred, 261
"Mothers of the Movement," 196
Movement for Black Lives (M4BL), 192
multidisciplinarity, 58
Murray, Joseph, 55

Napoleonic Wars, the, 230, 231
Nashville Fraternal Order of Police, 62n16
National Action Network (NAN), 198

National Advisory Commission of Civil Disorders, 69
National Alliance Against Racist and Political Repression (NAARPR), 183, 188, 191
National Institute of Justice (NIJ), 270
National Police Foundation, 59
National Socialism, 234
National United Committee to Free Angela Davis, 183
Nazi Germany, 222, 233. *See also* Third Reich, the
Nazi police, 18
Neocleous, Mark, 249
"New Policing," 223
Newton, Huey, 187
"New Wars," 222
New York City Housing Authority (NYCHA), 193
New York City Police Department (NYPD), 41–42, 69, 180, 193–194, 269
New York City Police Department Internal Affairs Bureau, 51
nonideal theory, 8
non-interference norm, 51
Norton, Ben, 195
Norwegian Police, 93
nulla poena sine lege (equality of citizens before the law), 233

Obama, Barack, 15, 183, 196
Obama administration, the, 192
officer behavior, 66
oligarchy, 162
Omnibus Crime Bill, 190, 196
O'Neill, James P., 194
Ontopower (Massumi), 259
On War (Clausewitz), 227–228, 230
oppositional ideology, 157
Ordnungspolizei (civilian police units), 241, 242
Orta, Ramsey, 188
Oyama, Susan, 253

palliative care, 55, 58
Panopticon, the, 226, 251
Pantaleo, Daniel, 186, 191, 194
Paoli, Pasquale, 231
paranoia, 237
"passport police," 232
past, the, 282–283
Pastore, Nick, 95
pathocentric medicine, 55
Payne, Jeff, 39, 53
peace, 229 – 230
peacekeeping, 96–97
Peel, Robert, 205, 231
Penal Code of 1810, 233
perception, 252, 253, 258
pereat mundus, fiat justitia (let justice be done, though the world perish), 234
Perez, Guillermo, 137–138
performance, 69–70
perpetual peace, 229
Persistent Surveillance Systems, 258
personal force injuries, 117
person-based modeling, 272, 276
Plato, 251
Podesta, John, 196
police, 234; as agents of maintenance, 99; civil society and, 232; confidence in, 9; conservative function of, 229; creation of, 206; cynegetic power and, 252; discretion of, 7; distrust towards, 205; etymology of, 4; experience of the state and, 6–7; as form of government of the polis, 225; governmentality and, 226; as helper, 238–240; law and, 233; as a "legalized gang," 153; militarization of, 234, 249, 256; military and, 228, 230, 237; as moral exemplars, 4, 6; the nation-state and, 231; in Nazi Germany, 232–244; perceived abandonment of, 163–165; the policed and, 153; as protecting innocent life, 140; resoluteness and soldierly loyalty to duty, 240; role of, 3; slave patrols and, 216;

police (*cont.*)
  as soldier, 238–240; soldiers and, 101–102; use of force and, 3; violence and, 235
police abolitionism, 15, 25, 31, 33
police administrators, 107, 116, 140
police brutality, 7
police culture, 81, 82
policed, the, 153
police drones, 248
police encounters, 158–162
police ethics. *See* ethics of policing
Police Executive Research Forum, 59
Police for the Future (Bayley), 26
police gunfire, 107
police injuries, 117
police interventions, 156
police malfeasance, 189
police officer death rates, 108
police officer risk of fatal assault, 109 fig.
police reform, 2, 9, 58, 180
police regulation, 28
police repression, 182
police shootings, 112–114, 118
police trainers, 131
police violence, 32, 32–33, 179
policing: adversarial and collective nature of, 49; adversarial nature of, 57; aggressive forms of, 66; as a childhood intervention, 158–162; Clausewitz on, 228; drones and, 249; equality and, 97; ethos of, 66; excess of, 32; gender and, 75–80, 82–83; goals of, 54–56; governance and, 179; history of, 4–5, 10; improvement norms and, 49; informal norms of, 40; as input, 168; as a mechanism, 168; in Nazi Germany, 224; as an outcome, 167–168; political philosophy and, 4; politics of, 180; as preventing crime, 270; private and public, 33; as a public good, 33; reduction in crime rate and, 99; slave patrols and, 34; soft approaches to, 80; technology and, 3, 13; temporality of, 229; war and, 223; "warrior" approach to, 73, 77, 100. *See also* lawful policing
political philosophy, 44
politics, 227, 236, 243–244
Polizei, 4–5
Polizeiwissenschaft, 232
Portals, 150–151, 155–158, 174
portals, 17
power, 224, 225, 251
Power to the Edge, 260
precarity, 199
predation, 250, 252, 253, 263–264
predator, the, 223
Predator drones, 248
predatory policing, 262
predictive policing, 257, 268; criticisms of, 274–276; the past and, 282; profiling and, 276–284
PredPol, 249, 256, 259, 271
preemptive policing, 19
prejudice, 98, 279
"President and the People, The: Race in America," 196
President's Commission on Law Enforcement and Administration of Justice, 26, 69
President's Task Force on 21st Century Policing, 81, 131
preventive detention, 241
priming, 260
principle of distinction, 101
principle of proportionality, 101
prison abolitionism, 32
prison admissions, 152 fig.
prison-industrial complex, 181, 190
proactive activity, 77–78
problem-oriented policing, 269
procedural justice, 29, 30; effective policing and, 31; guardian policing and, 73; lawful policing and, 31; legitimacy and, 31

professional ethics, 41, 44
professional obligations, 50
profiling, 276–277. *See also* racial profiling
propaganda, 237–238
proportionality, 43, 47
protective custody, 235
Prowse, Gwen, 151
public goods, 33
public health, 107
public safety, 184
public trust, 107

race, 152 fig., 206, 236, 278–281
race-based violence, 217
"race war," 242
racial bias, 17
racial capitalism, 182
racial injustice, 12
racial oppression, 218
racial profiling, 241, 277–284. *See also* profiling
racism, 45–46, 98, 190
racist perception, 263
Ramsey, Charles, 84
Rauber, Die (Schiller), 231
Reagan, Ronald, 191, 197
"real" police work: awards and, 77, 80; as crime fighting, 68–70; as dangerous, 70–71; incentivizing of, 72–74; informal rewards of, 74; as masculine, 71–72
reason, 228
reasonable suspicion, 273
recidivism, 275
Reconstruction, 35, 217
"red boxes," 257
Reed, Austin, 154
Reed-Veal, Geneva, 196
"Reflections on the Black Woman's Role in the Community of Slaves" (Davis), 183, 189–190
Reichstag, the, 234
Republic, The (Plato), 4, 251

Research Triangle Institute, 108
resistance to arrest, 123–124
respect, 105
restorative justice, 186
Rice, Tamir, 1, 51
right to bear arms, 94
Rise of the Warrior Cop (Radley), 95
risk, 129
risk profiles, 277
Risk Terrain Modeling, 271
Rivera, Oscar Lopez, 192
Rosenblatt, Josh, 48
Rousey, Dennis, 218
Rousseau, Jean-Jacques, 163
rules of engagement, 95–96, 100, 101–102, 105

Sanders, Bernie, 190–191, 195
Savali, Kirsten West, 200
Schauer, Frederick, 279, 280
Scheindlin, Judge Shira, 29
Schiller, Friedrich, 231
Schoolcraft, Adrian, 51
Scott, Walter, 1
Scott v. Harris, 104
SD (*Sicherheitsdienst*), 237
Seale, Bobby, 187
searchers, 209
Security, Territory, Population (Foucault), 226
Selbst, Andrew, 281
self-protection, 122–124
Shakur, Assata, 192
Sharkey, Patrick, 32
Sharpton, Al, 198
Sheehey, Bonnie, 283
Sherman, Lawrence, 160
Sierra-Arevalo, Michael, 16
Six livres de la republique (Bodin), 224
slave catchers, 212
Slave Catchers, Slave Resisters, 218
slave insurrections, 213
slave passes, 209, 214

slave patrols, 18; fear of insurrection and, 213; history of policing and, 34; the Ku Klux Klan and, 215–216; militias and, 207–208; as precursors to city and county police, 205; slave catchers and, 212
slavery, 10, 217
slaves, 207
Smith, Rick, 14
Smith, Sylville, 157
Snowden, Edward, 192
Snyder, Timothy, 242
social anxiety, 220n2
social identity, 30
social justice, 198
social network analysis, 272
social order, 229
social status, 30
soft power, 252
Soledad Brother Defense Committee, 182
Soledad Brothers, 180
Sonitrol, 62n18
Soss, Joe, 154
South African Truth and Reconciliation Commission, 219
sovereignty, 224–225, 227
SS Dirlewanger Brigade, 243
"stand your ground," 141n2
state baptism, 158–162
state lawlessness, 166
statelessness, 166
state responsiveness, 162
statistical discrimination, 278
Steinem, Gloria, 183
Sterling, Alton, 1
Stevenson, Bryan, 12
Stier, Gunther, 236
Stono Rebellion, 208
stop, question, and frisk (SQF), 28, 29; benefits of, 46–47; controversy of, 45; costs of, 59; equality and, 46; harshness of, 47; legitimacy and, 42, 46–48; proportionality and, 47; racism of, 45;

Ray Kelly on, 53; risks of, 59; *Terry v. Ohio* and, 45. *See also* Terry stops
stop and frisk, 61n8
Strategic Subjects List, 272, 282
subjugated knowledge, 170–172
super-predators, 255–256
surveillance, 226, 241
suspicion, 206
Susser, Daniel, 19
SWAT teams, 17, 71, 95, 131, 252
systemic racism, 2

Tag der Deutschen Polizei (Day of the German Police), 241
Tasers, 13, 14
Taylor, Breonna, 1
technology, 13, 15
Tennessee v. Garner, 103, 108, 141n4
Terry stops, 45. *See also* stop, question, and frisk (SQF)
Terry v. Ohio, 45
Third Enforcement Act, the, 216. *See also* Enforcement Acts of 1870 and 1871
Third Reich, the, 222, 232, 235. *See also* Nazi Germany
Thirteenth Amendment, the, 35, 180, 214
Thirty Years War, the, 224
"This is America" (Childish Gambino), 160, 173
threat perception failures, 142n7
three-fifths clause, the, 180
Town of Castle Rock v. Gonzales, 166
Tracy, James, 39
Trump, Donald, 194, 200
Trump, Ivanka, 200
truth, 261
2016 Democratic National Convention, 196
Tyler, Tom, 30

Uncle Tom's Cabin (Stowe), 212
understanding, 174
Union Army, the, 213

United States Department of Justice Civil Rights Division, 3
United States Holocaust Memorial Museum, 13
United States Supreme Court, 100
unjust laws, 8
US Customs and Border Protection, 248
use of deadly force, 107; administrative guidelines on, 121; during arrest, 108; criminal laws governing, 139; defined, 122; hostage situations and, 128–130; Innocent Aggressors and, 125; life prioritization and, 131, 136; as most profound power of the state, 120; obligation to protect others and, 130; paramaters on, 121; policy statements governing, 126; reform of, 118; resistance to arrest and, 123–124; self-protection and, 122–124; social tension surrounding, 140; states' permission of, 141n3; strategies for control of, 112–114; *Tennessee v. Garner* and, 141n4; Villainous Aggressors and, 125
use of force: body cameras and, 13, 14; as defining characteristic of American police, 127; encouragement of, 73; legitimacy and, 53, 57–58; necessity of, 17; predictive policing and, 273; protection of life and, 99; rules that govern, 96; Tasers and, 14; use of police car as, 104

Varela, Francisco, 253
Varieties of Police Behavior (Wilson), 254
vigilantism, 27
Villainous Aggressors, 125
violence, 224, 228, 235, 243
Violence Crime Control and Law Enforcement Act of 1994, 26
Vitale, Alex, 97
Vollmer, August, 40, 60n2
vulnerability, 251

Walker, Neil, 33
Walzer, Michael, 16
Wang, Jackie, 256, 264
war, 223, 227–228, 236, 241
"war on cops," 70–71
War on Crime, the, 101
War on Drugs, the: aggressive policing strategies and, 10; defeat of law enforcement in, 54; as metaphorical war, 101; militarized policing and, 94
War on Poverty, the, 94
War on Terror, the, 101
"warrior cop," the, 249
"warrior" policing, 73, 77, 100
Warsaw Uprising, the, 243
"war stories," 73
Washington, DC, 94
Watts riot, 156
weapons, 110–111. *See also* guns; knives
Weaver, Vesla, 17
Weber, Max, 127, 224, 226
Weimar Republic, the, 236
welfare, 224
When Police Kill (Zimring), 118
whistleblowing norm, 51
Whiteness, 262
White supremacy, 11
"Wild West," the, 93
Williams, Jeri, 116
Wilson, Darren, 261–262
Wilson, James Q., 101, 254–255, 258
Wilson, O. W., 68
Works Progress Administration (WPA), 211
World War I, 233, 236
wounds, 113–114
Wubbels, Alex, 39

Zimring, Franklin, 17, 132
zone of peace, 95, 97, 100, 101–105, 229, 235
zone of war, 95, 96, 235